Naval Warfare
IN THE
Age of Sail

NAVAL WARFARE
IN THE
AGE OF SAIL

BERNARD IRELAND

TED SMART

This edition produced for The Book People Ltd, Hall Wood Avenue, Haydock, St Helens, WA11 9UL

HarperCollins*Publishers*
77-85 Fulham Palace Road
Hammersmith
London W6 8JB

First published by HarperCollins*Publishers* 2000

1 3 5 7 9 10 8 6 4 2

© HarperCollins *Publishers* 2000

ISBN 0 00 762906 0

Airbrush illustrations © Tony Gibbons

Design: Rod Teasdale
Computer graphics: Richard Burgess

Printed and bound in Spain

The publishers wish to thank the National Maritime Museum, London and the Musée de la Marine, Paris for supplying photographs. All the paintings and ship models illustrated here come from the National Maritime Museum except for the images on the following pages which belong to the Musée de la Marine: 84, 91, 97, 122, 160 and 172

CONTENTS

INTRODUCTION: *King George's Navy*

It is not possible to write a book such as this without developing a deep admiration for the ordinary seamen of the Royal Navy. The stuff of legend is that the greater part were impressed against their will and, for a pittance, were sent to serve in damp and unhealthy conditions, subjected to discipline verging on the inhuman until, incapacitated or with health broken, they were cast ashore and forgotten. It is no credit to the nation that this was, all too often, the case. But then we have the paradox. How was such a body of men, apparently bereft of education, status or prospects, motivated to form a service respected the world around?

They were the raw material that was moulded by the system into a new creation of vastly different qualities, as clay is transformed by the process of firing. Much credit must lay with their officers, themselves recruited almost casually at an age when today's lads have yet to see a GCSE. Some from the aristocracy, some from the professional classes, they were virtually apprenticed to their captains and learned their trade from the bottom up. Some, but very few, "came aft through the hawse".

Captain William Rogers capturing the Jeune Richard (Samuel Drummond)

In August 1807 the French privateer *Jeune Richard* grappled the British packet *Windsor Castle* near Barbados. With 92 men, the enemy outnumbered the British three to one, yet the latter, led by their master, William Rogers, defended stoutly. Against all the odds, Rogers won the battle, eventually leading five of his men to clear the enemy deck. The privateer struck her colours.

This was the age when the man counted, rather than technology. To ghost toward an enemy line, without response to air thick with shot and shell, required discipline. It also required leadership, and the waiting upper deck guncrews were backed by their officers, moving unprotected, yet calmly and deliberately, encouraging and inspiring.

Following the unimaginable hell of a close-range, muzzle-to-muzzle encounter, and the crunch of ship against ship, it was the officers, often headed by the captain himself, who led a bloodied boarding party to swarm aboard the enemy, hacking and lunging, avenging their mates and clearing her deck.

It was the officers who guided their men when, in ship's boats with muffled oars, they silently navigated strange harbours to cut out enemies who believed themselves beyond reach. It was the officers who, time and again, pushed and heaved along with their men to haul naval guns over watercourses and through fetid jungle to commanding heights from which they could assist the military, only to see the territory for which they had fought handed back by politicians signing the eventual peace.

It was the men, however, that made a ship what she was. Well led, they performed prodigies. In the context of the times their discipline was severe, but little worse than life ashore. Food and pay could have been better but at least it was fairly regular. On a long commission the ship was home; they identified with her as a soldier does with his regiment. In a blow they cursed her wetness, her unhandiness. In action they blessed her strength. They pumped her, stored her, painted her and holystoned her. Following a heavy action they undertook tasks that, today, take some imagining, improvising rigging and swaying up spars and topmasts the size of telegraph poles.

There was, for the ratings, no concept of continuous service. A commission ended, a peace signed and it was back to the land or unemployment. In the meantime Jack ashore was a man liberated. Boisterous and pugnacious, he was loved more for the wages in his pocket than for himself. Kipling recognised it, but articulated it only for the soldier, although the sentiment is the same:

'O it's Tommy this, an' Tommy that, an' "Tommy, go away";
But it's "Thank you, Mister Atkins" when the band begins to play...'
It is, therefore, to this great body of largely unsung heroes that this book is respectfully dedicated.

At a more practical level, I would like to recognise the unstinting help of my editor, Ian Drury, together with the patience of the staff at the National Maritime Museum and of those administering the naval collections in the Portsmouth area. Lastly, as ever, my wife, both secretary and general encourager.

Bernard Ireland

Abordage du Nelson par le Bellone, 13 August 1804 (A. Mayer)

Attacked west of Brest by the French privateer *Bellone* on 13th August 1804, the East Indiaman *Lord Nelson* was boarded and taken. With a prize crew aboard, she was headed for Corunna when, on the 25th, she was intercepted by the British sloop *Seagull*. Despite every effort, *Seagull* proved too light to re-take her. Almost in sight of the Spanish coast, the *Lord Nelson* encountered Pellew with four ships of the line and surrendered to the *Seagull*.

CHAPTER 1: *The Royal Navy*

Building a Tradition

Neither a convenient path to somewhere else, nor even particularly accessible, the British Isles have been spared much of the misery of other peoples' wars. Located on the periphery of Europe, the islands are a cul-de-sac. Separated from the continental landmass by an unpredictable sea, they are not in themselves an attractive objective for casual assault. As European powers created vast armies to pursue their leaders' grand designs, Britain was able to stand aside, relying on shrewd alliances, effective diplomacy and a powerful fleet to enable her to decline or accept her moment of involvement.

The long reign of King George III extended from 1760 to 1820, an era of almost continuous war during which the Royal Navy was to achieve the highest reputation in its history. Perhaps surprisingly, this history had not been particularly long, for the fleet that George inherited had not come into being at some point in time in accordance with careful planning.

During the Middle Ages there was no 'royal' navy, indeed no real warships. In times of war the King had the right to demand the services of ships and men, taken from their routine occupation and blended with such forces, if any, that he had funded from his own pocket. Military campaigns on the continent were not infrequent; since the Norman Conquest, the English Crown brought with it large territories in France and claims to even more. Shrewd people saw that there were here good profits to be made. Individual wealthy merchants, then whole communities, made contract with the Crown to furnish a specified force when required in return for trading favours or tax exemptions, Bristol and the Cinque Ports being good examples.

Merchant ships, however, were built primarily to earn a living, and they proved expensive to hire on the regular basis that the Crown required to support its territorial claims in France. Henry V thus found it more economical to build his own fleet. This was not a fighting force, just a means of transporting his armies over neighbouring waters. With his death, it was sold off. Arrangements between the Crown and contractors continued into Tudor times, expanded and modified to accommodate the growth in regular foreign trade, for growing prosperity found the home base less than self-sufficient and imported wares attractive as well as necessary.

Trading forays to foreign parts quickly ran into trouble with would-be entrepreneurs discovering that the Iberian powers — Spain and Portugal — who had long-established maritime traditions, had neatly apportioned the resources of the New World to suit their own interests. Just two years after Columbus made his epic first voyage, and three years before Henry VII despatched John Cabot in the direction of Newfoundland, Spain and Portugal met at Tordesillas and agreed a line of demarcation, a meridian situated 370 leagues to the west of the Cape Verdes. All to the west of it would be Spanish, all to the east, Portuguese.

Henry VIII created a standing fleet but, for all his intimidating personal image, his navy was primarily a defensive force, for these were days of fundamental religious divisions. Both he and his father had made provision for the future by establishing facilities that would develop into the naval yards of Portsmouth, Deptford and Woolwich. Queen Elizabeth I gave whole-hearted encouragement to a new style of gentleman adventurer, not only motivated by the potential riches of trade but prepared to pursue them as required, in the process meeting and brawling with the disputing Spaniard. The inevitable result for England was war. It was about religion and it was about trade but, critically for our story, it was waged against the greatest naval power of the age. Elizabeth's warships acquitted themselves well except that, lacking the cash windfall available to her father, she could field only one in five of the ships that engaged the enemy. Far more appealing was the encouragement of privateering against the sprawling Spanish trade routes.

The English of the time were little interested in colonisation; territory was useful primarily as a forward facility for the maintenance of ships and crews. Huge fortunes were made for individuals and the Crown, the latter legalising activities through the issue of Letters of Marque. In times to come, when British trade was in turn preyed upon, this era would be recalled as a lesson in the need to devise a protective strategy. For trade sustained not only the population but also the means to prosecute the war itself.

Having apparently established justification for an active 'royal' navy the monarchy, in the pusillanimous form of James I, lacked both the resources and the will to maintain it. Britain's fortunes sank low until Charles I devised his controversial solution. A permanent fleet would be funded by a universally levied tax, the notorious 'Ship

'Men-of-War at Plymouth' -(Serres)
Dominic Serres the Elder was French, but settled as a marine painter in England, where he rose to become a founder-member of the Royal Academy in 1768. This characteristically serene Serres picture shows the principal types of Royal Navy ship of the late 18th Century. They are depicted typically with lower canvas furled, with minutely-observed detail and as a part of the greater scene, here Plymouth.

"Jack ashore"
was a man of basic pleasures, freely available in the scores of establishments that stood, virtually shoulder-to-shoulder, in the main streets of the dockyard towns. Since the second half of the 18th Century, seamen's dress had become more standardised but, in this 1825 cartoon, variations are still apparent.

Sailors Carousing, or a peep in the Longroom

HMS Bellona
The 74-gun Third Rate was the Royal Navy's workhorse. This is a demonstration model of the *Bellona*, launched by Chatham Dockyard in 1760. It is completed only with wales and partial planking to show the primary structure. The complex curvature of the hull is evident, and the sheer quantity of compass timber required soon put it in short supply.

Money'. That Charles intended the nation to pay, but himself control, proved to be the stumbling block. The fleet was built against a background of deteriorating relationships between Crown and Parliament. No sooner did it begin to achieve its objectives in support of England's near-sea interests than it became involved in the civil war. Supporting Parliament, the fleet guaranteed that the French, who were for the King, could not intervene. This barrier was critical to the eventual outcome.

The Commonwealth Government that followed the King's defeat was an imposed institution and a significant proportion of the fleet, with monarchist sympathies, defected under Prince Rupert. With this force at large Parliament set about the expansion of the remainder through an annual vote of taxpayers' money. It was from this point only that a regularly funded British fleet has been in continuous existence.

'Shipping a sea in the gunroom'
In a scene that would be familiar to
the small-ship sailor of World War II,
the midshipmen of the *Canopus'*
gunroom cheerfully find dry perches
when all goes awash. Servants try to
maintain order. Note the 32-pounder
at right, muzzle-lashed with the port
secured. While its gun-tackles are
taut, the heavy breeching appears
very slack for the conditions!

Like most dictators, Cromwell sought to divert public attention from his minority, and widely unpopular, administration. Lacking suitable leaders for his fleet, he simply created several 'Generals at Sea', who, surprisingly, proved very able. One, Blake, finally oversaw the end of Rupert's ambitions at Cartagena in 1650. Cromwell then sought a quarrel with the Dutch. With Elizabeth I's support, the Dutch had thrown off Spanish control and progressed to dispute Iberian hegemony of the high seas. As James had withdrawn from the partnership the Dutch had gone on to establish trading monopolies of their own. Lacking sentiment, they excluded the English along with all other competitors. In growing wealthy, they excited resentment.

The First Dutch War began in 1652. It was all about trade share and was fought almost exclusively at sea. Under the Generals at Sea, the new English navy experienced its first

Plymouth Dockyard - (Pocock)
Nicholas Pocock, whose life spanned
the period of the great wars with
France, was one of several merchant
seamen who went ashore as
accomplished marine painters. Dated
1798, this picture is one of a series
of bird's-eye views of the major
dockyards, here Plymouth.
Dominated by its storehouses and
long ropery, the yard has its five
drydocks, graving dock and three
building berths all occupied.

Rayo

All four of the Allied three-deckers at Trafalgar were Spanish. The smallest of them was the 100-gun *Rayo* which, as one of Dumanoir's division, was in the van. Blocked from the main action, she escaped to Cadiz. Emerging during the gale of 23 October, she was dismasted and surrendered to the *Donegal* 74, only to be driven ashore and wrecked.

triumphs and reverses but Dover, Portland, the Gabbard, the Kentish Knock and Scheveningen grace ships' honour boards to this day. In 1660 came the Restoration, King Charles II assuming the throne and using, for the first time, the term 'Royal Navy'. Between 1665 and 1680 there were to be two more fiercely contested maritime wars with the Dutch. Lowestoft, the Four Days' Fight, St. James' Day, Solebay, Schooneveld and the Texel added to the stature of the Service.

During the Third Dutch War the French had, briefly, been England's allies. There was no natural affinity and little trust. In 1673, the very year of the bloody battle at the Texel, English aversion to the French and the machinations of their monarch resulted in the beginnings of peace talks with the Dutch who, from the following year, became firm allies. The relationship was based on mutual respect and was cemented soon afterward by the marriage of William of Orange and Charles II's niece Mary. A critical development in tactical fighting during these wars was the final abandonment of end-on attack, followed by rapid boarding, in favour of 'the line'. The first harked back to the tactics forced on galleys; the second enabled broadside ships to come into their own.

Protestant opposition to the succession of Charles's Catholic brother James II was such that William was invited to take the throne. The resulting deep divisions brought about a further war, as James was supported by the French. This War of Succession lasted from 1689 until 1697 and again proved the value of a fleet. In 1689 a British squadron surprised, but were worsted by, a French force off-loading supplies in Bantry Bay for James' army. During the following year came the controversial action off Beachy Head where Torrington, commanding an Anglo-Dutch fleet but outnumbered 68 to 56, was content to contain the French rather than to seek their defeat. Since much criticised, Torrington knew that to lose the fleet would spell disaster, and he took no chances. In contrast to the vicious encounters of the Dutch Wars, where the outcome depended greatly upon opportunity detected and exploited, Torrington had written very precise fighting instructions, so thoroughly considered as to provide the basis of line battle for nearly a century.

Two years later the situation was reversed in the decisive encounters off Barfleur and la-Hougue, where the Anglo-Dutch force of Edward Russell, Earl of Orford, crushed the French under Tourville. On this occasion the Allied fleet had the huge advantage of 99 to 44. The destruction of the French fleet prevented their further free movement of military forces by sea, ensuring that James could no longer dispute the English throne. Again, a fleet action had greatly influenced the course of English history.

For a brief period, Spain was also being supported by the English against French ambitions. Operations designed to protect the Spanish seaward flank demonstrated advantages in maintaining a naval presence in the Mediterranean although, as yet, there existed no permanent base there.

The Dutch Wars marked the beginning of a century and a half of strife for the English. As the nation depended upon the fleet for its defence and for what, today, would be termed 'power projection', the Service steadily prospered. Although inevitably run down following the peace of 1697, the process was quickly reversed when Queen Anne involved the state in the War of the Spanish Succession, the French also having proclaimed James' son to be the rightful heir to the English throne.

Under Queen Anne the Royal Navy maintained an average of about 65 First to Third Rates, now termed Line of Battle ships, with a corresponding increase in Fifth and Sixth Rates, the indispensable 'cruising' ships. Still enjoying Dutch support, the English broadened their interests from influencing the course of west European successions to include the acquisition of their colonial holdings, together with the concomitant increase in trade and influence.

The dominant name in Queen Anne's naval war was that of Sir George Rooke. Rigid in doctrine but seemingly attended by good fortune, Rooke failed to seize Cadiz in 1702 but took a treasure fleet at Vigo, failed to take Barcelona in 1704 but secured Gibraltar at negligible cost. Rooke's Anglo-Dutch squadron was then counter-attacked off Malaga by a Franco-Spanish fleet. As in earlier times, huge and unwieldy numbers — over 50 per side — were involved. Rooke fought as unimaginatively as ever and the outcome was a draw. A major enemy objective, Gibraltar, however remained firmly in British hands.

Before the war was over the British had taken it to the Spanish in the West Indies, where Wager took a further treasure 'flota' off Cartagena (in present-day Colombia). By the peace in 1713 the fleet had performed well and with little loss, Britain gaining legal title to Gibraltar, Minorca and the Canadian territories (the latter's boundaries yet ill-defined).

During the thirteen-year reign of King George I there was, unusually, only one short war, this fought against Spain. George's dual role of King of Great Britain and Elector of Hanover had already, in 1715-17, caused complications in the support of the Danes and Russians against the Swedes. Paradoxically, ephemeral good relations with the French were instrumental in their employing their diplomatic skills to defuse the situation.

Britain, as a member of the so-called Quadruple Alliance with Austria, France and Holland, then embarked on a process of rationalising territorial and constitutional anomalies resulting from earlier peace settlements. Spain, feeling unfairly treated by the Alliance, sought to seize Sicily from Italy. Demonstrating the growing importance of the Royal Navy as an instrument of national policy, together with her increasing interest in Mediterranean affairs, Britain underwrote Italy's neutrality through the despatch of Sir George Byng with a powerful squadron. Although neither camp appeared to be certain of the existence of a state of war, Byng clashed with the Spanish fleet near Cape Passero in August 1718. Not only did the latter lose 22 ships but it was also now unable to support an army marooned in Sicily. Spain then accepted the terms of the Alliance, beginning a peace that persisted for nearly twenty years.

Renomée

Captured by the *Dover* 50 in September 1747, the 32-gun *Renomée* was a 9-pounder frigate. Noted as a good sailer, she was taken into the Royal Navy as the *Renown*. She is not to be confused with the next *Renomée*, of 1805, also captured, and re-commissioned as the *Java*.

Quasi-hostilities with Spain lingered around the West Indies and Gibraltar. The inevitable response by the British monarch (since 1727 King George II) in expanding the active fleet brought about a reluctant rapprochement, with Spain joining Britain, France and Holland in defensive alliance. This made little difference to day-to-day squabbling with the Spanish in the Caribbean, where continual outrages were perpetrated on British shipping and trading interests.

The so-called War of Jenkins' Ear broke out in 1739 as a result of one such depredation. A recent royal union between Spain and France saw the latter making loud protestations of support, but Britain moved firmly, despatching a small but powerful squadron under Vice-Admiral Edward Vernon who, with successors, demonstrated Spanish vulnerability in the isthmus by the seizure, with much booty, of several fortified towns. Consequent to the 1743 Treaty of Fontainebleau, however, France took a more active role. Her objectives, inter alia, were to divide Britain from her allies and, better, to eject British forces from the Mediterranean. More directly, despite no formal declaration of war, a French fleet attempted to reach Dunkirk to embark an invasion force and Prince Charles Edward Stuart, Pretender to the British throne. Battered by the weather and threatened by Sir John Norris and the Channel Fleet, however, the French abandoned the project and returned to Brest.

In the Mediterranean a Spanish squadron, which had been blockaded in Toulon by the British, emerged in February 1744 with the French in support. They were brought jointly to action by Admiral Thomas Mathews but, plagued by incompetence and petty jealousies, the resulting Battle of Toulon was not only indecisive but was followed by a spate of courts-martial. In 1745 the French successfully landed the Pretender on Scottish soil, much as a diversion to plans elsewhere. After his hopeless enterprise they succeeded also in evacuating him and his supporters to exile.

A slack British attitude in eastern Canada encouraged the French to attempt a re-occupation. The rapid transfer of a naval squadron from the West Indies to cooperate with a combined British and New England military and militia force restored the situation. Through taking the French main base at Louisbourg, they gained control of the strategically important Cape Breton Island.

Naval encounters between the French and British spread to the Indian Ocean and the West Indies and, in 1747, the French assembled separate expeditions, to recover Louisbourg and to attack British settlements in India. For mutual security they were to sail the first leg in company, and it was together still off Cape Finisterre that they were intercepted in the May by Vice-Admiral George Anson, recently returned from his

A French 74
Although rather more complete, this model of a French 74 contrasts nicely with that of the *Bellona* of the same period. The almost "apple-cheeked" bow of the Frenchman is conspicuous, as is the sweeping curve of the profile linking figurehead to forecastle. Note lack of chase fire and how the sided gangways linking quarterdeck to forecastle have widened so as to largely roof-over the upper deck.

triumphant circumnavigation. To cover their convoy the French formed line for formal action but when Anson, who had been in open order, conformed, they made for escape, the action becoming confused in a 'General Chase'. Considerably outnumbered, the French fought well, but strength ultimately prevailed. Both French commanders, a dozen assorted prizes and considerable booty were taken.

Barely five months later the same waters saw a second action. An enormous French convoy of better than 250 sail was intercepted by Rear-Admiral Sir Edward Hawke soon after its departure. Again the escort fought well, losing six of its eight ships in buying time for the convoy to disperse. The British squadron was left too heavily damaged to attempt pursuit of the merchantmen, although many of them were taken later in the West Indies.

The Dutch had made available a squadron at the outbreak of hostilities but had not participated in the major actions. In 1748 there was a joint operation to send Dutch forces on to the East Indies, their particular sphere of interest, while the British, under the Hon. Edward Boscawen, moved on Madras. Shortly before the peace the commander in the West Indies, Rear-Admiral Charles Knowles, intercepted a Spanish squadron off Havana. The forces were evenly matched but, where a little dash was required, Knowles engaged in formal manoeuvre. Time-wasting, misread signals and an adversary unwilling to be brought to action combined to stalemate the outcome and Knowles was subsequently reprimanded by court-martial.

This, the War of the Austrian Succession, was ended in 1748 by the Peace of Aix la Chapelle. It had been significant in maritime terms, the more so because, militarily, the war for Britain had not been successful. This, to British frustration, resulted in the peace largely restoring the status quo. In India and Canada, however, 'peace' was only a relative term, and the resumption of full hostilities was only a matter of time.

The French navy had lost substantially and was in need of both rebuilding and reforming. A naval academy was established to examine and improve fighting techniques. A foreseen shortfall in professional naval officers was met by a scheme to grant temporary commissions to capable men of the merchant marine, although these would never be accepted by the many of aristocratic background. Strained budgets were expended in supporting a huge administrative 'tail' while new ships lacked armament or the means to work up to fully-efficient fighting units. With the British still obviously spoiling for a fight it would appear to have been appropriate to use diplomacy to buy a little time to improve the state of preparation. That the French continued to create trouble in the colonies could lead predictably to only one conclusion.

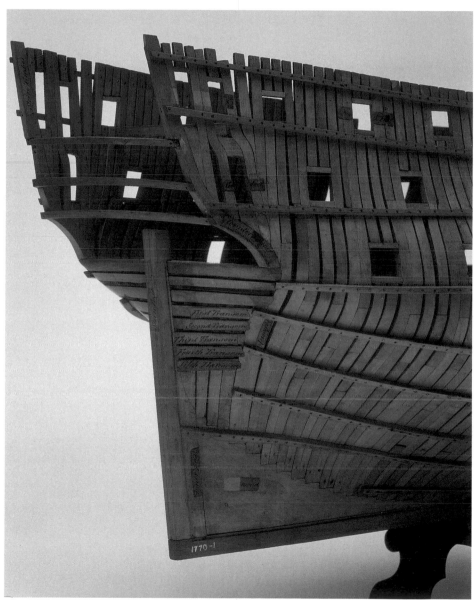

HMS Intrepid
This model of the *Intrepid* 74, launched at Woolwich in 1770, shows the overhung construction of the traditional square stern. Eight transverse transom timbers are in place forward of the sternpost, as are the transverse counters above. The curved timbers supporting the counter, and the vertical gallery timbers are yet to be fitted.

CHAPTER 2: *The Seven Years' War (1756-63)*

The Foudroyant,
an 80-gun Third Rate, was completed at
Toulon in 1750. Leading a force despatched
to assist de la Clue, blockaded at Cartagena,
she was brought to action off Cape de Gata
by the *Monmouth* 60 on 28 February 1758.
In over four hours of action, during which her
captain was killed, the *Monmouth* fought the
Foudroyant to a standstill, compelling her
striking to the *Swiftsure.*

Far right: The Battle of Lagos (Luny)
Admiral Boscawen's flagship, the *Namur* 90,
engaged the French *Océan* 80 for thirty
minutes, losing her mizzen mast and
remaining topsail yards. To retain control of
the action, and to prevent the enemy
escaping, Boscawen transferred by barge to
the *Newark* 80. Five French ships were
eventually taken or destroyed, both de la
Clue Sabran and Suffren being captured in
the *Océan.*

During the latter part of the 18th Century, the future map of the world was still being
defined. Voyages of exploration were being undertaken by European colonial powers,
which simultaneously disputed the controlling interest over territories still being settled.
When George III assumed the throne in 1760, his nation had been involved already for
several years in what came to be called the Seven Years' War. Although Britain gave
heavy financial support to Frederick the Great's Prussia in its struggle on the European
mainland, her primary objective was to defeat France's competing interests abroad,
particularly in North America, in India and in the Caribbean. With both parties
separated from these territories by thousands of miles of ocean, the importance of sea
power would be apparent.

Already steadily gaining in strength, the Royal Navy in 1755 comprised just under 300
ships, of which 134 were of the line, i.e. First to Fourth Rate. At a time when the
population of Britain was yet under eight million, the funded strength of the Navy's
seamen and marines was a considerable 70,000. The merchant service and fishing
industry, which employed many laid-off ex-naval personnel, required another 80,000.
Periods of hostilities, and the growing needs of the regular navy, had inflated a merchant
seaman's wages to seventy shillings monthly and, with little incentive to transfer, they
were impressed in considerable numbers.

Britain had observed a fragile peace with France and Spain since 1748, when the Peace
of Aix la Chapelle had ended the nine-year War of the Austrian Succession. Success at

sea, notably in Anson and Hawke's twin victories off Finisterre in 1747, had offset British misfortunes ashore in Europe. Neither camp gained much from the settlement; much remained unresolved and the period until 1756 was, at best, only a quasi-peace. In North America, the Aix terms restored to France the fortress of Louisbourg which, located strategically on Cape Breton Island, commanded the approaches to the St. Lawrence. In return, Britain had restored to her the valuable port of Madras, on the Bay of Bengal.

In India, Joseph Dupleix, Governor of the French East India Company, continued his efforts to create a colonial territory through alliances with local princes hostile to the rival British East India Company. Both organisations were increasingly well armed and a de facto state of war had existed since about 1751.

Powerfully established in Canada, the French were pursuing a strategy to gain control of the great basins of the Ohio and Mississippi rivers. This posed a continuous threat, part real, part imaginary, to the British settlements in New England. These adopted an aggressive stance, confident in the knowledge that both camps were dependent upon extended sea communications, which could only make the French the more vulnerable. Seemingly indifferent at first to their colonists' attempts to curb increasingly bold French-Canadian incursions, the British government reacted in 1754 by despatching a military force in two 50-gun ships under Keppel's flag. France responded massively with an expedition covered by sixteen ships of the line, commanded by Dubois de la Motte. In the spring of 1755 Boscawen was similarly despatched, and later reinforced. A clash was inevitable, coming in June 1755 when three French line ships encountered a superior force under Boscawen, east of Newfoundland. Refusing to salute the British flag, the French were attacked and two 64-gun ships, *Alcide* and *Lys*, were taken.

France delayed a declaration of war only because of the rundown state of her fleet and insufficient resources to expand it rapidly. Her new Secretary of the Navy, d'Arnouville, had instituted measures to increase line strength to 80 ships, but even this eventual strength would hardly menace that of the Royal Navy. France's strategy, therefore, was to tie down much of Britain's fleet in home waters by threatening invasion. This had the

Boscawen

Of privileged background, the Hon. Edward Boscawen was born in 1711. His father was Viscount Falmouth and he was related, through his mother's line, to the Duke of Marlborough. He entered the Royal Navy as a volunteer in 1726 and was, perhaps, fortunate to survive a three-year stint in the West Indies, where operations against the Spanish cost 4,000 deaths from yellow fever.

Promoted lieutenant in 1732 and junior captain in 1737, he commanded the *Shoreham* 20 under Admiral Vernon in further operations against the Spanish. Here, he showed a talent for operations ashore, leading naval parties at the reduction of both Porto Bello and Cartagena. In 1747 he had command of the *Namur* 74, a unit of a force under Admiral Anson which decisively defeated an inferior French squadron off Finisterre. Boscawen suffered a severe neck injury but was further promoted. Appointed a Lord Commissioner on the Board of Admiralty, it fell to him to sign the death warrant of the unfortunate Admiral Byng.

As an Admiral of the Blue, Boscawen had overall responsibility for the fleet that supported military operations for the final ejection of the French from Canada in 1759. Given command in the Mediterranean, he was soon in action again, pursuing a French squadron into Lagos Bay in Portugal. Although Boscawen's comment was "it might have been a great deal better", the ensuing action cost the enemy five ships.

Made the first General of Marines, he nonetheless remained at sea, blockading the French around Quiberon. In 1761 his career was cut short when he contracted a fatal dose of typhoid fever.

desired effect, creating virtual panic in some quarters. It also covered the build-up of the fleet at Toulon, for the purpose of taking British-held Minorca.

Formal war was declared when this expedition, escorted by a fleet commanded by Admiral de la Galissonnière, descended in April 1756. French intentions toward the base at Port Mahon had been well signalled however, and already on passage was a scratch squadron under Vice-Admiral the Honourable John Byng. With ships already on station, he could muster twelve of the line and four frigates, much the same as the French who had already landed 15,000 troops.

As the two battle lines squared up on 20th May 1756, Byng's flagship, the *Ramillies* 90, was laying ninth in line, the result of an earlier 16-point turn in succession. In a light breeze, he held the weather gauge but, in typical British fashion, his line was closing that of the French at a comparatively steep angle, of some 30-40 degrees. His intention was to engage formally, ship-to-ship, but, when he made the signal, only his half dozen van ships were in range, and still at such an angle to their opponents that only the latter could use their broadsides. As Byng, keeping his line, endeavoured to close, the *Intrepid*, sixth in line, had her fore topmast shot away, causing her to fly into the wind. Coming aback right across Byng's track, she threw the rear of the line into disorder as ships sought to avoid collision.

De la Galissonnière tried to take advantage of the situation by penetrating the resulting gap in the British line and isolating the van, but he was blocked. As Byng reformed, the

Sans Pareil

Battleships of their time, the great three-deckers were select commands on both sides. The French *Sans Pareil* here shows her full form and, unusually, a complete set of fair-weather canvas.

The Attack on Gorée.
29th December 1758 (Serres)

An important French outpost off present-day Dakar, Gorée Island had withstood an earlier attack by an inadequate British force under Commodore Marsh. In December 1758, therefore, Commodore Keppel was despatched with a larger squadron. Here the *Torbay* 74, wearing Keppel's broad pennant, prepares with others of the squadron to land troops. One of the two bomb ships also appears.

two fleets moved out of range. The primary duty of the French admiral was to cover his forces ashore and he had no reason to seek to renew the action, which had lasted about two hours. That Byng did not was a different matter. Brought home for court-martial, he was charged with not having done his utmost to either destroy the French fleet or to recover the situation ashore.

A major problem had been that the flagship had been stationed too far back in the line for Byng to have a clear idea of what was happening in the van and, when he did wish to exercise control, the available signal codes were not sufficiently explicit to convey his intentions accurately. Found guilty, Byng was executed, widely held to be a scapegoat.

It was an inauspicious start to a war that, for Britain, would be decided largely at sea. France had her attentions divided between events at sea and in the colonies, and in Europe with alliances and the need to beat Prussia. Britain, not so encumbered, was able to steadily convert naval superiority to naval supremacy. Although the Royal Navy enjoyed numerical superiority (and a further fifty line ships alone would be completed between 1756 and 1763), it would be sorely stretched in discharging its major policy duties:

(a) Maintaining forces in North American and Indian waters, capable of facilitating friendly operations while inhibiting those of the enemy;

(b) Blockading major enemy ports, to prevent formations putting to sea except at the cost of being brought to battle;

(c) Basing a squadron on Gibraltar capable of neutralising French forces based on Toulon;

(d) Conveying and supporting expeditions against enemy interests and territories world-wide, but notably in West Africa and the East and West Indies;

(e) Mounting raids on the French coast to oblige the enemy to deploy resources that could more usefully be deployed elsewhere.

There was also the on-going requirement to protect British coasts against the threat of invasion, and to safeguard vital British trade routes. With respect to the later, numerous British cruisers were committed to countering the many enemy privateers. These, making a good living from prizes, attracted the most able of seamen. Carrying the armament of a regular frigate, their apprehension often resulted in fierce ship-to-ship duels. The British 28-gun frigate *Tartar* was particularly successful, taking at least half a dozen privateers, including one 36 and three 26s.

France had several older-established bases in the Indian sub-continent and in neighbouring waters. In the Indian Ocean there were the islands of Madagascar, the Ile de France and the Ile de Bourbon (now the Malagasy Republic, Mauritius and Réunion respectively). On the mainland were Pondicherry, situated on the Coromandel Coast south of Madras, and Chandernagore, near Calcutta. Like their British equivalents, ships of the French East India Company were well armed, often having to defend themselves against pirates. Although pierced for many guns, however, they made indifferent warships, being slow and poor in manoeuvre. Their largest guns could rarely be deployed as the lower gundeck was usually cluttered with cargo.

Slow to look to their Indian interests, the French did not send a squadron of warships to the area until May 1757, and then only a 74 (the *Zodiaque*) and eight East Indiamen transporting 1,200 troops. Dupleix had fallen from favour and was being recalled. His successor, the Comte de Lally-Tollendal, was accompanying the squadron commander, the Comte d'Aché, with whom he had serious differences. With aristocratic hauteur, the latter in turn considered his command demeaning and took almost a year on passage.

British presence on the station was, nonetheless, inferior numerically. Vice-Admiral Sir George Pocock's squadron consisted of five line ships and a pair of 50s. During 1757 he had played a major role in Robert Clive's seizure of Calcutta and Chandernagore. In the June, Clive went on to defeat France's Indian allies at Plassey. Replacement by an Indian administration sympathetic to British interests was then pivotal in the latter's eventually taking overall control, and the part played by the Royal Navy should not be underestimated. Before this, however, a significant French force, under the Marquis de Bussy, was operating in Orissa, between Madras and Calcutta. D'Aché's reinforcement of de Bussy would have been of critical importance.

Acting on intelligence Pocock, with seven ships, intercepted d'Aché, with nine, off Cuddalore on 29th April 1758. He signalled 'General Chase' but, surprised when the French formed a line of battle, he countermanded the order and did the same. The *Fighting Instructions* allowed Pocock little latitude in tactics but, while the three van ships ahead of his flagship (the *Yarmouth* 64) engaged the enemy fiercely, the three in the rear persistently misread instructions and appeared reluctant to close. This Battle of Sadras was thus indecisive for, although d'Aché began to disengage after two hours of action, Pocock's four effective ships had been too cut-up about the rigging to attempt pursuit. While the French could point to a lack of formal naval training, Pocock's errant commanders well deserved the severe disciplinary sentences later handed down.

Ashore, de Lally had experienced some success and sought to invest the British base at Madras. As he argued in vain for d'Aché's support, Pocock refitted his damaged ships and brought his opponent to action again on 3rd August, this time off Negapatam. The fleets were of much the same strength, the British line led by Kempenfelt in the *Elizabeth* 64. He forced one Frenchman out of line afire and moved on to her neighbour. D'Aché in the *Zodiaque* moved in personally to intervene but, at a critical point, had his steering gear shot away and suffered a gun

Venus

The Spanish 28 gun frigate *Venus* was built in 1756 at La Carraca and armed with 12-pounder guns. The first Spanish 28/30 gun frigate *Juno* was completed in 1714 but the type was not followed by other navies for some time; although the term 'frigate' was employed by the Spanish navy for vessels carrying 22-40 guns from the early eighteenth century.

Kempenfelt

Of Swedish stock, Richard Kempenfelt was born in 1718. Lacking aristocratic connection, he was to make slow progress through the Royal Navy's ranks. In a junior capacity he was at the capture of Porto Bello in 1739 but it was only on commanding the *Elizabeth* 64 under Pocock that he first made his mark in actions against the French in Indian waters.

Kempenfelt finally made flag rank in 1780, proving his potential in the following year when, in the *Victory* 100, he led a squadron to take 20 ships of an America-bound French convoy, despite its superior escort, commanded by the capable Admiral Guichen. With Lord Howe taking the *Victory* as flagship when he assumed command of the Channel Fleet, Kempenfelt shifted his flag to another famous vessel, Hawke's old flagship *Royal George*. He was killed when she infamously foundered at Spithead in 1782.

Kempenfelt is noted, however, for being one of the Navy's better intellects. With Howe and others he greatly improved signalling methods. Deeply religious, he was much concerned for the welfare of his men and is often credited with proposing the divisional system. In truth, he was building on - as yet unregulated - attempts by others, notably Middleton (later Lord Barham) and Howe, to break down the large crews of the day into manageable groups. These would include individuals with all levels of experience, who would be the responsibility of assigned lieutenants, charged with both discipline and welfare. Kempenfelt produced many more papers on subjects as diverse as improvements to hygiene and health afloat, the tactical use of the Navy's various types of ship, and gunnery.

explosion. D'Aché cut his boats adrift and, crowding on sail, pulled away from the slower British, followed by his whole force. In light breezes, Pocock's signal for 'General Chase' was academic and a further 2½ hours of action proved indecisive. The French had, however, suffered over 250 fatalities.

Still defying de Lally, d'Aché landed his marines to fight as infantry and sailed his damaged squadron to refit at the Ile de France. De Lally laid siege to Madras in December 1758 but retired after eight weeks when Kempenfelt sailed into the port unchallenged with a relief convoy. Meanwhile, d'Aché's arrival at Ile de France was greeted locally with dismay as the island was destitute. The admiral did find three royal ships there but had to depart following only the most basic refitting.

Pocock was already back on the coast, having sailed around to Bombay for repairs. The French did not return until August 1759, having been obliged to seek materials from as far afield as Madagascar and South Africa. They now, however, had an advantage of eleven line ships and two frigates to nine British ships of the line and one frigate.

De Lally was now on the defensive, deployed around the French base at Pondicherry, and it was near here that Pocock brought d'Aché to action for a third time on 10th September. At what became known as the Battle of Porto Novo the British rear again experienced problems in getting into the fight which, elsewhere, was fierce and sustained. Three captains lost their lives and, following an interchange between the flagships, d'Aché himself was severely wounded. His flag captain was dead and, the next in command not having the will to continue, the *Zodiaque* pulled out, to be followed by the remainder. It was a bloody encounter, with 1,500 French casualties and nearly 600 British. Although, yet again, neither side lost a ship, d'Aché had had enough. He entered Pondicherry, landed what reinforcement he could and, ignoring all remonstrations from the besieged de Lally, sailed again for the Ile de France.

Pondicherry fell in January 1761 and, with it, the French challenge to dominance in India. On his return to France, de Lally's fate was to be imprisoned and, eventually, executed. The errant d'Aché died in comfort on a vice-admiral's pension. Pocock, though without a great victory to his credit, had succeeded in his aims, and was well rewarded with a KB and promotion to Admiral of the Blue.

Besides at Calcutta, mentioned above, the Seven Years' War provides several instances of successful combined operations between the Royal Navy and the military.

If Quebec was the key to Canada, then Louisbourg was the key to Quebec. Since its return to the French in 1748 (to the disgust of the New Englanders who had captured it) its fortification had been considerably extended. In the spring of 1757 the British moved 11,000 troops up from New York to Nova Scotia, there to await a delayed squadron from England. Learning of the move, the French had adequate time to garrison the town and to gather in its protected anchorage a force of 18 line ships and five frigates. Although his own attached naval force was slightly superior in numbers the British commander, Lord Loudoun, deferred an assault. Vice-Admiral Holburne therefore decided to institute a blockade, based on Halifax, both to prevent further reinforcement and to provoke his opposite number, the elderly Dubois de la Motte, to a fleet action.

Late in September, however, Holburne's force encountered hurricane-force winds, in which two ships were lost and many damaged, the majority having to sail for England and repair. Taking advantage, de la Motte sailed for Brest during November, the arrival of his typhus-ravaged crews creating an epidemic in that unfortunate town.

Pitt, on assuming power in the British administration, adopted a more resolute stance. In February 1758 Admiral Boscawen sailed with an expeditionary force commanded by Major-General Amherst. In conditions of heavy surf (in which 100 boats were lost) and some opposition, Brigadier-General James Wolfe conducted a satisfactory landing and, by mid-June, had Louisbourg besieged. Five French line ships, trapped in the harbour, for a time added their armament to the defence. A nocturnal cutting-out operation by Boscawen's men successfully captured the *Prudent* 74 and the *Bienfaisant* 64, their three colleagues being disabled by siege batteries. Excellent naval and military cooperation thus brought about Louisbourg's surrender on 27th July.

French forces about Quebec were cut off from re-supply. Although the French then tried to relieve such pressures abroad by increasing the threat of invasion at home, the British now had many more men under arms to resist this, while the Royal Navy had sufficient strength to blockade the enemy formations gathered at Morbihan, Le Havre

French fireships attacking at Quebec (Scott)

Although not a specialist marine painter, Samuel Scott was a founder member of the British school of marine art. This scene depicts British forces under Vice-Admiral Charles Saunders, whose blue ensign is worn by the *Neptune* 90, laying in the St. Lawrence prior to the assault on Quebec. At midnight on 28th June 1759 they were unsuccessfully attacked by French fireships, seen being grappled by British boats.

Far left: Model of 32-gun frigate. c1761
The date suggests that the model represents one of the British Lowestoffe (sic) class, whose lines were modified from those of the French *l'Abénakise*, a 'demi-batterie' frigate captured in 1757 by the *Chichester*. Although the French ship mounted a mixed 18- and 12-pounder armament, the *Chichester* was conventionally armed. Note the mizzen, still crossed with a lateen yard.

and Dunkirk. The French bluff was thus called, for their fleet was unable to contest control of Canadian waters. In contrast, the British transported sufficient forces to mount four separate shore expeditions for 1759. The sheer size of the wilderness across which these operated saw two of them enjoy little success, but the major effort, the assault on Quebec, was brilliantly carried through.

Staging, appropriately, via Louisbourg Vice Admiral Saunders' force of 20 sail of the line, two 50s, eight frigates and a score of smaller ships transported Wolfe and 9,000 men up the St. Lawrence river, arriving below Quebec by the end of June. The town was defended by some 14,000 French troops under the Marquis de Montcalm but such ships as he had in support had retreated further up-river. Profiting from capable hydrographic surveying, notably by James Cook, a decade before the commencement of his first great voyage, Wolfe was able to move formations up and down the river at will. Having prepared fixed bombardment works he unbalanced Montcalm by a series of feints along the river, and was able to land his main force without undue difficulty. In the ensuing action, in September 1759, both military commanders lost their lives, the French eventually surrendering to the British naval and military senior officers. The Navy had been the key to military mobility, while detachments of seamen had fought with distinction ashore.

Further up-river the French beleaguered in Montreal were in a hopeless situation. They capitulated a year later. Dominance in Canada was no longer disputed. As in India, only the flexibility of seapower had made possible the necessary movement and support of the military forces involved.

The war extended to the West Indies. Since early in the 17th Century the British had settled islands such as Antigua, the Bahamas, Jamaica, Montserrat and St. Kitts-Nevis; others had later been disputed with the Dutch. Beyond the capacity of the French fleet to defend them, Dominica, Grenada, St. Vincent and Tobago were added to the British flag by the Seven Years' War, together with others won but returned by peace agreement.

Cruiser warfare against French commerce in the Caribbean made it quickly adopt convoy. Intelligence on one of these sailings in October 1757 led Captain Arthur Forrest, in the *Augusta* 60, with two others in company, to an interception. The

San Genaro

A fine example of a Spanish 74, she participated in the Battle of St. Vincent in 1797. The name appeared to be unlucky. Her immediate predecessor was a 60-gunner, taken by the British at Havana in 1762 but subsequently wrecked on the Goodwins. An earlier galley of the name was one of five burned at St. Tropez in 1742 by the British fireship *Duke*.

strength of the convoy's escort, however, was a surprise, being three line ships, a 50 and three frigates, commanded by the Breton Commodore Kersaint de Coëtnempren. When Kersaint barred the way by forming a line of battle, Forrest boldly separated his three ships to tackle the enemy van, the centre and the rear. The French flagship, the *Intrépide* 74, after 2½ hours of battering from the *Augusta*, was in such straits as to order a frigate to tow her out of the line. This led to a general withdrawal, with a reported 500 French casualties. The British, with 120, were too cut-up about the rigging to follow up and, to their credit, the French had succeeded in their primary aim of safeguarding the convoy.

During this action the British centre was occupied by the *Dreadnought* 60, commanded by Captain Maurice Suckling, maternal uncle and, later, patron of one Horatio Nelson, born in the following year. The date of the action was, by coincidence, 21st October, forty-eight years to the day before Trafalgar.

High freight rates encouraged many British merchantmen to travel independently rather than wait for a convoy. Losses to French privateers provoked loud protest for action against their bases to eradicate the nuisance. By 1759, therefore, a powerful force was based on Barbados, its 28 ships including ten of the line, two 50s and seven frigates. In January of that year, 4,000 troops were put ashore on the French island of Martinique. It was a poorly-led operation and strong resistance from the garrison was sufficient to see the force recovered and moved on to Guadeloupe. A foothold here was successfully gained but it was a further three months before the mountainous little island was secured. Sickness ashore was rife and, because the French had reacted by sending a significant squadron, naval support had to fall back on Dominica.

With Guadeloupe taken and operations in Canada reaching a satisfactory conclusion, ground forces were available for other purposes and, towards the end of 1761, the appointment of Rear-Admiral Sir George Rodney to command the West Indies station signalled firmer action.

Spain, shortly before, had declared a compact with France. Pitt feared her intentions and urged a pre-emptive declaration of war. King George III, who had succeeded to the throne the year before, was only one of many deterred by Pitt's imperious manner but the latter's misgivings were justified. Spain had agreed a secret clause to declare war on Britain in May 1762 if the existing conflict had not already been resolved. The delay was caused primarily by want of funds, due with the annual arrival of the Plate fleet. Had Pitt's advice been followed, the two ships that arrived safely in September 1761 could have been seized by the Royal Navy. Pitt resigned in disgust the following month, only to see Spain's hardening attitude cause Britain herself to declare war in January 1762.

Spain's motives were based on sentimental ties between Bourbon courts, but France was in poor state as a partner. Ousted from Canada and India, she lacked a credible fleet, reduced to barely 40 of the line, and was losing ground elsewhere. While a welcome reinforcement, the Spanish fleet was not highly regarded by the French and despised by the British. Already flushed with success, the latter determined to deal hard and deal quickly with their new adversary. British squadrons thus cruised the Iberian coasts as a large expedition was being assembled to strike at Havana in Spanish Cuba.

Lacking French activity locally, the East Indies station instigated a move against the Spanish Philippines. A scratch collection of warships and East Indiamen sailed from India under the command of Rear-Admiral Samuel Cornish in the *Norfolk* 74. Staging via neutral Dutch Malacca the force arrived off Manila to find the Spanish unaware of the declaration of war. Although the defences were much run down it took the two available battalions of British troops ten days of desultory fighting to persuade the garrison that it could capitulate honourably. The town itself was ransomed for four million dollars, and the islands placed under the administration of the East India Company. A further three millions were secured when the *Santissima Trinidad* treasure ship was captured by the *Panther* and *Argo*. As a further argosy, with a reputed four millions, had been seized in the Atlantic, the impoverished Spanish awaited with some apprehension the next and obvious move against Central America.

The landings in the Philippines had been carried out in heavy ship's boats. Unsuited to heavy surf, many broached and not a few men were drowned, even though opposition was very light. The 150 fatalities were, nonetheless, considered a small loss, while the senior officers were awarded the usual generous prize money and honours.

As the war moved towards its climax, the British staged other major amphibious operations in the Caribbean, against the French in Martinique and the aforementioned one against the Spanish in Havana. Against Martinique Rodney had a large force of 40 warships, including 13 of the line. Early in January 1762 these transported about 14,000 troops to the island and, as these battles were over difficult terrain, ships closed the shore to pound strongpoints, to cover seaward flanks and to land naval brigades with field guns. It took a month to subdue resistance but, with the fall of Fort Royal, the enemy lost his major privateering base, said alone to have been responsible for the loss of 1,400 British merchant ships.

Although Rodney's success led also to the rapid taking of Grenada and St. Lucia the scale of the expedition against Havana saw the command given to Admiral Sir George Pocock, with Commodore Keppel as his second-in-command. Bearing in mind Rodney's reputation for the pursuit of booty and prize money, this must have been a severe personal blow.

With many more ships now available for deployment, Pocock had a virtual fleet, including 22 ships of the line. In May 1762 he utilised good surveying to move this armada unexpectedly quickly by the dangerously constricted Mona Passage and Old Bahama Channel. Covered by a feint move, he put ashore over 15,000 troops. These required to cross a river to reach their objective but the attempt by the Spanish to make this a main line of defence was defeated by ships, including the *Dragon* 74, coming close inshore to pour in enfilading fire.

The entrance to Havana harbour was dominated by the twin bastions of Morro Castle and the Castello de la Punta. Three third rates were detailed to close and pound these into submission but, not for the last time in history, it was found that ships were no

The Execution of Admiral Byng
Vice-Admiral the Hon. John Byng was despatched in April 1756 to raise a French siege of Minorca, then the only effective British base inside the Mediterranean. On 20th May he fought an inconclusive action with the French covering force, which was content to prevent his interference. Byng tried no further and Minorca fell. Condemned to death at a controversial court-martial, Byng was shot in March 1757.

Southampton

The four Southamptons were the Navy's first 32-gun 12-pounder frigates. Large for their time, they could be used for tasks earlier requiring a small two-decker. The crew were quartered below the gundeck, which made for more comfort while allowing the ship to be more quickly cleared for action. Wrecked in 1812.

HMS Southampton cutaway key

1. Mizzen
2. Mizzenmast
3. Mizzen topsail
4. Mainmast
5. Mainsail
6. Main topsail
7. Main topgallant
8. Foremast
9. Foresail
10. Foretopsail
11. Foretopgallant
12. Staysail
13. Spiritsail
14. Captain's cabin
15. Rudder
16. Rudder post
17. Food store
18. Spare chains
19. Water barrels
20. Powder store
21. Potato store
22. Flour
23. Chain locker
24. Capstan
25. Gun deck
26. Main deck
27. Orlop deck
28. Pump
29. Magazine
30. Rubbing strake
31. Long boat
32. Hull support
33. Deck beams
34. Ballast
35. Boat store
36. Cable bits
37. Spare rigging
38. Sail locker
39. Galley
40. Forecastle
41. Sick bay
42. Carpenter's stores
43. Keel
44. Prow
45. Bowsprit

The Capture of St. Lucia (Serres)

As the garrison capitulated honourably in the face of superior force, the taking of St. Lucia in February 1762 was something of a formality. Here, temporary Commodore the Hon. Augustus Hervey in the *Dragon* 74 oversees the landing of troops. The stylised appearance of the latter is due to the design of the special flatboats, aboard which troops stood in a double line along the centreline, flanked by seated seaman rowers.

match for fixed fortifications. Having taken heavy damage and over 200 casualties they withdrew, leaving the task to field batteries. Morro was eventually stormed and taken on 30th July, the city surrendering a fortnight later. The capture was equivalent to a significant naval victory for, of the twelve Spanish ships of the line in the harbour, three had been expended as blockships, and the remainder left for prizes. Two more hulls, still in frame, were destroyed.

The city yielded so much wealth that the then enormous sum of nearly three quarters of a million pounds was distributed as prize money. Never more obvious was the inequality of the system for, of this, Pocock and the military commander, the Earl of Albemarle, each received £123,000 while the average seaman was awarded less than four pounds. Disease ashore was so rife that it was estimated that barely 2,500 fit men remained when the city fell. Reinforcement by 4,000 New Englanders met with disaster when, on 24th July, their four transports and the escorting *Chesterfield* 40 were all wrecked.

If too high a proportion of Spain's fleet had been deployed abroad, the opposite was true for that of her ally. The French navy was run-down and in poor spirit. There was friction between the aristocratic officer corps and those recruited from the merchant marine to plug the gaps, despite the latter being the source also of the corsairs and privateers who caused British interests much grief. Ministers of Marine came and went, either incompetent or despairing of curing the general malaise. As we have seen, the French, realising that they could not resolve the struggle at sea, adopted the policy of threatening invasion. In home waters, therefore, the Royal Navy had a prime duty to ensure that the enemy could not assemble a maritime force large enough to transport the formidable French army. Much of the British coastline — East Anglia, Wales and Scotland — was virtually undefended. The endlessly dissident Ireland was also attractive to the French as an invasion objective.

Suitable shallow-water craft were being produced in numbers at such as Dunkirk, Le Havre and Rochefort while the fleet strove to improve both its strength and efficiency. Because the main strength of the Royal Navy was kept in home waters, so was that of the French, but its division between the major bases of Brest and Toulon was a handicap. The latter force had a certain freedom within the Mediterranean as the British still could not operate there in strength. That at Brest, however, became more of a fleet-in-being, blockaded in its base and unable to benefit from exercise or the experience of battle. It remained a powerful latent threat but its morale deteriorated knowing that its enemy cruised, unchallenged in its very approaches.

British 'close blockade' varied considerably in its closeness. When weather conditions were propitious for a French breakout, the Western Squadron increased its immediate strength but, because remaining at sea for extended periods reduced the ships' fighting efficiency through wear and tear, it was customary to maintain the fleet at short notice in an anchorage such as Torbay, relying on patrolling frigates to give warning. The system was far from ideal; the British lacked a completely satisfactory anchorage and, in a rapid weather shift, the French could break out with a head start if they moved smartly.

To keep French resources committed at home, and relieve pressure on their Prussian allies, the British mounted raids on the enemy coast, varying from operations lasting a few hours to actual occupation of French territory. They were an expensive way to annoy the enemy, moving Charles James Fox, later Foreign Secretary, to compare them with "breaking windows with guineas".

Operations in home waters saw the British succeed through patient attrition rather than by glorious battle, the opportunities for which were few. Nor were British operations always entirely creditable.

An early expedition was that of September 1757, when Admiral Sir Edward Hawke was charged with descending "at or near Rochefort ... and, by vigorous impression, force that place; and to burn and destroy ... all ... as shall be found there". Rochefort, situated near the mouth of the Charente River, lay in something of a marine cul-de-sac.

Barrington's action at St. Lucia - (Serres)

In December 1778, Rear-Admiral the Hon. Samuel Barrington took advantage of French indecision to land a superior force at the Carénage (now Castries) on St. Lucia. By capturing enemy fortifications on the promontary of la Vigie he was able to bring his squadron to anchor close inshore, enabling him to repulse a counter-attack by a larger squadron under d'Estaing.

The captured Spanish fleet at Havana (Serres)

The taking of Havana was the equivalent of a considerable naval victory for, of the twelve Spanish sail of the line there present, three were expended as blockships and the remaining nine surrendered. Taken into the Royal Navy were the *Infante, Reina, Soberano, Tigre* and *Aquilon*, all of 70 guns. With anglicised names, they all gave about a decade more of useful service.

Its approaches, the soon-to-be-famous Basque Roads, were dominated by fortifications on the sheltering Ile d'Oléron and the inshore Ile d'Aix. Hawke was given a formidable fleet, including 16 line ships, whose captains included such up-and-coming names as Howe, Keppel and Graves. The Ile d'Aix was quickly seized and its fortifications reduced but, although the fleet could now operate freely, the military leadership dithered for four days before deciding a landing to be too hazardous, and aborting the operation. Amazed at this, the French afterwards owned Rochefort to have been virtually defenceless.

Perhaps alleviating what must have been a frustrating experience, Hawke breached the same waters again in the following April. His objective was an assembly of half a dozen enemy line ships, as many frigates and a reported 40 transports, gathered to carry an expeditionary force for the relief of Cape Breton Island in Canada. Hawke's intentions were again thwarted, this time by a falling tide, whose considerable range enabled the French to scatter their ships into innumerable mud-bound inlets.

Where such British probes should have been vulnerable to interception by a considerable force issuing from Brest, the latter were still in poor shape and under close investment by Admiral Lord Anson. During the following June, Anson and Hawke provided deep cover for a considerable raid on St. Malo. Over the course of two days, some 14,000 troops were landed to the east, at Cancale, from specially-constructed, flat bottomed boats. Finding the town to be too well fortified to be taken easily, the force spent a week making a nuisance before being re-embarked. Having thus far achieved little, it cruised in the Channel for a fortnight before appearing at Le Havre. Finding the French well-prepared there, it moved on to Cherbourg, whereupon the weather turned unfavourable for a landing. A month after originally leaving, the army returned in a poor state of health.

The force sailed again a month later with a new military commander. Its objective was again Cherbourg, then undeveloped as a base. Following a week demolishing defensive works, it returned safely to England on 19th August, only to be ordered back to France just twelve days later. On this occasion it attempted to take St. Malo from the west. Again the resources available were found insufficient but, by now, the French had also deployed a field force. After a leisurely week ashore the British suddenly found themselves harried by cavalry and artillery and only regained the beach under considerable pressure. Re-embarkation cost the army 800 men and the navy four captains who had been landed as beachmasters. What had started as a successful exercise in annoying the enemy had been pursued to the point of complacency and punishment followed.

French forces based on Toulon were the responsibility of Admiral Osborn's Gibraltar command. Late in 1757 the French were ordered to despatch a relief squadron to North America. Short of materials they sailed a first part of the force under Admiral de la Clue Sabran. Learning that Osborn was cruising the Gibraltar strait, the French admiral ran into Cartegena to await the remainder of his strength. This, five line ships and a frigate, duly arrived on 28th February 1758. Two entered the Spanish port safely but the rest lagged behind and were intercepted by Osborn. They scattered, but only the frigate, *Pleiade*, escaped. The *Orphée* 64 struck to the *Revenge* and *Berwick*, each of comparable strength. The *Oriflamme* 50 was driven ashore by the larger *Monarch* and *Montagu* and was later saved. The major capture was that of the *Foudroyant* 80, wearing the flag of the French subordinate commander, Duquesne. She fought for 4½ hours with the *Monmouth* 64, capitulating only with the arrival of the *Swiftsure* 70. The *Monmouth*'s achievement was the greater as she was armed with 12- and 24-pounders against her opponent's 24s and 42s. The British ship lost her captain, but fought on under her first lieutenant. A fine ship, the *Foudroyant*, was refitted and went on to give the Royal Navy 30 years of service carrying, as was customary, her original name.

On a scale of actions fought, that off Cartagena would not rank very high, yet it typified the remorseless attrition that eroded the French will to seek decisive action. In this case, their intentions were frustrated — de la Clue returned to Toulon — and they lost valuable ships. French accounts speak also of the *Foudroyant*'s guncrews taking cover from the *Monmouth*'s broadsides.

Early in 1759 the French threatened to invade again. Royal Naval squadrons watched Dunkirk and lay in the Downs; others cruised the Channel off the Normandy ports and continued the close blockade of Brest. Vice-Admiral Thomas Brodrick, based at Gibraltar, was charged with monitoring de la Clue's activities in Toulon. As this French fleet grew to ten of the line, two 50s and three small frigates the Admiralty supplemented Brodrick's force with another under Admiral Boscawen, who assumed command at the end of April.

This reinforcement was timely as de la Clue had been ordered to sail for the Spanish Atlantic port of Cadiz, there to await instructions. As the British rotated ships for rest and repair the French admiral seized his chance. It was on the 17th August that the *Gibraltar* 24 sighted the French, hard by the African shore and approaching the strait before a favourable breeze. She raised the alarm at 7.30 p.m. and after frantic preparation, Boscawan's force was at sea by 10.00 p.m. He had two line ships more than the French, and also a dozen ships of 40 guns or less. Having put to sea in haste themselves, they were in some disorder, divided into two main groups.

De la Clue knew that his next order would be to link with the fleet at Brest. With Boscawen in pursuit and a fair wind he therefore decided to stand on rather than enter Cadiz. However, either through disaffection or, simply, not reading their admiral's night signals, the five rear ships put into the Spanish port as originally directed. Dawn on the 18th discovered de la Clue with only seven ships in company. When he saw a group of ships astern, he assumed them to be his own stragglers and slowed to allow them to rejoin. He then realised that they were the British lead group, pressing on under full sail.

Hawke

Born in 1705, Edward Hawke was the son of a barrister, although brought up by his uncle, a senior official at the Royal Mint. Joining the Royal Navy as a 15-year-old volunteer, he served on the American, West Indies and African stations before being promoted to third lieutenant in 1729. Junior captain followed in 1733, when he assumed his first command, the 14-gun sloop *Wolf*. His good connections saw him made post-captain in the following year, at the age of 29. Married in 1737, he eventually fathered six children.

It was 1744 before he had the chance to prove himself at sea. Commanding the *Berwick* 70 during an otherwise indecisive action off Toulon, he took a 60-gun Spanish ship. In doing so, he disregarded Fighting Instructions by breaking line, the success of which greatly influenced his future actions. His promotion to rear admiral in 1746 is said to have been by the direct influence of the King.

During 1747 he took temporary command of the Western Squadron. Encountering a French formation off Ushant, he ordered 'General Chase', which resulted in the capture of six of the enemy. Made a KB, Hawke also became MP for Portsmouth, simultaneously serving as Flag Officer of that command. Following an abortive combined operation against Rochefort in 1758 he struck his flag, but returned to serve under Anson. In 1759, in the *Royal George* 100, he led his squadron into the Bay of Quiberon in pursuit of Conflans, gaining a decisive victory in wild conditions among the shoals.

He finally came ashore in 1762, serving as First Lord from 1766 to 1768, when he was made Admiral of the Fleet. Created Baron Hawke of Towton in 1776, he died five years later.

The Capture of Havana (Serres)

A feint assault preceded the main landing, seen here, which went ashore some six miles from Havana. Here, the Earl of Albemarle's army is landing without opposition from transports and a squadron of Sir George Pocock's ships, the *Téméraire* 74, *Dragon* 74, *Orford* 66, *Edgar* 64, *Pembroke* 60 and *Ripon* 60. The capture of the town resulted in a bonanza of prize money and booty.

Throughout the forenoon, de la Clue was slowly overhauled and, at 2.30 p.m., the *Culloden* was sufficiently advanced to fire on the French backmarker, the *Centaure* 74. The British ships were under orders to turn the enemy van and the unfortunate *Centaure* found herself the first target for each as it overtook. The wind dropped and she found herself surrounded by British ships which she gallantly engaged in an effort to allow de la Clue to escape. Although she fought for five hours before striking her flag, her sacrifice was in vain. Boscawen slowly worked his flagship, the *Namur* 90, alongside the French flag, the *Océan* 80, only to have his rigging so badly damaged he transferred to the *Newark*.

Under a fitful breeze, the running action continued into the following night. In the course of this, and to their discredit, the French 74s *Souverain* and *Guerrier* managed to slip away, eventually making Rochefort. By dawn on the 19th the unfortunate de la Clue was left with only four ships. He was himself badly injured, his pursuers were three miles away and the Portuguese coast was visible. He decided to seek cover of neutral waters and made for an anchorage between Cape St. Vincent and the small port of Lagos. It proved to be no sanctuary. In the tradition of hot pursuit, Boscawen followed him in.

The *Océan* ran aground and carried away her masts. De la Clue and the bulk of his crew abandoned her before the British came up and burned the hulk. Admiral de la Clue later died from his injuries. The *Redoubtable* was burned too. The *Téméraire* and *Modeste* put up only a token resistance before being taken. Together with the battered *Centaure*, they were brought back to Gibraltar. Portuguese susceptibilities were soothed by a limited diplomatic apology and, with Brodrick blockading the five French survivors in Cadiz, the Toulon squadron was no longer a threat. Incidentally, the Battle of Lagos highlighted the deficiencies of signalling systems on both sides: Boscawen was displeased with the lack of enterprise shown by some of his captains. Faced with an unplanned 'General Chase', they tended to hang back awaiting instructions that the admiral's limited choice of signals could not convey.

Hawke remained in force outside Brest, using a small inshore squadron to watch both the base and the considerable force of invasion transports gathered in the Gulf of Morbihan to the south. The French admiral, de Conflans-Brienne, was much concerned for the latter and when, in November 1759, a spell of severe weather compelled Hawke's temporary withdrawal to Torbay, he broke out to chase off the inshore squadron and to bring out the transports.

Again it was McCleverty in the *Gibraltar* that raised the alarm, meeting Hawke who, fortuitously, was already heading back. Conflans had been sighted on a south-easterly heading and Hawke, correctly assuming Morbihan to be his objective, steered directly there. The anchorage in question is sheltered offshore by Belle Ile and contained by the curve of the Quiberon peninsula, the extremity of which continues as a dangerous line of half-submerged reefs, terminating in a distinctive group called les Cardinaux. Beyond is a hazardous patch known as le Four. What appears a safe and spacious haven is a boiling death-trap in a gale from the south-western quadrant. In this November of 1759 there was a rising gale from the south, with a hint of east.

Conflans had in company 21 sail of the line, organised in three divisions, and five frigates. Doubling Belle Ile, he turned northward to approach Quiberon at first light on the 20th. The blockading British squadron hastily decamped on sighting the approaching armada. Hawke, with 23 line ships, four 50s and six frigates, was hard put to make ground to the south until, on the 19th, the wind veered through west to north-west, increasing the while. Sending three fast sailers ahead to reconnoitre and to make a landfall, he was rewarded when, at 8.30 p.m. on the 20th, the *Maidstone* frigate reported the enemy.

Conflans had hoped to have the opportunity to draw his fleet up defensively at anchor but did not really believe that the British would dare enter the roadstead in poor

Bombardment of Morro Castle (Richard Paton)

To assist in the siege of Havana, Sir George Pocock ordered the bombardment of Morro Castle, one of the fortifications flanking the harbour entrance. On 1 July 1762 the *Cambridge* 80, *Dragon* 74 and *Marlborough* 70 exchanged close-range fire for some six hours. Warships rarely get the better of shore fortifications and all had eventually to retire, having suffered a total of 42 killed and 140 wounded.

Destruction of the Floating Batteries at Gibraltar (Thomas Whitcombe)

Gibraltar, victualled by Rodney in 1780 and by Darby in 1781, remained besieged. To blockade the Rock the Spanish built gunboats with oars and sails. These proved to be unsatisfactory and were replaced by floating batteries. In September 1782 these attacked before the arrival of Howe with a large convoy. All but one were destroyed by the defences.

conditions and without local knowledge. Seeing the leading elements of Hawke's fleet nonetheless overhauling him, Conflans wasted some time endeavouring to form a line of battle. Eventually, he changed his mind and his fleet made its way into the bay in no real formation, led, rather unfortunately, by his flagship *Soleil Royal*. In conditions of heavy squalls and a lumpy, breaking sea two fleets pressed on all possible sail, the one to engage, the other to survive. Hawke had sent on a flying squadron of seven ships (including Howe in the *Magnanime* and Keppel in the *Torbay*) and, even as Conflans rounded the Cardinaux, these were engaging his tail-enders, some eight miles astern. It was already after 2.00 p.m. and Hawke, realising that this was no time for a set-piece battle, wisely kept his instructions to a minimum.

Moving like terriers up the French line, the seven savaged particularly the *Formidable* 80, flagship of the Third Division. Shattered and with over 200 dead, including the rear-admiral, she was the first to strike. Hawke was taking a supreme gamble in allowing a mêlée to develop in such wild and dangerous waters. Conflans, who had believed himself safe, now found his fleet running out of searoom, pursued by an enemy apparently heedless of his own safety. Collisions and groundings became inevitable.

The *Thesée* 74, commanded by Kersaint de Coëtnempren, rounded on Keppel's *Torbay*, only to heel so far that her lower lee gun ports vanished under water. She foundered instantly, to be followed almost immediately by the 74-gun *Superbe* in similar circumstances. As darkness gathered matters became confused, with stranding a major risk to both sides. Howe took on the *Héros*, of similar strength to his own, and obliged her to strike. Such was the sea that was running, however, that no boat could be sent to claim her. She grounded on the Four bank, and her crew scrambled ashore.

Elements of the French fleet split away, a group of eight ships running inshore of the Four to escape southward to Rochefort. Most of the survivors, however, gathered in the entrance to the Vilaine River. As darkness fell, Hawke signalled his force to come to anchor but, as a double signal gun gave the order, it is doubtful if many comprehended it.

After a wild and uncomfortable night, Conflans himself anchored in the midst of his enemies at first light, while the Vilaine group were frantically lightening their ships to ascend the river further. Slipping in haste, the *Soleil Royal* grounded. Hawke sent the *Essex* 64 to complete her destruction but she, too stranded and was lost. Also aground, and eventually lost, was the *Resolution*, which had done well in the flying squadron.

Able to accomplish no more, Hawke retired in good order. The Royal Navy would fight many a tidier action but rarely a more effective one. The ferocity of the attack and the lack of concern for its own situation engendered a new respect for the Service. With three wrecked, two foundered and one captured, the material loss to the French was not overwhelming, but the moral effect was immense. Now split in two groups, the Brest fleet was blockaded for a year, making invasion plans impossible and freeing much of the Royal Navy's strength for operations elsewhere. To public acclaim, Hawke was awarded a generous pension for life and, among others, Boscawen, Howe and Keppel were honoured.

Freedom from the risk of general invasion did not guarantee Britain's long coastline from attack however. As part of the main French invasion plan, a diversionary force was to sail from Dunkirk to effect a landing in Ireland. Led by an ex-privateer named François Thurot, the force comprised six minor warships with 1,300 troops aboard. It slipped out of Dunkirk in October 1759, the month before Quiberon. Following a strange odyssey via Scandinavia, the Faeroes and the Hebrides it arrived, less three ships, off Belfast Lough in February 1760. Thurot landed his troops, who seized Carrickfergus but balked at going on to threaten Belfast. His situation was vulnerable, for three of Hawke's frigates were laying at Kinsale for stress of weather. On 28th February, the alarm raised, these rapidly intercepted and captured all three French ships, taking them into Ramsey.

In 1761 the British occupied Belle Ile, an island of little tactical use and whose re-supply and support was possible only through sea supremacy. Keppel, advanced to the rank of commodore to reflect his responsibilities, commanded a force of ten of the line and eight frigates, covering transports with about 7,000 troops. Arriving on 6th April after an eight day passage the troops had to undertake an opposed landing at three points, and were repulsed with heavy casualties. They were then crowded aboard their transports for a further fortnight. On the 22nd, supported by feint landings and a close barrage from four of Keppel's ships, the Marines secured a tiny foothold through which more powerful forces could be passed. Most of the island was quickly overrun but the citadel in the town held out until 7th June. British military losses, in action and from disease, ran into many hundreds but the island was held without incident for the remainder of the war.

Peace came unofficially in November 1762, being formalised by the Treaty of Paris in the following February. Although having to return some territory, Britain gained considerably. Despite hundreds of vessels lost to privateering, the nation increased in prosperity through the strengthening of trading networks. The Royal Navy enjoyed a surge of prestige while France, having absorbed the results of allowing her fleet to go into decline, relied on another new Secretary of the Navy, the able Duc de Choiseul, to rebuild it in spirit as much as materially. During the period of the Seven Years' War 1756-63, 39 seagoing British warships were lost. Of these, 31 were destroyed by wreck, foundering or accident. Of the remaining eight, taken by the enemy, four were eventually recaptured. By comparison, the French lost exactly 100 warships but, of these losses, only 23 were due to hazards of the sea. Spain lost 18 during her brief spell of hostilities. Only five were taken in action, the remainder being seized or scuttled at Havana.

Keppel

Augustus, 1st. Viscount Keppel, was something of a prodigy. Born in 1725, he joined the Royal Navy as a boy, serving under Anson during the circumnavigation of 1740-44. He was a post-captain at 19 and, by 1754, having commanded a squadron operating against the Barbary Pirates, he was a commodore, wearing his broad pendant in the *Centurion*, Anson's old ship. In the *Torbay* 74 he commanded a squadron that captured the important settlement of Gorée in French Senegal and, in the same ship, he was with Hawke at Quiberon in 1759.

Transferring to the *Valiant* 74 he commanded a considerable force that transported and covered 7,000 troops who seized Belle Isle as a forward base for operations against the French Atlantic coast. In 1762, the following year, he was second-in-command to Pocock in an even larger operation to take Havana. About a dozen Spanish ships were taken or destroyed, while the town yielded enormous riches. Keppel was awarded £25,000 and made Rear Admiral of the Blue.

Keppel would not operate against the Americans in the struggle for independence but, when the French intervened, he took command of the Channel Fleet. In July 1778 he encountered the French off Ushant and, with both sides having some 30 sail of the line, a major action should have ensued. The French Admiral d'Orvilliers, however, had conflicting orders and the result was indecisive. Unusually, the commander of the British rear, Palliser, brought charges against Keppel. It was a personality clash and, although both were tried by court-martial, both were acquitted.

In 1782, as Admiral of the White, Keppel was made First Lord of the Admiralty but, having been raised to the peerage, soon after retired. He died in 1786.

CHAPTER 3: *King George's Navy*

*Naval Review at Spithead 1767
(Francis Swaine)*

King George III showed great personal interest in the Royal Navy, in which served two of his brothers and a son. Fleet reviews were popular manifestations of his attention, being accompanied by distributions of favours and promotions. The florid detail of yachts, royal and otherwise, harked back to the Restoration and, here, Swaine portrays craft of both 'yacht rig' and a variation of 'ketch rig'.

When the Peace of Paris ended the Seven Years' War in 1763, the Royal Navy was in good shape. This was due in no small measure to the exertions of Lord Anson. In two spells as First Lord of the Admiralty (1751-6, and from 1757 until his death in 1762) he had proved to be one of the most effective administrators to date. His epic circumnavigation of 1740-4 and his victory off Finisterre in 1747 had secured his reputation, now sealed by considerable wisdom and judgement, exercised through his creation of a sympathetic Navy Board. Like the later First Lord Admiral Barham, his efforts went far to ensure that the Navy Board and the Admiralty pulled in the same direction.

The Ships

It was Anson who simplified the rating system, which divided the hotchpotch of existing classes into two main groups. First, Second and Third Rates served in the Line of Battle while the majority of Fourth Rates, together with Fifth and Sixth rates, acted in supporting roles. Although a measure of overlap inevitably existed, the 1763 rating resulted in a battle fleet of about 140 ships, with twice that number of lesser vessels, often lumped together as 'Cruisers'.

Complaints abounded that British-built ships were inferior sailers, or that they could not fight their full armament in such extreme conditions as their opponents. There was always a grain of truth in this and, occasionally, prejudice, for all ship design is a compromise and an ideal range of qualities is never realised in a single hull. In 1719, following much adverse comparison with French-built ships a new establishment of dimensions was prepared, with each type considerably increased in size. By 1740, these standards were being widely ignored, resulting in significant variations, even among supposed sister ships. Continued comment about their being 'crank', or unable to carry sufficient canvas in a blow, resulted in two further half-hearted efforts at reform in 1733 and 1741, but only in 1745 was a new establishment of dimensions firmly mandated. These, expressed in feet, were:-

	100gun	90gun	80gun	70gun	60gun	50gun	40gun	30gun
Length, gun deck	178.00	170.00	165.00	160.00	150.00	144.00	133.00	113.00
Length, keel	140.54	138.33	134.90	131.33	123.04	117.71	108.83	93.33
Breadth, extreme	51.00	48.50	47.00	45.00	42.67	41.00	37.50	32.00
Depth at hold	21.50	20.50	20.00	19.33	18.50	17.00	16.00	11.00
Tons, burthen	2,000	1,730	1,585	1,414	1,191	1,052	814	508
Complement	850	750	650	520	420	350	280	160

It was to be the last major attempt at achieving standardisation and, even by the time of Anson's first appointment, it was seen as too restrictive and was being circumvented.

At a time when a ship's fighting power was measured in terms of weight of broadside, the disparity between classes is rather greater than that indicated by the number of guns carried. This is simply because larger ships could accommodate heavier guns. Recommended batteries were:-

	100gun	90gun	80gun	70gun	60gun	50gun	40gun	20gun
Lower deck	28x42	26x32	26x32	28x32	26x24	22x24	20x18	-
Middle deck	28x24	26x18	26x18	-	-	-	-	-
Upper deck	28x12	26x12	24x9	28x18	26x12	22x12	20x9	20x9
Quarterdeck	12x6	10x6	4x6	12x9	6x6	4x6	-	-
Forecastle	4x6	2x6	-	2x9	2x6	2x6	4x6	-
Broadside (lb)	1,140	842	770	763	492	414	282	90

In this table the typical abbreviation (28x42) represents twenty-eight 42-pounders. The 40-gun type is represented by the 44-gunner, the nearest then built. Figures for broadside are theoretical, assuming the unlikely possibility of half the armament bearing on a target; they nonetheless serve as a comparison.

A. Flying jib
B. Jib
C. Fore topmast staysail
D. Spritsail topsail
E. Spritsail
F. Fore royal
G. Fore topgallant sail
H. Fore topsail
I. Fore sail or fore course
J. Main topgallant staysail
K. Middle staysail
L. Main topmast staysail
M. Main staysail
N. Main royal
O. Main topgallant sail
P. Main topsail
Q. Mainsail or main course
R. Mizzen topgallant staysail
S. Mizzen topmast staysail
T. Mizzen staysail
U. Mizzen topgallant sail
V. Mizzen topsail
W. Mizzen sail

STANDING RIGGING
Upper diagram: Stays

Stays supported masts against fore-and-aft forces from ahead. They were greatly interdependent. For instance, the loss of a jib boom would not only make the ship unmanageable through the additional loss of her headsails but would also bring down the fore topgallant mast. Important stays might be doubled and the inset shows how they were 'snaked' to prevent chafe.

Lower diagram:
Backstays and shrouds

Backstays helped support the masts from fore-and-aft forces from astern, while shrouds gave mainly transverse support. Both are led only slightly aft, so as to allow the yards to be braced to a maximum angle. Lower shrouds are led to the sides of the ship and are secured to chain plates, being set up taut by deadeyes and lanyards (see inset).

Quoted numbers of guns were often significantly inaccurate, particularly after 1779 and the introduction of the carronade. Probably because of its lightness and its short barrel, it was not reckoned as part of the main battery. Between eight and ten were carried by most classes of British ship; so a nominally 100-gun First Rate might carry 110 carriage guns. A Fifth Rate 32-gun frigate might, more importantly, have 40. A further anomaly was that even conventional ordnance was not reckoned in the total if mounted on the poop. Not until 1817 did the Admiralty revise the system, to give a more realistic yardstick.

Only 100-gunners and above were classed as First Rates. Until the closing years of the 18th century only four or five of them existed at any time, and were usually employed as senior flagships. The 42-pounder guns carried on their lower decks enabled them to deliver a very heavy broadside. Such cannon, however, demanded larger crews and suffered from a low rate of fire. From about the turn of the 19th century, it became customary to exchange them for the faster-firing 32-pounder.

In the line of battle, the senior flagship in the centre would be flanked ahead and astern by Second Rates. These were not numerous either, no more than 12-18 active at once. These 90-gunners followed the general trend to increase in size, eventually being designed as 98s. Used as general-purpose flagships, they became the equal in firepower and size to First Rates of only a few years earlier.

Ships pierced for 60 to 80 guns were classed as Third Rates and, from about 1755, were considered the smallest fit to lay in the line of battle. Eighty-gun ships devolved into two types, having either two or three decks. The three-decked variant attracted much adverse criticism. Shorter and deeper than the two-deckers, they were very tender and unable to open their lower gun ports in more than a moderate breeze. On the other hand, the extra length required to accommodate the same armament in only two decks resulted in problems with longitudinal strength, as depth was significantly decreased. Some two-deckers were decked-over in the waist to give a little extra stiffness but the fate of most three-decked 80s was either a short life or being cut down to two-decker 64s.

A successful design was, not for the first time, obtained from the French. The 80-gun *Foudroyant* was taken off Cartagena in 1758 following a magnificent single-ship action and, when measured, proved to be 12 feet longer than a contemporary British First Rate. Taken into the Royal Navy under her own name, her fine qualities made her a popular command, and she was associated with both Rodney and Jervis.

Far right: 'The Rivals'

At a time in British history when most able-bodied men were under arms, normal conventions were altered by an endlessly-shifting population. Any comely wench could enjoy the attentions of a variety of suitors. Here, Jack ashore has competition from a splendidly-attired military person, but has taken the precaution of bringing a mate...

R.Bunbury Esqr del.^t   G.Shepheard sculp.^t

THE RIVALS.

Published Jan.^{ry} 1809 by J.Dedey 9 Berwick St Soho.

Naval vessels could spend extended periods at anchor at such as St. Helens or the Nore and, by today's standards, a crew might be granted considerable licence. Among a wide variety of visitors were traders, many of them rascally, of whom one here gets appropriate deserts. Note Cruikshank's grasp of detail; the boats and spars on the skids and the Marine enjoying the spectacle but not participating.

Third Rates formed the backbone of the fleet, by far the most numerous group being the 74s. Probably influenced by the French *Invincible* and *Monarch*, taken at the 1747 actions off Finisterre, the joint Surveyors of the Navy, Slade and Bately, ignored the strictures of the 1745 establishment and lengthened a group of 70s then on order. Still ten feet shorter than the Frenchmen the British ships, beginning with the Dublins, proved popular. Handier than three-deckers, they carried their lower tier at a height which allowed them to be fought in heavy weather. While the versatile 64 also existed in considerable numbers until about the time of Trafalgar, it was the 74 that flourished, becoming the most desired command for a post-captain keen to achieve flag rank.

Fourth Rate two-deckers were anomalous in that the 60-gun types retained line status whereas the 50-gunners, although only six feet shorter, did not. 'Fifties' nonetheless made excellent leaders for frigate squadrons and often served as flagships on smaller foreign stations. While they enjoyed a late revival with the American War of 1812, they were really superseded by the large frigate.

The term 'frigate' was venerable but had no precise definition. Frigates were Fifth Rates, embracing a wide band of warships mounting from 22 to 44 guns and, confusingly, overlapped by the smaller Sixth Rates which could carry up to 28 guns. French influence was again evident for, in heavy seas, a British two-decked 44 was unable to cope with a larger single-decked French 40, which carried all of its battery higher. The disposition of the guns on upper deck, quarterdeck and forecastle became synonymous with the new generation frigate. Very influential in this development was the capture in 1746 of the French *Embuscade* by the *Defiance* 60. At this time the British were still building 28-gun Fifth Rates with a frigate layout but armed only with 9-pounders. In 1757 appeared the four Southampton class, armed with 32 12-pounders; this was the first real class of British frigates. They were followed immediately by the larger 36-gun Pallas and Brilliant classes. The Admiralty advanced the frigate slowly,

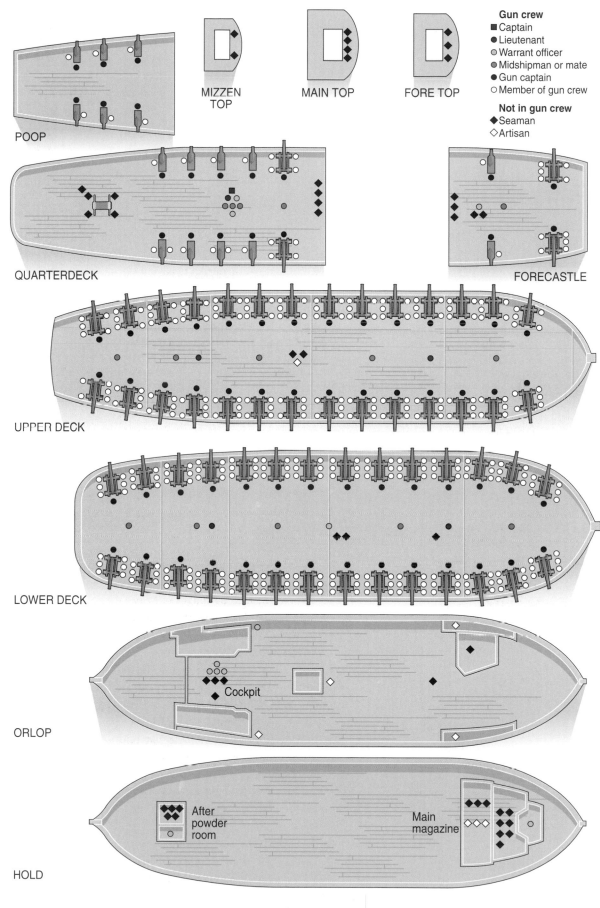

Gun crew
- ■ Captain
- ● Lieutenant
- ◐ Warrant officer
- ◑ Midshipman or mate
- ● Gun captain
- ○ Member of gun crew

Not in gun crew
- ◆ Seaman
- ◇ Artisan

MIZZEN TOP

MAIN TOP

FORE TOP

POOP

QUARTERDECK

FORECASTLE

UPPER DECK

LOWER DECK

Cockpit

ORLOP

After powder room

Main magazine

HOLD

The Quarters of a 74

Having beat to quarters, the ship is here with her crew at action stations. Note that the 32- and 18- pounders, on the lower and upper deck respectively, require crews of fourteen and eleven men. It is assumed that the ship will be engaged on only one side at a time, so guncrews were the combined personnel from the weapons on opposite sides. Specific men were detailed to be withdrawn at any time for more urgent duties, eg firefighting or boarding.

San Carlos

One of 69 ships of the line built by the Spanish navy at Havana, Cuba, *San Carlos* carried 98 guns: 30 x 36-pounders on the lower deck, 32 x 24-pounders on the middle deck, 32 x 12-pounders on the upper deck and four 8-pounders on the poop. Displacing 1,714 tons, she was built from the plans of Matthew Mullan, an immigrant from Ireland.

moving on to 36 and 38-gunners as foreign examples progressed from 40 guns to 44. Only with the experience of the war of 1812 did larger British frigates emerge in numbers alongside the still-common 32s; they had an additional advantage of mounting 18-pounders in place of 12-pounders.

Frigates were the Navy's multi-purpose ships. Attached to the Fleet, their speed made them indispensable as scouts or despatch boats. Independently tasked, under men such as Cochrane, they proved capable of harrying the enemy and causing him acute discomfort.

Subtle variations in type, construction and armament meant that a smaller, 28-gun frigate-built ship could be classed either as a Fifth or Sixth Rate and, from about 1790, even be termed a 'corvette'. To these handy little 9-pounder-armed ships were added numerous others, mostly lumped together under the term 'sloops of war'. Designated largely for inshore use, they were typified by their shallow draught and, at least in earlier years, the ability to be rowed.

Gunnery

As the primary task of a warship was to be able to carry and to fight her guns adequately, it is not surprising that armament was a major influence in ship design. From the table above it can be seen how the weight of the cannons dictated that they became progressively lighter the higher they were positioned aboard ship. The pronounced tumblehome of the hulls was not only to make boarding difficult but also to bring the upper tiers of guns further inboard — in the mistaken belief that this would improve the ships' stability.

Large guns required large crews. A standard 32-pounder, for instance, needed 13 men to serve it, a major reason for the enormous ships' complements. Even restrained by breeching tackles, guns recoiled a considerable distance. In smaller ships of limited beam, this often meant staggering opposite gun positions. By the era of the Seven Years' War, the Industrial Revolution had greatly improved British iron-founding. Muzzle-loaders looked much the same as ever, but their composition was far less variable in quality while better machining techniques improved accuracy of manufacture. Where precise casting had earlier called for 'brasses', cheaper iron was now almost universally used for ships' cannon.

A legacy from Tudor times was an enormous variety of weapons, a range that was progressively reduced to simplify supply arrangements. For most types of gun there was a choice of barrel length, to achieve a necessary balance between weight of broadside and weight of armament. The following major guns were prescribed under the establishment of 1743:

Barrel length	42-pdr	32-pdr	24-pdr	18-pdr	12-pdr	9-pdr	6-pdr
10	65	-	-	-	-	-	-
9.5	-	55	50	42	36	-	-
9	-	-	46	39	32	28.5	24.5
8.5	-	-	-	-	31	27	22
8	-	-	-	-	-	26	21
7.5	-	-	-	-	-	24	20
7	-	-	-	-	-	23	19
6.5	-	-	-	-	-	-	17
Bore (inches)	7.03	6.43	5.84	5.30	4.64	4.22	3.67

Barrel length is expressed in feet and weight of gun in hundredweights (cwt) of 112 pounds/50.9kg. Available also were 4- and 3-pounders, together with a swivel-mounted, anti-personnel half-pounder.

Securing the Guns

In heavy weather it was essential to adequately secure the guns. Just one coming adrift could smash through the side of the ship.

(a) Lashing alongside.

To increase space when a gun was located in a cabin, or on deck when a large number of personnel, eg troops, were being carried, the weapon was secured across the port. Heavy lashings secured barrel and cascabel to ringbolts flanking the port, while the gun-tackles were cross-connected from the trucks of the carriage to lighter eyebolts on the ship's side.

(b) Double breeching.

In a variation of the arrangements shown below at (c), a cable was run the length of the gundeck and secured to the cascabel of each gun. The gun-tackles were secured to this cable rather than to the carriage.

(c) Lower deck gun housed with port secured.

The quoins have been removed to drop the inboard end of the gun. The muzzle has been raised and secured to a permanent clamp on the side of the ship, using a 'muzzle lashing'. Gun-tackles and breeching have been tautened and frapped to barrel.

(d) Upper deck gun secured in run-out position

Gun-tackles have been tautened between the carriage and the side of the ship. A heavy breeching runs between ringbolts on either side of the port via ringbolts on either side of the carriage and the eye cast above the cascabel, or 'button', of the gun.

The Ordnance Board provided guns and associated equipment for both the British Army and the Navy. On paying-off, a ship returned her weapons to the gun-wharf for repair, refurbishment and re-issue. The Board did little to address the basic difference between Army and Navy gunnery; whereas military guns and their targets remained fairly static, naval equivalents were ceaselessly moving.

Naval gunnery remained a crude process. A large cannon might propel its shot for over a mile; with a well-trained crew it might fire again a couple of minutes later. Between 1660 and 1756, rate of fire had increased from one round every four or five minutes to something like one per minute for the best-drilled gun crews in perfect conditions. However, there was only the remotest chance of hitting the same place twice, even without the pressures of close action.

Effective fire called for broadsides, although opinions differed as to whether this should be directed at hull or rigging. The 'English way' was to withhold fire until the range was pistol shot or less before shocking the enemy crew with a crashing broadside to the hull. Ever more scientific in their approach, the French favoured disabling an opponent's rigging; once damaged aloft, an enemy had lost his power to manoeuvre, fight or flee. Although some British flag officers, such as Kempenfelt, supported the logic of this, the smashing attack to the hull continued to presage the process of boarding and taking. From admiral to ordinary seaman, the British sailor was always greatly attracted by the prospect of prize money!

The British stressed rate of fire rather than bother with accuracy. At close quarters this demanded cool discipline under severe pressure. It was on gun drill that the Royal Navy based its superiority. Gun sights — simply cast onto the reinforcing rings of the barrel — were making their first appearance at this time, but commanders such as Nelson had little time for them on the grounds that they slowed the rate of fire.

Gunpowder was an imperfect propellant. To prevent its ingredients settling during storage, and to reduce the tendency to dampness, the mixture was 'corned' or granulated. This also allowed an airspace around each tiny element of the charge, speeding and evening its combustion.

The resulting near-instantaneous release of energy accelerated the ball along the barrel but, unless adequate clearance (or 'windage') was allowed around it, the pressure behind the ball would burst the gun before it could be dissipated. Much of the potential energy in a charge had to be wasted.

Although the elevation of a gun barrel could be adjusted by setting a wedge (or 'quoin') at its inboard end, this was too slow for anything other than quasi-static bombardment. Firing at sea tended to be timed to a particular point on the roll cycle of the ship. Unfortunately, a cannon might not necessarily fire when expected. Thrusting a red-hot rod down the vent worked well but was liable to cover the deck with excess powder from the priming — an obvious safety hazard. Slow matches were safer but took an unpredictable time to initiate the charge. The quickmatch that superseded it was 'quick' only in a relative sense.

As is so often the case, it was the enthusiasm of one individual, which effected major improvement. Sir Charles Douglas improved the fighting efficiency of his ship, the *Duke* 98, by the adoption of goose-quill firing tubes and an improved flintlock mechanism, which gave near-instantaneous firing. Although proposed long before by Anson, the Navy would not generally adopt flintlocks until 1790.

Before this came the controversial carronade. Invented some time after 1760 by General Robert Melville, it capitalised on improved casting techniques to fire hollow spherical shot from a more precise bore. As windage was much reduced, a smaller charge could drive a large ball with great effect. Smaller charges resulted in lower stresses in the gun which, consequently, could be cast lighter. The weapon well met Melville's objective of creating a short, light gun that would fire the heaviest possible shot over the short ranges that typified British fighting tactics. Carronades were manufactured in the following principal sizes:-

Nominal weight of shot (lb)	68	42	32	24	28	12
Length (feet)	5.17	4.29	4.02	3.63	3.25	2.17
Weight of gun (cwt.)	36	22.25	17.13	13	9	5.96

Comparison with the figures quoted in the earlier table will show that carronades, in terms of both size and weight, could advantageously replace conventional cannon sited in upper deck positions.

Far left: Untitled (Reg. No. PU4772)
Regular naval seamen were employed on a short-term basis, and at about half the rate paid to merchant seamen. Rapid fleet mobilisation generated chronic shortfalls in manning. These conflicting factors brought about the iniquities of impressment, and the popular image of the man being torn from wife and family lingered until the introduction of improved conditions and continuous service.

'The Arethusa frigate in a Storm'
Sudden Spring blows are nothing unusual, and a squall here has ships sending down topmasts and scurrying in all directions under low canvas and bare poles. The shape of the tops on the subject suggest that she is of British design and is, therefore, probably the Bristol-built *Arethusa*, a 38-gun, 18-pounder frigate launched in 1781, rather than the ex-French prize which took the name and which was wrecked off Ushant in 1779.

'The Point of Honour' (Cruikshank)

'Hands to witness punishment' was an all-too-familiar pipe. A seaman is secured to a grating, awaiting the lash for a misdemeanour. A shipmate has the courage to intervene, to disagree with the due process of law. The likely outcome was that both would suffer, for to modify the scale of a proposed punishment would be seen as weakness. Note how the Marines were used to underpin the force of authority.

Popularly termed the 'smasher', the carronade's short range was offset by improved battering power. Where a solid shot often passed through a wooden structure, the (usually) fabricated ball of a carronade tended to break-up on impact. In coming to rest at this point it expended all of its energy, usually causing a damaging spall rather than a clean hole; this delivered a grisly secondary effect against the enemy crew, who were showered with lethal splinters of wood and metal.

Requiring fewer men to work it, the carronade proved popular in frigates and armed merchantmen. It differed from standard cannon in most respects. Its carriage, solid and without wheels (or 'trucks'), slid along a timber bed. As the latter's capacity for absorbing recoil was limited, it was customary to secure the weapons to the ship's structure with double lashings. The bed was fitted with a pivot at its outboard end and rollers inboard, making it easy to traverse the weapon within the limitations of the gunport, and causing thinking captains to modify their ideas on the concept of rigid broadside fire. (This was taken further by Douglas' innovation of extra training tackles on long guns.) A further carronade feature was its barrel being pivoted, not on conventional trunnions but from below at about its centre of gravity. It was elevated by the use of a substantial vertical screw at its inboard end.

Frigate captains championed the weapon because it increased their hitting power in close combat without a weight penalty. Some complained that its lack of sufficient projection through a gunport caused it to set fire to standing rigging, but others were so taken with its battering power as to install it in place of much of their regular armament. Some were caught out badly when an astute opponent recognised the fact and used superior sailing qualities to stand off and 'play long bowls' with broadside of conventional cannon.

Interestingly, the fabricated spherical shot made for carronades resurrected earlier ideas for explosive-filled 'shells'. Centres of gravity of such projectiles could be

'The Proserpine Frigate' (Serres)

Early in 1799 the 28-gun *Proserpine*, carrying a diplomatic party for Berlin, stranded in snow and heavy drifting ice on the Scharhörn, at the entrance to the Elbe. The gale of wind and press of ice prevented her being warped off. Beginning to disintegrate, the ship was abandoned, personnel crossing miles of sand and gullies of icy water to seek refuge on Neuwerk. Fourteen people, including a woman and child, froze to death, many others were badly frostbitten.

considerably eccentric, resulting in wayward trajectories. This, in turn, promoted thought on spin stabilisation but, although first mooted in Benjamin Robins' '*New Principles of Gunnery* in the 1740s, these concepts were still far ahead of their time.

Tactics and Signalling

The line of battle has been criticised over the course of three centuries for its lack of flexibility, its tendency to produce indecisive results, and the manner in which it discouraged initiative in subordinate commanders. As with much else, however, the system was a product of its time. An admiral would commonly lead a force of 30 or more First to Third Rates. As most of their firepower was mounted broadside, the line ahead formation made sense not only in leaving a clear field of fire for each ship but also in providing strength in numbers. A closed-up line of battle presented a continuous line of fire that was daunting to approach, while protecting the vulnerable ends of individual ships.

In fairly open order, and taking into account the general lack of handiness of many large warships, the line might be a dozen miles in length and very ragged in nature. It comprised three divisions, the Van, the Centre and the Rear, denoted by their respective colours of White, Red and Blue. The senior flag officer commanded the centre and was often beyond visual contact with the extremities of his line. With the codes of signals available to him, moreover, he was often unable to convey his more subtle intentions.

Unless blown up or burned a warship was rarely sunk. Most were lost either through boarding or by being battered into submission — often after major damage to their rigging. The heavy timbers of a major warship could resist considerable smashing by solid shot. At close range, however, personnel on the upper deck were vulnerable to grapeshot while Marine sharpshooters, positioned in the tops, were tasked with picking off key people. By such means, a ship's ability to board, or to resist boarding, could be eroded.

Boarding required coming to close quarters, of course, which the line of battle and associated fighting instructions were not bound to do. The only real alternative, if circumstances were favourable, was to signal for 'General Chase' and to accept that the result would be a disorganised mêlée, where chance would play a greater part in the outcome. This, perhaps, is where the merely proficient admiral differed from a truly

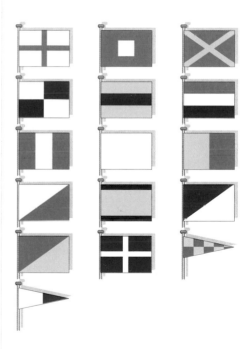

Howe's Signal Code (1790)

Lord Howe was only one who contributed to the progressive refinement of the naval signalling code. Note how the design of each flag is unique; even seen against the light so that its colours were distinct, a flag's design left its identity unambiguous. Although the individual signal flags represented numerals, they would be read as such only if preceded by the numeral pendant. Otherwise, hoisted in groups, usually of one to four flags, a group represented a word or command which could be read directly from a common signal book.

great one. To see an opportunity, and to seize it by disregarding the rulebook, required courage, for to succeed was to be honoured (for being far-sighted) but to fail was to be damned (for disobeying written instructions).

Formal battles fought in two parallel lines were the stuff of textbooks and they rarely decided anything. Some encounters found the lines passing in opposite directions, the action being over almost before it had begun. Good intelligence from scouting frigates might allow time to decide an angle of convergence, not with the objective of the van attacking its opposite numbers but to observe and take advantage of any looseness in an enemy formation; part of the enemy line might be isolated and destroyed in detail. If there was superiority in numbers, or if the lines overlapped, unengaged ships could be used to double around the extremity of the opposing line and engage it from the opposite side simultaneously.

The upwind end of an enemy line might be engaged by superior numbers by dint of leaving the remainder unengaged. To assist their colleagues, the latter would need to make extra way upwind and, delayed further by a blocking force, would arrive, if at all, too late to affect the outcome.

This era of almost continuous maritime warfare provided the confidence-building experience necessary to experiment with more flexible tactics. A broadside-armed ship took a considerable chance approaching a line of similar ships at right angles. During her final approach, she would become the target of several broadsides; end on, she would be virtually unable to reply. If she could survive the pounding and break the enemy line, however, she immediately assumed the advantage; passing through a gap, she could use her full broadsides to rake the vulnerable bow and stern of adjacent enemy vessels. In attempting to respond and evade this fate, the latter would turn out of line and create a knot of confusion, which could be further exploited.

As in chess, an admiral needed to think several moves ahead. He could find himself having created a desired situation but unable to develop it. His ships might find themselves unable to support him or, worse, his signalling system would prove inadequate to convey his intentions. Successful leaders developed a close working relationship with their captains, the latter being able to act intuitively when direction was lacking. An important ingredient for success, when an action had been reduced to a mêlée, was for individual commanders to watch for the need or opportunity for mutual support.

Today, when data interchange is taken for granted, it requires some effort to comprehend the primitive methods available to an admiral of the late 18th century. Signals, being few, were almost synonymous with commands. Signal books were printed and distributed, but signals were actually made only by the commander-in-chief and designated repeating ships. They were an integral part of his fighting instructions but lacked subtlety — to the point where a council of war before an action was desirable in order to explain the finer points of his intentions. Flags varied in meaning, depending upon where they were flown, 17 positions being used at various yardarms, topmasts and shrouds. The firing of one or more guns (inaudible in battle) was supposed to highlight a signal being made, but any deviation from pre-arranged instructions was often attended by much scurrying of boats between ships, even in the heat of battle. Signalling by night was limited to light groups and the discharge of guns.

By the end of the Seven Years' War about 50 signals were listed, with some flexibility added by addresses for individual ships. Lord Howe takes credit (although most of the work was Kempenfelt's) for the development of a numerical system, whereby 28 flags were allocated different numbers. Used in two-or-three flag hoists they could, by reference to a signal book, convey a significantly larger range of meanings. By 1799 numerical-based signalling embraced over 300 combinations, to be usefully extended in 1803 by Home Popham's modifications, which added a limited vocabulary.

VICTORY 1805

1. Fore sail	19. 32 pounder gun
2. Fore topsail	20. Riding bits
3. Fore topgallant	21. Rope store
4. Fore mast	22. Store
5. Buntlines	23. Magazine and filling room
6. Bowsprit	
7. Prow	24. Cable locker
8. Carronade	25. Sail locker
9. Forecastle	26. Orlop deck
10. Marines' walk	27. Shot locker
11. Cat tail	28. Capstan
12. Galley area	29. Pump
13. Belfry	
14. Upper deck	
15. Middle deck	
16. Gun deck	
17. 12 pounder gun	
18. 24 pounder gun	

30. Mast foundation
31. Main mast
32. Main sail
33. Main topsail

34. Main topgallant
35. Hanging magazine
36. Water
37. Powder

38. Poop
39. Captain's dining room
40. Captain's day cabin
41. Admiral's quarters
42. Wardroom
43. Steerage area
44. Flag locker
45. Mizzen mast
46. Mizzen topsail
47. Mizzen topgallant
48. Mizzen
49. Netting

50. Rudder
51. Officer's cabin
52. Tiller room
53. Ballast

The only three decker to survive to the present day, *Victory* continues to undergo preservation work at Portsmouth. Note the hanging magazine between decks, a feature intended to reduce the effects of an explosion. Fortunately, it was never tested.

Trimming the yards

Braces are used to swing, or trim, the yards to various angles for the purposes of shiphandling or to take advantage of wind from a given direction. Some terminology is as follows:

(1) Yard 'braced up' as wind direction moves farther forward.

(2) Yard 'braced in' ('squared') for running directly before wind, which direction has moved farther aft.

(3) Yard 'braced aback', bringing wind on forward side of sail to take way off ship.

(4) Yard 'braced about' as wind moves to opposite side on going about.

(5) Yard 'braced by', the forces in the backed mainsails balancing those in the foresails, causing the ship to 'lie-to', or be 'hove-to'.

(6) Yard 'braced abox', the foresails being backed, again to slow or stop the ship.

(7) Yard 'braced to', easing the sail as the ship comes more before the wind.

'In irons for getting drunk'

Attitudes to drunkeness in the Royal Navy were strangely ambivalent. In port it was usually tolerated, to a quite astonishing degree on some ships. The daily allowance of rum or grog was more than generous and beer was freely available, yet to bring liquor aboard was a grave offence. To be drunk at sea meant almost certain flogging, but the pair shown are probably being cooled-off, having returned aboard a little too incapable.

Points of sailing

(1) Ship in eye of wind. Fore and aft sails not drawing. Square sails 'flat aback'. Ship makes sternway.

(2) Ship 'all in the wind'. Yards not braced and sails shivering. Ship slowly drifts to leeward.

(3) Ship on the wind. Yards braced, everything drawing, she is close-hauled on the starboard tack.

(4) Ship off the wind. Sheets eased, she is sailing free with a quartering sea.

(5) Ship further off the wind. With full quartering breeze she is 'sailing large'. Studding sails may be set or weather clew of main course may be lifted, depending upon wind strength.

(6) Ship running before wind. Forestaysail not drawing and taken in. Main course brailed up to reduce strain on mainmast. Spanker brailed up to reduce risk of broaching-to, ie slewing suddenly and uncontrollably across wind and sea.

WIND

All competing fleets of this era developed signalling systems of roughly similar capabilities, and none established any particular pre-eminence. The task of signal staff could never have been easy, with flags fluttering end-on, their spars shot away or the flags themselves obscured by sails or the voluminous clouds of smoke that accompanied any engagement.

Recruitment by Press Gang

Impressment in the Royal Navy was abandoned only after the Napoleonic Wars, when the number of volunteers at last exceeded the requirements of a rapidly-shrinking fleet. Until then, crews were a mix of volunteers and pressed men, the relative proportions of which varied widely with time and between ships. At the outset of a drive for new personnel, enlistment in foreign merchantmen could be forbidden; in an emergency even in British ships.

Volunteering for the Navy was encouraged by a number of incentives. Permanent recruitment teams, comprising regular officers and petty officers, and locally-recruited assistants, operated in many towns, many well inland, and provided a continuous trickle of men. Bounties offered appear quite generous for the times. In 1770 an Able Seaman volunteer might be offered 30 shillings but, with the shortage of personnel by the turn of the century, this could increase seven-fold. The prospects of prize money, which could double a year's pay, were good. Compared with pressed men, volunteers enjoyed higher rates of pay, the right to shore leave and, technically, the right to request transfer to a ship of choice.

The impressment of genuine landsmen was forbidden by law, although the definition of who it was that actually 'used the

Tacking

Unable to point very high, a square rigger could make ground up-wind only by following a zig-zag course in a series of 'boards'. To commence each board a ship normally 'tacked', going about to put the wind on the opposite bow. At (1) the ship is on the port tack and, ready to go about, is pointing as high as is consistent with her moving at her best speed. Head sails and spanker (the mizzen fore-and-aft sail) are eased at (2) as the helmsman begins to bring her into the wind. Keeping way on the ship, fore and head sails are let fly at (3) and (4), taking the weight of the wind out of them and allowing the ship's momentum to take her head through the wind (5). To keep her head swinging, and to avoid getting 'in irons', ie stuck head to wind, the foresails are quickly backed, while main and mizzen are braced onto the new, ie starboard, tack, leaving the spanker free. The ship's head falls off onto the starboard tack (6), foresails being braced around and spanker sheeted in smartly to maintain as much way as possible, to minimise loss of ground through leeway.

Boxhauling (right)

A square-rigged vessel, caught 'in irons', could regain control by boxhauling. In the diagrams, the ship at (1) points up-wind with no way on. Her main and mizzen are squared off and headsails sheeted in. She therefore gathers sternway. In this case, her foresails are braced around to port. This will bias her head to starboard (2), assisted by holding port rudder. Momentum carries the ship across the wind (3) and, as she comes stern to wind (4), her main and mizzen are braced in to prevent her being slowed, while the rudder is gradually brought amidships. By squaring off the main and mizzen, and freeing the headsails, the ship may now be made to gather headway on the starboard tack (5).

Making a sternboard (below)

Many ships were 'dull' sailers, particularly liable to miss stays when going about. Making a sternboard enabled them to go about in the least space, although at the expense of losing some ground. The ship, on the port tack in (1), turns into the wind. At (2) her main and mizzen yards have been smartly braced about, the foreyards remaining unchanged. The backed sails bring her to a standstill. As, at (3), she gathers sternway, her rudder is reversed from port to starboard. The foresails, the only ones drawing, help push her bows over to port, assisting the new rudder direction. As the ship comes across the wind at (4) her main and mizzen sails fill, the foreyards are smartly braced about and she gathers way on the starboard tack. A sternboard constituted the primary part of a boxhaul.

sea' was very flexible. It behove any able-bodied man who could claim immunity to acquire a 'passport', or certificate establishing his employment in a reserved occupation. Men of British extraction could be impressed from merchantmen, and probably enjoyed better treatment than those taken up ashore who, once in the system, were confined to prevent their escape. They were then transported, in the most miserable of conditions, to further confinement in 'receiving ships', which were little better than floating prisons, until being allocated to a commissioned ship. Here, their unfamiliarity with their surroundings and lack of skills saw them the butt of petty officers and shipmates alike.

With such a wide range of men and attitudes below decks it is not surprising that petty crime and the general flouting of regulations was common. Discipline was therefore maintained with considerable ferocity. Under some commanding officers, well marked throughout the Service, it was with an iron intensity that drove men to mutiny. Much has been written about crime and punishment in the Royal Navy. Severe as justice could be, however, it should be viewed in the context of the wider social conditions of the time. Afloat or ashore, life was rigorous to a degree that would be unacceptable today, indeed very difficult to imagine.

The 'bible' was the Naval Discipline Act but, like most bibles, this was frequently ignored. Only seamen could be flogged, in theory, up to 12 lashes, beyond which it was

Numerous reefs, swift-running currents and a large tidal range made the long watch on Brest very hazardous. Among many ships lost was the frigate *Blanche*, wrecked near Ushant on 4th March 1807. As the *Anfitrite*, she had been captured from the Spanish in 1804, and had, in turn, taken the French *Guerrière* in July 1806, an action for which her captain, Thomas Lavie, had been knighted.

a matter for court-martial. Although it has become the stuff of Hollywood legend, flogging was certainly the universal deterrent to common misdemeanours such as drunkenness, insubordination, stealing, quarrelling or neglect of duty. Some captains maintained discipline with a minimum of such punishment; others, perhaps afflicted with persistent offenders, would pursue via courts martial sentences of up to 150 lashes or the barbaric 'flogging round the fleet'

Drunkenness was widely tolerated in an off-duty crew when alongside, yet dealt with savagely at other times. Considering the high incidence of the problem, it comes as something of a surprise to discover the sheer quantity of liquor dispensed and consumed aboard. For impoverished seamen it was, illegally, something of a universal currency. Punishment returns, required of each ship by the commander-in-chief on a quarterly basis, make interesting reading. That of a typical 74, for instance, lists 187 misdemeanours in a 12-month period. Of these, no less than 123 involved drunkenness with others attempting to smuggle liquor aboard. Being drunk was usually rewarded with 12 lashes, with repeat offences attracting 18 or 24. Again surprisingly, over a quarter of recorded cases were forgiven, with a handful resulting in disrating.

Effects of heel on a sailing ship

Heel, unavoidable in a sailing ship, lowered the efficiency of the hull by resulting in an asymmetric waterplane. As the greatest beam of the hull was usually above the waterline it rapidly increased the volume submerged, opposing further heel. The greatest beam, and maximum transverse section, were also forward of amidships and so, as the submerged volume must always be constant, the centre of buoyancy moved forward with heel, in turn changing trim.

On 1 May 1795 the flagship of Sir John Jervis, the 98-gun three-decker *Boyne*, caught fire while laying at Spithead. Grounding opposite Southsea Castle, she burned for seven hours, the heat discharging her loaded guns, until the forward magazine exploded 'offering', according to one eye-witness, 'one of the most magnificent sights that can be conceived'.

Desertion was potentially a capital offence, with some captains, Lord Howe included, being quite ready to hand down the full sentence via court-martial. Hanging was to be hoisted by the neck from a block at the yardarm end. The victim's neck was not broken and death was not quick.

One aspect of naval life that receives little attention is the question of women at sea. In port, considerable numbers might be tolerated or even accommodated aboard but, depending upon the whim of individual captains, they might go to sea, although this was against General Instructions. They had no victualling allowance or service pay, so that their food was 'lost' within the general issue and their income earned by services rendered. Surviving references speak of women 'belonging to the ship' being allowed ashore twice weekly on market days. Elsewhere, their greater water consumption attracted official disapproval, although suggesting a regular laundering service. Others again were known to have dressed wounds after an action.

Dockyards

The direction and administration of the Royal Navy at this time were the separate responsibilities of the Admiralty and the Navy Board respectively. Not until 1832 were their functions subsumed into a single entity, which retained the 'Admiralty' label. The awkward, divided responsibility dated back to the tumultuous period following the English Civil War, when the fleet reverted to the nation, as opposed to being an instrument of the Monarch's personal authority. The Board of Admiralty comprised what were known officially as Lords Commissioners. They were a judicious blend of the political and the professional, in an age when the one could merge seamlessly into the other. On one hand, for instance, Russell and Barham were noted as politicians more than as fighting admirals while, on the other, Cochrane, Hawke and Rodney typified those whose glittering naval careers paralleled duties as Members of Parliament.

Right: Active and Alceste v. Pomone

This lacklustre impression gives little idea of the ferocity of the action when, on 29 November 1811, the British frigates *Active* and *Alceste* intercepted the Franco-Venetian *Pauline* and *Pomone* near Corfu. Nearly three hours of action saw three ships fought virtually to a standstill. The *Pauline* escaped, but the *Pomone*, Italian-built for presentation to Jérôme Bonaparte, was taken. Although re-named *Ambuscade*, she was scrapped in 1812.

Below: The Glorious First of June 1794

Howe's flagship, the *Queen Charlotte*, breaks through the enemy line, raking the *Eole* as she passes. As Vice-Admiral of England, Howe wore the Union Flag at the mainmast head. Just five years later, the *Queen Charlotte*, a 100-gun First Rate, suffered a fate similar to that of the *Boyne*, 673 of her people were lost when she blew up in a fire off Leghorn (Livorno).

The Navy Board was, with the Board of Admiralty, originally subordinate to the overall control of the Lord High Admiral. It comprised five members - the Treasurer (its senior member), the Comptroller (responsible, inter alia, for dockyards), the Surveyor, the Clerk of the Ships and the Master of the Ordnance. To these were later added the offices of the Storekeeper-General, the Controller of Victualling, the Physician-General and others, the composition of the board changing constantly to reflect the growing size of the fleet.

There were six major royal dockyards at home. Deptford (founded 1486), Woolwich (1512), Chatham (1547) and Sheerness (1665) reflected not only the ancient relationship between the Royal Navy and the defence of the capital but also the fact that the Thames remained the nation's primary centre of shipbuilding and ship repair. On the south coast, Portsmouth rivalled Deptford in its antiquity, but was joined by Plymouth only in 1660. With the slow silting of the London River, and with France assuming the Netherlands' role as major European threat, the two south coast yards had, by the time of American independence, become the primary fleet bases.

The succession of wars brought the Royal Navy wide-flung commitments which, in turn, resulted in the establishment of foreign bases. These often stemmed from simple store depots created by the local commander-in-chief. Such depots already existed at home; activity in the Downs during the Dutch Wars brought about the creation of one at Deal. This was followed by others at Leith and at Kinsale in Southern Ireland, both remote from regular dockyards. Abroad, Gibraltar dated from 1704, the year that it was captured, although Port Royal in Jamaica could claim to be older. Antigua, Bombay and Halifax, Nova Scotia followed, with Falmouth and Yarmouth in Britain.

Port Mahon in Minorca grew in importance with extended British

Clubhauling (below)

As it meant the loss of an anchor and cable, clubhauling was used only in desperate circumstances as a means of going about. At (1) the ship is close-hauled on the port tack. It is anticipated that she will miss stays, so the lee (here, the starboard) anchor is made ready to drop. It hangs from its cable but, from the anchor ring, a second line (or 'spring') is led back to the lee, or starboard, quarter. The ship comes into the wind (2), misses stays, loses headway and begins to fall off astern. The starboard anchor is dropped and both cable and spring are let out (or veered) quickly to allow her to gather sternway. At (3) the spring is stopped while the anchor is still paid out. With yards braced in on the starboard tack, the ship comes around starboard side to wind. The moment that her sails fill and she starts to gather way, both anchor cable and spring are severed by axe, leaving the ship to gain headway on the starboard tack.

WIND

'Sir James Saumarez leaves Gibraltar 12 July 1801'

Following his hot inshore action against the French at Algeciras on 5 July 1801, Saumarez had to retire to Gibraltar for repair. The French admiral, Linois, appealed for and received reinforcements from Cadiz and, on 12th July, made to sail. Rapidly patched and stored, Saumarez' squadron followed post-haste and won a fine victory. Seen are the *Caesar* 80 (flag), *Venerable*, *Superb*, *Spencer* and *Audacious*, all 74s, and the *Thames* 32.

dominance of the Mediterranean, only to be superseded by a combination of Gibraltar and a newly-acquired Malta at the beginning of the 19th century, with coverage being completed by the establishment of facilities at Alexandria in Egypt. For the duration of the wars, short-lived ventures served at Barbados, the Cape, Haiti, Martinique, Madras, Mauritius, Penang, Sydney and even Rio de Janeiro. Others, at Bermuda, Trincomalee and Pembroke Dock, went on to provide the facilities of minor dockyards in their own right.

As might be expected, such piecemeal development resulted in an organisation that had not a few inefficiencies and shortcomings. Graft and wastage certainly existed and, due to the intensely political atmosphere of the time, attracted more than their fair share of opprobrium. As a result, the generally excellent work performed by the yards in support of the fleet was much obscured by the publicity generated by a series of commissions of enquiry and endless calls for reform.

The figures speak for themselves. Early in 1793, for instance, the commissioned strength of the Royal Navy was only 26 ships of the line and 109 others. Three years later, the totals were 105 and 281 respectively, for which much credit was due to Charles Middleton (later Lord Barham) in his capacity of Comptroller.

Before hulls were coppered, ships were docked and refitted about every third year but, from about 1775, cleaner hulls tended to extend this period by a further year. To strip and refit the average 74 took some four months, a frigate only two. A major bottleneck at times of rapid mobilisation was the availability of docking facilities, particularly for larger ships, which often needed to await spring tides to clear the dock sills.

Emergencies saw the refurbishment of ships that would otherwise have been scrapped. Decay could affect frames or planking and, when sufficiently advanced, could require bracing frames with added members or completely 'doubling' the hull by overlaying it with sound planking. Shortage of grown timbers encouraged their substitution with selected iron components from 1805, and also increased the practice of dismantling condemned ships for spare parts rather than simply disposing of them for scrap. By the end of the Napoleonic Wars, two thirds of major warships were being cannibalised for useful timbers.

Despite their unremitting criticism of dockyards, serving naval officers acknowledged that yard-built ships were superior to those from mercantile builders. Dockyards were obliged to maintain a three-year timber stock, guaranteeing its proper seasoning. Under normal conditions, dockyards would allow a partially-planked hull to stand on the ways to allow for settlement. Contractors could not afford the cash outlay for the one or the time for the other.

On behalf of the dockyards, the Navy Board was one of the nation's largest consumers of materials. It required about 20,000 tons of oak annually, half of it from home sources (although the proportion diminished steadily) the remainder imported from the Baltic. About 1,000 large mast timbers per year, increasingly from Canada once the United States became independent. Up to 13,000 tons of hemp each year for cordage; Russian was preferred but politics demanding that much be sourced from Australia, Canada, India and Spain. Some 100,000 bolts of canvas, each of 39 yards' length and up to 2½ feet width, for sail lofts, most from Scotland and India. Rigging blocks, 100,000 of them annually, were an expensive hand-made product until Brunel's production line machinery was installed at Portsmouth, which then supplied the needs of the whole service. Iron, tar and softwood again came mostly from the Baltic. Copper, for fastenings and hull sheathing, was mostly home-produced. It was always expensive and Portsmouth was equipped with a metal mill for recycling it.

The hostilities that spanned much of the reign of George III put the royal dockyards under great pressure, which hastened the process of reform. Management, procurement, accounting, the control of wastage, recruitment and training were all greatly improved. The foundation of the School of Naval Architecture in 1811, and the fostering of apprenticeship schemes, pointed to a new, long-term perspective. Most importantly, the yards proved equal to their most exacting trials to date.

'French frigate *Tribune* captured by *Unicorn* 1796'

West of the Scillies on 8 June 1796 the British frigates *Unicorn* and *Santa Margarita* encountered two French frigates and a corvette. The ex-Spanish *Santa Margarita* re-took the ex-British *Tamise* and, after a ten-hour pursuit, the *Unicorn* came up with the *Tribune*. In a 35-minute night action the British 18-pounders out-gunned the French 12s. Under the British flag, the *Tribune* was wrecked off Halifax, Nova Scotia in 1797.

CHAPTER 4: *Exploring the World*

'Tahiti revisited' - (William Hodges)

First visited by a British navigator in 1767, Tahiti was duly claimed by Captain Samuel Wallis for the Crown. He stayed seven weeks for rest and recreation and, despite renaming their home King George III Island, he enjoyed good relations with the Queen and her people. Descriptions of an earthly paradise on their return to England triggered a series of expeditions.

The world map of 1760 still featured extensive blank areas, bordered by detail that owed much to conjecture and imagination on the part of the cartographer. Britain at the time was in an intellectual ferment as new wealth produced a class with the leisure and money to pursue exotic interests. Learned societies were formed for the study of every conceivable subject, while individuals indulged themselves with extensive collecting of such as shells, plants or insects. Interest in astronomy and botany extended up to the monarchs themselves.

This surge of interest in strange lands and strange peoples was part of contemporary culture and the higher echelons of the naval establishment were not immune. Earlier long-distance British voyaging had been predatory rather than scientific, limited to the activities of men like Drake and Dampier. With Spain re-emerging as a serious rival at sea, it was felt that an effort should be made to dispute the accepted notion of the Pacific Ocean being a Spanish lake. Anson was despatched on his epic circumnavigation of 1740-44. The account of the voyage, published four years later, caused immense public interest containing, as it did, all the ingredients of true adventure — storm and shipwreck, disease and the capture of treasure that exceeded any expectation.

Sharing Anson's privations were several junior officers who later were to make their own contributions to exploration. One, the Honourable John Byron, who had then been a midshipman was, as a captain, given a modest force of two minor warships (the *Dolphin* 24 and *Tamar* 14) to undertake another circumnavigation to 'make discoveries of countries hitherto unknown' in order to 'redound to the honour of this nation, the dignity of the Crown and the advancement of trade and navigation thereof.'

Byron sailed in June 1764, his great ambition to discover the long-rumoured 'Great Southern Continent'. He followed the South American coast to the latitude of

Patagonia, then struck out eastward into the Atlantic. He came to the conclusion that the Falklands were what had been reported as continental landmass and made a rough survey to determine their extent. In doing so, in January 1765, he formally named them and annexed them for the Crown. Leaving the Falklands, he proceeded through the Magellan Strait, but was then content to follow Anson's track across the Pacific, showing little interest in the island groups except for a two-month break in the Marianas to allow his scurvy-afflicted crews time to recover. Threading through the Indonesian archipelago, he called at the Dutch settlement at Batavia, on Java, before doubling the Cape to arrive back in England in May 1766. In nearly two years away, Byron had achieved little and, perhaps realising this, he spiced his report with an allusion to a substantial land mass to the south, which he had never had the fortune to sight. His fame was thus less as an explorer than as grandfather to the poet.

The Admiralty's interest whetted, the *Dolphin* was refitted for a further voyage, this time commanded by Captain Samuel Wallis. Accompanied by the *Swallow* sloop, under the able Philip Carteret, he sailed in August 1766. By December, in the southern summer, the expedition was compiling sailing directions for the Magellan Strait but, on entering the Pacific, the ships became separated. Rather short-sightedly, no rendezvous had been arranged in case this happened.

In June 1767, a year before Bougainville's French expedition arrived, Wallis 'discovered' Tahiti, enjoying local hospitality for a month. The islands of the group are mountainous and distant peaks on the southern horizon, sighted but not investigated, perpetuated the myth of a southern land mass. Like Byron, Wallis proved a timid explorer and lost little time in heading across the Pacific to the known stopover in the Marianas. By May 1768 he was back in England.

World Map 1785 (Henry Roberts)

A cursory glance at this map could, forgivably, assume it to be a modern edition as Cook's three voyages had contributed so much that was new. Closer inspection, however, reveals that knowledge was still lacking of Australia's southern coastline and of Tasmania as an island, the Chilean archipelago and the Aleutian chain.

'War boats of Otaheite' - (William Hodges)

Hodges' images of Tahiti portray wild, jungle-clad islands overlaid with a serene classical aura. The noble savage, often strangely clothed, combines beauty with a warlike edge. Here, he is credited with the construction of huge, somewhat threatening craft, of shape fantastic to European eyes. The impact of such pictures on the popular English imagination can only be conjectured.

Carteret showed more mettle. His little ship was not intended for independent wanderings and he headed for Juan Fernandez to acquire fresh produce. He found that a powerful Spanish garrison had been installed there following the publicity surrounding Anson's voyage. With scurvy a growing problem, Carteret discovered and named Pitcairn Island and carried out a running survey of the northern shore of New Guinea before reaching Dutch Macassar. He was unlucky in encountering hostility everywhere that he called, but arrived home safely in March 1769.

A further Admiralty-supported expedition had already sailed. This had been stimulated by the Royal Society's request for astronomical observations to be undertaken, but Wallis' new hints regarding a southern continent added a search to the scientifically-based brief of the expedition. The Admiralty's choice of leader was James Cook, whose earlier work surveying the St. Lawrence River and Newfoundland had been well received. Cook's background had been the East Coast coal trade and, at his instigation, the Admiralty purchased one of the sturdy little collier brigs, converting her into His Majesty's bark *Endeavour*. Of about the dimensions of a modern harbour tug, on which a dozen men spend a working day, the *Endeavour* housed 94 men for months on end. Cook's humble beginnings made him the most humane of commanders, greatly concerned for his crew's welfare, yet technically uncommonly able.

An interesting sidelight to the attitude of the Royal Society was its injunction to Cook to seek the agreement of local natives before annexing new lands for the Crown for 'they are ... the legal possessors of the several Regions they inhabit. No European Nation as a right to occupy any part of their country, or settle among them without their voluntary consent'.

Sailing in July 1768, Cook rounded the Horn and, in the following April, reached Tahiti. Following six weeks of scientific observations, surveying and collecting, he headed the *Endeavour* southward. Reaching the latitude of 40 degrees South without sighting land he encountered the huge oceanic swells of the region, which convinced him that no land existed within a considerable distance. In October 1769 Cook sighted the North Island of New Zealand. He then spent six months circumnavigating the islands and executing a surprisingly detailed survey of their 2,500 miles of coastline. Four months were then spent surveying the east coast of Australia and the Great Barrier Reef, upon which *Endeavour* stranded and was almost lost. She rounded Cape York in August 1770 and threaded the hazardous Torres Strait, south of New Guinea, and on to the now-customary call on the Dutch at Batavia for rest and refit. Cook had kept his crew in a remarkably good state of health but here they contracted fever and dysentery, from which 40 men died. The survivors returned to England in June 1771.

Cook's work was widely published, both to satisfy popular interest and to counter claims by the French and Spanish, who were also active. Officially, British interest was in fostering trade rather than in colonisation but the new charts were liberally besprinkled with features named unashamedly for senior Admiralty figures, politicians, sponsors and, of course, the explorers themselves. At one stage even Tahiti was labelled 'King George III Island' and its main anchorage 'Port Royal'.

Promoted to commander, Cook was immediately appointed to head a second expedition. Sailing on this occasion in two ex-colliers, *Resolution* and *Adventure* (Lieutenant-in-Command Tobias Furneaux) the group again included scientists and artists and, following John Harrison's recent achievements, had the benefit of a chronometer for more accurate calculation of longitude. Sailing in July 1771, Cook had been instructed to settle, once and for all, the vexed question of the southern continent's existence, particularly as the French navigator Bouvet had now reported land at 54 degrees South.

HMS Resolution off Cape Stephens, with waterspout' - (William Hodges)
Cook's *Resolution* beats offshore in a setting worthy of a Verdian opera. The viewer cannot escape the impression that, as today a scientist may exaggerate the implications of his findings in order to justify the grant of further research funds, so Hodges, with his fantastic images of new worlds, was easing the way for yet further voyages of exploration.

Cook

James Cook was born in Yorkshire in 1728. Largely self-educated, he went to sea aged 18, as an apprentice in the east coast colliers. His quick brain gained him advancement to mate by 1752 when he joined the Royal Navy as an able seaman. By 1757 he was sailing master of the *Solebay* 24. Drafted to the *Pembroke* 60 in 1758, he undertook the critical survey of the St. Lawrence River that permitted large warships to approach Quebec. Cook remained with the flagship for three years, surveying the estuary and adjacent coasts. He was then given the armed Schooner *Grenville*, spending five more years mapping Canada's eastern seaboard. His work caught the attention of the Royal Society, for whom he was sent to Tahiti to observe a transit of Venus. His command was a converted collier, renamed HMS *Endeavour*. Sailing in August 1768, Cook was absent for nearly three years, having gone on to survey much of New Zealand and Australia's east coast.

Replacing the worn-out *Endeavour* with the similar *Resolution*, the Admiralty then despatched Cook to establish, or otherwise, the existence of the rumoured great southern continent. In company with the *Adventure*, Cook sailed in July 1772. Sweeping the southern ocean at high latitudes he found only ice but went on to cover the Pacific from New Zealand to Easter Island, returning in 1775.

As post-captain and newly-elected Fellow of the Royal Society, Cook left for the Pacific again in 1777. His primary purpose was to seek the fabled North West Passage but, having run up the Alaskan coast, he was thwarted by ice in the Bering Strait. He returned by the familiar waters of Polynesia but became involved in a dispute with previously friendly natives. This culminated in a skirmish in which Cook was killed. It was February 1779. His voyages have secured him a unique place in the story of the world's exploration.

Proceeding via the Cape of Good Hope Cook's ships were in company with numerous huge icebergs by December, some measured at miles in extent. They probed down to 67 degrees South, at which latitude they tracked from the meridian of the Cape to that of New Zealand without sighting land. The ships then separated to undertake solo surveys of New Zealand and Van Diemen's Land (now Tasmania). Thence, in company, they moved to Tahiti to re-establish earlier relationships before moving on to other island groups. In heavy weather the ships became parted, the *Adventure* returning home. Cook returned to New Zealand, hoping for a rendezvous but, when this did not materialise, he headed southward again. In November 1773 he exceeded 71 degrees South before being halted by continuous ice. He saw no land.

His enlightened dietary regime maintained a healthy crew, so Cook went on to spend seven months testing unconfirmed sightings by various Dutch and Spanish navigators, criss-crossing the Pacific to visit territories as far removed as Easter Island and the New Hebrides (now Vanuatu) before returning to New Zealand's Queen Charlotte Sound for a final refit. Returning on the long haul via the Horn he maintained a southerly track, establishing the existence of South Georgia (54.5 degrees South) and the South Sandwich Islands (57 degrees South), named for the King and the First Lord respectively. Calling at the Cape, Cook finally arrived at Portsmouth in July 1775, over three years after his departure.

The second voyage had been a tremendous achievement, not only hydrographically but also in keeping his crew healthy by diet and correct routines, for only one man had died of sickness. As another full account rapidly went to press, Cook was promoted post-Captain and elected Fellow of the Royal Society (FRS).

Capitalising on success, the Royal Society now had little difficulty in enthusing the Admiralty with the prospect of a North-West Passage, the long-conjectured short cut to the riches of the Orient. Any such waterway would possess great strategic and commercial significance. The only known route to the Pacific, that via the Horn, could possibly be controlled from the Falklands but, between Byron's visit in 1765, and 1771 there was feuding between the British, who claimed the islands, and the Spanish, who had taken over a derelict French settlement on East Falkland. In order to reduce the prospect of war, both parties abandoned the territory in 1774 and this, possibly, added to the attraction of any northern route.

After a year on home soil, Cook sailed on a third voyage, again in the *Resolution* but now accompanied by the 300-ton *Discovery*. Proceeding via the Cape, he first investigated the desolate French island of Kerguelen in the south Indian Ocean before moving on to the more familiar and equable territory of Tasmania and Tahiti. Early in 1778 his ships were off the western seaboard of Canada, moving northward, through the Aleutian chain to the Bering Strait where, keeping to the American shore, Cook nearly entered the yet-unnamed Beaufort Sea, exceeding 70 degrees North. He looked at the Asiatic side but, still in the Arctic winter, he was much hazarded by ice. Having sketched-in an important waterway, but without having proved or disproved the existence of the passage itself, Cook moved southward. The year previously, he had stumbled across the Sandwich Islands (present-day Hawaii) and returned in January 1779. Within a month, he was dead, killed by the natives in a misunderstanding stemming from cultural differences. His ships returned safely under the command of subordinates in October 1780 but Cook's enormous contribution to mapping the world was finished.

Far left: 'The Resolution in the Marquesas' (William Hodges)

As the Marquesas had been visited by the Spanish navigator Mendana as early as 1595, Cook's visit in 1774 only added to the sum total of knowledge of the group. This little monochrome study shows Hodges the observer, making visual notes for a later work. He has, however, over-emphasised the loftiness of the masts and has consequently taken the shrouds to a point well below the tops.

Monuments on Easter Island (William Hodges)

Silently watched-over by its enigmatic, red-capped monoliths, Easter Island was another spot much favoured by romantic artists. Desolate and isolated, the island was first visited by Europeans when the Dutch navigator Roggeveen landed on Easter Day, 1722. With few resources and of no strategic value, Easter Island was never contested by the maritime powers.

Resolution and Discovery at Nootka Sound (John Webber)

Unlike the romanticism of Hodges' work, that of Webber during Cook's third voyage has a realistic touch. En route from the Central Pacific to the Bering Strait, Cook's two ships spent a month in 1778 refitting at Nootka Sound on Vancouver Island. Rigging sheerlegs to shift a complete foremast was a normal evolution to seamen of the time.

Southern continent or no, the vastness of the Pacific continued to attract British interest. During 1778 Cook had spent a month refitting on the Canadian coast, at what was called Nootka Inlet after the local inhabitants. Following the flag, a British trading post was established, but this was seized by Spanish forces seeking to re-establish their hegemony. Diplomacy at home secured a note from the Spanish Prime Minister requiring the post's return and this was conveyed by a further expedition, with Commander George Vancouver in the *Discovery* (a new ship) accompanied by a tender, the *Chatham*. Sailing in April 1791 they tracked eastward via the Cape and Australasia. En route to Hawaii, the *Chatham* came across, and gave her name to, an island east of New Zealand. On arriving in Canada in April 1792 Vancouver was courteously received by the Spaniards, who accepted the situation although apparently engaged in settling the coast from Mexico north. They had completed a considerable amount of surveying but, unlike the British and, to an extent, the French, they kept the data to themselves.

Vancouver cruised down to the area of modern San Diego before returning to spend several seasons on the complex fjord coast around the present-day border at 49 degrees North. Names such as Vancouver Island, Puget Sound and Johnstone Strait all result from this survey. Following instructions, Vancouver examined the Alaskan coast to a point 60 degrees North before heading south again to visit Mexico and the Galapagos before calling into the thriving Spanish settlements at Valparaiso and Santiago in Chile. He had been away for four years and here he discovered that an anxious Admiralty had sent HMS *Rattler* on an unsuccessful search for him in 1793-4. Arriving safely back in England in October 1795 Vancouver had maintained Cook's standards both in surveying and in care of his crews.

In truth, the Pacific was no longer lonely and unknown, being exploited rapidly by settlers, traders, missionaries, whalers and sealers, of which latter there was a veritable explosion following the arrival of the First Fleet at Botany Bay in 1788. Cook's work on the Australian coast was continued thoroughly by Bass and Flinders. One striking aspect of this activity is the continuity of the personalities involved. For instance, Cook's

The death of Captain James Cook (Zoffany)

Having failed to discover the fabled North-West Passage, Cook returned via Hawaii to effect repairs. Here, following native pilfering, a full-scale clash occurred on 14 February 1779. Cook was one of several killed. The manner of his death, an anti-climactic end to expeditions of such value, was soon romanticised, not least by the contemporary artist Johannes Zoffany.

Poedooa, the daughter of Oree (John Webber)
Webber was official artist to Cook's third, and fateful, voyage. Standards had been laid down regarding contact with indigenous peoples and the conditions under which territory could be claimed for the Crown. Webber's work thus emphasises friendly contact with natives, although the reality was increasing friction and not-infrequent clashes. The chief of Raiatea and his daughter were probably hostages when this portrait was made.

expedition botanist in 1768 was one Joseph Banks, a gentleman of means. Banks' abilities achieved him eminence and, by the close of the century, he was President of the Royal Society, in which capacity he was instrumental in persuading the Admiralty to despatch Flinders. With the latter was a midshipman named John Franklin, the future Arctic explorer. Vancouver, too, had served as a midshipman on Cook's last two voyages and, on his own later expedition, the *Chatham* tender had been commanded by Lieutenant Broughton. In October 1794 Broughton was given the *Providence* sloop to look at the Asiatic coasts of the Pacific. Two years later he had achieved little but had, fortuitously, purchased a tender to aid in survey work. In May 1797, when the *Providence* was wrecked near Formosa (Taiwan), the tender was able to rescue the crew. Most were returned home but, retaining a handpicked nucleus, Broughton undertook a courageous voyage, proceeding as far north as Sakhalin, and sketching-in the coasts of Japan, Korea and the Pescadores. He terminated his voyage at Macao, returning in a merchantman in February 1799 after an absence of nearly four and a half years.

In 1795 (a century after the French) the Admiralty established a Hydrographic Office to coordinate surveying activities and to publish results for the benefit of all. The first Hydrographer to the Admiralty was Alexander Dalrymple, who had worked in a similar capacity for the East India Company. Dalrymple served for thirteen years, it then being felt more appropriate to appoint a serving officer. The post has been thus occupied ever since.

The surveying career of Flinders (who first coined the name 'Australia') ended abruptly with his detention and seven-year incarceration by the French. The Admiralty, engaged in the long struggle with Napoleon, lost much of its enthusiasm for scientific voyaging. In 1804, however, a new and influential figure appeared in the person of John Barrow. Like Cook a man of humble background, Barrow had served in China and South Africa before being appointed Second Secretary to the Admiralty, a post that he was to occupy for about 40 years. Once Napoleon had been defeated, the Board was presiding over a Royal Navy vastly expanded by years of war. Much had to be culled, but Barrow saw the opportunity of using some of these excess assets to investigate a few of the blanks, which still disfigured the world map. Having been elected FRS, he was much influenced by Sir Joseph Banks, now in his sixties, and their interest centred on Africa and the Polar regions.

The enormous African rivers had long been romantic enigmas, potential highways flowing majestically through unexploited wilderness, but leading heaven knew where. An investigation of the Congo was instigated, not least to establish whether it and the Niger were separate rivers. A bold step (for 1814) was to construct a steamship for the task, but her machinery proved inadequate and she was converted to sailing. Named *Congo*, her necessarily-restricted draught and dimensions made her a crank sailer and she was horribly cramped for the over-large body of 56 personnel. Appointed to command was James Tuckey, a man of already frail health. Accompanied by a small tender the *Congo* sailed in February 1816, reaching the mouth of the river in the following July.

The expedition was appalled by the impoverished state of the land and people that it passed, the result of unrestricted slave-raiding over centuries. Reaching the known cataracts at Yellala, the *Congo* could proceed no further. From here success depended upon small boats and foot-slogging. Unfortunately, the party began to succumb to a particularly virulent strain of mosquito-borne yellow fever. Invariably fatal, it spelt total defeat. Less Tuckey and his second-in-command the survivors sailed for home early in October. They had penetrated about 250 miles up-river but had lost many good men. Depressed by the result, Barrow's interest shifted to high latitudes.

To the west of Greenland lies the wide Davis Strait, leading to the huge expanse of Baffin Bay. A noted whaling master, William Scoresby, reported the ice unusually broken for several seasons, and offered to take advantage of this by leading an expedition to investigate whether the North-West Passage did, in fact, lead out of the bay. Barrow liked the idea, but selected two naval officers, Captain John Ross and Lieutenant William Parry, to command the purchased ships *Isabella* and *Alexander*.

Sailing in April 1818 they did, indeed, make good progress, reaching the head of Baffin Bay, beyond 75 degrees North, by the end of July. A south-easterly wind then piled ice into the bay, the two ships being fortunate to survive. The experience seemed, however, to unnerve Ross. There were three known sounds proceeding from the head of the bay but Ross, on the scantiest observation, declared them to be closed bays and of no interest. Despite the disagreement of Parry and others, Ross decided to return. Barrow, predictably irritated at Ross's performance, put Parry at the head of a further attempt, to leave in May 1819 in the *Hecla* and *Griper*. Again progress was excellent and, from Baffin Bay, Parry took the west-leading Lancaster Sound. He intended to over-winter in the area, which allowed him to penetrate to Melville Island (named for the First Lord). Had he known, beyond Banks Island that lay across his path was the exit into the Beaufort Sea. The freeze set in rapidly however, and the expedition was able to break out only in the following August.

With his crews healthy and in excellent spirit, Parry returned in October 1820. He had almost broken through the fabled route and had surveyed over one thousand miles of coastline. On returning he heard, for the first time, that the King had died some months previously. Parry was to gain fame with years of Arctic exploration, but he was never able to prove conclusively that the North-West Passage actually existed.

This brief, necessarily incomplete, review concentrated on the activities of the Royal Navy. Although this service achieved most, it must not be forgotten that others, too, made great contribution. Notable French expeditions were those of la Pérouse, Bougainville, Kerguelen and d'Entrecastaux. State security prevented Spanish navigators, such as Malaspina, from receiving their just recognition but the Russian Bellinghausen's activities in high latitudes added extra urgency to British efforts.

Wreck of the Astrolabe

Six years after Cook, the French navigator Jean-François la Pérouse also failed to find the Pacific end of the North-West Passage. With his two ships, *Astrolabe* and *Boussole*, he sailed via Hawaii to the seas around Japan and Russia before heading south. After visiting the British settlement at Botany Bay in 1788 his expedition vanished. Not until 1826 was the wreckage of his ships found on the reefs of Vanikoro.

CHAPTER 5: *The American War of Independence*

Forcing a passage of the Hudson River 1776 (Thomas Mitchell)

General Howe's operations to defeat Washington's army about New York depended greatly upon control of the many waterways. The East and Harlem Rivers were difficult or inaccessible for larger ships but Long Island Sound and the Hudson River were wide and navigable. Here, bunched by a light and fickle breeze, Hyde Parker's ships *Phoenix* 44, *Roebuck* 44 and *Tartar* 28 brave hostile batteries to force the Hudson on 9 October 1776.

The causes of rebellion in Britain's American colonies were complex but, although incidental to this account, they set the Royal Navy's task in context. Enormous British territorial gains from the Seven Years' War caused a great burden in administration, policing, defence and essential investment. This was additional to servicing the national debt, which had been doubled by the war. The American colonies were reasonably content, with comparatively mild taxation and their defence underwritten by Britain. However, the authorities in London regarded Britain's growing empire as a mutually beneficial trading bloc, bound by the Navigation Acts. Endlessly growing in number and complexity, these reserved trade between the home country and the colonies for British and colonial-flagged shipping. More irksome were British requirements that specific trades between the colonies and states outside the bloc were conducted via British ports. This resulted in lucrative British transshipment business but caused great resentment, manifested in a thriving smuggling industry that the expensive and corrupt customs service could not prevent.

Nonetheless, an increasingly industrialised Britain benefited the colonies through the supply of cheap manufactured goods and a high demand for raw materials, a trade which favoured the shipping industries of each. While demanding access to European markets Britain also, unashamedly, used the Royal Navy to enforce the requirements of the Navigation Acts. Seeking to reduce its level of debt the British government, arguing that the colonies had also gained from the war, sought to tax them more equably. Tightened controls and restrictions, particularly those in the sugar trade, contrasted with the previous lax attitude, resulting in further discontent.

For the colonies' defence, the British decided to station a standing army of some 10,000 troops in America. As the only real threat, that from the French, had only recently been defeated, the colonists felt this to be an unnecessary imposition. Worse was the Stamp Duty of 1765, imposed largely to pay for the soldiers. Colonial protest was met by the 1766 Act of Declaration, reminding citizens that, although they were not represented in the British parliament, they were subjects of the Crown and would be governed on its behalf 'in all cases whatsoever'.

It was over a century and a half since the landings at Plymouth Rock and a great number of colonials, some fourth or fifth generation, thought of themselves simply as 'American'. Britain and Europe were increasingly irrelevant and the colonies wanted local government, legislating for the local good. The new British administration of 1766 improved matters by repealing the widely flouted and unenforceable Stamp Act. It nonetheless left the colonists feeling rebellious and the government thwarted. Taxes on staples were thus imposed but direct refusal of their payment, orchestrated by Massachusetts, resulted in their abolition, except on tea.

Bent on reforming local government the British suspended the New York assembly. British military presence was centred here although, by the provisions of the 1765 Mutiny Act, each state was responsible for the support of the military quartered in it. None welcomed it; New York refused to consider it.

There still existed a 'frontier' attitude among many citizens, manifested in a tendency to form mobs to settle local, and even inter-colonial, disputes. The resulting disturbances often required the intervention of militia or even British troops, with disapproval of the latter being fanned by exaggerated reports of 'massacres'.

Profitable to the British exchequer, deeply unpopular in America, the tax on tea represented a tariff imposed on a commodity traded within the general framework of the Navigation Acts. Parliament thus involved the East India Company in its bulk shipment and local retail. The interests of merchants, smugglers and consumers alike were overridden and a boycott resulted. In 1773 ships in Boston were boarded and their tea cargoes dumped in the harbour. Outraged, and in no mood for further appeasement, the British government passed a series of Coercive Acts in 1774, resulting in the colonies forming the so-called Continental Congress. Moderate proposals for power-sharing with the British were narrowly defeated in favour of demands for full colonial government, with a common constitution and the power to levy taxes and to raise militia. In a further rebuff, the congress drew up a Declaration of Rights, and new trade laws beyond the structure of the Navigation Acts. Faced with this overt defiance the British offered concessions but these were rejected as insufficient. Matters had progressed too far. Like naval mutineers, the colonists knew that they had to win or go under.

Events came to a head in the spring of 1775 when the Massachusetts governor, General Gage, sent troops to seize a cache of stockpiled weapons. Resisted by force at Lexington, the military responded and, moving on to Concord, destroyed the weapons, but only at the cost of a major clash. Following a fighting retreat, the force was then besieged in its base at Boston. The Continental Congress met again, authorising the colonies to adopt a 'state of defense', with an army of 20,000 under a newly-promoted General George Washington, who was also Commander-in-Chief. In June 1775, only two months after Lexington, the British won their pyrrhic victory on Bunker's Hill, where 1,500 fell. Two American columns marched into Canada and their defeat before Quebec transformed British public opinion. Widespread disquiet among moderate Americans had Congress approach the British government to seek a rapprochement but even a direct appeal by loyalists to the King himself received no response. The rebellion was to be put down by force.

Unfortunately, the British had difficulty in grasping the scale of such a task. A purely naval war, it was argued, would blockade American interests and achieve the aim with no further bloodshed. As the colonies had a population of about three million people, however, this would take some time. Military operations, for the moment, were out of the question, with Boston under siege and outposts in up-country America and Canada being mopped-up. Limited to policing and the enforcement of the Navigation Acts, the Royal Navy's strength in American waters was not great. Despite the developments of the previous year, Vice-Admiral Samuel Graves had only 30 warships. None was of any great size and their number was spread thinly over a seaboard that stretched from Newfoundland to the Floridas.

Bon Homme Richard
A converted French East Indiaman, she was the command of John Paul Jones during his celebrated 1779 duel with the British frigate *Serapis*. The latter was taken after a three-hour battle but the *Bon Homme Richard* foundered from the damage that she had received. Note the old-style lateen mizzen sail.

The besieged army in Boston was in no great danger as long as store ships could run in. This suited the rebels well for, in the absence of any escorted convoy system, which Graves should have organised, many (a reported 55 in total) were captured. Most were taken by ships of the Continental Navy, a force which Washington was authorised to raise through the hire of vessels suitable for use as privateers. One such, an 80-ton schooner named *Hannah*, reputedly funded from the General's own pocket, can fairly claim to be the very first American warship.

Boston eventually capitulated with the arrival of heavy siege artillery, which was installed on commanding high ground. Gage's successor, Lt.-General Sir William Howe, brother to the vice-admiral, negotiated an unopposed withdrawal in return for sparing the town the need for bombardment. In March 1776, the British and many American loyalists were withdrawn by the Royal Navy to Halifax, Nova Scotia.

For the trials that lay ahead, the Navy suffered from two major drawbacks — a widespread sympathy for the rebels, who were never thought of as 'foreign', and an unshakeable belief in its own invincibility.

A new C-in-C, Rear Admiral Molyneux Shuldham, had the dilemma of how best to deploy his slender resources. His ships found themselves acting as safe havens for beleaguered officials or loyalists but, otherwise, were most useful in conferring mobility to the military, particularly as many rivers allowed navigation for a considerable distance inland. Early action included punishment bombardments of coastal towns, but that on Falmouth (now Portland), Maine proved so distasteful that the practice was abandoned. New York was yielded rather than have it destroyed by dispute. Offshore naval patrols were effective neither in apprehending American privateers nor in safeguarding transports. The razor edge of the Royal Navy of 1763 had dulled with time, and general attitudes on the American seaboard were those appropriate to a backwater. The one clear success took place at Quebec, which the Americans besieged after the failure of their initial assault. With the spring break-up of ice on the St.

Hancock

This 32-gunner was one of the US Navy's original thirteen frigates. Captured by the *Rainbow* 44 in 1777, she became the British *Iris*. As such, she captured the American frigate *Trumbull* before, herself, being taken by de Grasse's squadron in the Chesapeake in 1781. Her final fate, ironically, was to be burned by the British when they evacuated Toulon in 1793.

Bushnell's Turtle

History's first submarine attack was carried out in 1776. The target was HMS *Eagle*, Lord Howe's 64-gun flagship which was anchored below New York. The submersible, called the American *Turtle*, was the creation of Doctor David Bushnell. Built of wood, it looked like an egg-shaped barrel, ballasted upright with a lead mass, part of which could be released on a line in an emergency. At the top was a 'swell', or dome, fitted with observation windows.

The sole crewman opened a valve to admit water to an internal tank, trimming the vehicle down until the dome was awash. This dome was fitted with short breathing tubes, containing non-return valves and working much like a modern swimmer's snort tube. To eject water in order to surface, the operator had a pair of brass 'forcing pumps'. In the gloom of the interior — there was insufficient oxygen to permit candle or lantern — he had to watch both his compass and a water-tube indicator. The operator needed to be fit for, with steadily deteriorating air, he had to control his depth with a hand-cranked vertical propeller while inducing forward or astern motion with a second, horizontal propeller. A large rudder was necessary for low-speed course control.

Having approached the target, the *Turtle* needed to be forced deeper with the vertical propeller in order to feel its way beneath the target's hull. As its residual buoyancy then held it in contact with the bottom of the target, the operator used an auger, set in a vertical tube, to bore into the wooden hull. Once the auger bit was deeply attached, it was released from the *Turtle* by the latter submerging a little further. Attached to the bit were a short line and a sealed wooden box containing 150 pounds (about 67kg) of gunpowder. It is assumed that the act of release activated a clockwork firing mechanism which allowed the *Turtle* time to get clear.

In September 1776 the operator was one Sergeant Ezra Lee who was towed by rowing boats to a point up tide of the *Eagle*. Released, the *Turtle* drifted so rapidly that Lee exhausted himself in gaining an attacking position. He was unable to attach the auger bit to the hull and, was obliged to come awash. Spotted by a guard boat he was pursued, but escaped.

Lawrence River the *Isis* 50, supported by a corvette and smaller units, arrived directly from England with a regiment of troops to resolve the issue.

Determined to crush the rebellion with one decisive campaign in 1776, the British government embarked on the huge task of assembling the 500-odd transports necessary to ship nearly 30,000 troops, half of them German mercenaries. As several return trips were required, using both Quebec and the New York area, the administrative system was severely over-stretched. The build-up before New York was assisted by 2,000 troops from the Carolinas, following an unsuccessful attempt to take Charleston. Cooperation between the naval and military commanders had been virtually non-existent there. Without awaiting military assistance, Commodore Parker's ships attempted to subdue fixed fortifications. Not for the first, nor for the last, time in history this evolution failed.

From late August Howe's forces enjoyed considerable success, using the navy and deep waterways to continually shift their centre of gravity. Washington's tactic was always to yield ground in the face of superior strength, while the British, in the wake of Bunker's Hill, were reluctant to undertake frontal assaults. By October, Washington had been eased northward, from the New York environs to White Plains. From the north, advancing from Quebec, the forces of Lt.-General Sir Guy Carleton sought to squeeze the rebels between themselves and those of Howe, to force a decisive battle. Their only route across otherwise trackless wilderness was along the valley occupied by the rivers Richelieu and Hudson, which flowed north and south respectively from a watershed near Fort Ticonderoga. To the north of the fort lay the 60-mile long Lake Champlain, the control of which was essential to any advance. As sitting tenants, the Americans made huge efforts to collect and construct craft that could be armed to prevent Carleton moving southward. For their part, the British expected the Navy to sail suitable vessels up the St. Lawrence, thence up the Richelieu, a tributary, to access the lake.

Rapids and shallows, which characterised the Richelieu, delayed the effort and it was to be October 1776 before battle was joined. Small, oared sailing craft, appropriately referred to as 'galleys', were stiffened by a few larger ones: Benedict Arnold's Americans with three schooners and a sloop; Captain Thomas Pringle's Royal Navy by five of various types, including the 18-gun sloop *Inflexible*. Three days of scrappy encounters saw Arnold lose 10 of his 15 craft, but his tactical defeat was more than offset strategically. The 'naval race' had so delayed the British that they ceased operations for the winter. Their intention to resume in the spring was forestalled by Washington's winter offensive, which caused the British abandonment of much of New Jersey. This, in turn, meant that British forces could no longer be sustained locally, necessitating the diversion of much merchant shipping and naval protection to bring supplies from Europe.

Now under Lt.-General Burgoyne, the military advance southward from Lake Champlain was resumed early in 1777, complemented by a looping movement to the west, via Lake Ontario. Better organised, and armed by the French, American forces disputed their every move. Howe, expected to advance northward from New York to meet Burgoyne, decided to distract Washington by seizing Philadelphia. For this, he required the Navy to transport his forces coastwise via Chesapeake Bay. Thus, at a time when an estimated 200 American privateers were swarming offshore (560 British supply ships were taken in 1776-7 alone) already inadequate naval strength was diverted to an operation which left British land forces dangerously divided. Philadelphia was duly taken but Burgoyne, unsupported, his strength whittled down, his supply lines long and vulnerable, was brought to action at Saratoga by an American army now twice his strength. On 17th October 1777 Burgoyne surrendered.

France supported the rebels with supplies and 'volunteers', seeking revenge for the Seven Year's War in a new war by proxy. Uncertain of the outcome, she was reluctant to make a full commitment until the British surrender at Saratoga. In February 1778 France entered into commercial and defensive alliances with what had been, since the Declaration of Independence the previous July, the United States. As the latter alliance guaranteed each other's territories in America, Britain and France were again at war.

This had an immediate effect on the conduct of hostilities. A colonial war was one thing: France's massive army threatened Britain with invasion. British priorities had to change. Sir Henry Clinton, who had succeeded the uninspiring Howe as Commander-in-Chief, was instructed to bring Washington to battle. As the American's strategy made this unlikely, the British were also to consolidate, provide an expeditionary force to defend the Floridas, and to take the war to the French in the West Indies. As the outcome against France would hinge on maritime war, the bulk of the Royal Navy would, as was traditional, remain in home waters. French intentions were less to assist the Americans than to defeat the British. As the threat of invasion was a major plank of their strategy, the greater part of their fleet, too, would be home-based. Assistance to the Americans would, however, keep the Royal Navy dispersed.

Far left: 'Monsieur sneaking gallantly 27 July 1778

On 27 July 1778 Keppel met d'Orvilliers in the Battle of Ushant. A popular response here shows the French, sternsheets ablaze, being driven into the safe haven of Brest. The reality, however, was an inconclusive action, following which mutual recrimination between Keppel and his second-in-command, Palliser, brought about courts-martial for them both.

Concorde v. Minerva 22nd August 1778

Prizes taken by either side, confusingly, tended to keep their names under a new flag. During 1761, for instance, the British frigate *Minerva* captured the *Warwick*, an *en flûte* 60 gunner taken by the French five years earlier. In August 1778 the *Minerva* was, herself, captured by the French *Concorde*, remaining in enemy hands for only three years. The *Concorde*, seized by the *Magnificent* 74 in 1783, carried the name in the Royal Navy until 1811.

John Paul Jones

One of the American navy's first heroes, John Paul was a Scot born in Galloway in 1747. At 14 he went to sea from nearby Whitehaven, graduating early to command. In 1773 he was involved in a scuffle in which a man was killed and Paul fled to Virginia, a wanted man. Here, he changed his name to John Paul Jones.

With the armed struggle for independence, Jones was commissioned as lieutenant into the new Continental Navy. Commanding the 18-gun sloop *Ranger* he sailed from Brest in 1778. He took several prizes in the Irish Sea but failed in an attempt to burn the collier fleet at Whitehaven and also to kidnap the Earl of Selkirk. A successful duel with the 20-gun sloop *Drake* resulted, however, in the latter's capture. Feted on his return to Brest, Jones was given command of an old 43-gun East Indiaman, renamed *Bonhomme Richard*. As commodore, Jones now took a small Franco-American squadron on a circumnavigation of the British Isles. He took several prizes and caused consternation by an unsuccessful attempt to seize the port of Leith.

Off Flamborough Head his squadron encountered a large British convoy but allowed it to escape through becoming embroiled with its two escorts. Both were captured, although the *Serapis* 44 had so injured Jones' ship that she foundered. Jones returned to France a hero. The Americans gave him command of a 74 but she was still incomplete when the end of the war brought him unemployment with the disbandment of the navy. He briefly served the Russians but his irascible nature made him influential enemies. In 1790 he settled in France where, surrounded by the turmoil of revolution, he lived in comparative poverty, dying in 1792 at the age of only 45.

In 1905 John Paul Jones was honoured by his adopted country, which re-interred his remains at the US Naval Academy in Annapolis.

To this end the soldier-turned-sailor, the Comte d'Estaing, sailed from Toulon in April 1778 with a dozen sail of the line and five frigates. His task was to transport a body of troops and to secure Washington's seaward flanks as required. In winter, British naval activity permitting, he was to operate in the Caribbean, with the ultimate objective of recovering lost island territories. From Gibraltar, d'Estaing's progress was tracked by a British frigate which remained in company long enough to establish his likely destination.

Within days Vice-Admiral the Hon. John Byron (late circumnavigator) sailed in the *Princess Royal* 90 to reinforce the American station. His force comprised 13 line ships and a frigate. In the June the British army was leaving Philadelphia for New York, its heavy equipment following by sea. On the 28th. Lord Howe was appraised of d'Estaing's imminent arrival and of Byron's despatch. Howe had six 64s and four 50s and, concerned that the Americans and French might have planned coordinated moves against British bases such as New York or Newport, Rhode Island, he gathered his forces sufficiently to place heavier units in Lower New York Bay and set a patrol line as far south as the Chesapeake.

It was near the latter that the French squadron was sighted on 5th July and shadowed to Sandy Hook. Here it dithered for nearly a fortnight before heading north for Newport. As Howe, in inferior force, was about to follow, the *Cornwall* 74 of Byron's force arrived to say that the squadron had been dispersed by a severe storm and, like herself, most ships had been considerably damaged aloft. Arriving first, the French boldly entered Narrangansett Bay on 29th July. From both the east and west sides of Rhode Island they cannonaded the British garrison as American troops crossed the narrow channel to the northern end. Caught in the harbour at Newport, four frigates and a sloop were stripped of their guns to assist in the defence and then, with some transports, either scuttled as blockships or burned. This loss alone equated to a sharp naval defeat.

Battling on, the outnumbered defenders were cheered on 9th August by the arrival of Howe. Although, without Byron, he too was in inferior strength, his arrival caused d'Estaing to abandon his activities quickly in order to get some sea room. Howe, who could accept action only on favourable terms, fell back, and a manoeuvring contest began, with neither side wishing to move far from Newport.

Concorde v. Minerva.

Matters were again decided by the weather, a full gale over two days causing extensive damage to the rigging of ships of both sides. D'Estaing collected his scattered ships and returned to Rhode Island only to inform the American army commander that the squadron would withdraw to Boston to refit, prior to sailing for Martinique. Howe was unable to intercept the French but had achieved his purpose. Deprived of French support, the American army had to abandon its investment of Newport. With inferior numbers, Howe had preserved his fleet-in-being while safeguarding British military forces, both in Newport and New York, from overwhelming attack. This could not disguise the fact that the British army in America was totally dependent upon the Navy, but the Navy was never given the strength required to discharge its responsibilities on the American station. Howe returned home deeply disenchanted with the Admiralty. He found little enthusiasm in Britain for pursuing the war further, being advised by peer opinion that the territory was too vast to be contested in the face of popular opposition.

In European waters, Admiral the Hon. Augustus Keppel had assumed command of the Channel Fleet. One of many senior officers to have refused to serve against the Americans, he considered the French a different matter. Early summer of 1778 had seen him compelled to avoid action due to insufficient strength but, by July, his force had been extended to 30 of the line. Based on Brest were 32 French sail of the line, commanded by the Comte d'Orvilliers. The French admiral laboured under contradictory instructions. With invasion the ultimate objective he needed to keep his fleet intact in order to link with another French squadron at Rochefort and, it was hoped, the Spanish fleet. He had also to instil a 'fight to the last' mentality and eradicate the tendency of his aristocratic officers to dispute between themselves.

On the afternoon of 23rd July, when he sighted Keppel, d'Orvilliers decided to decline action. Spending the night pressing hard to the north west, he succeeded in getting to windward of the British, thus being able to avoid an engagement except on favourable terms, but at the cost of having Keppel between his squadron and its base. Keppel tried to cut off two enemy stragglers to force an action but, disappointingly, these made for Brest, leaving the fleets with 30 sail apiece. For four days d'Orvilliers remained beyond reach but, early on the 27th, squally conditions with frequent windshifts allowed Keppel to close him.

Barrington's action off St. Lucia 1778

On 14 December 1778 Admiral the Hon. Samuel Barrington, learning of the approach of d'Estaing with a superior force of twelve of the line, herded over 50 transports into the small bay of the Carénage on St. Lucia. Across the entrance to the bay, in a tight line, he anchored his seven ships of the line and two frigates. In this defensive formation he successfully repulsed two attacks.

Left: Action between the Quebec and the Surveillante 1779 (Robert Dodd)

In July 1779 the 32-gun frigate *Quebec* grounded in the Channel Islands and had to jettison her 12-pounder guns to refloat. Returning to Portsmouth for repair, she could be rearmed only with 9-pounders. Meeting the French 12-pounder frigate *Surveillante* on 6th October she had insufficient firepower to prevail. Both ships were dismasted but the *Quebec* caught fire and eventually blew up, only 68 surviving.

Wearing ships in succession, the French found the British, in a ragged line of bearing, suddenly upon them. D'Orvilliers tried to form a battle line, his rear leading, while exchanging furious fire at very close range. Drawing slowly ahead, the French admiral was concerned that Keppel would concentrate on his rear. He signalled his fleet wear together, passing down the lee side of Keppel's line. With several ships already badly cut up aloft, Keppel countered by tacking away together, signalling to preserve the line.

At this stage, the British rear, under Vice-Admiral Sir Hugh Palliser, became separated. D'Orvilliers awaited a further attack but Keppel had to spend a critical period in reconstituting his fleet, with individual captains appearing to prefer following their divisional commander rather than their admiral. It was too late to resume the action when Keppel had finally reformed and, by daylight on the 28th, d'Orvilliers was beyond reach. The indecisive action, known later as the Battle of Ushant, found the British out-manoeuvred but having the better of gunnery and casualties inflicted.

There were furious repercussions on both sides. D'Orvilliers accused his rear commander, the Duc de Chartres, of not supporting him wholeheatedly. More vociferously, Keppel levelled much the same charge at Palliser. In a politically polarised service the two were from opposite sides of the floor but subsequent courts martial acquitted both. Where Keppel's reputation was enhanced, however, Palliser —although found to have fought well —was damaged to the point where his seagoing career was at an end.

Then one of the world's most valuable markets, the West Indies were again to be the scene of major confrontations between the British and French fleets during the War of Independence. Following repairs at Boston, the Comte d'Estaing sailed for Martinique on 4th November 1778. In this theatre, too, the British had been woefully prepared for war and, in seizing Dominica in the September, the French had enjoyed a virtual walkover. Its possession gave them a group of four islands (the others being Guadeloupe, Martinique and St. Lucia) which acted as their power base.

Ranger

In the 18-gun sloop *Ranger*, John Paul Jones made his first foray into British waters. On her arrival at Quiberon, she became the first American ship to have her ensign recognised and saluted by a foreign government. She was taken by the British when Charleston capitulated in 1780, and served briefly as the *Halifax* before being sold out.

Comte de Guichen (1712 - 1790)

Although he joined the French Navy at eighteen, the promotion lists were clogged and he was still a frigate captain at 36. As a contre-amiral he led the French centre at the inconclusive 1778 Battle of Ushant. As lieutenant-general (vice-admiral) he skirmished three times with Rodney in the West Indies. During December 1781 he was out-manoeuvred by an inferior force under Kempenfelt, which cut out much of a large convoy. In 1782 (aged 70) he was unable to prevent Howe from running a huge re-supply convoy into Gibraltar.

L'Indien

Built in Amsterdam, apparently to the account of the French Navy, *l'Indien* was acquired by the Duke of Luxembourg before being loaned to the state of South Carolina. Serving under that name, she was over-gunned with 28 x 32-pounders and twelve 12-pounders. This probably contributed to her capture in 1782 by the British frigates *Astraea*, *Diomede* and *Quebec*.

Immediately to the south of the group lay the important British island of Barbados and, for its immediate protection and a projected invasion of St. Lucia, 5,000 troops were stripped from the already inadequate forces in North America. Convoyed by Commodore Hotham, they left New York on the same day as d'Estaing's departure. In inferior strength, with only five of the line, and slowed by transports, Hotham was in considerable hazard of being overtaken and discovered by the unsuspecting French. A straggling British transport was taken by them in heavy weather near Bermuda. The crew told d'Estaing of Hotham's presence but, as they had not been informed regarding their convoy's destination, the French admiral guessed, wrongly, that it was Antigua, neighbouring Guadeloupe to the north. With the enemy squadron fortuitously diverted, Hotham arrived at Barbados. Here he joined Rear-Admiral the Hon. Samuel Barrington with two more of the line.

Moving quickly on to St. Lucia, Barrington landed the troops in an enclosed bay on 13th December, seizing the high ground and existing fortifications that surrounded it. In the expectation of rapid French reaction, the transports were herded inshore and the warships anchored in close line ahead across the bay's mouth. D'Estaing's squadron arrived in due course, and made two passes along the British line, after which it retired to nearby Martinique for 7,000 troops. These were landed to the north of the British defences, now reinforced by naval guns. Three frontal assaults were repulsed with heavy loss of life. On the 29th d'Estaing pulled out, the remainder of the St. Lucia garrison surrendering on the following day. By acting so rapidly, Barrington, had seized territory of great value despite his inferior strength.

Both sides then spent a period reinforcing the West Indies. Vice-Admiral Byron arrived from Rhode Island with ten ships of the line and took command of the station. The French, however, maintained superiority, with d'Estaing lucky to count such stalwarts as Suffren and la Motte-Picquet among his divisional commanders.

A large and politically-important British convoy had been assembling to the north, at St. Kitts. When it sailed, early in June 1779, Byron needed to escort it for a safe distance. Profiting by his absence, d'Estaing landed in force on the small island of St. Vincent, immediately south of St. Lucia. Its seizure was to facilitate the taking of Barbados. Because of contrary winds d'Estaing could not make Barbados but, in full strength, assaulted the more accessible Grenada. Its small garrison was overrun in two days, demonstrating again that, in the absence of naval support, smaller islands were indefensible.

Still encumbered by the transports, Byron arrived at Grenada on 5th July—too late. D'Estaing got under way in the small hours. In the steady north-easterly trade wind, the French formed line, standing to the north west on the starboard tack. Broad-reached on

Rodney

Born in 1719, George Brydges Rodney entered the Royal Navy at the age of 13 years. Well-connected, he was a lieutenant at 19 and a full post-captain at 23, commanding the *Eagle* 60 at Hawke's action off Finisterre in 1747. Rodney's character was one of contradictions. Quick to make enemies, he was, nonetheless, a dedicated socialite. Although appearing to favour appointments ashore, he was a brilliantly innovative tactician at sea. Endlessly in debt, his quest for prize money was ruthless.

Following a spell as Governor of Newfoundland, he was back at sea in 1758, playing a key role in the taking of Louisbourg. The following year he was made Rear-Admiral of the Blue, unusually jumping to Vice-Admiral of the Blue just three years later. During this period he had commanded a squadron charged with reducing a potential invasion fleet at le Havre, before being transferred to the West Indies. Here, he led a force which seized Martinique and the Grenadines.

Again going ashore, Rodney became governor of Greenwich Hospital in 1765, only to be shifted, against his will, to Jamaica. Financial problems drove him to live in France during the later 1770s, despite France and Britain being at war. Back at sea in 1780, he was instrumental in lifting a protracted siege of Gibraltar, en route defeating a Spanish squadron in the so-called "Moonlight Battle" of St. Vincent. In 1781 he was appointed Commander-in-Chief West Indies, crowning his career with the defeat of Guichen off Martinique and of de Grasse at the Saintes. All his later actions succeeded through deviation from rigid line tactics.

Having finally amassed considerable wealth in the West Indies, Rodney was made KB in 1780 and a peer in 1782. He retired as an Admiral of the White and died in 1792

the port tack, Byron was heading south along the Grenada coast. He detached the convoy, with suitable escort, and signalled his rather ragged formation to 'General Chase'. With the French rear still in something of a ruck Byron did not realise that he was outnumbered by 24 line ships to 21.

'General Chase' often led to the fastest ships drawing ahead, unsupported. In this case, Byron's second-in-command, Barrington, in the *Prince of Wales* 74, headed for the disorganised French rear in company with two other fast sailers. Approaching end-on, they suffered badly when the French offered their broadsides, but wore ship and headed up the weather side of the enemy line. As it arrived, Byron's main group did likewise, although three ships misjudged the manoeuvre and were severely punished as the French swept past. Signalled to 'Close Engagement' by Byron, the British van was soon under such heavy pressure that the *Suffolk* 74, supported by the *Monmouth* 64, stood in to assist. They prevented any French attempt to double the head of the line, but were heavily damaged.

Byron needed to stay between d'Estaing and his convoy, but also to safeguard four crippled line ships, now trailing. The French admiral could have moved against either or brought the British line, now only 17 strong, to further action. He did none of these, his objective being to preserve Grenada from attack rather than to seek a naval victory. Byron had fought a poor tactical action, and the time that many of his ships were off-line for repair hazarded other territories.

As part of the invasion plan, d'Estaing was ordered to leave in the West Indies detachments of ships under de Grasse and la Motte-Picquet, and to return to France with the remainder of the Toulon squadron. The veteran admiral had received disquieting news of events in the United States. In November 1778, as the northern winter set in, the British military switched its attention to the southern states. Although the resulting division of strength was ultimately to prove fatal, the campaign in Georgia and the Carolinas initially went well. It still depended upon naval support, however. The Admiralty recognised that Howe's successor, the widely-detested but well-connected Rear-Admiral James Gambier, was the wrong man for the job, and replaced him during 1779 with the uninspiring Vice-Admiral Marriott Arbuthnot, who arrived with a small reinforcement.

For the moment, d'Estaing had heard of the fall of Savannah, with pleas for help from the hard-pressed Americans and, worse, reports that they believed that their French ally had forsaken them. Feeling that his own, and his national honour was at stake, the old soldier ignored his orders and made for the Savannah River. With 22 of the line, he intended to relieve pressure in the south before heading north to support Washington in a drive against British-held New York. D'Estaing's arrival at Savannah achieved surprise but, having landed his troops, the admiral, as was his custom, led them himself. With American support, an ill-considered assault was mounted on the town. It failed and the admiral was wounded. As a result, he returned with his squadron to France as originally ordered, leaving the disillusioned Americans to yield further ground.

The replacement French Commander-in-Chief in the West Indies was the able but 67-year-old Comte de Guichen. Arriving in March 1780 he moved immediately against St. Lucia. With 22 of the line he arrived to find Rear-Admiral Sir Hyde Parker with just 16, but occupying the same easily defensible anchorage. Guichen did not attack and within the week Sir George Rodney, now a full admiral, arrived as British C-on-C.

British hopes of reinforcement in the West Indies had been dashed when, in June 1779, Spain had also declared war. With Brest un-blocked, 30 French line ships rendezvoused with 36 Spanish and cruised off the English coast. In French Channel ports, over 50,000 troops and 400 transports had been assembled. A predictable invasion scare gripped the British, who could muster only 35 ships for the Channel Fleet. Fortunately for the British, the Franco-Spanish fleet had no common signalling system and could not agree where to land. They vacillated throughout August until struck by an easterly gale and an epidemic. Unable to goad the inferior British fleet to action, the Franco-Spanish fleet dispersed.

Spain was not in the war through any sentiment for American independence; indeed, this threatened to challenge her territorial claims on the Gulf. As allies of the French, the Spanish sought the recovery of Gibraltar and Minorca. Gibraltar was immediately besieged and, although the British feared little from a direct assault, this raised the

Destruction of the American fleet at Penobscot Bay 1779 (Serres)

A fort being built by British and Loyalist forces on Penobscot Bay, Maine was fronted on 24 July 1779 by a mixed force of 17 Continental Navy and State warships, privateers and 19 transports with troops. The American attack developed so slowly that, on 13 August, they were surprised by a scratch British squadron of one 64, three frigates and three smaller ships. In the ensuing rout two American ships were captured and the remainder burned.

Left: Quebec v. Surveillante.

The opening stages of the epic duel between the two frigates in 1779 (see p82)

problem of keeping it supplied. Rodney's passage to the West Indies was not, therefore, direct. His own small squadron of five line ships was boosted to 22, with 14 frigates, by a detachment from the Channel Fleet. These escorted a large convoy for both Gibraltar and Minorca, with further contingents for Portugal and the West Indies.

On 7th January 1780 the West Indies group was detached as planned, the remainder standing on. The following morning they encountered a large group of ships which Rodney pursued. With little trouble he seized the whole of the Spanish squadron — a 64, four frigates, two sloops and a dozen supply ships, all bound for the fleet base at Cadiz. His prizes were brought to Gibraltar.

Speaking passing ships, Rodney learned of another enemy squadron, reported to be off Cape St. Vincent. This comprised 11 ships of the line and a pair of frigates under Admiral Juan de Langara. When the Spanish commander observed a mass of sail approaching from the north on the afternoon of the 16th he assumed that it was an unescorted convoy. Seemingly not warned by his frigates, he stood his ground, realising too late that it was Rodney's fleet and that he was outnumbered two to one. De Langara formed line and made for the distant haven of Cadiz. Rodney signalled 'General Chase' to give his fastest ships their head. As the winter dusk set in, the British took grave risks by standing inshore. In what became known as the Moonlight Battle of Cape St. Vincent the Spaniards were overtaken one by one. Conditions were very boisterous but, after ten hours of action, de Langara's flagship, the *Fenix* 80, and five 70s had been captured. A further 70 had blown up with the loss all hands. Rodney, himself crippled with gout, managed to extricate his squadron off the lee shore. He had scored two successes, but against opponents so negligent that they were severely criticised even by their French allies. Rodney's victories had a powerful effect on enemy morale. He remained for a fortnight at Gibraltar, awaiting the return of the Minorca convoy escort. During this time no action was taken against him by a superior Franco-Spanish force laying in Cadiz, just 60 miles distant.

The British run of good fortune continued. Rodney and the West Indies convoy sailed finally in mid-February 1780. It was accompanied part way by the Channel Fleet contingent which, with their prizes, then broke off for home. En route it encountered a French convoy bound for the Indian Ocean islands. One of its two escorting 64s and three transports were taken, the other 64 sacrificing herself to buy time to allow the remainder of the convoy to scatter. Rodney's arrival at the end of March brought the strength of his Leeward Islands station to 20 of the line. Both he and his opposite number, Guichen, who outnumbered him with 22, were noted for their tactical skills. On 16th April 1780, when he sighted his opponent some 30 miles west of Dominica, Rodney resolved on a decisive engagement. The winds were light but, by the following morning, the fleets had formed battle lines. As the French formation was notably ragged, Rodney concentrated on its rear, but Guichen reversed direction by wearing his ships together, preventing the British achieving a concentration against part of his line. With the advantage of the weather gauge, Rodney eventually succeeded, and signalled his captains to engage their opposite numbers in line. Not for the first time, unequal numbers caused confusion. Convention called for the van to engage the van and the leading British ships strove to make ground on their opponents. The British centre, including the flagship, the *Sandwich* 90, became very hotly engaged but the admiral was later highly critical of inadequate support from both van and rear. His irritation was compounded by Guichen's success in bearing away when his fleet was on the verge of being divided.

The French admiral had two objectives: to recover St. Lucia and to keep the sea 'without too far compromising' his force. Rodney wished simply to defeat him, but he was too wily to be caught out by an opponent with fewer ships. Two more clashes

Washington
Representative of the varied fleets operating on the lakes, in this case Champlain, the *Washington* is lateen-rigged to buck headwinds blowing down the lake. Normally carrying ten guns, including two 18-pounders, she is pierced for more. Note the rowing ports interspersed with the closed portlids.

occurred — on 15th May and 19th May — after days of manoeuvre as formal, a stately but potentially deadly court dance. Both ended indecisively. Rodney had safeguarded St. Lucia at the expense of several crippled ships. Guichen had kept the sea as ordered, although the strain of being in close proximity to his enemy for over a month broke his resolve. He requested to be relieved of his appointment.

As Napoleon was yet to discover in Russia, some undertakings are just too vast in scope to be practicable. The British in North America had a low ratio of force to space. Ashore, inadequate military forces moved hither and thither across limitless territories. Any local effect disappeared the moment they moved on. Offshore, the fleet upon which their survival depended was unable to enforce a declared blockade on so long a coastline. While the Continental Navy and American privateers could never develop a threat to the Royal Navy, and even their capture of scores of storeships was never more than a nuisance, these self-same supplies and those of foreign war materials were enough to sustain the American effort.

In endeavouring to enforce the blockade, the British infringed the rights of neutral shipping. Rigorous stop-and-search went against the principles of free navigation. The definition of contraband was never exact, resulting in contentious seizures and interminable wrangling at law. It was because so many materials vital to shipbuilding and ship repair originated in the Baltic that Russia, Denmark and Sweden were driven to form the so-called Armed Neutrality, the better to protect their rights. They were later joined by Austria, Prussia and even the Kingdom of the Two Sicilies. The Dutch, as universal carriers, were also moved to join, a development actually welcomed by the British who eyed Dutch foreign possessions with covetous interest. They could legitimately be acquired within a legal state of war, which began in December 1780.

COUNT DE GRASSE *delivering his Sword to the Gallant* ADMIRAL RODNEY.

De Grasse and Rodney

One of the French Navy's most successful commanders, the Comte de Grasse was directly responsible for the final British defeat in the American colonies when he out-manoeuvred Graves in the Chesapeake in 1781. He met his match, however, in that wily tactician Rodney who, at the Battle of the Saintes in 1782, famously broke his line, taking de Grasse's flagship and four others.

Among the most northerly of the Leeward Islands were three small Dutch-owned islands, which the British had suspected of using neutral status to profit greatly from an entrepôt trade with the Americans. Rodney's notoriously acquisitive instincts led him quickly, and in person, to seize the islands in February 1781. Large numbers of merchantmen were captured and well-stocked warehouses particularly on St. Eustatius, added to the loot. The admiral did his personal reputation no service by remaining there for nearly three months. He was still there when, in the March, the Comte de Grasse arrived at Martinique with an important French convoy escorted by 20 ships of the line. Rodney had left Rear-Admiral Sir Samuel Hood, with 17 line ships, to watch the islands, but his explicit instructions to Hood had caused the latter to be caught well downwind. De Grasse thus had no difficulty in interposing himself for the safe conduct of the convoy, while preventing every attempt by Hood's inferior strength to force an action. Hood, a comptetent fighting admiral had arrived early in the year with a convoy and welcome reinforcement of eight of the line. Now, with four ships damaged and the worst of the casualties, he was deeply unhappy with his commander-in-chief.

In this theatre of war the enemy did not always wear French colours. A late hurricane in the previous October had wrecked a dozen warships, including two ships of the line and several frigates. Others were grounded and dismasted, totally beyond the capability of local resources to repair.

In March 1781 the British moved against the Dutch in Cape Colony. A troop convoy of 10 armed Indiamen was escorted by Commodore George Johnstone in the *Romney* 50, with a further two 50s, two line ships, three frigates and eight lesser warships. To frustrate the operation, the French despatched Commandeur de Suffren St. Tropez with a pair of 74s and three 64s, also carrying troops.

On 11th April Johnstone put into Porto Praya in the Portuguese Cape Verdes. Although aware that Suffren was behind him, Johnstone accepted the protection afforded by a neutral anchorage and allowed his ships to anchor at will. It was by chance that the French squadron called, in order to top up with fresh water, and was as surprised as the British, which had many personnel ashore and ships masking each other's field of fire. Suffren seized the moment, entering the wide shallow bay to engage in a messy, confused scrap. Ill-supported by their colleagues, the two French 74s took the brunt of the fighting. One, the *Annibal*, was totally dismasted but, so unprepared were the British, Suffren extracted her under jury rig. One East Indiaman was taken but recaptured.

Neither side lost a ship but, despite their heavier armament, the French took far more casualties. Suffren's strategical sense did not fail, however. As Johnstone effected repairs, the French pressed on for the Cape. When the British squadron did arrive it found its opponents in such a powerful defensive position that it dared not attack. Having saved the colony from certain capture, Suffren was well rewarded by promotion. In the meantime, his orders were for India.

The year of 1781 saw a renewal of the invasion scare in Britain, whose Channel Fleet, while outnumbering the French Brest squadron was, in turn, inferior in strength to the Cadiz-based Spanish. The Dutch remained an unknown quantity, but ominously positioned off British home waters.

Gibraltar had not been re-supplied since Rodney's operation of February 1780 and was still under siege. In something of an anti-climax, Vice-Admiral George Darby ran in unchallenged with a large convoy in March 1781. Chagrined, the Spanish enlisted French help for an ineffectual demonstration against Minorca, which was not relieved and fell a year later. This led to the interception by la Motte Picquet of the British convoy returning with the plundered spoils of St. Eustatius. Two thirds of its ships were captured.

Le Bailli Suffren de St. Tropez (1729 -1788)

Suffren joined the French Navy as a midshipman in 1743 maintaining, through his aristocratic family, a lifelong connection with the Order of Malta. Still a junior, he spent a year as a prisoner of the British. Slow promotion saw him yet a captain in 1781, but the death of his commander, d'Orves, gave him command in the Indian Ocean. He died a vice-admiral, having never really suffered defeat nor gained a victory.

COMBAT DE LA FRÉGATE FRANÇAISE LA BELLE POULE ATTAQUÉE PAR LA FRÉGATE ANGLAISE L'ARÉTHUSE LE 17 JUIN 1778.

Das See Gefecht der Französische Kriegs Fregatte die Schöne Hehe mit der Englische genannt Arethuse, wie letztere 1778 d. 17 Iuni die erstere angegriffen | Combat de la Fregate Française la Belle Poule attaquée par la Fregate Anglaise l'Aréthuse le 17 Juin 1778.

Arethusa v. Belle Poule 1778

From February 1778, when France concluded an alliance with the American rebels, a state of near war existed with the British. This flared in the June when a small French patrol group encountered Keppel in the western English Channel. Keppel demanded to speak them. All refused and were made to comply by force. Resistance by the *Belle Poule* resulted in 45 French dead and effectively signalled the outbreak of hostlities.

Convoys of sail often involved huge numbers of ships by 20th century standards and their escort resulted in several fierce actions, including the only real confrontation with the Dutch. In August 1781, while bringing home a Baltic convoy, Vice-Admiral Hyde Parker fell in with a Dutch fleet under Rear-Admiral Johannes Zoutman, also escorting a convoy, near the Dogger Bank. Tactically, both sides accompanied their charges with a small close escort, supported by a free-ranging, heavier fighting group. The strengths of the latter were similar, each with seven line ships and five or six smaller. Since the maritime wars of a century earlier, the British and Dutch had rubbed along well enough as somewhat grumpy neighbours and, on this day, Zoutman's attitude was one of a man reluctant to fight but prepared to defend stoutly if molested. In contrast, Hyde Parker sought to expunge the criticism heaped on him by Rodney in the West Indies a year previously.

In a fair north-easterly breeze, the British convoy was packed off on the shortest course to its own coast while the admiral signalled, unnecessarily, 'General Chase'. His scratch squadron, mostly of old ships fit only for convoy escort, ran down in a ragged line abreast on Zoutman. The latter, his convoy safely to leeward, formed an exemplary line of battle and might have punished the British severely with broadsides as they closed head on. Instead, the Dutch earned great admiration by holding their fire.

Hyde Parker rounded-to, forming his line to windward and only on the 'execute' signal by his flagship, the *Fortitude* 74, to open fire did hostilities commence. Etiquette demanded that flagship engaged flagship but, as these were placed differently in their respective lines, there was some confusion. Following near three hours of toe-to-toe combat, the battle ceased by mutual consent. No ships were sunk but many were severely damaged and one Dutchman later foundered. With enormous casualty lists to both sides it had been an entirely ineffective display of gallantry, with neither convoy affected. Predictably, Hyde Parker was again criticised by Rodney. He had, however, been able to discuss with the King himself, who visited the squadron on its return, the inadequate size and condition of a Royal Navy expected to conduct a major war in several theatres simultaneously.

Having abandoned their base at Newport in 1779 in order to concentrate around New York, the British began an ambitious attempt to win back the southern states. Charleston was taken with naval assistance, and a squadron of the Continental Navy was captured there. The Americans had just lost heavily in an ill-planned operation in Penobscot Bay.

Concerned at British success, the French landed a further 5,000 troops under the command of the Comte de Rochambeau at Newport in July 1780. En route, the convoy's covering force, under d'Arzac de Ternay, was engaged by the inferior British squadron of Commodore the Hon. William Cornwallis. Having had much the advantage, de Ternay was heavily criticised for not punishing the British more severely. He successfully maintained that discharging his mission was of greater importance.

Learning of Rochambeau's arrival the British commander, Clinton, left 8,000 troops with Major General the Earl Charles Cornwallis, and hurried back to cover New York with the remainder. By August 1781, a meandering and generally successful campaign found Cornwallis with a somewhat depleted army at Yorktown. Watched by 5,000 Americans under the Marquis de Lafayette, the British were separated from Clinton's 17,000 strong army but, being on Chesapeake Bay, they could be reinforced by sea.

Covering Clinton in the north, Washington and Rochambeau had about 10,000 men and, wishing to move against Cornwallis, the Americans needed to ensure that he was cut off from naval assistance. Agreement was reached that de Grasse, who had 28 sail of the line in the West Indies, would sail north in full strength, with a further 3,000 troops. Simultaneously, Washington hurried south with 7,000 men. Rodney, the ever-shrewd tactician, was unhappy at developments and, having himself to sail for England, he despatched Rear-Admiral Sir Samuel Hood for the Chesapeake with 14 ships. Hood left Antigua on 19th August 1781, five days later than de Grasse but, as the latter sailed a long, deceptive route, he arrived first. Finding all well with Cornwallis he proceeded, as instructed, to New York. In command here was the more senior Rear-Admiral Thomas Graves, with a further five line ships and a 50. Uneasy that Cornwallis was about to be attacked, Graves sailed for the Chesapeake with the combined squadron.

De Grasse arrived on 30th August and disembarked his troops while he awaited a convoy from Newport, bringing siege guns to batter Cornwallis' defences. When sails hove into view on 5th September, the French assumed it was their convoy. That it turned out to be Graves and the British fleet was a disagreeable surprise, but de Grasse had a five-ship advantage. Graves did not hesitate. With a favourable breeze he swept down on de Grasse's fleet which got into disorder, beating out of a confined channel. As a French line formed, the British wore together, forming a parallel line but in reverse order.

At too great a range, Graves might have been expected to bear away together to close as a complete line but, instead, ordered the lead ship, the *Shrewsbury* 74, to incline in the direction of de Grasse's van. As the flagship, the *London* 98, was still flying the 'line' signal, each ship followed the Shrewsbury in turn. The result was that the British line was inclined at an angle to that of the French and, while the vans became heavily engaged, the centres and rears were beyond all but long-range pot shots. At the rear, the

The Battle of Nagapatam 1782

During 1782-3 Vice-Admiral Sir Edward Hughes and then-acting Commodore Suffren fought a series of five actions of the Coromandel coast of India, reminiscent of those between Pocock and d'Aché in 1758-9. Again, both had scratch squadrons, poorly supported by their governments, and neither dared risk defeat. The action of Nagapatam was fought on 6 July 1782; 255 men died, nothing was taken.

perfectly able Hood was strictured by the need to maintain line, and his seven ships were reduced to bystanders.

The battle rumbled on until sunset whereupon Graves hauled off, with five of his van in a crippled state. Despite Hood's urging him to tackle de Grasse again, Graves stood off for four days. From his standpoint, it had been just one more indecisive encounter. Unfortunately, urgent despatches revealing the deteriorating situation at Yorktown never reached him. He was unaware that de Grasse's intentions were merely to keep him at a distance.

On 11th September de Grasse entered the Chesapeake to find his Newport convoy had arrived safely. Graves, now aware of his situation, was both outnumbered and with damaged ships. He scuttled the *Terrible* 74, which was in a sad state, and hurried north to New York to repair. He returned on 24th October with over 7,000 troops, but five days before he arrived Cornwallis was obliged to surrender.

Franco-American strategy had worked brilliantly. Through temporarily losing local command of the sea, the British lost an army. In losing the army, they lost the will to retrieve the hopeless situation in America. Although desultory fighting continued for another year, the die was cast. So long underrated, the French Navy had scored the success that really mattered. In the West Indies, too, the British had much to lose and, following Yorktown, de Grasse returned to Martinique. On his arrival, on 26th October 1781, he was heartened by the news that French troops had seized St. Eustatius.

December saw five of the line sail for the West Indies with a large convoy, bearing military stores and troops. As far as Cadiz it was to be covered by the Comte de Guichen with 14 line ships. During thick and boisterous weather in the Bay of Biscay, Guichen uncharacteristically allowed himself to drop to leeward of his charges. A sudden clearance disclosed sails to windward. It was a powerful British squadron commanded by Rear-Admiral Richard Kempenfelt in the *Victory* 100. Despite his numerical advantage, Guichen could only watch helplessly as the convoy sought refuge in scattering. Kempenfelt, who had been awaiting it, seized 15 transports. Guichen's discomfiture deepened as the violence of the weather intensified, scattering the whole assemblage. Most returned to France, only two ships of the line and five transports reached de Grasse.

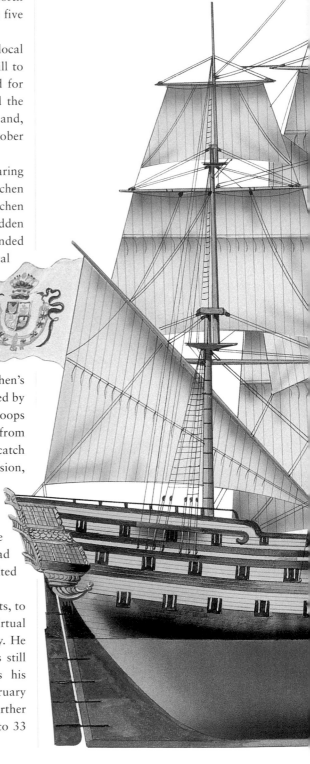

The French commander was ordered to join forces with a Cuba-based Spanish squadron to mount a coordinated assault on Jamaica. Awaiting Guichen's convoy, de Grasse decided to fill his time constructively by taking Barbados. Defeated by the consistent trade wind, however, he turned north-westward and landed 6,000 troops on St. Kitts on 11th January 1782. Hood hurried from Barbados to collect troops from Antigua, then sailed for St. Kitts. In the minority by 22 line ships to 26, he hoped to catch the French at anchor off Basse Terre early on the 23rd, but delayed by a minor collision, his approach was signalled to de Grasse. The French sallied forth to meet him.

Hood briefed his captains on his intentions before engaging in a manoeuvring match to gain the advantage of the wind. Seizing the opportunity when it came, Hood caught de Grasse on the wrong tack and slid inshore of him along the neighbouring island of Nevis. Running smartly into the bay that the French had recently vacated the British anchored in a hooked defensive line in the very limited shallow water.

Even reinforced to 32 line ships, de Grasse was unable, in two determined attempts, to shift Hood. Having suffered a damaging repulse, he learned also of the virtual destruction of his convoy. As he needed to re-store he allowed Hood to slip away. He was not unhappy, for he had lost no ships and the large body of French troops still ashore guaranteed the island's eventual capitulation. Of more concern was his knowledge of Rodney's imminent return as Commander-in-Chief. On 25th February 1782 Rodney arrived with 12 ships of the line and met Hood near Antigua. Further reinforcement boosted Rodney's strength to 37 of the line and that of de Grasse to 33 of the line plus a pair of 50-gun ships.

Fenix

A beautifully-built Spanish 80-gun Third Rate, the *Fenix* wore the flag of Admiral Langara when she and five others were taken by Rodney near Cape St. Vincent in 1780. Renamed *Gibraltar*, she had a busy career in the Royal Navy serving, for instance, with Hood against de Grasse, and with Hughes against Suffren. Hulked in 1813, she served in harbour duties until 1836.

Relief of Gibraltar by Earl Howe (Richard Paton)

By his own estimation this was Howe's finest achievement. Gibraltar, beleaguered, was on the verge of famine. A combined Franco-Spanish fleet of 49 of the line awaited, at Algeciras, the inevitable staging of a relief operation. This, a convoy covered by 34 of Howe's Channel Fleet, arrived during an October gale which drove most merchantmen through the strait. Howe successfully held off the enemy and marshalled the convoy safely into harbour.

Far right: Comte de Grasse (1722 - 1788)

Of aristocratic stock, he began his naval career at sixteen. He saw early action in the War of the Austrian Succession and the Seven Years' War. As a commodore he was at the Battle of Ushant in 1778. His ability was noted and he was given command in the West Indies. His outmanoeuvring of Graves in the Chesapeake in 1781 brought about the British surrender at Yorktown. His failure the following year against Rodney at the Saintes caused him to blame many of his aristocratic subordinates. The resulting social banishment saw him retired as a vice-admiral.

With the move against Jamaica imminent, de Grasse left Martinique on 8th April 1782, accompanying an immense convoy carrying 20,000 troops. He was to meet the Spanish from Havana off the Haitian coast but had Rodney immediately on his tail from St. Lucia. In light airs the following morning the French ghosted up the western, or lee side of Dominica, the British almost becalmed further offshore. As the French neared the Saintes, a small island group in the channel between Dominica and Guadeloupe, they picked up a fresher breeze from the east, but two warships had fallen badly to leeward. In the British van, Hood found the breeze and made for this pair in order to commit de Grasse to their rescue.

The tactic worked almost too well for, as Hood eased ahead with eight ships, de Grasse made for him with 15, having detached his convoy to the haven of Guadeloupe. Hood was now in considerable peril and slowed to avoid getting further separated from Rodney. His opponent, the Marquis de Vaudreuil, held the weather gauge and collected the two laggards. The Marquis then formed his ships in a continuous loop, which could pass along the near-stationary British line in sequence. De Grasse could have moved in to guarantee Hood's annihilation but considered his subordinate equal to the task. In any case, de Grasse wished to preserve his main body undamaged for the operation against Jamaica.

Probably out of exaggerated respect for the carronades, recently introduced to some British ships, de Vaudreuil kept at too great a range to seriously damage Hood. Indeed, it was one of the French ships, the *Caton* 64, that received damage sufficient to warrant her withdrawal to nearby Guadeloupe.

De Grasse needed to divert Rodney's attentions if he were to be able to move his convoy on to Haiti. Unfortunately for him, with both fleets drifting in the Dominica Channel, he suffered two collisions, which cost him ground to leeward. The culprit in both cases was the poorly-handled *Zélé* 74 which, damaged, was packed off to Guadeloupe in tow of the frigate *Astrée* (whose commander, Captain le Comte de la Pérouse, later disappeared on a voyage of exploration). Seeing the pair at first light on the 12th, Rodney detached Hood with four ships to cut them off. De Grasse countered immediately. With the breeze at about south-east the British, now superior in numbers, were already in battle line, close hauled on the starboard tack. On their port bow, de Grasse steered a collision course as he formed line on the port tack. As they met, Rodney appeared unconcerned that the French held the advantage of the weather and, as he had not tacked together, Hood's division found itself at the rear.

The British lead ship, the *Marlborough* 74, reached the ragged enemy line at about the sixth ship and eased to run down its lee side on the opposite tack. As the remainder followed, the British line assumed a dogleg. Having failed to get his line to wear together to take a parallel course, de Grasse ordered it to wear in succession. Action was already close and only a few of his captains appear to have noted the signal. Possibly due to a windshift, a large gap developed opposite Rodney, who promptly rammed his flagship, *Formidable* 100, into it. Five ships followed him through, each in turn raking the unfortunate French 74s, *Glorieux* and *Diadème* that flanked the gap.

Six ships astern of the flag, Commodore Edmund Affleck in the *Bedford* 74 saw a similar gap and led through it the 11 ships of the British rear. Broken in three, the French line fell apart, ships grouping for mutual defence. Also in three parts, the British remained in order and concentrated on two enemy groups. De Grasse's flagship, the much-admired 110-gun *Ville de Paris*, became something of a magnet, defending herself for several hours against up to eight British ships until, out of powder and with over 300 casualties, she was taken and the French admiral made prisoner. Hood's division took three 74s and a 64.

As the Battle of the Saintes ended, so too did what had been an excellent day for Rodney. Hood nonetheless criticised him for not capitalising on French disorder by ordering 'General Chase' and, more pertinently, for not following up on the demoralised enemy on the morning of the 13th.

The great unorthodoxy of the Saintes, the breaking of the French line, was probably not due to Rodney's initiative, for he was a sick and cautious leader. He may have been persuaded to it by his Captain of the Fleet or it may have been boldness in the heat of battle. Although Hood later accounted for the French cripples in Guadeloupe, the Battle of the Saintes was far from decisive. However, although it failed to prevent Vaudreuil's force and its convoy from rendezvousing with the Spanish, their 20,000 troops were never unleashed on Jamaica. The greater part of the force went on to Boston, leaving the West Indies dominated by Rodney. Following the agreement of a peace treaty, the British withdrawal from the United States was already well advanced. It would, however, be November 1783 before HM frigate *Ceres* left New York with the very last personnel.

Politics still greatly influenced naval affairs and a change in administration in July 1782 saw Rodney relieved by Admiral Hugh Pigot, while Howe came out of retirement to assume command of the Channel Fleet. He foiled a Franco-Spanish attempt to link with the Dutch to form a concentration of over 50 ships of the line. Next, Howe planned to re-supply Gibraltar. Although it had seen no convoy for over a year the Rock was in fine fettle. In the September it defeated a determined Spanish assault, in the course of which the latter had employed floating batteries with massive slope and overhead protection, a concept also employed on the American rivers. During the same month

Howe escorted down a massive assembly of over 130 merchantmen, 30 of them for Gibraltar. His 34 ships of the line, with a dozen smaller, were outnumbered by the returned Franco-Spanish squadron which, having returned and been reinforced to a strength of 49, lay threateningly across the bay at Algeciras.

A slow passage and adverse weather delayed Howe's arrival at the Strait until 11th October 1782. Poor discipline then saw all but four of the Gibraltar merchantmen carried past and into the Mediterranean. Howe had to proceed 50 miles in that direction to keep them covered and was still engaged in this when, on the 13th, the enemy emerged. The Franco-Spanish fleet should have enjoyed easy pickings but, over several days, it allowed Howe to manoeuvre defensively until, achieving the weather advantage, the British admiral slipped his charges into Gibraltar. This non-action guaranteed the bastion's survival for the remainder of the war, an achievement of which Howe himself was extremely proud.

Having frustrated Commodore Johnston's move at the Cape in July 1781, Suffren sailed for Ile de France (Mauritius) and on to India, where he was to act as the Comte d'Orves' second-in-command. On the Comte's untimely death in February 1782, however, he assumed overall command in the rank of Commodore. Like d'Aché before him, Suffren was charged with loosening the British hold on India. On the commencement of hostilities against France in 1778 the British had again seized Pondicherry. The action further inflamed an ongoing rebellion in which the Governor-General's forces were barely containing the Marathras under Haidar Ali and Tipu Sultan. Until Suffren's arrival the French had tried no naval intervention to exploit British difficulties. Indeed, the new commander found d'Orves' force so lax in discipline that he decided to keep clear of the Ile de France as far as was possible. For his purposes he had a dozen ships of the line, mainly 74s and 64s, and about 3,000 troops. For his own reasons, he refused to cooperate with the Indians.

The British had over-stretched themselves and the Royal Navy's presence on the station comprised nine line ships, of which only two were 74s. However, it was commanded by Rear-Admiral Sir Edward Hughes, whose portly frame belied an aggressive spirit. He had been supporting the besieged port of Madras, north of Pondicherry, and the main British outpost on the Coromandel coast. Suffren approached Madras on 15th February 1782 but discovered Hughes anchored under the guns of the fortress. The French admiral saw no profit in attacking. He headed southward, causing Hughes to fear for Trincomalee in Ceylon, recently taken from the Dutch.

Sailing in pursuit, Hughes found himself between Suffren and the French convoy at first light on the 16th. The British snapped up six transports without intervention. In fickle breezes the following morning, however, the French were within striking distance with the advantage of both the weather gauge and superior numbers.

Hughes, in the *Superb* 74, was fifth in line, while Suffren led the French in the *Héros* 74. Suffren's intention was to overhaul the British to windward with half his force, his own ship stopping opposite and engaging the *Superb*. As the four ships in the British van would then be cut off down-wind, his own rear could double the British rear by overhauling to leeward. The rear five of Hughes' squadron would be annihilated. Suffren's plan went awry through the petty jealousies that plagued the French fleet. His signal to double the rear was repeated but acted upon by only one ship, the *Brilliant* 64. She progressed no further along the British line than its rear marker, the *Exeter* 64. Lagging somewhat, this ship acted as a block, putting up a stout resistance to as many as three adversaries simultaneously.

The encounter, off Sadras, thus ended indecisively but, once again, both commanders knew the importance of preserving their squadrons. Loss of either would entail repercussions out of all proportion to the value of the ships. Their flexibility was immediately apparent: Suffren landed his troops to assist Haidar Ali's successful assault on Cuddalore, while Hughes shuttled between Madras and Trincomalee, reinforcing the latter.

Hughes well understood Suffren's need of a sheltered harbour closer than the Ile de France and covered Trincomalee closely. On 9th April 1782 the French arrived but found the British off Providien. Hughes formed line allowing the French to attack. Advancing before the wind in two groups, Suffren's ships became disordered. They were signalled to put up their helms to form a parallel line, with one extra ship doubling the British rear. The resulting line, however, was so badly bowed that only the centres ever became heavily engaged. Although heavy casualties were incurred, with Hughes also being forced into shoal water, neither side again lost a ship.

Suffren repaired his ships in the Dutch port of Batticaloa, overcoming the improvidence of his own government by stripping his merchantmen for replacement cordage, spars and timber. Sailing up the Coromandel coast, he re-embarked his troops for an attack on Nagapatam. On his arrival on 5th July 1782, however, he found Hughes awaiting him at anchor. Hughes formed line of battle but found his rear at too great a range and was still remedying this when the wind shifted, to head both lines. Most ships responded by steering outward, momentarily opening the range. Four British and two French, however, turned inward toward each other. A furious little action resulted, the French 64s *Brilliant* and *Sévère* being so shot up that the latter struck her colours, only to re-hoist them following a heated exchange between her officers.

Hughes frustrated Suffren's designs on Nagapatam. Both fleets came to anchor for repairs to cripples. An interesting comment on the manners of the time is that Hughes,

Surrender of the Ville de Paris at the Saintes 1782 (Thomas Whitcombe)

Flagship of de Grasse at the Saintes, the *Ville de Paris*, variously described as having 104, 110 or 120 guns, was isolated in a small centre group by Rodney breaking the French line in three. Poised for an annihilating victory, Rodney then moved cautiously, leaving it to Hood to pressure the enemy. The *Ville de Paris* was a main objective, incurring more casualties than the British fleet in total, and running out of powder before striking.

HMS Mediator engaging French 1782 (Thomas Luny)

The *Mediator* was one of a class of small 44-gun two-deckers. On 12 December 1782 she encountered a mixed group of five French and American ships bound for the West Indies. Carrying stores, they were armed *en flûte*. With her 18- and 12-pounder armament, the British ship first overcame the *Alexandre*, with twenty-four 9-pounders, then took the *Eugène* and the *Menagère* (taken into the Royal Navy as the *Albemarle*).

in close proximity to the French, sent word to Suffren demanding the handover of the *Sévère*, on the grounds that she had surrendered in action. The French admiral refused, citing her then inability to signal.

Although in full nominal strength, the French were by now in poor material state. A relief convoy of 19 ships was intercepted in the Bay of Biscay, losing 13 transports and two line ships. One of the latter, the *Actionnaire* 64, had struck her armament below in order to stow a full cargo of spars for Suffren. It was a good example of how the relentless British blockade in home waters influenced events in distant waters.

A second convoy was more successful, however, reaching Batticoloa on 21st August 1782 with a small military force and two more ships of the line. Turning around quickly, the French were off Trincomalee within 48 hours, where they landed their troops and compelled its speedy surrender. Hughes arrived two days later, and dawdled around to entice Suffren to action. Although reinforced by the *Sceptre* 64, the British were inferior by 14 to 12 ships of the line, but the admiral had great faith in his captains, both as ship handlers and as fighting men. By now, six of his commanding officers had been killed yet he was able to replace them confidently by promotion of their subordinates. Suffren had an intuitive tactical sense, but was let down by his disaffected captains. As an acting commodore he had already exceeded his authority by dismissing several, but individual dash counted more with them than group discipline.

Both sides were anxious for action when they met off Trincomalee on 3rd September 1782. Hughes deliberately engaged in manoeuvre, staying just beyond Suffren's reach. The French eventually advanced with their ships on a line of bearing, a favourite British evolution but one which was not easy to maintain. Seeing the French getting into some disorder, Hughes stood his ground. The British rounded together, but the French came into a very ragged line with some ships masked and others out of range. Only the centre, including Suffren himself, became fully engaged and suffered badly. *Héros* and her next in line were left with only their foremasts standing. Hughes might have better exploited the situation but for the flat calm conditions. The engagement petered out as dusk fell. Suffren made for nearby Trincomalee, where he lost the *Orient* 74 by stranding. Hughes, with several ships hulled and leaking, had first to make for Madras, thence round to Bombay for permanent repairs.

In the severe and unpredictable weather of winter an unofficial truce was declared for some months. During late October, Hughes was reinforced by Commodore Sir Richard Bickerton with five of the line. Suffren, less a further stranded 64, retired to Sumatra for refit. Here, in March 1783, he was joined by three more of the line, with 2,500 troops, under the redoubtable, but by now elderly Marquis de Bussy.

The French cause in India was not faring well. Haidar Ali died the previous December and his son was failing against British forces. By early summer de Bussy was confined to a defensive pocket around Cuddalore as Hughes cruised offshore with 18 of the line. Suffren, with only 15, needed to force the British squadron to withdraw in order that Cuddalore could be relieved.

On 20th June Hughes allowed himself to be engaged in a straightforward line action. The British and French blasted each other indecisively for three hours. Nothing was sunk, nothing taken. A total of 201 men died and 820 were injured for their flags, and for nothing. Neither side was aware that a preliminary peace agreement had been signed five months earlier.

In September 1783 a peace treaty was finalised at Versailles. The antagonists were awarded much of what they had lost, but with the important difference that the independence of the United States was recognised. France gained little but satisfaction for the losses incurred in the previous war. For the moment, Spain retained Minorca and the Floridas, but had failed to gain Gibraltar. Burdened by war debt, saddened by losses, the United States embarked on its existence as a sovereign state. Although now responsible for safeguarding her own trade, her Continental Navy had been whittled down to just one ship. Two years later, even she was sold and, for a decade, America was without a warship. The global aspect of the war was emphasised by the significant losses incurred by belligerent fleets. Ships lost between 1775 and 1783 may be summarised as follows:-

Fleet	Captured	Wrecked, Foundered, Burned, Scuttled, etc.
British	89	113
French	60	12
Spanish	10	14
Dutch	7	?
U.S.	15	24

When these numbers are broken down by type, the contribution made by the 74s, 64s and the frigates is evident:

Rate (approx.)	1st	2nd	3rd	4th	5th	lesser
No. of Guns	100+	80-90	63-79	50-62	28-49	>28
British	2	-	14	4	36	146
French	1	-	18	-	23	30
Spanish	-	1	7	-	10	6
Dutch	-	-	-	4	3	2
U.S.	-	-	-	-	15	24

King George III was concerned that the loss of the American colonies would mark the beginning of wholesale loss of territories elsewhere, and the descent of Great Britain into insignificance. However, many political leaders were of the opinion that the tendency of the Americans to baulk at the authority of legitimate government made them a liability of which the British were well rid. The truth lay somewhere between the two. There was certainly no lasting enmity; by 1790 British exports to America increased by 50 percent over those at the outbreak of war, and by 150 per cent by 1800.

Probably because its pivotal role was ill-understood by the politicians, the Royal Navy in American waters had been under-resourced to the extent that the service could not realise its true potential. However, when pitted against more traditional enemies the Navy performed well despite being badly stretched. Its containment of the fleets of the Bourbon alliance and its deterrent effect against invasion continued to improve its standing in the eye of the general public.

CHAPTER 6: *From the American War to the Frenc*

EQUITY or a Sailors PRAYER before BATTLE. *Anecdote of the Battle of Trafalgar.*

Prize money,

A great incentive in the Royal Navy, was also the cause of great discontent owing to its grossly unfair distribution. In a typical case, in which a combined operation resulted in a payout of some £750,000 the two military commanders received £250,000 between them, leaving the average matelot or squaddie with less than £2 apiece!

In the British public perception, the loss of the United States was diluted somewhat by the continuing struggle against, and eventual triumph over, the real threat to the nation posed by the Bourbon alliance of France and Spain. As the American colonists themselves were still predominantly of British extraction, strong links remained at personal level, although the general intransigence of the colonies themselves had, for years, signalled approaching problems. With hindsight, it is readily apparent that a better accommodation should have been reached with the Americans in the matter of self-government. In fairness, however, Great Britain was not yet a great imperial power, and yet lacked the experience and confidence to grant such concessions. The result, to use a rather crude analogy, was to deny a long-standing toothache the treatment necessary to avoid the trauma of the inevitable abscess.

Close of hostilities found the nation at large, therefore, not so much in a mood of despair at having lost valuable possessions as of relief at having, yet again, defeated the more immediate enemy. In higher places, however, the backwash was rather more serious. Two years of political chaos saw the fall of a succession of administrations while the King himself, then still closely involved with the political scene, contemplated abdication. Anti-monarchist and pro-republican voices were to be heard yet were little heeded in the general racket. The most important yardstick, trade, had continued to thrive and expand with scarcely a stumble and Britain relaxed again, a nation with no cause for revolution.

Revolution

Britain emerged from the war with the national debt, already thought horrifying at the end of the Seven Years' War, almost doubled. There was the customary chain of mass demobilisation, financial strictures, rising unemployment and, inevitably, a crime wave. To end the period of diplomatic isolation in Europe the nation sought new alliances and was pleased to find itself in far better shape than its late adversary. For France had made an enormous effort in the war, succeeding in her secondary objective of gaining a measure of revenge through relieving Britain of some of her most valuable possessions, but failing in the primary goal of defeating Britain herself. The huge expense of her military adventures, and of extensive loans, contributed to a financial collapse that opened the way to the social upheavals of a few years later.

Britain's situation then, and one which greatly affected the Royal Navy, was that of the 'first' empire; she retained her major interests in the West Indies, the loss of the United States being compensated by the stabilisation of her footholds in Canada and India. With the end of French contention for these territories they formed, with Australia, the nucleus of the 'second' empire. Their still-remote situation and their potential for trade could only be hugely beneficial to maritime interests.

Voices in Britain were also beginning to be raised against the practice of slavery, their volume now no longer countered by the powerful demands of the southern states. It was only a beginning, for the ports of London, Bristol and Liverpool in particular had grown rich on it and still conducted a lively trade with the West Indies. Until the turn of the

Royal George at Deptford (John Cleveley the Elder)

Fifty years to the day before the Battle of Trafalgar the 80-gun three-decker *Cambridge* is launched at Deptford. Up-river for the occasion is the *Royal George* Second Rate. This ship dated from 1715, had been reduced from a First Rate in 1745 and, in 1756, was re-named *Royal Anne* in order to release the name for a new *Royal George*, to be lost tragically at Spithead in 1782.

century the trade actually continued to increase, before the long years of its abolition provided the cruising navy with one of its major tasks.

Despite its many difficulties, the Royal Navy had, in general, discharged itself well in the war.

Necessary detachments to foreign stations had left the Channel Fleet so outnumbered by the combined forces of France and Spain that it had to be employed with great circumspection. In view of the continuing threat of invasion, the fleet needed to be preserved, and an expensive victory would have been a disaster. The detached groups were in much the same situation. They needed to be greatly self-sufficient and were rarely of a strength that could be used confidently to seek decisive action.

With the commander of neither opposing squadron daring to expose it to real risk the upshot was, inevitably, a series of sterile skirmishes; the British were unable to attack confidently, while the French were content not to engage as long as they were allowed to pursue their mission.

Nor was the Navy even able to contain the onslaught on British trade and military transports mounted by a host of privateering craft of various flags and varying degrees of legitimacy. Irregular, guerrilla-type wars, whether ashore or afloat, are notoriously difficult to counter but here, although individual loss may occasionally have been considerable and comfort thus given to the enemy, although insurance rates may have rocketed and complaint voiced long and loud, the commerce of Britain, to take the wider view, was on so vast a scale and spread over so many bottoms, that this determined *guerre de course* never posed anything like a mortal threat.

Strenuous efforts were made to increase the strength of the fleet, the usual panic rectification of political money-saving decisions, lightly made in times of peace. The eventual success of the exercise may be gauged from the following table:-

Rate	First	Second	Third	Fourth	Fifth	Sixth	Lesser
No. of Guns	>100	84-98	60-80	50-60	22-44	20-28	<18
Available 1775	4	17	99	23	42	44	38
Available 1783	5	20	142	30	116	59	85
Building 1783	3	5	29	3	33	10	6

In the immediate aftermath of war the fleet attained a record level of strength. Under the new administration of the younger Pitt building programmes were continued, although the fleet decreased numerically because of a cull of older vessels. A number of worn-out hulls was retained and fitted out as accommodation ships for the crews of vessels under refit or for any surge intakes of new recruits. (Large shore barracks for the purpose, at each of the home dockyards, were still a century away.)

The intention was a higher degree of readiness, furthered by ships 'in ordinary' being partly stored, while being kept warmed and ventilated by shipkeepers. The same accommodation hulks could be used for the considerable influx of labour associated with rapid mobilisation and, later, for large numbers of prisoners of war.

A hard lesson re-learned by the administration was that the dispersal of strength to cover every eventuality was to invite defeat in detail. Any enemy capable of causing Britain mortal damage was inevitably European, and it was only in European waters that a decisive fleet action would be fought as a necessary precursor for any serious attempt at invasion. The priorities for the Royal Navy were thus quite clear: firstly, the defence of the home islands against invasion; secondly, the defence of trade; and thirdly, the defence of the colonies. It followed that the main fleet should continue to be home-

British mortar ketch 1750

1.	Rudder	17.	Powder
2.	Stern post	18.	Powder room
3.	Tiller	19.	Carpenter's store
4.	Capstan	20.	Boatswain's store
5.	Officers' quarters	21.	Crew
6.	Lamp room	22.	Anchor
7.	Potato store	23.	Bulwarks
8.	Anchor cable	24.	Mizzen mast
9.	Wine store	25.	Top
10.	Mast foundantion	26.	Main mast
11.	Shrouds	27.	Mizzen sail
12.	Mortar	28.	Main sail
13.	Mortar bed	29.	Main upper sail
14.	Ammunition	30.	Bowsprit
15.	Ballast	31.	Fore sail
16.	Spare sails		

'Bombs' were designed to carry one or two mortars for lobbing explosive shells into fortifications. Notable for their splendid names, eg *Sulphur*, *Tartarus* or *Explosion*, they combined sturdy construction with very little accommodation. The mortars here can be trained.

Sailors on a Cruise

Pub.d by J.s Robins & Co Ivy Lane Paternoster Row. Sep.r 1.st 1825.

'Sailors on a Cruise'

Whether the picture truly applied to the men of the 'saucy *Arethusa*' or to Jack in general is not clear but, having survived the Service's iron discipline and enemy shot for yet another cruise, the average matelot was more than ready to let his hair down on coming ashore. The old sailor, with his wooden leg and fiddle, the pipe-smoking matron and the free-range livestock are noteworthy.

based, a first line of defence but with a hard offensive edge. Maintaining pressure at home on a European maritime power would, in any case, much reduce its capability to wage war against trade or the colonies. In the last resort, however, the latter were as to the branches of a great tree, their loss grievous but acceptable to safeguard the whole. It is against these aims that the continued improvement in the quality and support of the Service should be assessed.

Despite the decade's events in Europe, and in France in particular, the size of the Royal Navy continued its decline:-

Rate	First	Second	Third	Fourth	Fifth	Sixth	Lesser
Available							
1789	6	22	116	19	92	43	42
Available							
1793	5	16	92	12	79	35	40
Building							
1793	2	5	5	3	3	-	2

In comparison, the French were credited with only 86 of the line and about 75 frigates. Actually ready for sea were an estimated 115 British liners and 76 French.

The French themselves were not unduly chastened by the outcome of the war, which they had been pleased to terminate because of its crushing expense rather than through inferiority at sea. Indeed, the French fleet was well regarded by the nation and entered a period of reorganisation against what appears to have been accepted as the next inevitable war against Britain. Under the direction of able Ministers of Marine, the Marquis de Castries and his successor, the Comte la Luzerne, and the talented ship designer Jacques-Noël Sané, who was Inspector-General of Marine Engineering, the material side of the navy was in good hands. Line of battle ships were divided into First Rates of 110-120 guns, Second Rates with 80 and Third Rates with 74. The 80's, carrying 24-pounders on the upper gun deck, had considerably more fire-power than the 74s, which had only 18-pounders. Like the British, the French relied greatly on the 74 and, during the coming war, would build nearly 100 of them to the basic Sané draught, together with 35 80s and 18 First Rates, most of which were 118-gunners.

Offsetting this was the generally sad state of personnel and morale. The officer corps remained polarised around its social divisions, those of aristocratic connection and the '*bleus*', recruited when required from the merchant service or, more rarely, from the lower deck. An officer of the so-called Grand Corps would not willingly accept orders from a '*bleu*' of senior rank, while those of the nobility, whatever their rank, considered themselves as equals and were prone to view an order as a basis for discussion. De Castries had recognised the problem and had set about a reorganisation for recruitment of junior officers, but this would not show results for a considerable time and would be overtaken by events.

Manning the Navy 1790

A captain and his officers had to crew their own ship, and a good reputation would go far in attracting volunteers, who were eligible for a bounty and better conditions than pressed men. To these were added 'Quota Men' from the counties, and Boys from such as the Marine Society. Conscription added such minor malefactors as debtors and drifters. To make up numbers, perhaps yet 50 per cent, the captain took pressed men or convicted criminals.

ATTIC MISCELLANY.

Drawn by Collings.   Publish'd as the Act directs by Bentley & Co June 1, 1790.   Etch'd by Barlow.

MANNING THE NAVY.

La Flore

Built in 1780, *La Flore* was a typical French frigate of the period, shipping 30 x 18- and 12-pounder cannon. French and Spanish frigates tended to be larger and better armed than their British equivalents. Those captured and bought into the Royal Navy became much sought-after commands.

UNCLE GEORGE AND BLACK DICK AT THEIR NEW GAME OF NAVAL SHUTTLECOCK 1787.

'Uncle George and Black Dick ... '

An Order in Council of 1718 directed their Lordships to promote senior captains to flag rank with regard only to their qualifications. This was modified by an Order of 1747 providing for disqualification on grounds of age and infirmity, but rewarding long and meritorious service by retirement as Superannuated Rear-Admiral known, from the colour of the list, as 'Yellow Admirals'. Much resentment was felt by many thus retired. The issue involved the Crown and both Houses during 1787, with the King having to field direct appeals and Howe ('Black Dick'), as First Lord, supporting superannuation.

The lot of the average crew member was as wretched as ever with many, who had been pressed into service during the late hostilities, being retained against their will, not only in poor conditions but also with low and irregularly-paid wages. Ironically, it had been the necessary material expenditure on the fleet, falling on an already war-impoverished treasury, that resulted in the wages of seamen and dockyard workers not being paid. The provision of spares and, indeed, dockyard support in general was to be a major problem in the coming period of hostilities.

From a present-day perspective British naval officer recruitment appears to have been positively eccentric, but it was very much a product of its time. It was the privilege, particularly of post-captains and commanders-in-command, to assume responsibility for what were collectively termed 'captain's servants'. While a few actually were servants, most were protégés, the sons of families seeking to set them on a naval career. In return for a privately agreed consideration, the lad became a sort of sea-going apprentice. Less than 10% of officers at that time were promoted from seaman grades, with a few more coming through the Portsmouth Naval Academy. As the Admiralty had no mechanism for recruiting the remainder it was reliant upon the above informal system with individuals, after 1796, acquiring the more regular title of Volunteers, First Class.

Depending upon the status of the sponsor, his 'servants' might be of the aristocracy, the landed gentry or the professional classes. While servants might be limited officially to, say, 400 of the ship's crew strength there was, in practice, little check on numbers. The practice could, therefore, be extremely lucrative to the sponsor, who was not even formally bound to any particular standard of instruction. Abuses of the system were, therefore, commonplace.

Of Admirals and Ensigns

Since early in the 17th century, a fleet sailing in Line of Battle was of a size that made its control by a single flag officer, situated near its centre, impracticable. It was, therefore, organised in three squadrons, namely the centre, commanded by the Admiral, and the van and rear, commanded tactically by Vice- and Rear-Admirals respectively.

Further extension to the line and the need for tighter local control saw the introduction of an admiral of each rank in each squadron. By early in the 18th century, therefore, the line could include a theoretical nine flagships. The nine flag officers also comprised the complete Flag Officer List and, as there was no compulsion to retire from it on grounds of old age, it grew increasingly venerable. Senior captains, given extra responsibility through, for example, the command of squadrons formed outside the main battle fleet, might serve as Commodores but this was only a temporary rank.

Flag officers, as their title suggests, flew distinctive flags to identify their ships. Each squadron had its own colour. In order of seniority, the centre was red, the van white and the rear blue. Flagships thus wore red, white or blue ensigns, sited at the main, fore and mizzen tops respectively. So-called 'private' ships, such as frigates attached to a squadron but not part of the line of battle, wore pendants of the appropriate colour. An exception to the general rule was the admiral of the red squadron who, as Commander-in-Chief, carried the title of Admiral of the Fleet and flew the Union Flag in place of the red ensign. The specific rank of Admiral of the Red was not created until early in the 19th century.

Until the enlargement of the Flag Officers' List in the mid-18th century, advancement through it was automatic. A senior captain entered it in the most junior grade of Rear-Admiral of the Blue. On promotion, he served successively through the ranks of Rear-Admiral of the White and Red before becoming Vice-Admiral of the Blue and repeating the process. In practice, there were so many outside factors involved that ranks were frequently skipped. In the case of Admiral Sir George Rodney, for instance, progression was via Rear-Admiral of the Blue (May 1759) directly to Vice-Admiral of the Blue (October 1762), of the White (October 1770) and of the Red (also October 1770, six days after his previous promotion). Thence he moved directly to Admiral of the White (January 1778), just before his 70th birthday. He was unable to achieve the Navy's highest rank before his death in 1792 as the sole post was occupied successively by Hawke and Forbes.

Exigencies of war also saw the main fleet form line of battle with considerably less than the planned flag officer structure. At the Saintes in 1782, for instance, a rare example of a full fleet action outside home waters, Rodney commanded a total of 37 line ships and 19 attached frigates and lesser rates. In the *Formidable* 98 he controlled the centre, with the assistance of Commodore Affleck in the *Bedford* 74. The van and rear had a single flag officer apiece, respectively Rear-Admiral Hood in the *Barfleur* 98 and Rear-Admiral Drake in the *Princesa* 70

As a footnote, it may be added that, with the changing shape of the Navy and the manner in which it did battle, squadronal colours were abandoned finally in 1864, the White Ensign being adopted for all regular warships. Admirals then adopted variations on the St. George's cross flag while Admirals of the Fleet retained the Union Flag.

Officially, a boy was required to be 11 years of age in order to commence his career as a 'young gentleman'. To be promoted lieutenant he needed to have served at least six years' sea time and to be at least 20 years of age when he passed his qualifying examination. It was nothing, however, to have prospective boys' names entered into a ship's muster book several years before attaining the age of 11 and to turn a blind eye to obviously forged birth certificates. Until 1794 boys received no official pay, which simplified such fraud. Once regular wages were involved, however, captains needed to be circumspect if the recipient was still under age and living at home.

During periods of peace, being 'passed for Lieutenant' was no guarantee of being offered a post, and there were many midshipmen of mature years. Rapid wartime expansion, however, saw further corners cut. None too stringent examination of aspirants' documentation resulted in cases of lieutenants being appointed at 16 years of age. Patronage and influence helped even more, with one well-known admiral's son becoming a lieutenant at 15 and a post-captain before his 16th birthday! It remains a small miracle of the age that such a system could support such a Service.

Although the welfare of the British seaman was better attended to than that of his French counterpart, his lot aboard the average ship was no sinecure, hard and uncomfortable, yet often with long periods spent at anchor. As it was necessary to keep large crews occupied, many captains became obsessed with cleanliness, the men being employed for long hours in excessive washing down, scrubbing and holystoning. Damp and cold on generally unheated ships were already the norm and this practice, maintained in all weathers, contributed much to individual states of health. Personal cleanliness was also apt to figure largely in captain's standing orders, but the provision of soap, fresh water and drying facilities for clothes was woefully inadequate.

Nonetheless, failure to observe arbitrary standards would be, at best, met with an abusive response from above or, worse, spot punishment such as stoppage of grog. If hair was unkempt, it was subject to summary cropping. Crews could spend years afloat without the simple pleasure of a walk ashore.

Not surprisingly, therefore, unrest was comparatively common. In many ships it took the form of petitions presented to the Admiralty in the name of an affected group of individuals. Those who appended their signatures well understood the possible consequences of their action and any complaint, particularly when made about specific officers or petty officers, was invariably prefaced by protestations of loyalty to both Crown and Service.

Deep-seated grievances, if unaddressed, could and did lead to mutinies. From about 1755 marines had formed a significant part of a ship's complement. A 74, for instance, might have two officers and 120 marines, with a smaller frigate two officers and 45 marines. In unhappy ships, such bodies were viewed less as an important part of the vessel's offensive capacity than as a means to the officers' protection from the crew. The marines themselves were not happy about their perceived role as upholders of imposed discipline and were well aware that, as 'landsmen', they were, in general, viewed in some contempt by experienced seamen.

Mutinies resulted most commonly from unreasonable or eccentric punishments, or arrears of pay. What today seem justifiable complaints, however, were met with disproportionate harshness. When, in 1779, seven men on the *Egmont* 74 refused duty until their arrears were paid, three were sentenced to death, although the sentences were later reduced. In the following year, a similar complaint precipitated a more general 'down tools' aboard the *Invincible*, another 74. Resolution of the problem was by

French First Rate Océan

Flagship successively of Vice-Admirals Willaumez and Allemand during the affair in the Basque Road in 1808, the 120-gun *Océan* was one of those that grounded in the panic following Cochrane's night attack but which was allowed, by Gambier's indicision, to be refloated by the French and towed safely into the Charente. Gambier survived censure by court martial. Allemand was never blamed, his subordinates being judged at fault.

authorities who dragged their heels for six months to demonstrate where ultimate power resided. Four ringleaders were then court-martialled, two of them being sentenced to an unbelievably savage 500 lashes apiece. Punishment this severe was administered in several regular doses, inflicted fortnightly.

Events in revolutionary France cast their shadow even over the Royal Navy, with unrest cropping up in widely separated but isolated incidents. One of the most serious, late in 1794, occurred at Portsmouth, where the captain of the *Culloden*, later to be one of the best-drilled ships in the fleet, but at this time a poor performer, felt constrained to hang five of the eight seamen sentenced for leading dissent.

It was three years later, however, that unrest came to a head with a general mutiny at Portsmouth, involving at least 16 ships. Again, complaints seemed reasonable enough: a petition for a rise in pay that had seen no increase in a century and more; that men incapacitated by wounds should be paid while recovering; improvement in provisioning

Naval Ranks

A lad destined for a naval officer's career would be entered at about 12 years of age as a captain's servant; a position re-designated in 1796 as Volunteer, First Class. After three years of service, which may have included a period ashore, studying at the Portsmouth naval college, he would be automatically re-rated Midshipman. A further three years would see him eligible to take the examination for Lieutenant. To be appointed, he had also (in theory, at least) to be 20, later 19, years of age. Granted his commission by the Admiralty, he would thereafter appear, with seniority date, in the forerunner of the Navy List and, if unemployed, be entitled to half-pay.

Equalling a lieutenant in rank at this time were certain warrant officers, including the Master, whose task was the ship's navigation. Emphasising the divided nature of the Navy's administration, warrants were issued by the Commissioners of the Navy Board. Only exceptional candidates ever graduated from warrant to commissioned rank, a good example being James Cook. Masters or lieutenants, when given their own ship, were known as Lieutenants-commanding, a title foreshadowing our present-day Lieutenant Commander. Other than in exceptional circumstances, this command would not be larger than an un-rated cutter or brig-rigged sloop.

Our officer's next grade would depend on how well he had made his mark. A routine appointment would be to a Sixth Rate, where he would be ranked Master and Commander, later simply 'Commander'. Both Lieutenants-commanding and Master and Commander would have the courtesy title of 'Captain', although not yet of that rank.

A Lieutenant-commanding who had done exceptionally well might be rewarded with being given a Fifth Rate, otherwise the next logical step for a Commander. Fifth Rates were 'post' ships and were commanded by what were then termed Post-Captains, as distinct from the 'captains' of lesser craft.

As a post-captain progressed in seniority and status, he commanded successively higher rates of ship. Until the middle of the 18th century, the Post-Captains' List was very long and the Flag Officers' List very short. Because progression from one to the other was purely on seniority, the upper reaches of the Captains' List contained many aspirants of advanced age. During the 1740s, however, the system was changed so that aged and infirm captains could be superannuated and pensioned as Rear-Admirals. Captains of lesser ability might now also be passed over to allow more able candidates to be promoted to an extended Flag Officer's List.

Organization of Crew

Individuals usually worked in those areas to which they had been allocated on the ship's watchbill. The topmen were the most skilled, requiring courage and agility to work aloft in all weathers, day or night. Forecastle and afterguardsmen usually 'pulled and hauled' but had individual skills in anchor and boatwork respectively. The waisters were the least capable, the unskilled and those of limited intelligence. They were made useful as required.

and in care of the sick; and rights to liberty when ships were in harbour. Perhaps surprisingly, the Commissioners of the Admiralty made concessions to the majority of the demands (an able seamen would still earn only a shilling a day) and offered a pardon to the mutineers. Because of outstanding items, however, and because the concessions had not been enshrined in legislation, the men still refused to sail from Spithead, where they lay at anchor. An attempt to hold a meeting aboard the flagship was resisted by the admiral's order. Boats approaching with delegates came under fire from marines and at least one person was killed. The incident changed what had been a peaceful refusal to sail into an active rising, with violence barely held in check.

Alarmed, the government hastily passed the necessary bill to approve the mutineers' demands, and despatched the 71-year old Lord Howe to present it to the seamen and to persuade them to return to work. The choice of plenipotentiary was a happy one, for the veteran admiral was both popular and trusted. Following a month's inactivity the fleet put to sea.

Properly handled, the settlement at Spithead should have put an end to it but, almost immediately, a new mutiny broke out at the Nore. Although based on much the same grievances, it was an altogether uglier affair. Its leaders were much more active, inciting widespread insolence and aggressive behaviour, with the plundering of stores and merchantmen for the dissidents' subsistence. Parliament again approved hasty legislation, this time to permit armed suppression. Faced with obvious preparations for the use of force, the mutineers' resolution crumbled. The ships involved should have been part of the Admiral Duncan's force blockading the Dutch at the Texel and the Admiralty was fortunate that the enemy did not move quickly to take advantage of the situation. Its seriousness, however, was marked by 36 executions and several floggings around the fleet, not least for their deterrent value.

Despite the likely consequences, further outbreaks occurred in various individual ships throughout the summer of 1797, the contagion spreading to foreign stations. Probably the worst case was that of the frigate *Hermione*. Cruising off Puerto Rico, she was taken over by her crew, who murdered the captain, the officers and the boatswain. Following this, they sailed her to a Spanish South American port. The arm of the Admiralty was long, however. Just two years later, the boats of the *Surprise* 28 cut out the defecting ship in the harbour of Puerto Cabello. Having seized her in a savage hand-to-hand fight, the boarding party sailed her from the port under fire from its protecting batteries. In this case, the mutineers were not only hanged for their actions but their corpses were suspended in gibbets at prominent points as a warning to others.

Except in the ports of the Home Command, the courts trying such cases were of naval personnel only. Judgements, based on the consideration of all known evidence, were held to be generally fair.

Divisions of a Ship's Day

The routines for the Starboard and Larboard watches would be regularly interchanged to equalise the periods of duty and leisure. 'Idlers', some 25-30 personnel aboard a 74, are those who are excused regular watches through being on call throughout each day. They include the armourers, sailmakers, carpenters, cooks, etc.

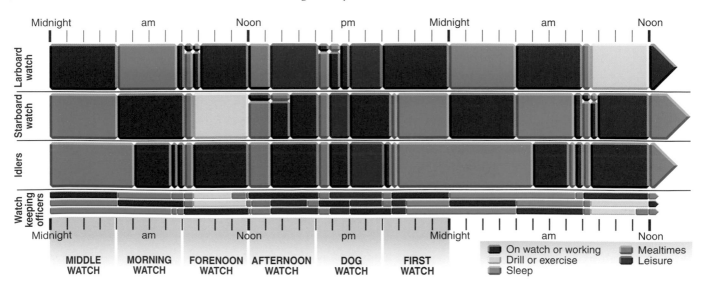

MIDDLE WATCH   MORNING WATCH   FORENOON WATCH   AFTERNOON WATCH   DOG WATCH   FIRST WATCH

■ On watch or working   ■ Mealtimes
□ Drill or exercise   ■ Leisure
■ Sleep

Above:

Brunswick, Vengeur and *Achille* seen on the morning of 2nd June 1794 after their prolonged action (see p130)

A 'guilty' verdict would almost certainly infringe one of the 36 Articles of War, for each of which the punishment was prescribed, sometimes mandatory, sometimes with a scale of severity that could be levied at the discretion of the court.

By 1783 the 64-gun Third Rate had been virtually discontinued by the British as being under-gunned for its position in the line of battle. In this the French concurred. Where, however, French expertise in superior ship design allowed them to build 80-gun two-deckers with confidence, the British found that the considerable length and lack of depth of their own design resulted in excessive working in a seaway which, in turn, demanded high levels of maintenance and repair while enjoying a relatively short service life. The two-decked 74, on the other hand, could be built strongly and to dimensions that allowed for a well-proportioned hull that handled well, while carrying its lower tier at a height above the waterline that permitted it to be fought in adverse conditions. Economical both to build and to maintain, the 74 proved popular, proliferating at the expense of other and larger types.

Three-decked First and Second Rates combined length, which made them tolerable sailers, with depth, which gave them the necessary strength. Being expensive, however, they tended to be regarded as flagships by the British, who always preferred numbers to size. An impetus for their continued construction was that the French and Spanish were still building excellent examples. The 1790s, therefore, saw not only the first British 110-gun First Rate, confusingly named *Ville de Paris* (after her French predecessor which, captured by Rodney, in 1782, foundered through her weakened condition while returning to Britain) but also the ordering of the first 120-gunner, the *Caledonia*.

Fifth and Sixth Rates had such a wide variety of roles, as independent 'cruisers' or in direct support of the fleet, that it is not surprising that they were subject to much innovation by both the French and the British. Where, in the earlier years of the 18th century, the Royal Navy had favoured small two-deckers of 40 to 44 guns for independent operation, the need for the maximum number of hulls for the outlay saw the single-decker of 32 to 36 guns gain increasing popularity. This also meant the end of that occasional throw-back from an earlier era, the so-called '*demi-batterie*' two-decker, whose lower deck was pierced over the greater part of its length with rowing- rather than gun-ports.

Although still building the occasional small two-decker, the French adopted a single-decked type with a 12-pounder battery. However, most of their existing ships of similar class mounted only 8-pounders. When the British went in suit with significant numbers of 12-pounder single-deckers, therefore, the French inevitably found themselves at a disadvantage.

Ship design has usually evolved through efforts to squeeze yet more into a given size and the struggle against France during the American War of Independence had seen the emergence of the 18-pounder cruiser. Such heavy weapons required an increase in ship displacement but a brief British reconciliation with the 44 proved unsuccessful, with several being cut down by a deck ('razeed') to carry fewer weapons of the same size.

During the war the Americans had shown an individual line of thought, indicating a preference for a considerable increase in size. This improved both sailing qualities and weatherliness, although the main battery still comprised 12-pounders. The loss of maritime superiority during the war persuaded an alarmed Admiralty to invest in more powerful individual ships, the immediate result being the 18-pounder single-decked frigate with either 36 or 38 guns. This type of vessel remained the standard British Fifth Rate over the period between the wars, its rated firepower enhanced by the siting of carronades on the quarterdeck.

The French progressed to favour a mix of 12- and 18-pounder frigates, the more numerous former type being cheaper and the latter being smaller than its British counterpart. Their more moderate armament allowed, however, for a hull better optimised to sailing performance, the Hébé type being so successful in this respect that the British later lifted her lines for their own purposes.

The wars to be fought shortly against the French and the Americans were to see the introduction of the large 24-pounder frigate, but these were as expensive as larger Fourth Rates, and with hulls loaded to the extent that their structural strength was somewhat suspect. The British never liked the large frigate, but this prejudice was to prove a liability when hostilities again commenced against the Americans, who built them to offset their lack of numbers.

Ships with 20 to 28 guns comprised the bulk of the Royal Navy's Sixth Rates and, for the most part, were scaled-down frigates, mounting a primary battery of 9-pounders, with a few 6-pounders on the quarterdeck. While the term 'corvette' was in use, it was never graced with a precise definition. In English usage, the term could cover both small, frigate-type warships and larger examples of the sloop, the most numerous of the non-rated combatants. British 'sloops' could range from three-masted, ship-rigged craft carrying 14 to 18 6-pounders, to two-masted brigs (although brigantines, ketches, snows and schooners were not unknown). The latter could vary from 300-tonners armed with 16 6-pounders to 220-tonners with only a dozen 4-pounders. A short-barrelled 6-pounder, developed for the

Boyne

Third ship of the name, the *Boyne* 98 was the flagship of Vice-Admiral Sir John Jervis in 1794, during the capture of Martinique and St. Lucia. On 1st May 1795, whilst laying at Spithead under a new command, she took fire, drifted aground and blew up, causing considerable damage to neighbouring Portsmouth.

smaller sloops, was overtaken by the widespread introduction of the carronade, of which 24- and 32-pounders were commonly shipped.

As the American war progressed to a struggle against the Bourbon alliance, sloops of various types proliferated. Apart from being a cheap alternative to larger ships, and pursuing the Navy's inshore duties, particularly against widespread smuggling, they were used in the on-going campaign against privateers. In the course of this they were likely to encounter their French naval equivalents, which provided the 'regular' component of the rag-tag collection of craft that made a good living preying on British commercial shipping.

An even smaller command was a bomb-vessel, a type so specialised that it virtually disappeared from the list in times of peace, its number increasing rapidly with hostilities. Mortars, firing projectiles in a high trajectory, had featured in siege warfare for many years, but it was not until the late 17th century that the weapons were taken afloat for the purpose of attacking such as fortified harbours. For this innovation the French are given the credit, its first major use being in the chastisement of Algiers by Duquesne in 1682.

The weapon itself was short-barrelled and, in British service, usually of 13 inches bore. It fired an explosive-filled spherical projectile weighing over 200 pounds, which could be lobbed over fortifications impervious to conventional low-angle fire. As its range was short it required the bomb-vessel to stand well inshore. For this reason a shallow-draught Dutch galliot-style hull was first used. Of no more than 150 tons, the French version featured two mortars, mounted side by side just forward of amidships. Crude weapons, they were fixed in elevation and could not be traversed, so that the whole craft had to be aimed at the target, and at a range dependent upon the weight of firing charge. The steep firing trajectory precluded any mast or permanent rigging being sited forward of the mortars. The mainmast was, therefore, stepped well aft, and its position, in conjunction with a mizzen, was not conducive to the design of an efficient sail plan, the craft being very dull sailers. Going about was assisted by a spritsail, spread below the bowsprit, sometimes supplemented by headsails set on the necessarily long forestays.

As adopted for British use the bomb-vessel favoured a ketch rig, becoming known as a bomb ketch, or later, just 'bomb'. The major innovation was to mount the two mortars on the centreline, the aftermost between the masts. This was possible through siting the weapons on rotating platforms, which permitted firing on either beam through a training angle sufficient to obviate the earlier requirement to aim the whole ship.

Mortars generated enormous reaction forces on firing. With no provision for recoil movement to absorb it, the instantaneous energy pulse was transmitted through the hull as a considerable shock. The problem resulted in odd combinations of massive timber sub-structures, beds of earth or packed masses of old cordage to give an element of resilience.

From about 1760 the British tended to ship-rigged bomb-vessels for their superior sailing qualities. Hulls with already limited internal space were much devoted to the mortar sub-structures and the considerable stowage for the large spherical projectiles. Gun crews, provided by the army, were therefore usually accommodated elsewhere, and joined the naval sailing crew only for action.

What is perhaps surprising is that the bomb-vessel brought together the concepts of revolving gun mountings and explosive projectiles. Yet it was to be more than a further half century before the combination would be developed further, with devastating results, by such as Paixhans and Cowper Coles.

Caesar

First of the new-style 80-gun two-deckers, the *Caesar* first commissioned in 1793. No ship had a finer fighting record. She led Howe's line at the Glorious First of June, she wore Saumarez' flag at Algeciras and its following action, and she was the command of Strachan, whose squadron accounted for Dumanoir's division after Trafalgar.

CHAPTER 7: *The Revolutionary War 1793-1801*

HMS Scourge capturing the Sans Culotte 1793 (Thomas Yates)

The ferocity of single-ship actions was not related to the size of the ships involved. On 13 March 1793, west of the Scillies, the British brig-sloop *Scourge* met up with the French privateer *Sans Culotte*. In the first action of the Revolutionary War the *Scourge*, reputedly carrying only eight 6-poounders although pierced for sixteen, took the Frenchman after a three-hour battle. The prize was found to be armed with eight 8-pounders and four 12-pounder carronades.

France's intervention in the Americans' struggle for independence from Britain had been decisive, but it cost her dearly. She gained little from the war and neither did her ally, Spain. Lacking the dynamism of her larger neighbour, Spain tended to be tied politically to France while relying overmuch on income from her American interests. Britain may have lost control of her American colonies but her trade with them continued to expand. The British merchant marine provided the basis for recovery from the war, while the Royal Navy that safeguarded it could equally well cut off Spain's source of income. From the turbulent political scene that followed the peace appeared the stable and sure ministry of the younger Pitt, under whose leadership the nation rebuilt its wounded morale and reduced assets.

The comparative calm of Britain contrasted with the mood in France. With the successful example of America before it, the nation was ripe for change, embarking on the nightmare transition from monarchy to republic via bloody revolution. Facing national bankruptcy the King, Louis XVI, called a meeting of the States General in May 1789. The commons appropriated this ancient gathering of nobility, clergy and commoners, which had last convened early in the previous century. The so-called Third Estate resolved not to stand down until an acceptable American-style constitution had been produced. Illegally doubling their numbers and voting rights, the Third Estate kept in session what was now termed the National Assembly, whose major consideration was the creation of a constitutional monarchy to replace the current despotic regime that favoured a privileged nobility at the expense of an over-taxed and resentful population. The deliberations of the National Assembly were overtaken by events when, in July 1789, a Paris mob stormed and occupied the prison-fortress of the Bastille, symbolic of oppressive rule.

Order collapsed. Landowners became a general target for attack, tolerated largely by militia newly recruited by empowered local councils, known as 'communes'. Tapping the popular mood, the National Assembly began to assume powers of state, but at too fast a rate for their adequate replacement by new arrangements. In the absence of real authority, hotheads and even criminal elements dominated communes. Beyond the control of the National Assembly that had spawned them, they oversaw the hounding of the aristocracy (in many cases well-earned). From the security of foreign soil the latter sought to involve other powers in counter-action.

Importantly, from the point of view of events to come, the French armed forces were badly affected. The extensive aristocratic element of the naval officer corps was no longer able to control abusive and insubordinate crews and, with lack of support from authorities and facing direct threats to their very existence, deserted in great numbers. They were replaced by politically-acceptable appointees or junior officers from the merchant service, whose lack of experience would shortly be exposed by war.

A recent major naval reform had been the creation of a corps of seaman-gunners, with fixed-term enlistment. This concept of a disciplined body, however, ran counter to the revolutionary ideas of the ruling councils, which disbanded it, replacing its numbers with army drafts, whose experience was of a very different type of gunnery.

With the National Assembly still deliberating on his future the King, subjected to successive humiliations, resolved in June 1791 to go into exile. He and his family were, however, intercepted and returned to virtual house arrest. Louis' queen was Austrian and it was to this power and to Prussia that the exiled French aristocracy turned for assistance. While sympathetic, they were already bound by a complex of defensive alliances. The combined monarchies did, however, declare that the situation in which the French king found himself gave cause for common concern. Although in September 1791 Louis accepted the revised constitution, the National Assembly immediately re-invented itself as a Legislative Assembly, the elections for which fanned revolutionary fervour to new extremes. Other monarchies were insulted and forces for active intervention began to gather on their soil. In April 1792 the King was forced by the Assembly to declare war on Austria, which quickly involved Prussia.

Early reverses led the mob to demand, successfully, that the Assembly violate the new constitution by suspending the monarchy, for which action the British ambassador was recalled. To Europe's surprise, fervour compensated for general lack of direction, the French defeating the Prussians at Valmy and Jemappes. The Austrian Netherlands were overrun, Antwerp besieged and British interests confronted over rights of navigation on the Scheldt river.

In the south, the French navy supported military operations against Savoy in September 1792, when nine sail of the line landed troops from Nice eastward. *Contre-*

Le port vieux de Toulon

Like Brest, Toulon is very much a product of Richelieu's drive and Vauban's genius. Principal naval base on the French Mediterranean coast, it has an inner and outer roadstead, the former protected by narrows covered by the Great Tower and la Guillette batteries. The approaches are dominated by the rocky peninsula of St. Mandrier. Note that the newbuilding is ready to launch bow-first, according to continental practice.

amiral Laurent Truguet, their commander, had been newly promoted by the Minister of Marine, whose post he was shortly to occupy. An attempt to land a revolutionary army in Sardinia collapsed in disorder, with two line ships being lost through poor seamanship.

Matters with the British finally came to head when, in the December, the French king was arraigned. Tried, found guilty and sentenced, Louis XVI met his death in January 1793. The French ambassador to London was given eight days' notice to quit, his masters responding by a declaration of war. Britain, together with the Netherlands, Russia, Spain and Sweden, formed a loose alliance that became known as the First Coalition.

Anti-religious as well as anti-royalist, the revolutionary councils caused considerable disunity in France, resulting in open discontent in the provinces, notably the important naval city of Toulon and the Vendée. To quash dissent the central government embarked on the so-called Reign of Terror. Although this achieved its goals, it ended appropriately with its perpetrators themselves becoming victims. Under a new Supreme Committee, termed the Directory, France entered a more peaceful internal spell. In practice there existed a power vacuum that would ultimately be filled through the seizure of power by a dictator. But that is to anticipate.

If the developing crisis in France were not sufficient, events elsewhere also contrived to put Britain and her fleet at an enhanced state of readiness. An earlier chapter made mention of Captain George Vancouver's visit to Nootka Inlet in 1792. His courteous reception was achieved only after intense diplomatic activity, backed by a limited naval mobilisation. Trivial in scale, the incident nonetheless created an important precedent. Spain was prepared to enforce her 300-year old claim to exclusive exploitation of the complete American Pacific seaboard from the Horn to Alaska. The establishment of fur-trading interests at Nootka by the British East India Company was a direct challenge to Spanish sovereignty. Spanish warships arrived from Mexico in May 1789 to seize the company's assets, their personnel being treated rather as prisoners of war.

Representations by the Spanish ambassador were met firmly by Pitt and the British government, which upheld the right to establish posts and to trade in any area not yet actually settled by Europeans. The whole principle of territorial rights being at stake, both sides reacted forcefully. Spain appealed to her fellow Bourbon court in France for support. It was the spring of 1790 and Louis was still able to react positively, approving the Assembly's proposal to mobilise 45 ships of the line. Commanding the considerable Brest contingent was the capable and well-regarded Commodore de Rions, but he faced a state virtually of open mutiny. Unable to exert any authority, he resigned his commission and quit the country, which thus lost another able officer that it could ill afford.

In April 1790, meanwhile, the British mobilised 29 of the line, together with supporting ships, all placed under Lord Howe's command. Spain, disappointed at her ally's preference for revolution to loyal support, was in no state for a solitary war against the leading maritime power, and backed down. In the October, the Nootka Sound Convention saw Spain agree to pay reparations and also to recognise the British demands. It was to underscore these rights that Vancouver was despatched to undertake an extended survey of the coast.

An unlikely partnership between Austria and Russia also sought to instigate the break up of the Ottoman Empire in Europe, awakening an old British phobia regarding direct

Russian access to the Mediterranean. Powerful diplomatic pressure forced Austria to come to terms with Turkey early in 1791, with an agreement to restore pre-war boundaries. This diplomatic coup was, however, ruined by the Russian leader, Catherine the Great, refusing to cooperate. Britain and Prussia threatened joint military action, the former mobilising a further 36 of the line under Vice-Admiral Lord Hood. This, together with concessions, achieved Catherine's acquiescence in the following August. Between them, the two incidents had ensured that about 60 of the Royal Navy's 87 listed line ships were on a 'ready' footing.

Prime Minister Pitt's reciprocal declaration of war on France was altruistic in that a European monarchy was avenging the regicide of a foreign sovereign and because the French occupation of the Austrian Netherlands threatened the existence of the Dutch United Provinces. A practical underlying desire, however, was the destruction of French naval power, seen as responsible for the loss of the American colonies. In the course of achieving this aim, the seizure of French overseas territories, particularly the wealthy Caribbean islands, would be a bonus. As French relationships with Spain had been strained, it was doubtful that she could rely on the support of the not-inconsiderable Spanish fleet.

War with France also caused problems with the United States. Allied to the French since 1778, the Americans were bound to assist in the defence of the very West Indian islands that the British proposed to take. Washington the pragmatist, however, weighed cause and effect, and opted for neutrality in April 1793. Officially the reason was that regicide had invalidated the alliance but, in practice, there remained strong pro-British sentiment in influential places, while Britain herself was a market of prime importance. Britain, nonetheless, rewarded this action in a cavalier fashion by seizing scores of

Brunswick v. Vengeur 1794

During Howe's action of the Glorious First of June, the *Brunswick* and the *Vengeur du Peuple*, both 74s, became locked and fought, literally, to a finish. The *Brunswick* lost most of her upper-level guns, but her lower deck battery slowly eviscerated the *Vengeur* at point-blank range. Wrenched away, the Frenchman foundered under valedictory fire from the *Ramillies*. The French captain, Renaudin, received as much British approbation as his opponent, John Harvey.

Eole

A good example of the French 74, the *Eole*
was the sixth ship from the rear of the
French line at the Glorious First of June, at
the exact point at which Howe broke through
in the *Queen Charlotte*. In company with the
Trajan 74 she engaged and badly damaged
the British 74s *Bellerophon* and *Russell*
before making her escape.

American-flagged ships engaged in trade between metropolitan France and the Caribbean, a trade soon to be extinguished by a full blockade.

France had hardly been preparing for an all-out maritime war for, of her reported 82 available ships of the line, barely a dozen were ready for sea in each of the northern bases of Brest and Lorient, three more down the coast at Rochefort and a further half dozen at Toulon. Possibly 15 more were close to commissioning. As was customary, the bulk of British naval strength was concentrated in home waters, most of it in Lord Howe's Channel Fleet. Foreign stations still supported small peacetime squadrons. Those of greater importance — the Mediterranean, Jamaica and the Leeward Islands (still separate commands) and Halifax (Nova Scotia) — had, typically, a 50-gun flagship, a frigate or two and a handful of sloops. Lesser stations, such as the East Indies, supported nothing above a frigate.

The French fleet's numerical inferiority was offset somewhat by its no longer having to safeguard Indian and Canadian interests. Revolution had, however, taken a severe toll of the officer corps, while the energies of the crews were as much likely to be directed towards furthering the revolution as to meeting a powerful and familiar adversary whose establishment was not so afflicted. Similar discord affected also the all-important French naval bases, greatly reducing their capacity and flexibility in support of the fleet.

Responding tardily but energetically to the demands of war, Britain expanded naval manpower from 16,000 to 25,000 and, by the close of 1793, had 85 commissioned ships of the line. About a dozen were allocated to the West Indies stations with, for the moment, the remainder divided approximately equally between the Channel Fleet and Lord Hood's Mediterranean command. There existed an immediate reserve of about 25 line ships.

Sizeable pockets of French territory retained overt monarchist sympathies, to the extent that the extreme ruling party, the Jacobins, feared their defection to the British. From June 1793 a nationwide network of regional deputies whose authority was backed by the ready and indiscriminate use of the guillotine enforced the leaders' requirements. To prevent British involvement in the pro-monarchist insurrection in the Vendée or, possibly, the hand-over of the port of Brest, the French maintained a standing patrol by 21 of the line between the Quiberon peninsula and Belle Ile. Its commander, Vice-Admiral (new style) Morard de Galles, had earlier fought under Suffren in the Indian Ocean. He was expecting also the arrival of an important convoy from North America and, following usual French policy, did not seek a major engagement with the British as long as he was left to pursue his mission. Howe, for his part, made no great effort to bring him to action, probably believing, as many in Britain did, that France would collapse in turmoil at any time.

Defection, when it came, was not at Brest but at Toulon. Following great effort, the French here had now 17 sail of the line ready for sea, four more completing refit, nine under repair and one building. Hood, watching offshore, could dispose of 21 of the line. It being early in the war, the force had a textbook command structure, with vice- and rear-admirals of the red, white and blue embarked in five three-deckers. Hood could also draw on reinforcement from a Spanish squadron under Admiral Langara.

Late in August French plenipotentiaries seeking British support in the re-establishment of constitutional monarchy met Hood aboard his flagship. Hood issued a proclamation that the allies would afford protection in return for cooperation. Following this, the ships in port were moved to an inner basin, largely disarmed and their rebellious crews repatriated under a flag of truce. Royalist support, however, was patchy and Provence did not rise in a general counter-revolution. Concentrating on holding Toulon, the British and Spanish, themselves at loggerheads, received contingents of Piedmontese, Sicilian, Neapolitan and Maltese to assist in manning defensive works around the long, 15-mile perimeter. They faced two republican armies, fresh from bloodily subduing dissent in Marseilles. Outnumbering the defenders some three to one, they were soon pressing into the city. By December they were able to bring the naval base under fire (their artillery being under the direction of one Bonaparte, then still a captain) and Hood began to make preparations for demolition and abandonment.

The considerable number of French ships had to be removed or destroyed under fire. Another rising star, the controversial Captain Sir William Sidney Smith, was given the task which, together with a Spanish force, meant towing a fireship into the inner harbour, covered by a rearguard ashore. The night of 18th December was chaotic. The fireship touched off a group of moored ships, by the light of whose conflagration the shore parties set about blowing up stores. Unfortunately, a frigate laden with powder was set off with a hugely damaging explosion which sank a British gunboat. Smith and his party barely escaped with their lives. Their effort had been left far too late. Only nine French ships (one 80 and eight 74s) were destroyed, and four (three 74s and the 120-gun *Commerce de Marseilles*) taken by the British. Left behind were a further 120-gun First Rate, three 80s and 14 74s.

As the British left with their rearguards and 15,000 royalist sympathisers, the revolutionaries commenced their revenge, over 6,000 being slaughtered. Hood, for the moment, retired on Hyères, in the unusual situation of having inflicted greater damage than a major engagement but under widespread criticism for failing to have done more. Royalist support also varied widely in French overseas territories. Investigation by the Royal Navy at Corsica and Martinique received short shrift but Tobago, San Domingo and enclaves in India were simply occupied.

General tumult, combined with a poor harvest, produced great shortages in France. Imported produce was desperately required, but British blockade measures had seen a large number of loaded French merchantmen driven for protection into American ports. Eventually, these would need to be sailed over in an immense and valuable convoy. The task would be a searching first test for several of the newly-created *Contre-amiraux* (Rear-Admirals) of the French Navy. At Brest, the Comte De Villaret-Joyeuse had replaced Morard de Galles. Lately a lieutenant, the latter, despite an aristocratic background, had received enhanced promotion and now wore his flag in the *Montagne* 120. This ship had been the *Etats de Bourgogne* but, as with many other larger units, had been given revolutionary re-naming, the *Montagne* in this case being the pseudonym for the ruling Jacobins.

With so many ships now commanded by political appointees rather than seamen of proven abilities the authorities could no longer count on their willingness to fight. It was decreed that any captain striking his flag to anything other than overwhelming odds would face the death penalty. To enforce this, the so-called Committee of Public Safety put afloat a political commissar to exercise ultimate authority.

Early in May 1794 Lord Howe's Channel Fleet, with 34 of the line, escorted about 100 merchantmen to the latitude of Cape Finisterre. Here, they divided into three separate convoys, Howe returning with 26 ships of the line. Off Ushant his frigates detected Villaret-Joyeuse in the Brest roads and assuming this gathering to presage the arrival of the all-important American convoy, Howe stood out into the Atlantic along its anticipated track. After a fortnight's fruitless search he returned on the 19th to find the French had sailed.

The convoy itself, of 117 sail, had left the United States on 2nd April escorted

San Telmo

San Telmo was one of six Third Rates built to the plans of Director of Naval Construction, José Romero y Landa, between 1785 and 1794. Completed in 1789 and displacing 1,640 tons, *San Telmo* was rated as a 64; others in the series were *San Ildefenso* (1785), *San Francisco De Paula* (1788), *Europa* (1789) and *Monarca* and *Montaes* (both 1794).

by *Contre-amiral* Pierre-Jean Vanstabel with four of the line. It had rendezvoused with a similar Rochefort force under *Contre-amiral* Joseph Marie Nielly. This group, en route, had encountered an inward-bound British Newfoundland convoy, capturing much of it along with its sole escort, the *Castor* 32. As the fleets tracked about in foggy conditions some of these were recovered. Villaret-Joyeuse, with 25 of the line, had left Brest on the 16th May, encountering a Dutch convoy, from which he took a score of sail. As the French were in several groups, Howe began to make sightings, first a 74, then a pair of corvettes, which he captured. Then, at 6.30 a.m. on the 25th, some 400 miles west of Brest, persistence was rewarded. In a fresh wind, south by west, and rough sea, his frigates sighted sail to windward.

Rear-Admiral Thomas Pasley in the *Bellerophon*, with three further 74s, was sent to investigate. He found the French main force and, by 9.00 a.m., both fleets were in full view, exactly equal in numbers at 26 ships of the line each. The French admiral had been instructed to join battle only if necessary to safeguard the convoy, and headed slowly westward on the port tack, interposed between Howe and the convoy, and endeavouring to lure the British from it.

With Pasley still ahead, the British pressed slowly to windward in two groups. The ragged formation of the French testified to lack of experience and, as several ships had become separated, the whole force tacked shortly before 2.00 p.m. to rejoin them. It was now heading about east-south-east. Howe, assuming the manoeuvre to be a prelude to escape, ordered 'General Chase' with Pasley to worry the enemy rear. Coming about to parallel the French course, it was apparent to the British that a large First Rate, the 110-gun *Révolutionnaire* (ex-*Bretagne*), was trailing. As, at about 6.00 p.m., the *Bellerophon* took her under fire, it was clear that her purpose was to cover the rear of her line.

For 75 minutes Pasley engaged his huge adversary, until he was relieved by his three squadron mates, which had finally worked up against the wind. Damaged aloft, the *Bellerophon* pulled out but had the satisfaction of seeing the Frenchman's weakened mizenmast go by the board. Coming into the wind, she was then attacked by two further British 74s. By 10.00 p.m. she had suffered over 400 casualties but had caused great damage to her attackers.

As the night progressed, Captain William Parker in the *Audacious* 74 had made a particular effort to take the *Révolutionnaire* but daybreak on the 29th found him nursing badly weakened masts while his great adversary, with no mast standing, was being tended by a French 74 and a frigate. Parker, too damaged to renew the action had to make for Plymouth. The gallant *Révolutionnaire*, at the end of a towline, also made Rochefort, her reward being to have her officers clapped in jail for leaving the action!

With Villaret-Joyeuse obliged to cover his convoy, Howe was able to gain a windward position on the 29th. He could now choose his moment and, for three days, was content to skirmish, mainly with the French rear, but causing sufficient damage to oblige several to drop out. These, fortuitously, were replaced when Nielly joined the flag in very thick weather. Dawn of Sunday, the 1st June, was fine with a moderate swell and a fresh breeze from the same quarter, south by west. Both fleets had formed line and, under easy sail, 25 British slowly closed 25 French. Howe's stated plan was to concentrate on the enemy centre, each ship to pass under the stern of its opposite number and, bearing up, to engage from the lee side, thus preventing damaged enemy ships from escaping down-wind.

At a stately five knots, the British van came under opening French fire at 9.24 a.m. Howe signalled for 'Close Action' but, by 9.50 a.m., only a few ships had succeeded in carrying out his intentions. The admiral himself, in the *Queen Charlotte*, barged through the French line astern of the flagship *Montagne*, engaging two neighbouring 74s in the process. Directly to leeward of the *Montagne* ranged the 90-gun *Jacobin* which,

Commerce de Marseille
One of several First Rates funded by the great French commercial ports, the 120-gun *Commerce de Marseille* was one of those removed by the British from Toulon during the panic evacuation. Although commissioned into the Royal Navy, she appears not to have suited, and was hulked as early as 1796.

Howe

Perhaps the most respected commander that the Royal Navy has ever produced, Richard Howe stemmed from Irish aristocracy in 1726. A post-captain at 20, he was badly injured in an engagement with a French privateer. He made his mark in 1755 when, in command of the *Dunkirk* 60, he assisted Boscawen's flagship in the taking of the French *Alcide*. At Quiberon in 1759 he led Hawke's line in the *Magnanime* 74, accounting for the French *Héros*.

During a protracted spell as captain and commodore, Howe was responsible for combined operations. He reached flag rank in 1770, becoming a vice admiral by 1776. In this capacity he cooperated militarily with his brother, General Sir William Howe, Commander-in-Chief during the American War of Independence. Here, the British fleet, comprising cruiser-sized ships, could do no more than contain the French under d'Estaing. In common with the bulk of the Navy, Howe disliked hostilities against the Americans, lately his countrymen. Disagreeing with the administration, he spent four years ashore.

In 1782 political change encouraged him back. As Commander-in-Chief, Channel Fleet he successfully eluded a combined French and Spanish fleet to run a sizeable convoy into a long-besieged Gibraltar. Becoming First Lord of the Admiralty in 1783, he held this post until 1788, when he was elevated to the British peerage. Despite age and failing health he returned to sea in 1790 and, four years later, enjoyed his greatest success in the tactical victory known as the Glorious First of June.

He was made Admiral of the Fleet in 1796 and had the task of quelling the developing mutiny in the Fleet. This, resulting from years of injustices, he solved through strength of character and reputation for fairness. He was created a Knight of the Garter and died, Earl Howe, in 1799.

endeavouring to close the gap in the line, had overrun the flag. Deftly handled, the *Queen Charlotte* forced her way between, blasting on either broadside. Raked from the quarter, the *Montagne* suffered heavy damage and over 300 casualties on her packed decks. By 10.00 a.m. the action had degenerated into little better than a mêlée and the French, less damaged aloft, added sail to disengage.

Some had already dropped out downwind and were firing on opportunity through the pall of gunsmoke. Howe signalled 'General Chase', but 11 British and 12 French were already disabled. The ferocity of the actions was typified by the long duel between the 74s *Brunswick* and *Vengeur du Peuple*, which fought each other to a standstill, the latter sinking at about 6.15 p.m. with only three dozen of the 400 survivors uninjured. It says much for the toughness of sound wooden ships that the *Brunswick*, with every mast and yard shot through, a quarter gallery sheared off, 23 guns dismounted and three fires extinguished, should not only be repaired but serve until 1812, following which she was decommissioned to serve yet another 14 years in harbour service.

Other notable duels were being fought out — between the *Leviathan* and the *América*, and between the *Marlborough* and the *Mucius* and *Impétueux*. Rear-Admiral Alan Gardner, in the *Queen* 98, lost both main and mizzen masts in subduing the *Jemappes*, following engagements with the *Patriote* and the *Scipion*, and was having difficulty in getting clear. At this point the French admiral rallied a dozen ships to round up and recover his cripples. His course took him toward the *Queen* but Howe, noting her pending predicament, also moved in with a group. Thanks to his intervention the *Queen* suffered no more than sporadic bombardment while Villaret-Joyeuse contented himself with towing away five dismasted ships.

For no loss, Howe had captured six and sunk one in an action which, having no close geographical reference, became known to the British as the Glorious First of June but, to the French, with their new revolutionary calendar, as the Battle of 13th Prairial.

King George himself visited Howe aboard the *Queen Charlotte* on her return to Spithead. Honours, awards and promotions abounded. Despite a three-to-one casualty list, the French had cause for satisfaction in that Villaret-Joyeuse' action in defence of his convoy allowed it to arrive unmolested. Despite being slowed by towing crippled ships, he was not brought again to action on the following day, owing to the elderly Howe's reluctance to renew the battle. All but nine of the British ships were immediately

Spanish Montanes
1794 74 guns

1. Stern lamp
2. Counter
3. Transon
4. Rudder
5. Stern post
6. Tiller
7. Gun room
8. Poop
9. Signal flag locker
10. Mizzen mast
11. Captain's quarters
12. Captain's pantry
13. Wardroom
14. Officers' quarters
15. Shot lockers
16. Quarter deck
17. Upper deck
18. Gun deck
19. Flour store
20. Rope
21. Chain locker
22. Dry store
23. Powder magazine
24. Water storage
25. Ballast
26. Capstan

27. Crew quarters
28. Main mast
29. Well
30. Step
31. Floor riders
32. Ribs
33. Keel
34. Rubbing strip
35. Anti-fouling plates
36. Pump machinery
37. Main deck
38. Navigation light
39. Fore mast
40. Oven
41. Belfry

42. Topsail bits
43. Knighthead
44. Bits
45. 32 pounder gun
46. 12 pounder gun
47. Fore peak
48. Pillar
49. Bowsprit
50. Manger
51. Powder store
52. Breast hook
53. Fore deck
54. Position of figurehead
55. Stem
56. Sail locker

Capture of Fort Royal 1794

Jervis's initial landings on Martinique were made on 5th February 1794. Six weeks later, with seamen supporting the troops ashore, the island, except for Forts Royal and Bourbon, was in British hands. On 17 March boats from the *Boyne* 98 successfully cut out a French frigate inside Fort Royal as the *Veteran* 64 and *Rose* 28, seen here, landed troops in a successful outflanking movement.

battleworthy and a further interception would also have caught *Contre-amiral* Montagu's cruising squadron, newly rejoined. The ageing British admiral was content for a victory, where annihilation had been possible.

As the first major fleet encounter of the wars, it was important in showing that French gunnery, seamanship and discipline had suffered because of the new order, while dockyards were unable quickly to repair and refit the sudden influx of damaged ships. It would be October 1794 before a squadron again sailed from Brest, when Nielly sortied with five of the line. His objective was a convoy but, in seeking this, he met two British 74s. Successfully dividing them, he took the *Alexander* after a two-hour resistance. As happened on several occasions, the ship was repaired, taken into the captor's navy under the same name, only to be recaptured later, in this case in June 1795.

French islands in the Lesser Antilles were not only valuable in their own right but also as potential springboards for mischief against British interests. The disturbed state of France herself, however, left the station ill-prepared and the appointment of Vice-Admiral Sir John Jervis as Commander-in-Chief with five of the line saw the British naval presence as by far the more powerful, supported as it was by 7,000 troops. Not one for idling, Jervis sailed from Barbados in February 1794, landing over 6,000 troops at three separate points on Martinique. Humid, mountainous and jungle-clad, the island was garrisoned weakly by a few companies of French regulars and militia who, nonetheless, manned properly-prepared fortifications.

Inter-service cooperation was excellent. Naval detachments, led by their captains and supported by marines, toiled mightily to bridge streams and to cut tracks through forest in order to haul cannon, mortars and ammunition to commanding heights. The bulk of the island was secured within six weeks leaving the strongly-held Fort Royal and Fort Bourbon (which retained their pre-revolutionary names).

Secured in the carénage under the very walls of Fort Royal was the French 32-gun frigate *Bienvenue*. In broad daylight, and using nothing but rowing boats, naval personnel boarded and took her but, swept as she was by musketry and grapeshot, they were unable to get her to sea. She had to be abandoned. A week later, when both forts fell to combined naval and military arms, the *Bienvenue* was again taken. She hoisted the White Ensign as the *Undaunted* and, as was the pleasant custom of the time, her command was given to the man instrumental in her capture, in this case Captain Robert Faulknor of the sloop *Zebra*.

Following a further multi-point landing, the neighbouring island of St. Lucia was carried within four days. Leaving a small garrison, Jervis maintained his momentum, landing on Guadeloupe on 11th April, just a week on. The surrender of Grande Terre was assisted by the *Winchelsea* 32 closing to silence batteries from 'half musket-shot' and by the indefatigable Captain Faulknor leading his matelots in support of infantry scaling near-vertical heights to storm the enemy strongpoint at Fort Fleur d'Epée. As three frigates were able to secure the adjacent islands of the Saintes, forces from Grande Terre were free to switch quickly to overrun neighbouring Basse Terre. Well-organised combined operations had resulted in the overall campaign taking just ten weeks.

As far as Guadeloupe was concerned, success was ruined by complacency. On 3rd June a small French squadron with transports put ashore a battalion-sized force which overcame a weak British garrison that was over-reliant on local royalist support. Only lack-lustre attempts were made to counter this enemy incursion and the island was finally abandoned again to the French in December 1794, by which time Jervis had been succeeded as station Commander-in-Chief by Vice-Admiral Benjamin Caldwell.

Lord Howe did not believe in wearing out the Navy's ships of the line in blockading Brest, instead maintaining a close watch with frigates while holding his main strength in Torbay or, in severe weather, at Spithead. Reaction to any enemy initiative was slow, a fact not lost on the French. In the main Biscay ports of Brest, Lorient and Rochefort now lay a total of 46 line ships. Of these 35 were at Brest, their considerable crew strength contributing to a desperate local shortage of food and other staples.

As Hood's activities had left the Toulon squadron under-strength, the French decided to reinforce it by six of the line, commanded by *Contre-amiral* Renaudin, late commander of the *Vengeur du Peuple*. To be accompanied to a safe latitude by Villaret-Joyeuse and the whole Brest fleet, they sailed shortly before Christmas in a gale of wind, only to return having lost the 110-gun *Républicain* on a well-documented shoal. A further, successful, attempt was made to sail a week later. Word reached the British only on 2nd January 1795 and further frigates were despatched from Falmouth to investigate. It was on this occasion that Captain Sir Sidney Smith took the *Diamond* to the very

Howe on deck of Queen Charlotte (Mather Brown)

Howe was 68 years of age when he fought Villaret-Joyeuse on the Glorious First of June. Throughout the protracted build-up to the action he never more than rested in a chair for five days. Codrington recalled, however, that, when the enemy obviously decided to fight, he 'expressed an animation of which, at his age I had not thought capable'. Following the action, he was so weak he had to be supported. Ill-health forced him ashore soon afterward.

Jervis

Born in 1735, John Jervis was of a respectable, rather than wealthy, family. He joined the Royal Navy at 13, but, as a midshipman, suffered impoverishment. Thus obliged to associate himself with the lower deck rather than the gunroom, he developed a powerful bond with the Navy's lower orders.

A junior captain by 1759, he was noted for taking his command, the *Porcupine* 14, under heavy fire during the landing of troops above Quebec. As a post- captain commanding the *Foudroyant* 80 he was next in line to Keppel at Ushant in 1778. In the same ship he distinguished himself in taking the French *Pégase* 74 single-handedly after a three-hour duel. In recognition, he was made Knight of the Bath and five years later, in 1787, he gained flag rank.

As vice-admiral in the *Boyne* 98 he led the sizeable expedition to the West Indies that, in 1794, took Guadaloupe, Martinique and other islands. He was appointed Commander-in-Chief, Mediterranean in 1795, hoisting his flag in the *Victory* 100. With an out-numbered fleet, his responsibilities included also the Iberian Atlantic coast and it was here, off Cape St. Vincent in February 1797, that he encountered a Spanish squadron of near twice his strength. Thanks greatly to the initiative of his subordinate commanders - an illustrious list that included Nelson and Collingwood, Troubridge, Calder and Saumarez - the general state of disorder of the Spaniards was exploited. Jervis, no Nelson, disengaged while he was winning, settling for a good victory rather than annihilation. For this he was created Earl St. Vincent, with a life pension.

It was Jervis who despatched Nelson to find the whereabouts of the French fleet, resulting in the Battle of the Nile. In 1799, a sick man he was returned home, becoming First Lord of the Admiralty in the following year. Made an Admiral of the Fleet in 1821, a rare honour, he died two years later.

gates of Brest under French colours, actually speaking anchored enemy ships in the process.

The French, however, were already at sea. They took a reported 100 British mercantile prizes and the 20-gun sloop *Daphne* but suffered badly in successive gales. So poor was their material condition that two 80s and a 74 foundered, and a further 74 had to be beached. The force returned with two three-deckers deeply flooded. Only at the end of February 1795 was Renaudin able to get away, reaching Toulon early in April. The addition of his 80 and five 74s gave the French superiority in the Western Mediterranean.

That the French fleet had enjoyed free rein caused disagreement at the Admiralty between Earl Spencer (who had succeeded the Earl of Chatham as First Lord) and Howe, now suffering ill-health and the caution of old age. The Admiral was obliged to exercise command from ashore at Portsmouth, whence the Admiralty could communicate quickly with him via the new overland semaphore chain. Tactical command afloat was given to Vice-Admiral Sir Alexander Hood, created Lord Bridport, who, however, was of the same age as Howe.

In June 1795, *Contre-amiral* Jean Gaspar Vence sailed from Brest with three 74s and a half dozen frigates to cover a coastal convoy from the Gironde. He encountered Vice Admiral the Hon. William Cornwallis in the *Royal Sovereign* 100 and four 74s, which squadron seized eight merchantmen before the remainder anchored under the guns of Belle Ile. Although Brest and Lorient flanked his line of retreat, Cornwallis remained in the offing. The French reacted strongly, Villaret-Joyeuse moving down in the *Peuple* 120 (the ex-*Montagne*, renamed again following the execution of Robespierre and the end of the Terror), nine more of the line and a pair of 50s, meeting Vence off the Ile de Groix, near Lorient.

Cornwallis, having covered the return of his prizes, was returning and encountered the enemy off the Pointe de Penmarch, as they 'rounded the corner' en route to Brest. With the wind west of north-west, Cornwallis had the weather advantage and, apparently mistaking the mass of sail as the convoy, closed on them. Warned by one of his frigates of his peril, he formed his five ships into line and went about. The French split into two groups, one of which forged ahead under the land. Dawn on the 17th saw the British in full flight, their pursuers now in three groups. Two of Cornwallis' ships, *Bellerophon* and *Brunswick*, had to jettison weight to improve their sailing but their enemy's weather division closed the tail of the British line. Cornwallis, accepting that action was inevitable, brought the *Bellerophon* farther up the line for safety.

The new tail-ender, the *Mars* 74, began to suffer from the tactics of the *Zélé* 74 and *Virginie* 40, which repeatedly ran up to her quarters before yawing and raking her. As she was in danger of losing spars and falling back, Cornwallis changed course and came to her aid with the flagship and the *Triumph* 74. Slowed, the British squadron was in danger of being surrounded.

Closer pursuit was discouraged by the British cutting away much of their stern galleries to bring more guns to bear while the frigate *Phaeton* went ahead and conducted a series of flag exchanges with an imaginary British squadron over the horizon. Villaret-Joyeuse then had only to sight some sail, perfectly innocent, to convince himself that he had pressed matters far enough. A very relieved Cornwallis was allowed to return to Plymouth relatively unscathed.

Villaret-Joyeuse' magnanimity was, however, poorly repaid for he again had to shelter under Belle Ile, this time from the weather. Emerging on 22nd June he encountered Bridport and the Channel Fleet, again off the Ile de Groix. The British were interposed between Brest and a force under the now-Commodore Sir Borlase Warren, mounting an operation against Quiberon. Warren sighted the French, now in very light conditions, off Belle Ile and alerted Bridport, who despatched his best sailers ahead of his main force. Cornwallis' late situation was now reversed, with 12 French sail of the line endeavouring to make Lorient, pursued by 17 British.

Admiral John Jervis (John Hoppner)

Joining the Service at thirteen, Jervis was a post-captain within eleven years, having made an impression at Quebec. Captain of the *Foudroyant*, he took the French *Pégase* in 1782. Following a successful campaign as vice-admiral in the West Indies in the early 1790s, he took the Mediterranean command and led the fleet to the great victory off Cape St. Vincent. As Lord St. Vincent, he came ashore in 1799, aged 64. Appointed First Lord in the following year, he finally retired as Admiral of the Fleet in 1804.

Waiting Room at the Admiralty (* No misnomer) P. 6.

"'Tis the curse of service, that preferment goes by favor & affection" Othello.

'Waiting Room at the Admiralty'

Huge wartime increases in the number of junior officers meant a surfeit in peace, when available commands decreased rapidly. Any hope of promotion from lieutenant to commander, and thus command of a vessel smaller than a Sixth Rate, required either political or aristocratic connection or, alternatively, a visit to the Admiralty and an interminable wait for a chance to impress the selectors.

Dawn of the 23rd saw the French, fairly well grouped, being overhauled by the widely-scattered British. Trailing the French was the *Alexandre*, captured from the British a year earlier and still sailing badly. Following abortive attempts to tow her to safety, she was abandoned to her fate. The old flagship, *Queen Charlotte*, was a fast sailer and, getting among the enemy's tail-enders, caused the *Formidable* to strike. With the *Tigre* also being taken soon afterward and the British leaders well in contact, a good day was on the cards but, at 8.00 a.m., Bridport, perhaps mindful of his primary duties, ordered the action to be discontinued. Three Frenchmen had been taken but the result was disappointing, with even the French themselves commenting on their good fortune. The relative casualty lists bore witness to the effectiveness of the British practice of firing into the hull. On the three prizes alone the French had suffered 670 casualties, while the overall British total was 144.

Ashore, French arms had prospered. By early in 1795, Belgium and much of a largely sympathetic Netherlands had been occupied. German territory as far east as the Rhine had mostly been abandoned by the Austrian and Prussian armies. Before the year's end Prussia concluded a separate peace with France, while Spain was seeking terms. From the British standpoint, the fleets of Holland and Spain had become hostile but the foreign possessions of those nations offered new prospects for seizure. The year 1795 also saw the significant acceptance by the French that they could no longer contest mastery at sea. Their navy would be maintained as a fleet-in-being, exerting a continuous threat but being used only on opportunity.

Following the loss of Toulon the British Mediterranean Fleet once again relied on

Destruction of the Droits de l'Homme (Ebenezer Colls)

The fleet supporting Hoche's disastrous expedition to Ireland in December 1796 was scattered by poor weather. Transporting General Humbert, the *Droits de l'Homme* 74 was returning to Brest when, on 13 January 1797, she encountered the *Indefatigable* 44 and *Amazon* 36. Hounded incessantly by the smaller ships the 74 drove ashore in the Bay of Audierne and broke up with huge loss of life. The *Amazon* was also wrecked.

Gibraltar as a secure base, a location remote from French activity. Corsica looked a promising alternative. Although garrisoned by republican troops, it appeared solidly royalist in its sympathies. Following assurances from local leaders, Lord Hood made preparations to use its northern anchorage of San Fiorenzo (the modern Golfe de St. Florent).

A modest combined operation in February 1794 dislodged the local garrison, which withdrew into nearby Bastia. Hood wished to secure his flank by taking Bastia but, when his military commander refused to move without reinforcements, the admiral landed a force of sailors and marines under Captain Horatio Nelson of the *Agamemnon* 64. Six weeks and 53 casualties later, the Navy held the town and citadel.

Hood returned to watch Toulon, leaving Nelson to move against Calvi, the other republican base in the region. A seven-week siege proved successful, although Nelson lost his right eye when struck by fragments during an artillery exchange. With the republican threat lifted the island's General Assembly pledged allegiance to Great Britain. A viceroy was appointed but Corsica was too close to France, and too large to be adequately defended. Like Toulon, it became a liability.

In November 1794 Lord Hood was relieved by Vice-Admiral William Hotham. French activity in Toulon had built up a total of 15 of the line, including the 120-gun flagship *Sans-Culotte* (ex-*Dauphin Royal*), three 80s and the remainder 74s. Considering the weakness of the British position in Corsica, it was unwise of Hotham to sail in February 1795 for Leghorn (now Livorno), the main base of his Tuscan allies. The French moved quickly, but their fleet commander, *Contre-amiral* Pierre Martin, lacked any experience;

The Inshore Blockading Squadron at Cadiz July 1797 (Thomas Buttersworth)

Following the Battle of Cape St. Vincent upward of 26 enemy ships took refuge in Cadiz. They were blockaded by Nelson's inshore squadron, which made every effort to goad the enemy to further action through annoying the town by bombardment. Having been promoted Rear-Admiral of the Blue in February 1797, Nelson here wears his flag in the *Captain* 74.

Cape of Good Hope. The expedition was too weak to overcome Dutch resistance until, a month later, a convoy of 14 East Indiamen brought reinforcement.

Small-scale expeditions also took the Dutch possessions of Ceylon, Malacca and Cochin, while Vice-Admiral Sir John Laforey, who had succeeded Caldwell as Commander-in-Chief of the Leeward Islands station, seized Demerara, Berbice and Essequibo, constituent provinces of the future British Guiana.

France emerged from her internal strife with a new constitution. Ultimate power was now vested in a five-strong executive Directory, presiding over a two-chamber legislative body. The Directory first appointed Bonaparte as general of the French army in the south and his energy quickly showed results, putting the Austrians on the defensive and forcing Naples and Sardinia from the coalition opposing him.

Jervis in the Mediterranean faced a difficult problem. With 18 of the line he faced the French Toulon squadron of 15 with, conveniently beyond the Gibraltar Strait at Cadiz, a further six. These, sharing the port with the major part of the Spanish fleet, comprised a squadron commanded by *Contre-amiral* Joseph de Richery which had slipped out of Toulon the previous September during Hotham's lacklustre watch.

With his main strength based on San Fiorenzo, Jervis detached Nelson with a small squadron to operate on the Ligurian coast against French shipping supporting their army. Nelson depended upon Leghorn as a forward base but, in June 1796, this fell to the French. As Corsica was now threatened, and would be impossible to defend, Nelson was ordered to establish facilities at Portoferráio on Elba. In August the situation became critical when Spain, awed by French military success, entered into an alliance, which led to a formal declaration of war in October 1796. While Spanish naval expertise was not highly regarded, their fleet included 50 ships of the line, mostly of excellent construction. Of Jervis' 22, seven were watching de Richery at Cadiz and when, at the end of July, these were recalled by Jervis, the French sailed on their original mission to Newfoundland where, with negligible opposition, they wreaked havoc on shipping and coastal communities alike.

Admiral de Langara joined with the French at Toulon to create an allied fleet of 38 of the line, with a score of frigates. Rear-Admiral Robert Mann, whose squadron had been recalled from Cadiz, and who recently had served under Hotham, had been ordered to Gibraltar to store. Pursued thence by a superior Spanish force, Mann made the extraordinary unilateral decision to sail for Britain rather than risk the return to San Fiorenzo. When one recalls the fate of Byng, just 40 years earlier, Mann was fortunate to earn only the disapproval of Their Lordships. Ordered to strike his flag, he never again held a seagoing appointment

Jervis had lost a third of his force through Mann's retirement. Short of supplies and in insufficient strength to establish an early moral superiority, he had to abandon Corsica and fall back on Gibraltar by the end of November. Although, for the moment, Elba and southern Italy remained, the Royal Navy's retreat from the Mediterranean gave the French great heart.

France and Spain put pressure on Portugal and Jervis was moved on to the Tagus. He arrived on 21st December 1796, his strength reduced by a series of mishaps to only ten of the line. On the 10th, the Spanish contingent had left Toulon for Cartagena, while a French squadron of five line ships under *Contre-amiral* le Comte de Villeneuve broke through the Strait, en route to Brest, under cover of an easterly gale. Expatriates such as Theobald Wolfe Tone had persuaded the French administration that disaffection in Ireland was such that a small invasion would trigger a popular revolt against the English. Thus, at Brest, Villeneuve would join with de Richery's squadron (returned from Canadian waters) and take aboard a large contingent of troops. The remainder of these, a total of 18,000, would be transported by the Brest squadron, under *Vice-amiral* Morard de Galles. The latter had succeeded Villaret-Joyeuse, who openly expressed his opposition to any Irish adventure and his disenchantment with the state of the French navy in general. Military command was vested in General Hoche, fresh from putting down Royalist insurrections in Quiberon and the Vendée.

Already delayed two months by the activities of British squadrons offshore, the expedition sailed on 17th December. An element of farce was introduced by de Galles having taken passage in a frigate. This was pursued far to the westward by a British frigate, causing command to devolve on *Contre-amiral* Baron Bouvet in the 74-gun *Droits de L'Homme*. In thick weather, Bouvet succeeded in evading the watching British, arriving off the Irish coast on the 21st. Here, awaiting de Galles, he was much scattered by days of stormy weather. His ships, with their large military complements, rapidly ran short of provisions.

Bridport's Channel Fleet was now alert and abroad, and only the continuing tempestuous weather saved the French from being mopped-up as, piecemeal, they abandoned the project and made for home. About 150 miles off Ushant the *Droits de l'Homme*, with General Humbert aboard, was intercepted by two British frigates. The two-decker, her rig storm-damaged, was well able to keep her smaller assailants at bay but the latter, led by Pellew in the *Indefatigable* 44, were very persistent. Using their superior speed and manoeuvrability, they sought continually to work-up on to her quarters before yawing and raking her with their light broadsides. Accumulating damage themselves from the enemy's 36-pounders and the wild weather, the British hounded their larger adversary eastward, not to safety but to the iron-bound Breton coast. Stranded near Audierne the ship disintegrated over three days, with the loss of about 900 of the possible 1,500 aboard. Pellew's accompanying ship, the *Amazon* 36, was also driven ashore, but lost only six of her complement. For the French Navy the Irish enterprise had been a disaster, with six ships wrecked or foundered, and a further seven captured.

January 1797 saw Lord Bridport confirmed as successor to the ailing Howe as Commander-in-Chief of the Channel Fleet. His immediate preoccupation was with the wave of mutinies then current but he maintained Howe's practice of using English bases from which to cruise the western Channel, ready to respond to Pellew or Warren, whose frigates kept a close eye on Brest. During February Sir John Jervis, still based on the Tagus, was reinforced by Bridport to a respectable 15 of the line, including six three-deckers. His usual cruising ground was off Cape St. Vincent, well-placed to prevent any intended junction between the French and Spanish fleets.

While at Cartagena, Admiral de Langara was superseded by Don José de Cordova in command of the Spanish fleet. On 1st February he sailed with 27 of the line for Brest, via Cadiz. Jervis' frigates tracked it through the Strait before a strong easterly took it well out into the Atlantic. Only on the 13th did Jervis get a full report, when Nelson rejoined in the frigate *Minerva*, having been briefly pursued, and then by the *Niger* 32, which had followed Cordova for some days.

Having finally gained a fair wind to make Cadiz, the Spanish, with very relaxed cruising discipline, cracked on sail. Jervis entertained his captains to a pre-battle dinner on the evening of the 13th and, as a new dawn broke, was some 24 miles west of St. Vincent. Closed up in two compact lines, his ships were close-hauled on the starboard tack.

From the British flagship, *Victory*, the approaching Spanish appeared to spread across most of the horizon. A formidable force, it was commanded from the huge 130-gun four-decker *Santissima Trinidad*. There were also six 112-gun three deckers, two 80s, 18 74s and a dozen 34-gun frigates. Cordova had spoken to an American ship which reported that Jervis had only nine of the line. When Cordova sighted the British in misty conditions, he stood on, anticipating battle with an inferior squadron. At about 10.00 a.m. the haze lifted and both sides discovered the true strength of the other.

At this stage the Spanish were heading about east-south-east, with a group of six well ahead of a ruck of 21. Jervis headed southward for the gap ordering, at 11.00 a.m., a single line of battle to be formed as convenient ahead and astern of the *Victory*. Most of the leading Spanish group (the 'lee division') turned north-westward, joined by three ships that had crossed ahead of Jervis. The latter's plan was that his van and centre would tackle the enemy's 18-strong weather division, his rear blocking any attempt by the lee division to beat upwind to its aid.

At 11.31 a.m. the two main groups began to pass on reciprocal courses. Led by Troubridge in the *Culloden*, the British line opened fire in succession. As the *Culloden* passed the enemy tail-enders at 12.08 p.m. she was ordered to come about, followed in succession as each ship reached this point. Sensing here a vulnerability, the Spanish lee division made as if to cut the British line but its leader, a three-decker, was closed off by the *Victory*, then seventh in line, and badly raked. Acting singly, her consorts fared no better as, although some British ships were cut about aloft, they gave effective mutual support. It was nearing 1.00 p.m. when the British tail-ender, Collingwood's *Excellent*, passed the enemy tail. The Spanish lee division had been held off but the British line still formed a 'U', and Cordova's main body was drawing well ahead.

The action may have petered out in a sterile pursuit except that two ships ahead of the *Excellent* was the 74-gun *Captain*, to which Nelson had transferred from the *Minerva*. Taking Jervis' signals to offer mutual support and to engage the enemy in their very widest sense, he ordered his captain, Ralph Miller, to wear ship. Cutting across the British 'U', ahead of the approaching *Culloden*, the *Captain* passed close under the bows

Battle of Camperdown

Much troubled by the mutinies, Admiral Duncan maintained a long blockade of the Dutch fleet at the Texel. When, in October 1797, the Dutch emerged, Duncan intercepting them off Camperdown. In an untidy but fiercely-fought action, most of Admiral de Winter's ships were taken. The Dutch were, at best, unwilling allies of Napoleon and many were uncommitted to his cause of the Spanish, causing some confusion, as Nelson made directly for Cordova's towering flagship.

Nelson risked Jervis's wrath, but his admiral immediately grasped the significance of the move and ordered the *Excellent* to support him. As the Spanish checked their flight, the *Culloden*, *Blenheim* and *Prince George* were also far enough ahead to get into the action. In the mélée that developed the untidy Spanish formation saw its ships masking each other's fire. The *Captain* was, however, soon suffering and unmanageable. Covered by his friends Troubridge and Collingwood, Nelson made emergency repairs before rejoining the battle. Jervis' order was to 'fill and stand on', i.e. to attack and move ahead, so that each enemy ship would receive attention. This became more difficult to follow as ships took more and more damage aloft, making manoeuvre sluggish.

Spanish gunnery was deplorable, enabling British 74s to take on far larger adversaries. The 112-gun *Salvador del Mundo* struck following an hour's savaging by the *Blenheim* and *Prince George* 98s, joined by the 74s *Orion* and *Excellent*. Collingwood then moved on to assist Nelson with the *San Nicolas* 80. In taking avoiding action, the latter ran foul of her colleague, *San Josef*. The latter, a 112-gun three-decker, had already suffered badly and, as the *Captain* was barely capable of manoeuvre, Nelson laid alongside and personally led a large boarding party to seize both the Spaniards.

Jervis' blow had fallen on the Spanish rear but, towards 4.00 p.m., the approach of the latter's lee division made obvious how outnumbered the British were. The admiral decided, therefore, to consolidate his gains by forming a line between his prizes and the still numerous and uninjured enemy.

Cordova had ten ships, including his own *Santissima Trinidad*, with moderate to severe damage and did not seek to renew the battle which, in material terms, he still had every chance of winning. Jervis, for his part, had taken two 112s, an 80 and a 74 and, with the short winter day ending, did not wish to hazard his damaged force in the lottery of a night action.

Despite individual courage, the enemy had suffered a severe blow to his morale. Captains were punished and Cordova replaced by Admiral Massaredo. At a point in the war when British fortunes were low, the Battle of Cape St. Vincent came as a national tonic. Jervis assumed the title of Earl St. Vincent and was awarded a handsome life pension. Captains and First Lieutenants were all rewarded, Nelson being made Rear-Admiral and a KB for his bold actions.

The now Lord St. Vincent retired to the Tagus for repair and to watch the enemy at Cadiz. Although he was still outnumbered, the Admiralty was niggardly with reinforcements. Those arriving were infected to various degrees with the mutinous behaviour then prevalent in the home commands. 'Old Jervie', however, was a stern disciplinarian, and a few very public hangings ordered to be carried out at the hands of their own shipmates demonstrated to would-be hotheads that there would be little future in trouble-making.

As a diversion, and to keep the fleet occupied, some of the best ships were combined as an inshore squadron under Nelson's command. By night he would provide cover for bomb-ketches, virtually to the walls of Cadiz, whence they would lob their ungainly missiles into the arsenal. This would provoke Spanish counter-attack by armed launches, resulting in fierce hand-to-hand combat. It was no place for a rear-admiral, but his men loved him for it.

Nelson's fearlessness led him into involvement in some desperate scraps, and his early demise was widely anticipated. The lure of Spanish treasure ships was irresistible and St. Vincent had word that the annual Manila galleon would, rather than risk the British blockade, berth at Santa Cruz de Tenerife. In July 1797, therefore, Nelson was sent there with three 74s, a 50 and supporting craft. A weathered volcanic cone, the island offered steep-to-rocky shores, beaten by heavy surf and approaches too deep for a ship to anchor. As the force had to remain in the offing awaiting suitable weather, there was no advantage of surprise. Minor landings then failed to secure key points.

Rather than abort the operation, Nelson opted for a direct frontal assault late on the 24th. As was the custom, captains led their ships' contingents in person, exposed to equal risk. Despite a murderous short-range fire, the invaders seized the mole and adjacent battery, only to be pinned down by a further barrage from the citadel and houses on higher ground beyond. Scores, including Captain Richard Bowen of the *Terpsichore* 32, were killed. Nelson had his right elbow smashed by a ball and the arm had to be amputated.

Their boats smashed and their ammunition wet, Troubridge, Hood and several other captains fought their detachments to the town square, where they found themselves hopelessly surrounded. Bluff and effrontery served only to amuse the Governor who, in victory, displayed exemplary magnanimity, offering the British every assistance. The latter's 146 dead or missing, with over 100 seriously wounded, was a toll scarcely less than that incurred by Jervis at St. Vincent, and with nothing to show for it.

HMS Triton and other vessels (Nicholas Pocock)

The fragile grace of a sailing frigate has seldom been captured better than by Pocock in his portrait of the *Triton* 32. Shown hove-to, the main subject is balanced by two distant vessels. These may well be the same ship on different points of sailing, a common artistic device of the time. Built of softwood, the Triton enjoyed a short lifespan of some seventeen years.

General Bonaparte, now a figure of considerable influence and beyond the Directory's power to control, began to put into practice his ideas for the domination of the Mediterranean. Certain island territories he saw as essential but the key to the Levant was Egypt. Sea power he recognised as critical to such a move and the French fleet and its infrastructure began noticeably to improve from its earlier depressed condition.

Britain was now France's only active enemy and her defeat remained the Directory's priority. Invasion was a necessary option and Napoleon was given command of an 'Army of England'. While he threw himself overtly at the planning and preparation for the project, it is obvious from papers addressed to his masters that he considered it impossible without command of the sea. To defeat the British it was required to defeat them militarily on their own soil yet, in 1798, Napoleon was suggesting such alternatives as an intense *guerre de course* or a campaign to secure control of the Levant. The former had already been shown to be a nuisance rather than a decisive factor in winning a war while the latter, although the General might argue that it would sever Britain's direct links with the East, meant little in those pre-Suez Canal days to a power that controlled the sea routes. In practice, the Directory adopted Napoleon's misgivings regarding invasion and, while maintaining the pretence of preparation, quietly backed a move against Egypt, with its vague promise of use as a springboard to regain a foothold in India.

As the Royal Navy, lacking base or ally, had virtually withdrawn from the Mediterranean, direct action was difficult. But it was impossible for the French to conceal the assembly of some 350 vessels, spread between ports from Marseilles to Civitavecchia, and whose naval cover was the responsibility of *Vice-amiral* Brueys d'Aigalliers.

By April 1798 Nelson had recovered from the amputation of his arm and had rejoined St. Vincent in his watch on Cadiz. The Admiralty, unsure of enemy intentions, directed the Commander-in-Chief to detach him, with three of the line, to institute a patrol outside Toulon. He was to be reinforced later. As Nelson was a mere 39-year-old Rear-Admiral of the Blue, with barely a year's seniority, this appointment caused some rancour. He left Gibraltar on 9th May but, on the 21st, off the French coast, his squadron was scattered by a severe mistral that left his own ship, the *Vanguard* 74, almost dismasted. Barely saved from grounding, she was towed to Sardinia for a rapid self-refit. Nelson was back off Toulon in four days but the French had already sailed.

Moving coastwise, west to east, the French armada grew, its 30,000 troops for conquest complemented by large numbers of civil servants for government and, reflecting the enlightenment of the age, a wide range of artists and academics.

Some reinforcement from home waters enabled St. Vincent to despatch ten of the line and a 50 to Nelson's aid and, on 7th June, with no frigates to assist, the latter went in search of the French with no more information that that they had sailed with a north-westerly wind.

Napoleon had, in fact, made for Malta. Although its fortifications were formidable, the Knights of St. John were an organisation in terminal decline. They capitulated following a token resistance and, leaving a 3,000-strong garrison, the French sailed on 19th June. One day later, in the Messina Strait, Nelson learned of Malta's capture and, with the wind still firmly from the north-west, inferred that Egypt was a likely objective. Pressing on, he reached Alexandria on the 28th. All was quiet. Believing himself mistaken, Nelson sailed the following day, to waste weeks visiting Turkey, Sicily and Greece before learning that the French had made for Egypt. They had arrived barely a day after his earlier departure, defeating the Mamelukes in short order. Having run the risk of moving an army by sea, Napoleon's temerity had paid off; Egypt was his.

'Battle of the Nile' (Mather Brown)

Brown's artistic penchant was to see a major battle as a spectacle, a vehicle for mass activity against which the putative subject of the work appears almost incidental (see also the portrait of Lord Howe). Here, the cataclysmic detonation of the *L'Orient* at the Nile serves not to stun the action into momentary silence so much as to provide infernal illumination for the panic abandonment of ships.

Alexandria was packed with shipping and Brueys, unhappy with its shallow anchorage, moved his squadron along the coast to Aboukir Bay which Brueys felt was close enough to render assistance to the army if called upon by Napoleon, anticipating a British reaction.

Nelson arrived on 1st August, his squadron of 13 74s and a 50 well matched by Brueys' 120-gun flagship *L'Orient*, three 80s and nine 74s. Aboukir Bay is sandy and shallow. Roughly semi-circular and open to the north, its eastern extremity borders the Rosetta mouth of the Nile. At its western limit is a slight re-entrant caused by the rocky promontory upon which is situated Aboukir town. This point continues as an extended line of shoals and Aboukir Island. Very shallow water lay between the island and the point, both of which had been fortified by French batteries.

Brueys elected to fight from an anchored position. He moored in a close-spaced line ahead, aligned roughly north and south, with the head hard under Aboukir Island and its axis slightly dog-legged to bring its tail close to the five-fathom line. Following three weeks at the location, French guard had relaxed but Brueys had ordered that, in the event of attack, heavy cables were to be passed between adjacent ships to create a physical barrier. Satisfied that his line could neither be turned nor pierced, Brueys rested content that his combined broadsides could keep any opponent at a distance. His first miscalculation was that the British would take time to plan an attack. Having arrived, Nelson's assault was instant and ferocious, catching many French ashore on water duty.

The British approach, in a light onshore breeze, was first noted by the French at about 2.00 p.m. on 1st August. Brueys signalled for the return of the shore parties but, as a precaution for their not making it in time, ordered the transfer of gun crews from the four frigates berthed inside the main line. Nelson's tactical genius and rapport with his captains was about to be demonstrated. On his approach, he observed that the French were moored only by the bows. Each, therefore, must have had room to swing with wind and current. Ahead of the lead ship in the line, therefore, there had to be sufficient water to prevent her grounding. Such a gap was large enough to sail through.

He made just two signals. Firstly, to prepare to anchor by the stern. (This would enable each ship to engage her French opposite number without slowly swinging around head to wind). Secondly, to engage the French van and centre. (Brueys' tail-enders, being downwind, would have difficulty in coming to their colleagues' aid.)

It was already 6.30 p.m, the sun very low, when Captain Thomas Foley ghosted the *Goliath* across the bows of the *Guerrière*, raked her heavily and turned inside the French line. He was followed by four others, the remainder of the force (less the grounded *Culloden*) anchoring outside the line. It was Bruey's second miscalculation. Not only were his five weak lead ships being engaged from either side by a total of eight British but their inboard batteries were unmanned and encumbered by piled stores.

The French fought gallantly but were shot to pieces. Cables were cut and dangerous gaps opened in the line. On the other hand, the British lead ships, moving down the line, repeatedly engaged fresh enemy vessels and began to incur serious damage and casualties. Thus, the *Bellerophon* 74 was virtually wrecked in tackling Bruey's three-decked flagship, and the *Majestic* 74 badly damaged by the *Tonnant* 80. Darkness brought no relief for the French. Nelson's ships exhibited fixed light groups and wore White Ensigns to be more immediately recognisable to each other. (Nelson's ships usually wore Blue Ensigns, virtually invisible at night).

As night deepened the *L'Orient* was seen to be heavily afire. Brueys, hit three times, was already dead. Modern evidence suggests that the ship was loaded with powder reserves for the army; in effect, a giant bomb. Adjacent French ships cut their cables. At about 10.00 p.m. she was blasted into three separate sections by an explosion so fearful that it momentarily halted the battle. Several ships had to extinguish fires caused by a hail of blazing debris.

The *Tonnant* was fought to a standstill but, one by one, her colleagues were striking their colours. Although the tail of the French line had barely been engaged the British guncrews were, by the small hours, dropping with exhaustion. Soon after 4.00 a.m. a dreadful dawn showed the French line to have been reduced to dismasted hulks and floating wreckage. Inshore, the frigates still showed fight, the *Artémise* blowing-up resisting the *Theseus* 74, and the *Justice* having to be dissuaded by the *Zealous* from molesting the badly damaged *Bellerophon*.

Five British vessels were engaged in securing the remains of Brueys' fleet but were unable to prevent the relatively unscathed *Guillaume Tell* 80 and *Généreux* 74, together with a pair of frigates, from beating out of the bay. *Zealous*, true to her name, engaged the group single-handedly, but was recalled.

"Victory is not a name strong enough for such a scene", said the justifiably elated Nelson, but his own ships had suffered greatly. Between nine of the line, only two masts remained standing. Eventually, seven were detached to escort the prizes to Gibraltar but three French 74s were burned as being damaged beyond repair. Unable to feed his vast haul of prisoners, Nelson put them ashore to join a dejected army which, master of Egypt, was now marooned there, together with their general and some of his ablest lieutenants.

What became known to the British as the Battle of the Nile had cost the French 1,700 dead, the British 200. Several senior officers were killed, Nelson himself having his forehead laid open by a splinter, an injury that he later blamed for allowing any enemy to escape. Honours were heaped on the victors but, more importantly, states disposed toward seeking terms with France were given new heart to resist, united as the so-called Second Coalition.

Action off Madagascar

The French expedition to Madagascar in 1811 led to one of the last major clashes between the Royal Navy and the French. The two frigate squadrons fought in line of battle, note the ships' boats on the disengaged side.

*'The Battle of the Nile 1798'
(Nicholas Pocock)*

The spectator has been given an imaginary elevated viewpoint, the better to assess the situation as the action commenced. The close-anchored line of Bruey's fleet is prominent, with the larger bulk of his flagship at the centre. Inside the line are anchored Ducrès' four frigates. Under fire from Aboukir fort, the *Goliath* 74 is seen squeezing past the bows of the *Guerrière* at the head of the French line.

Nelson's two smallest ships, the *Leander* 50 and the sloop *Mutine* were sent home with duplicated dispatches. Already damaged and short-handed, it was the ill-fortune of the former to fall in with the *Généreux* off Crete and, after a six-hour resistance, she was captured.

A small British squadron, initially under Captain Samuel Hood in the *Zealous*, was left to watch Alexandria, wherein the mass of merchant shipping was protected by two French 64s, eight frigates and a dozen smaller. These had sailed out *en flûte*, (acting as cargo carriers) but had now reinstated their armament, originally shipped as ballast. Ashore, Bonaparte could reach no accommodation with the Turks and, not waiting to be struck first, moved in February 1799 against Syria. Advancing against feeble resistance, the French had reached Haifa by 17th March. Ahead lay the powerfully-fortified port of St. Jean d'Acre, off which lay two British ships, the *Tigre* 80 and the *Theseus* 74.

The *Tigre* was the command of the now Commodore Sir William Sidney Smith, who was well trusted by the Turks and who held high rank in the Porte. Smith was a man of immense personal courage and ability, but his general demeanour and self-promoting activities left him deeply unpopular with his superiors. He was also well known to the French, who assessed him as something between knight and charlatan, intelligence and insanity, wearisome and originality. From the walls of Acre it was this complex character that now watched the approach of Europe's mightiest commander at the head of some 13,000 troops.

Smith had relieved Hood but, taking orders from the Foreign Office was, to Nelson's disgust, outside his control. Following two years of incarceration, Smith had escaped a French gaol with the assistance of a French royalist named Phélippeaux. Known personally to Napoleon, the latter was an expert on fortification and, granted the rank of colonel by the British, had been improving Acre's defences. To assist in the reduction of Acre, French artillery and heavy equipment was sent coastwise from Alexandria, only to be neatly taken by the *Tigre* and added to the batteries defending the town. On the 5th April, while Smith had withdrawn to re-victual, *Contre-amiral* Perrée successfully offloaded ships' guns and ammunition, but left his own squadron under-armed. When, a few weeks later, they had to return to Toulon, they encountered a British squadron just 60 miles short of the port. This had been mounted by Lord Keith (who had superseded the sick St. Vincent) and took Perrée's whole flotilla.

Acre was besieged for 62 days. Stiffened by British sailors and marines, the wildly courageous Turks resisted every French attempt to break in. At times the fighting was desperate with the enemy beyond the outer defences but, gradually sheer attrition demoralised the French, who had to mount each attack over the piled bodies of their comrades. When, finally, a plague visited their encampment, Napoleon decided to abandon the siege.

Although the gallant Phélippeaux had been killed, and the *Theseus* almost destroyed by an accidental explosion which killed 40 men, the British suffered few casualties in the actual siege, during which hand-to-hand fighting Smith's presence had been prominent. The besiegers had suffered over 500 dead in action and 700 by disease. By early June they were back in Egypt; their leader, anxious at the effect of the setback on his reputation, denounced Smith as a lunatic.

With Napoleon and his army thus engaged in the Near East, the Directory continued its attempts to foment revolution in Ireland. In the late summer of 1798 a French expedition was expected to combine squadrons from Rochefort and Brest but, in the chaotic tradition of these enterprises, only the former was ready on time. Three frigates and a corvette sailed with General Humbert, over 11,000 troops and sufficient materiel to equip 3,000 United Irishmen. Landing in County Mayo on 22nd August the force defeated local fencibles but failed to attract a following. Its eventual demise was inevitable, regular British Army units obliging it to surrender on 8th September. Commodore Savary's attached naval force was fortunate in evading the Royal Navy in both directions.

Notwithstanding Humbert's fate the much larger Brest component duly sailed on 16th September. Commodore Jean-Baptiste Bompart, in the *Hoche* 74, was accompanied by nine large frigates. The force was immediately spotted by British frigates, which tracked it and reported to Bridport who, assuming correctly that Ireland was the objective, despatched Commodore Sir John Borlase Warren with three of the line and five frigates. After following a long evasive track, Bompart duly turned up off Tory Island, County Donegal on 11th October. A north-westerly gale was blowing, preventing Warren from attacking immediately, several ships of both sides taking weather damage.

In moderating conditions on the 12th both squadrons formed battle lines. After a four-hour exchange, Warren's extra firepower had its effect; the *Hoche* and three frigates were captured. Aboard the *Hoche* was Wolfe Tone. Although all the remaining French frigates scattered and escaped in the wild conditions, three more were subsequently intercepted and taken. Still not knowing the fate of either Humbert or Bompart, the French on 12th October despatched Savary with four frigates. Landing in Sligo on the

27th the commodore learned the worst and sailed immediately for home, returning unscathed. Wolfe Tone's capture and subsequent suicide reduced for a time the potential of Ireland as a French invasion springboard.

In the July, Sir Sidney Smith and a Turkish squadron landed a Turkish army in Egypt, only for it to be roundly defeated at the battle of the Pyramids. Napoleon, however, had heard of a string of setbacks inflicted on French arms by those of the Second Coalition, and decided to return. Taking advantage of Smith withdrawing to replenish, he sailed with a select entourage in the frigate *Muiron*. The party landed at Fréjus and the general, hailed as a victor, made straight for Paris. In the famous coup of 18th Brumaire he swept aside both the Directory and the assemblies. A new constitution established a ruling Consulate of three, with Napoleon as First Consul. Again, vague proposals for peace were floated before the British but, as they offered no concessions, were not taken to be serious. The war went on.

In the Mediterranean, the Royal Navy was not in strength sufficient to exert sea control except in a limited, local sense. Leaving the French army in Egypt to live off the land, the British moved against Malta. By early 1800 the French garrison had been penned into parts of Valletta and, having received no supplies for a year, was half-starved and disease-ridden. In February, therefore, a relief convoy was sailed from Toulon, covered by an escort under *Contre-amiral* Perrée in the *Généreux* 74, one of the survivors from Aboukir Bay. As Keith was closely investing the island, Perrée stood little chance. He was mortally wounded and both escort and convoy captured.

Blockaded in the Grand Harbour were the three other survivors of Aboukir Bay, the *Guillaume Tell* 80 and two frigates. Verging on starvation, General Vaubois filled the *Guillaume Tell* with sick and non-productive mouths and sailed her on a dark night in March. She was taken, mainly by the exertions of Captain Henry Blackwood in the frigate *Penelope*, after a stout defence lasting several hours. The French garrison was starved into submission in September 1800. To be annexed by the British Crown in 1814, the island would remain firmly associated with the Royal Navy for the next century and a half.

Following an unsuccessful attempt by the French to land 5,000 relief troops in Egypt in January 1801, Keith covered the transport there of 16,000 British in the March. Six months of military operations induced the French, by then in a hopeless situation, to capitulate.

The Netherlands were believed by the British to be increasingly disenchanted with republicanism and, in great secrecy, a large expedition was assembled, the ultimate objective of which was the restoration of the House of Orange. Lord Duncan, now Admiral of the White, was still Flag Officer for the North Sea Command in 1799, and was still blockading the Dutch fleet that lay inside the Texel. Vice-Admiral Samuel Storij, commanding the latter, again entertained no particular animosity toward the British, being content to take no action unless himself attacked. Further units, however, whose temper was unknown to Duncan, lay at Amsterdam and in the Maas. Half the 37,000 troops assembled for the enterprise were Russian, although paid for by the British. In mid-August they were transported from a variety of ports by upwards of 250 ships. As these lay offshore in stormy conditions, Duncan sought Storij's acquiescence, which was refused.

Landing on the 27th the British army secured the area of den Helder including 13 old ships laying in ordinary. They also commanded the only channel by which Storij's force could get to sea. The Dutch, their loyalties divided, were finally persuaded to surrender without resistance. Minor warships of the Royal

Minotaur
Based on the design of the French 74
Courageux, the *Minotaur* was completed in
Woolwich Dockyard in 1793. Long the
command of Captain Thomas Louis, she
was present at the Nile where, with the
Theseus, she compelled the surrender of
the French *Aquilon* 74. In 1801 she
participated in Keith's expedition to Egypt.
In 1810 she was wrecked off the Texel.

Navy established control over the Zuider Zee and assisted the army on the numerous waterways. They could exert little influence on the military campaign, however. This failed badly, culminating in a combined Anglo-Russian force under the Duke of York being defeated by the French General Brume on 7th October.

With the courtesies of the time, the invaders were allowed to withdraw unmolested, none of the expedition's objectives having been met. The Dutch fleet, however, was no longer a force to be reckoned with, although British success here was offset by having suffered four ships wrecked on the coast.

As was customary, Britain waged economic war on the French through tight controls on sea-borne trade. The protracted period of hostilities had cost neutral shipping much in being forcibly prevented from carrying cargoes for the French bloc. Exasperated, Russia and the Scandinavians formed in 1801 a so-called Armed Neutrality, closely encouraged by the French. Denmark, seeking to conclude a separate agreement with the British, was sternly dissuaded by Russia and Prussia. The former was an ally of Britain but was offended by British actions. It was rumoured, too, that the Tsar was piqued by the British occupation of Malta, an island upon which he himself had designs.

Prussia in particular could damage British trade with the continent and being a land power was, militarily, effectively beyond British reach. The latter, newly unified with Ireland, resolved on a show of strength, euphemistically termed an 'armed negotiation'. In early spring, while ice still prevented any rapid concentration of the fleets of the neutral powers, a powerful British squadron was ordered to enter the Baltic. It would confront Denmark, Russia and Sweden in turn, presenting each with an ultimatum to withdraw from the union, a condition to be accepted within 48 hours on pain of having their fleets summarily attacked.

The First Lord, Earl Spencer, selected for his negotiating skills Admiral Sir Hyde Parker as senior officer, with Vice-Admiral Lord Nelson and Rear-Admiral Thomas Graves as subordinates. Of the Baltic fleets, Denmark could muster an estimated ten of the line, Sweden little more and Russia perhaps 20. Not holding their abilities in high regard and with an eye to shallow-water operations, the Admiralty allocated for the project just 18 of the line, supported by a strong force of frigates and smaller. The 98-gun *London* and *St. George* were designated flagships for Parker and Nelson respectively.

There was some disagreement in that Nelson proposed defeating the Russians first, following which the Scandinavians would probably come into line with no further action. Parker would not contemplate leaving undefeated hostile fleets in his rear. Sailing on 12th March 1801 the fleet concentrated in the Skagerrak while a frigate went ahead with an envoy to negotiate in Copenhagen. Again, Nelson disagreed, arguing that negotiations should be conducted from a position of strength, the fleet in full view of the capital. Not surprisingly, the Danes rejected British demands while overtly strengthening their defences.

It was now the 23rd. Nelson urged his superior to attack but chafed as the cautious Parker established whether the Danes and Swedes really did intend to resist actively. Only on the 30th did the fleet move, encountering nominal opposition from the Narrows' defences before anchoring short of the city. Copenhagen was fronted by shallows, on which the substantial Tre Kronor battery dominated the approach from the north. Seaward of the shallows, and parallel to the coast, lay two navigable channels, separated by a long middle ground. Along the inner channel, fronting the city, the Danes had established a line of 18 floating batteries, mostly older warships. Nowhere was there an appreciable depth of water, shoals abounded and navigation marks had been removed or shifted.

Nelson transferred his flag to the lighter draught *Elephant* 74 before reconnoitring from a small craft. As the wind backed from north-west to the southerly quarter he decided to attack from the south, navigating down the outer channel before rounding the lower extremity of the middle ground to engage the Danish line. Once the batteries were neutralised the way would be clear to confront and, if necessary, bombard the city itself. The nights of the 30th and 31st March were spent in surveying the approaches.

For the attack itself, Nelson was given seven 74s, three 64s and a 50, with 18 lesser. Parker, left with eight of the line, would lay just beyond gunshot to the north-east, ready to intervene as necessary, although faced with unfavourable wind and current. Late on 1st April Nelson moved his force to an anchorage near the bottom end of the middle ground and held a final briefing. With the fair wind, larger ships would require to anchor by the stern to maintain their heading and position while engaging the Danes. Gun-brigs would be positioned in groups to enfilade the enemy line. Captain Edward Riou of the *Amazon* would command a frigate squadron and a brace of fireships, and be ready to exploit any developing situation.

At 9.30 a.m. on the 2nd the fleet entered the inner channel and moved northward, less three ships, two of which had grounded. The absence of these three was critical, the now over-short British line having to employ Riou's frigates to take on the Tre Kronor. From 10.05 a.m. until about 1.00 p.m. the carronade was continuous, moving Nelson to write

Capture of the Guillaume Tell

The only French ships to escape the horror of the Nile were two of the line and two frigates. Of the former, the *Généreux* 74 was captured by the British on 18 February 1800 when the enemy tried to put a relief convoy into Malta, where the besieged garrison was starving. Laying at Valletta was the other Nile survivor, the 80-gun *Guillaume Tell*, with Ducrès aboard. Breaking out on 30 March she was captured, after a fierce resistance, by the *Foudroyant* 80, the *Lion* 64 and *Penelope* 36, entering the Royal Navy as the *Malta*.

Monmouth

Building as the East Indiaman *Belmont*, the *Monmouth* was purchased on the stocks and completed as a 64-gun Third Rate. As a new ship she was one of the most militant of those participating in the 1797 Nore mutiny. Eventually rejoining Duncan's flag, she fought at Camperdown and took part in subsequent operations to secure the Dutch fleet at the Texel in 1799.

later: "Here was no manoeuvring; it was downright fighting." The Danes resisted stoutly, reinforcing their gun crews from ashore. If a battery looked ripe for taking, British boats were unable to approach through the crossfire.

Parker had detached three further 74s to make up Nelson's strength but these could not make headway. The Commander-in-Chief, apprehensive of the outcome, signalled to discontinue the action. This resulted in the celebrated incident of Nelson invoking his blind eye to avoid seeing it, leaving the order for 'Close Action' flying. His judgement was correct for although some of his ships were by now badly cut up, the enemy's were, for the most part, virtually untenable. Only Riou's squadron, hopelessly outgunned, took advantage of Parker's signal. In disengaging, they were severely and continuously raked and Riou, a most promising officer himself, was killed.

Nelson sent a letter ashore under a flag of truce and addressed to the Danish Crown Prince. Two of Parker's 74s had at last got into the action but the Tre Kronor was adjudged too powerful to storm although the vice-admiral had to be firmly convinced of the folly of launching these ships at the fortification. By 3.00 p.m. the parleying was accompanied by a scaling-down of the ferocity of the action. It was to the benefit of both sides as some of the British ships had incurred damage to the point where it would be difficult to extricate them.

It was agreed that hostilities would be suspended for 24 hours. The Danes yielded their ships, aboard which the carnage exceeded anything that the war-seasoned British officers had yet witnessed. Nelson commented that the Danes had resisted for four hours what the French, however brave, would not have resisted for one. Retaining one ship for hospital duties, the British burned the remainder. Rated one of Nelson's great victories, Copenhagen could easily have been a disaster. Over 250 British dead and 700 wounded well exceeded the casualty list of the Nile. The Dane's total casualties lay between 1,600 and 1,800. As the Danes consented to an extended armistice and British reinforcements arrived, Nelson urged Parker to move quickly against the Russians, but the admiral dallied, unwilling to act without instruction.

Fortuitously, from the expedition's standpoint, the Tsar was assassinated on 23rd March. It was, however, the 5th May before Parker was effectively censured; Nelson was ordered to replace him. Nelson wasted no time. Leaving a force to watch the Danes, he despatched his best ships to the Gulf of Finland. It was far too late to catch the Russians icebound and the fleet had withdrawn to the secure base at Kronstadt. The Armed Neutrality was now, in any case, a dead letter. The firm lesson of Copenhagen and the accession of a Tsar of more conciliatory disposition resulted in a series of new agreements. With 22 of the line and 46 supporting ships, the Royal Navy remained in the Baltic until the following summer as a powerful instrument of policy. Nelson, never of robust health, had returned home in June 1801, and was relieved by Admiral Sir Charles Morice Pole.

Nelson's withdrawal had political undertones in that the nation was again apprehensive of French preparations for invasion. While it is probable that Napoleon had no intention of actually carrying out such an operation, Nelson's new appointment as anti-invasion supremo greatly calmed public nerves. Both nations were war-weary and, as the Pitt administration had fallen, the French threat was aimed at influencing his weaker successor, Addington.

*A Two-Decker and a Frigate
(Charles Brooking)*

The two-decker has her sternchaser gunports open. The cabins above could be transformed into gun positions too, but firepower ahead or astern remained very limited.

As mentioned above, the French during 1801 had made an unsuccessful attempt to relieve their army in Egypt. They were to make two further attempts before the arrival of General Abercromby's army made further effort superfluous. As this forlorn hope was being played out, a further French force slipped out of Toulon. *Contre-amiral* Durand-Linois with three of the line was bound for Cadiz, where six more ships of the line had transferred to French colours. With six Spanish, the force had been destined to raid the Tagus, but Portugal had by now been intimidated into accepting allied Franco-Spanish demands. It would either, therefore, be used for a further means to relieve Egypt or as a means of interdicting the continuous flow of British shipping using the Strait.

Sir John Borlase Warren, now based on Malta, was watching French activities, his frigates reporting Linois' departure on 13th June. The latter, believing Cadiz to be watched only by a pair of British 74s, was fortunate to learn from a prize that, in fact, a detachment of the Channel Fleet was present. Rear-Admiral Sir James Saumarez had arrived in the *Caesar* 80, accompanied by a half dozen 74s. The news made Linois divert to the bay of Algeciras, capturing en route the 14-gun brig sloop *Speedy*, commanded by the later-famous Lord Cochrane, then a commander.

Saumarez, alerted by the only British ship at Gibraltar, the 14-gun polacre-rigged sloop *Calpé*, responded immediately but, in calm conditions, could not arrive before 6th July. He found Linois anchored in line, close inshore in shallow water and covered by shore batteries whose location permitted flanking fire. His force was also supported by inshore gunboats, a potent nuisance in windless conditions. Efforts by Saumarez' ships to anchor precisely by the stern were frustrated by the lack of wind and, when the action began at about 9.00 a.m., they were not well located. The French were intent on warping closer inshore to prevent the British cutting inside.

The British *Pompée* 74, able to bring only part of her main battery to bear, was being worsted by Linois' flagship *Formidable*. Saumarez ordered the *Hannibal* 74 to "get athwart the Frenchman's hawse", i.e. into a raking position. This put her right on the edge of shoal water and, with no wind for proper control, she grounded under the guns of two Spanish forts. It was about 11.00 a.m. and, after about two hours of battering, the *Hannibal* surrendered. By then, the French were themselves deliberately grounded under the protection of the shore batteries and Saumarez, his ships increasingly damaged, was concerned at sharing the *Hannibal*'s fate. He called off the action at about 1.30 p.m., having to use ship's boats to tow the *Pompée* clear.

As Saumarez furiously refitted in Gibraltar, across the bay Linois was reinforced on the 10th by five Spanish line ships (including two 112-gun three-deckers and a 94) and a French-crewed Spanish 74. On the afternoon of the 12th this combined squadron sailed, followed by Saumarez with an 80 and four 74s. With the day well advanced, Saumarez feared that he would lose the enemy during the coming night and ordered the *Superb*, a fast sailer, to bring the enemy rear to action. Clapping on all sail Captain Richard Keats was, by nightfall, virtually out of sight of his colleagues.

At about 11.00 p.m. Keats could make out one of the Spanish 112s, the *Real Carlos*, in the darkness to port. Beyond was another, the *Hermenegildo*, and the *St. Antoine* 74.

The cutting-out of HMS Hermione 24th October 1799 (Nicholas Pocock)
Cruising off Puerto Rico on 22 September 1797, the *Hermione* frigate was seized by mutineeers who bloodily disposed of the deeply unpopular captain and nine others, mostly officers. She was sailed to La Guaira and joined the Spanish. On 24th October 1799, however, she was cut out by the boats of the *Surprise* 28. Retaken, she was renamed *Retaliation* (later *Retribution*). The mutineers were hunted down and hanged.

'The Explosion of the l'Orient'

The illustration shows the moored French line at the Battle of the Nile, doubled by Nelson's fleet. The fearsome blaze on the French flagship eventually reached the magazine, blowing her to pieces. Parts of the ship have been found recently, scattered all over the bay.

What followed bordered on farce. Yet unchallenged, the *Superb* put three broadsides into the unsuspecting *Real Carlos*, felling her foretopmast and setting her afire. She and her nearby colleagues then began firing at random, possibly at each other. Keeping clear, the *Superb* closed the *St. Antoine* and, by 1.00 a.m., had caused her to strike. This did not prevent her being additionally punished in error as each of Saumarez' ships caught up.

Unmanageable with her damaged rigging, the *Real Carlos* fouled the *Hermenegildo*, setting her alight. Soon after midnight both exploded and sank, killing some 1,700 officers and men. First in strong winds, then in light offshore airs, Saumarez pursued the allied main body. Both followed an inshore track and, by 5.00 a.m. on the 13th, the *Venerable* was able to open fire on the French *Formidable*. The latter had the better of the exchange, however, damaging the British ship's rigging to the extent that she grounded some 12 miles south of Cadiz. While her colleagues were delayed by her salvage, Linois safely gained the sanctuary of Cadiz. Saumarez was rewarded with a KB and a life pension for what had been a very smart action against considerable odds.

As the war drew to its close the Royal Navy had strength to spare and proceeded to relieve of their foreign possessions those powers that had supported Napoleon. Thus the

Virgin Islands from Denmark, St. Bartholomew and St. Martin from Sweden, St. Eustatius, Saba and Ternate from the Netherlands, and even Madeira and Timor from the Portuguese. It was the final lesson in unfettered sea power.

Following months of negotiation the warring nations finally agreed acceptable terms to declare a peace. On the 12th October 1801, King George III proclaimed the end of active hostilities, although the full instrument of peace was signed at Amiens only in the following March. Napoleon was more than a match for the timid Addington ministry, which yielded most territorial gains, although retaining the valuable islands of Trinidad and Ceylon. Most importantly for Britain, however, was that she had isolated and defeated the contagion of anarchic revolution which, for a considerable period, had threatened the very survival of the nation.

From the bruising years of war the Royal Navy emerged incomparably stronger than its primary opponent. Commencing hostilities with 135 ships of the line and 133 frigates, it finished with 202 and 277 respectively. By comparison, France had begun with 80 and 66, and ended with 39 and 35. What the Royal Navy had truly gained, however, was a complete belief in itself, a tradition of victory.

CHAPTER 8: *The War against Napoleon*

Cutting out the Chevrette 21 July 1801
(John Schetky)

Boats from the frigates *Beaulieu* and *Doris* made an unsuccessful attempt to cut out the French corvette *Chevrette* in Cameret Bay on the night of 20/21 July 1801. Unable to sail, the Frenchman was run under the protection of shore batteries and took aboard a party of troops. Nonetheless, the British, with further boats from the *Uranie*, attacked again during the following night and carried the ship. Twelve British and 92 French died.

The Peace of Amiens determined that the shape of Europe would not be decided by popular revolution, but it could not contain the activities and ambitions of Bonaparte. Shortly after the treaty was ratified in 1802 he was declared Consul for life with the overwhelming support of the French people. He used his mandate to deal ruthlessly with the remaining dissident elements, both Jacobin and royalist, and attracted back much French talent that had been forced to flee. He re-established relations with the Church and created a new aristocracy by elevating each of his 18 marshals to the status of Duke, with appropriate holdings and power. He re-cast the Executive, increasing the size of the Senate, the loyal upper house, while reducing that of the Tribunate and Legislative Corps, which opposed some of his early reforms. Difficult measures called for Orders in Council, but he did not hesitate when expedient to by-pass the Executive and appeal directly to the populus by holding referenda.

France re-discovered her pride and, justly drawing strength from his achievement, the First Consul again moved on to grander designs. Astute diplomacy, backed by real strength, saw France acquire the Louisiana Territory from Spain, enlarge Guiana by purchase from Brazil and, cheekily, to gain commercial privileges from Turkey for the 'return of Egypt'. Italian territory was added, while Spain ceded her portion of San

Domingo. Large French expeditions were despatched to this territory and to Haiti, long abandoned to insurrection. The scale of these enterprises was such as to cause the British to reinforce their Jamaica station. Crews that had been promised they would be paid off were ordered to the West Indies instead, triggering further fleet mutinies.

Armed intervention in Switzerland acquired France the Valais region while moves were made to take Malta, still British-occupied pending an effective means of guaranteeing the island's future non-alignment. Pseudo-scientific expeditions were despatched to India and Tasmania, Muscat and Egypt. To Addington's troubled ministry, French influence seemed everywhere. British tolerance was tried particularly by the continuing French occupation of Antwerp and the Dutch delta region. Nonetheless, gold reserves had been reduced to such a degree through the subsidising of foreign armies in the late war that ominous portents were ignored in the search for economies.

The Royal Navy, upon which so much depended, was a prime target. Earl St. Vincent, who had been created First Lord in 1801, carved ruthlessly into an organisation that was in peak condition. By concentrating on reducing manpower and material stocks, however, he was able to keep hull numbers virtually unchanged.

Public feelings were whipped-up by the popular press on both sides, that of the French demanding the return of reluctant emigrés and the British abandonment of Malta. Fully aware of the strategic value of these islands, Britain insisted on a further ten-year extension of tenure. As the French would not agree to this, nor to withdraw from Dutch and Swiss territories, the British ambassador was recalled from Paris in May 1803. On the 16th Britain declared war on France, anticipating its leader's similar intention once his fleet had been sufficiently re-built.

The Battle of Copenhagen 2nd. April 1801 (Robert Dodd)

The action at Copenhagen was unusual in being conducted against a fleet whose ships, for the most part, were unrigged and incapable of movement. Moored in a tight line, with shoal water close inboard, they could not be doubled, as at the Nile, while fresh guncrews could be brought from ashore. His own fleet depleted by several ships running aground, Nelson here leads his line in the *Elephant* 74

*Loss of the Magnificent 25 March 1804
(John Schetky)*

The watch on Brest was always fraught with
danger, the coast of Brittany being rocky,
with many outlying rocks and reefs, and
fierce tidal streams. The prevailing direction
for wind and weather is south-west, so that
the very conditions that prevented the
French breaking out presented the
blockaders with a lee shore. Just one of
many casualties, the *Magnificent* 74 was
wrecked on 25 March 1804.

Pitt, in opposition, had re-stated the historic truths that Bonaparte could triumph only
through direct invasion or by a sustained and successful onslaught on the British
economy. Addington understood this but did not intend to over-burden a successful
economy with an all-out war. He would not, therefore, contest French military
superiority within continental Europe, but the oceans, the narrow seas and the trade
routes would be British-controlled.

When his prestigious expedition to Haiti failed through the pernicious effects of yellow
fever, it dawned on the First Consul that overseas holdings could be a defensive
embarrassment in a new war. Jefferson's United States was thus surprised to receive a
French offer to sell Louisiana and the city of New Orleans for $15 million. Stripping
their treasury to pay for it, the Americans doubled their territorial area in December
1803, with lands extending from the Gulf to the Canadian border, from the Mississippi
to the Rockies. The so-called Louisiana Purchase greatly improved relations between
France and the United States which, between 1798 and 1800, had waged an undeclared
maritime war. France, convinced by the notorious Jay's Treaty of 1794 that the
Americans were bound by British demands, had commenced the seizure of British
cargoes from American merchant ships. This had provoked armed American retaliation
by a fledgling force re-created by the Navy Act of 1794.

In the wake of his Egyptian experience, Bonaparte determined to improve the state of
the French Navy. The revolutionary era had largely destroyed the base organisations,
and new supremos, termed Maritime Prefects, were appointed for each primary naval
port (Brest, Lorient, Rochefort and Toulon) as well as for Le Havre and Antwerp, which
were significant to plans for an eventual invasion of Britain. Answering directly to the
Minister of Marine, Admiral Decrés, each was senior to the port admiral and could
closely control all departments. A healthy ship replacement programme was initiated
and maintained stocks began to grow. The list of serving officers was culled of
deadwood, although many of those remaining had gained middle rank during the
upheavals and were of dubious quality. Like a later dictator, however, Bonaparte
followed a foreign policy which prompted a war before his plans for a fleet worthy of
his ambitions had come to fruition.

The British Admiralty, meanwhile, aware of coming hostilities, used impressment unmercifully to reverse the recent run-down in manpower. Orders had been given in early March for the Royal Dockyards to expedite ship commissioning. They responded well, for the 32 of the line available in early spring 1803 had grown to 53 by the opening of hostilities and 60 by early June. Proof of the innovatory quality of the yards came in their building of steam-powered bucket dredgers as early as 1802. These were invaluable in keeping open the approaches to the larger dry- docks, whose silting up had previously limited their availability to larger ships.

In France, the Low Countries and the German estuaries, every available yard was turning out small craft for Bonaparte's planned invasion. Their numbers were swelled by requisitioned fishing craft, while the public, buoyed by 'invasion fever', subscribed huge amounts. Logistics were such that the 100,000-strong 'Army of England' would need to be transported in two waves. "Let us be masters of the Strait for six hours", wrote the First Consul, "and we shall be masters of the World". His leadership was inspiring; he even struck a victory medal in anticipation of taking London. All that was required was to distract Admiral the Hon. William Cornwallis and the Channel Fleet.

The French fleet was not in a good position to do this. It was the intention to station ten Dutch-type 74s as an 'Escadre du Nord' at Flushing (Vlissingen), a satellite port to Antwerp, but these were not yet ready. Of 23 available French line ships, the unexpected British declaration of war caught ten of them overseas, nine of them supporting the Haiti operation and one at the newly-returned Indian enclave of Pondicherry. Twenty were completing refit in the major yards while 25 more were in various stages of construction. Only six ships of the line were ready for sea at Brest and seven at Toulon, although Britain had also to count as hostile ships of the so-called Batavian Republic.

The French ships of the line were recalled from the Caribbean. Cornwallis established a standing watch on Brest, together with cruising squadrons, but all the French ships made port. However, they were badly separated: five ended up at Ferrol/Corunna and a sixth at Cadiz. All were immediately blockaded.

With little immediate prospect of action for its major squadrons, the Royal Navy concentrated on using its smaller warships to disrupt French invasion preparations at the many small ports between Ostend and Granville. Any craft venturing to sea was liable to be quickly intercepted or, if run aground, cut out. While the sum total of damage inflicted was probably not great, it was excellent training and fostered an offensive spirit, while denying the same to the enemy.

Vice-amiral de Latouche-Tréville and the Toulon squadron was covered by Vice-Admiral Nelson in the *Victory* 100, with five more of the line present and four on detached duties. This squadron was in poor material state, for which Nelson was highly

The French 74 Rivoli

The ship is modelled as supported by a 'camel' on either side. Camels were rectangular, tank-like structures which could be ballasted with water, attached to a ship and then pumped out to give the ship extra stability or a reduced draught. They were used either in salvage operations, to refloat a grounded and flooded vessel, or to move her in shallow waters. Note how shrouds obstruct the quarterdeck guns.

Barham

Charles Middleton, later Lord Barham, is remembered for his organisational abilities rather than for high-profile action at sea, and the success of the Royal Navy during the long years of hostilities between 1793 and 1815 owed much to his precise control and attention to detail. He was also the greatest force for reform in the Navy during the later years of the 18th century.

He was born in 1726 to a Leith family without influential connection. His time at sea was comparatively undistinguished but he gained his commission in 1745. Thirteen years later he shone sufficiently to be promoted directly to post-captain, commanding the *Emerald* and *Adventure* frigates in the West Indies. The peacetime years of 1763 to 1775 saw him on half pay but, with the outbreak of the American war, he was again afloat in a succession of ships. In 1778 he was made a Comptroller of the Navy, a post that he was to hold for the next 12 years.

Even without further sea time his progress was steady. He was created a baronet in 1781 and won the parliamentary seat for Rochester in 1784. Already over 60, he attained flag rank in 1787. As vice-admiral in 1794 he was appointed to the Board of Admiralty, achieving First Lord in 1805. A full admiral already for ten years, he was now elevated to the peerage, taking the title of Lord Barham, by which he was latterly known.

Barham restored a sense of correctness to the post of First Lord, his predecessor having been impeached for misappropriation of public funds. He was responsible for the Service's administration and strategy, the latter never better than when, soon after his appointment, he made the correct fleet dispositions to bring about Trafalgar. Having never flown his flag at sea Barham, for all his ability, was widely regarded in the Service as a 'political animal'. He finally retired in 1806 aged 80, but lived on for a further seven years.

critical of the dockyards. To be closer to Toulon than either Gibraltar or Malta, he used a new anchorage at Maddalena on the Strait of Bonafacio, using his frigates to cruise outside the French base.

French colonies, so recently returned by treaty, were quickly seized again. Thus, between June and September 1803, small expeditions took St. Lucia, Tobago, Dutch Guiana and the Indian enclaves. The disastrous French operation in Haiti and San Domingo had already cost the interception and seizure by the British of several useful corvettes and gun-brigs. Hard-pressed by well-led native forces, the remaining French on the island faced massacre. A British-brokered agreement averted this by arranging that the packed French ships that remained could sail, discharge a nominal broadside, then hoist British colours in surrender. Not only did France thus lose control of this large and valuable island but their attempts to hold it had cost some 40,000 lives, including those of 20 field officers.

In the Indian Ocean *Contre-amiral* Durand-Linois, with the *Marengo* 74 and three frigates, was tasked with re-establishing French administration in Pondicherry before basing himself on the Ile de France. A scratch, but more powerful British squadron, possessed of poor intelligence or insufficient energy, was unable to prevent Linois from creating nuisances as far apart as Muscat and Java. Early in 1804 Linois intercepted one of the East India Company's periodic China convoys. Indiamen carried light armament

Chasse-Marée

The three-masted, standing lug rig of the Chasse-Marée does not look particularly elegant but offered high speeds on some points of sailing, although requiring a large crew. The type was used widely by the French for privateering and smuggling. Note the characteristic long bumpkin extending aft to spread the mizzen.

East Indiamen repulse French squadron 1804

Early in 1804 a French squadron under *Contre-amiral* Linois intercepted the annual British convoy from China. Unescorted, this valuable group of 16 Indiamen and 15 others were all armed and painted-up like warships. Under their commodore, Nathaniel Dance, the Indiamen manoeuvred as a squadron, covering the remainder whilst engaging Linois with their weak armament. The bold face unnerved Linois, who broke off the action.

and were accustomed to defending themselves from pirates and privateers. They were painted-up warship style and operated with much of the regular navy's discipline. On being approached, Commodore Dance adopted a tight formation which left Linois uncertain. When the three largest Indiamen were detached to imitate an escort line, the French commander did not risk calling the bluff and withdrew.

Earl St. Vincent's reforms of the Royal Dockyards following the Peace of Amiens included appointing Commissioners to examine every aspect of fleet support. Ever the disciplinarian, the Admiral saw everywhere 'abuses and frauds', and castigated the Chatham yard as a vile sink that beggared all description. Transparently honest himself, he was naive in failing to comprehend that graft was not confined just to contractors and artisans but reached to the very top. Frustrated in being unable to dismiss existing Commissioners, he had the Navy Board censured for failing in its duty. The ever-fragile relationship between the Admiralty and Navy Board was sorely tried, to the embarrassment of the Prime Minister, Addington.

At the other end of the scale the First Lord also alienated the timber contractors. Grouped as the powerful 'Timber Trust', they retaliated by converting a general shortage of ship timber to an outright dearth. Ships, including Nelson's, were being brought forward by patching main timbers or using second-hand sections. Cordage began to face a crisis for the very same reasons. As the rate of commissionings fell, St. Vincent, well-meaning but inflexible, began to attract wide criticism.

Addington's hopes for an inexpensive war also looked like foundering as recruitment was grossly mismanaged. Losing an important vote, Addington decided to step down and, in May 1804, Pitt was again in power. A stern critic of the First Lord he had him replaced by Viscount Melville. Melville promptly threw his predecessor's policies into reverse. Appeasement of contractors came expensively, but ships again began to re-commission at better than two per month. St. Vincent, however, made loud and continuous justification for his policies while the Commissioners uncovered earlier financial irregularities, dating from the period when Melville had been Treasurer. Unsuccessfully impeached, Melville resigned, to be replaced by probably the greatest-ever senior administrator, Admiral Sir Charles Middleton, later created Lord Barham.

Throughout 1804 French Channel ports, from Ostend to Etaples, hosted ever-increasing numbers of invasion craft. Against the thronged anchorages the British even used fireships and craft packed with powder, but to little effect. There remained to the French Navy the problem of assembling a force powerful enough to hold the Strait for sufficient time. At Toulon, Latouche-Tréville could still muster less than a dozen of the line, and ignored Nelson's enticing withdrawals. The French commander's untimely death that summer left the Emperor (as Napoleon had crowned himself) in a quandary. With few likely candidates for his successor, *faute de mieux* he promoted *Contre-amiral* Villeneuve. Stolid, rather unimaginative, never one to take risks, Villeneuve was not inspirational and Napoleon down-rated the role of the Toulon squadron to one of diversion.

Only five ships of Villeneuve's late squadron were at Rochefort, which left the 20 at Brest as the primary force. These

Christian VII
In September 1807 the Danes were obliged to surrender their fleet on pain of Copenhagen being destroyed by Gambier's expedition. The *Christian VII* was a 90-gun two-decker taken into the Royal Navy, initially as the *Blenheim*, and subsequently widely copied. Her structure predated Seppings in featuring a type of round stern, and for the same reasons.

were commanded by *Vice-amiral* Honoré Gantaume, who lived under something of a cloud as 'The Man who Failed to Relieve Egypt', and they were closely invested by detachments from Cornwallis's Channel Fleet.

To distract Cornwallis and to release the five line ships still in Spanish ports, the French proposed an elaborate diversionary plan. Despite Nelson's presence, the Toulon squadron would transport a strong military force to the West Indies, seizing the island of St. Helena en route. They would be met in the Caribbean by the Rochefort squadron, now commanded by *Contre-amiral* Bourges-Missiessy, and take St. Lucia and Dominica on opportunity. Such activities would, it was anticipated, cause the British to send a substantial force in response. This would find nothing for, having reinforced the garrisons of Guadeloupe and Martinique, the combined French force would have doubled back to Spain, released the five trapped ships and returned to Rochefort, a base difficult for the British to blockade closely.

Spain's close defensive alliance with France, which obliged her to provide up to 15 of the line and military support when required, was an embarrassment at a time when the nation wished to remain neutral. Napoleon, however, was not in a forgiving mood. He

gave her three options: join him against the British, pay him a subsidy of like value, or have France declare war on her. Spain opted for the second. Unusually, the British recognised that she was acting under duress and continued to respect her neutrality in spite of advantages to the enemy, including haven for his ships and a ready market for prizes taken by French privateers.

Napoleon then obliged Spain to repair and refit his ships. When their crews, as belligerents, were allowed freely to cross Spanish territory, Britain issued a formal warning. Recognising that Spain's attraction lay not in her military potential but in her wealth, and that such wealth comprised mainly bullion shipments from Spanish South America, the government instructed the Admiralty to order squadron commanders to allow general Spanish shipping to pass freely, but to bring those carrying bullion to a British port. There they were to be detained as surety for Spain restricting her assistance to France to within treaty limits.

The inevitable clash occurred in October 1804. Four Spanish frigates, suspected of carrying bullion, were intercepted by four larger British frigates outside Cadiz. As the latter did not constitute 'overwhelming force' the senior Spanish officer was honour-bound to resist. Following an exchange of fire, one of his frigates blew up. On 12th December 1804, Spain declared war on Britain.

The grand combination movements of the Rochefort and Toulon squadrons did not go smoothly. On 11th January 1805 Missiessy sailed in the 120-gun *Majestueux*, with four others of the line, three frigates and 3,500 troops. The force failed in an attempt to take Dominica and, as Villeneuve did not arrive within the specified period of 35 days, Missiessy returned, arriving back at Rochefort on 20th May. Villeneuve sailed on 17th January with 11 line ships, seven frigates and 3,500 more troops. Four days out, his squadron was overtaken by a violent storm which scattered his ships, caused extensive damage and obliged him to return to port. The admiral was depressed by both the material state of his ships and by the poor standard of seamanship evident throughout the squadron. Nevertheless, Villeneuve's sally caused Nelson great problems. His

Top left: Amiral Villeneuve (1763 - 1806)

A victim of his own success under the Republic, the Comte de Villeneuve was promoted contre-amiral at age 33. Commanding the rear at the Nile battle just two years later, he escaped with four ships, but the experience left him an indecisive pessimist. For lack of choice, he was given command of the Toulon squadron in 1804. Believing that, even combined with the Spanish, his fleet was no match for that of the British, he fought Trafalgar only under threat of being superseded. Placed under house arrest on returning to France in 1806, he committed suicide.

watching frigates had raced back to Maddalena with the news that the French had sailed from Toulon, heading south. Nelson, fearing a military operation against Sicily or even Egypt, wasted weeks sailing as far as Alexandria, and back via Malta.

Gantaume, with 21 of the line and 20,000 troops, was ready at Brest, but closely watched. Napoleon's new plan was for Gantaume to break out, link with the Rochefort squadron and raise the British blockade at Ferrol. Here, he would collect *Contre-amiral* Gourdon's five French ships and such Spanish ships as were available, and make for Martinique. There he would rendezvous with Villeneuve, who was to sail from Toulon via Cadiz in order to pick up a further Spanish contingent. Having drawn off the major part of the British fleet in pursuit, Gantaume would double back and, with the combined

The Battle of Trafalgar 21 October 1805 (Turner)

Turner was less interested in accurately portraying a historical incident than using it as a vehicle for his experiments with the effects of light. Scale here counts for little than to magnify the three-decker, the loftiness of her masting, and the billowing of collapsing towers of canvas. Like Mather Brown, Turner reduces his human detail to a medium through which is expressed the mood of the moment.

Santissima Trinidad

This 130-gun four decker, built at Havana, was fortunate to escape after the action at St. Vincent in 1797. At Trafalgar she was engaged by a succession of British ships, finally striking to the *Prince* 98. Badly damaged, she was scuttled on Collingwood's orders on 24 October 1805.

allied fleet, sweep up the English Channel to establish command of the narrows. At the Texel, nine ships of the line and 80 transports were poised to embark 25,000 troops. A second major group around Boulogne would bring the total to 130,000 troops, who could be shifted within two tides.

With the slow maturing of this threat Melville, the then First Lord, had bolstered the building programme with orders to bring forward every reserve ship capable of being commissioned. For the moment, Keith was guarding the narrows from the Downs anchorage with only 11 small ships of the line. Cornwallis, with the major task of blockading Brest, disposed of anything between 11 and 24, depending upon commitments. On 23rd March 1805 there were just 15 British ships present and Gantaume proposed using his extra strength to break out and start the operation. This was forbidden by the Emperor. Napoleon's view was that there was no justification for risking the force to win a naval victory that would serve no purpose. The Brest squadron was required complete and was, therefore, to escape without fighting. As usual in French naval policy, the mission was paramount.

Fatigued and frustrated, Nelson was re-victualling at Palma on 31st March when the frigate *Phoebe* arrived with word that Villeneuve had left Toulon. Hampered by light conditions, the French took until 6th April to reach Cartagena, only to find the Spanish contingent yet without orders. With Nelson's whereabouts unknown, Villeneuve did not dally. Passing the Strait during the night of 8th/9th April he proceeded, as instructed, to Cadiz. The small British blockading force could not prevent him collecting a French 74 and six Spanish ships of the line under the able Vice-Admiral Federigo Gravina. The combined squadron sailed immediately for Martinique, arriving on 14th May with the instruction to await Gantaume for 40 days. Poorly served by both intelligence and weather, Nelson did not sail from Gibraltar in pursuit until 11th May.

Although Cornwallis had to go ashore for health reasons, his successor, Admiral Lord Gardner, kept the grip on Brest as tight as ever. Gantaume, ready to break out in mid-April, desisted on learning that his 21 of the line would be met by 24 British. Napoleon chafed, despatching *Contre-amiral* Magon de Médine from Rochefort with a pair of 80s to tell Villeneuve to extend his wait to a month after Magon's arrival, which was on 29th May. After one month, he should return to Ferrol to rendezvous with 15 French and Spanish sail of the line. Gantaume was instructed that, if he was unable to sail before 20th May, he should remain at Brest until Villeneuve, now with 35 of the line, arrived from Ferrol and drove off the British squadron. Then, with a combined strength of 56 ships of the line, they could drive up Channel.

Nelson, blessed by a good passage, arrived in Barbados on 4th June, but could get no news of Villeneuve's whereabouts. The latter had done little to further the seizure of British islands and when, on the 8th, he heard of Nelson's arrival, he abandoned a planned landing on Barbados, despatched his military force to Martinique by frigate and, on the 9th, sailed for France. Learning of this, Nelson left on the 13th for Gibraltar, which lay in his Mediterranean command. Critically, Nelson despatched a fast brig to inform the Admiralty of his progress and intentions. Taking a more northerly track, the brig sighted Villeneuve and her captain, appreciating that he alone knew the location of both fleets, made all haste. Barham, in receipt of the information on 8th July, assumed the French to be bound for Brest or Ferrol, and made dispositions to cover both. Cornwallis, back in command, was to leave frigates to watch Gantaume and to cruise with his main strength to the south-westward. Rear-Admiral Sir Charles Stirling was to lift his watch on Rochefort and take his five liners to reinforce Vice-Admiral Sir Robert Calder's force off Ferrol. Once combined, the group was to cruise about 100 miles off Cape Finisterre. In the event of either Cornwallis or Calder intercepting

Collingwood

Cuthbert Collingwood was born in 1750 in Newcastle-upon-Tyne. With no influential connections he joined the Royal Navy as a volunteer. His gallantry while in charge of a naval party supplying the military during the 1775 battle on Bunker's Hill earned him an instant commission. Strangely, this was offset in the following year through his being tried, and admonished, by court-martial. While both lieutenants, Collingwood and Nelson became firm friends. Gaining the attention of the Commander-in-Chief, the former began a succession of moves that shadowed those of his colleague. These included to the brig *Badger* as commander and to the *Hinchinbrook* 28 as post-captain. Both were fortunate to survive the disastrous Nicaragua expedition of 1780, following which Collingwood took command of the *Pelican* 24, only to be wrecked during a hurricane off Jamaica. For a further five years he held commands in the West Indies but was at home on half pay between 1786 and 1790.

War in 1793 brought him a post of flag-captain to Admiral Bowyer and in his ship, the *Barfleur* 98, he fought at Howe's victory of the Glorious First of June in 1794. During Jervis' victory at Cape St. Vincent in 1797, Collingwood and Nelson fought shoulder to shoulder in their own commands, the 74s *Excellent* and *Captain*. Drearily employed in blockading Cadiz, Collingwood missed the Battle of the Nile.

He gained flag rank in 1799 but enjoyed a quiet spell until 1803, when a new war saw him with Cornwallis, blockading Brest. Made vice-admiral in 1804, he hoisted his flag in the *Royal Sovereign* just ten days before Trafalgar. At that battle, he led the lee line, smashing the Spanish flagship *Santa Anna*. It was his sad duty to take command following the death of his friend.

Raised to the peerage, he was kept on in the Mediterranean. Here he fell ill in 1810, dying on that station

Villeneuve, the location would be far enough out to sea to prevent the latter being reinforced from Brest or Ferrol.

Late in the morning of 22nd July 1805 Calder was steering southward in patchy fog which cleared to reveal the Franco-Spanish fleet. In three divisions and with a following breeze it was heading about east-south-east for Ferrol. The British were approaching at right angles from the northward and both fleets re-formed into line of battle. In poor visibility, the action opened at about 5.00 p.m.. Neither admiral could exert proper control and a mêlée developed, with some ships fighting at odds, others being unable to see the enemy. Copious gunsmoke hung in the wet air so that some ships were reduced to firing at the 'sound' of guns. Most of the damage to Calder's ships was to their rigging, although there were also 200 casualties. Two Spaniards, an 80 and 74, were dismasted and taken, having alone suffered 500 casualties, but the action was unsatisfactory.

By the dawn of the 23rd the fleets were separated by some 17 miles, the conditions hazy, with very light airs. Outnumbered, Calder formed up between his cripples, his prizes and Villeneuve but the latter, obeying his injunction to avoid battle, took no further action. By evening the fleets were beyond visual contact. Calder faced heavy criticism and later a court-martial. There he was severely reprimanded for being too intent on safeguarding his two aged prizes and making insufficient effort to renew the action which, if decisive, might have ruined French intentions there and then.

Villeneuve, who appears to have been in a state of almost clinical depression, put into Vigo on 28th July to land about 1,000 sick personnel. Calder had to stand offshore in a storm, enabling the French admiral to slip out with 15 of the line, arriving off Ferrol on 2nd August. Having here augmented his strength to 29, he was exhorted by his Emperor to link quickly with the Rochefort squadron and go on to raise the blockade of Brest. Such official expectations, however, seem to have unnerved the unfortunate admiral who, instead, anchored at nearby Corunna. Here he remained, undiscovered by the British until a frigate sighted him on 9th August.

In sufficient strength to keep the allied fleet blockaded, Calder sailed northward, joining Cornwallis on the 14th. Fortunately, Nelson had heard of the French fleet's arrival in Spain and had returned on his own initiative. Arriving on 15th August with 11 of the line, he increased Cornwallis' strength to 34. The allies were, of course, still divided, with 21 ships of the line at Brest, 29 with Villeneuve and the five from Rochefort still somewhere at sea.

Villeneuve had left Corunna on 10th August and was sailing half-heartedly northward. Unknown to him, dispositions were suddenly in his favour, for Cornwallis committed a strategic blunder. Having effected a concentration in the Western Channel, in exactly the right place, he now divided it, despatching Calder southward with 18 of the line, leaving 16 in the Channel. Villeneuve, with 27, was in a position to defeat the British in detail. The Emperor was ready with his Army of England at the Strait. Politically, he needed a significant victory to offset increasing isolation. Russia and Sweden had aligned with Britain, while Prussia was a very hostile neutral. Following the Emperor's recent coronation as King of Italy, Austria then joined what became known as the Third Coalition. To the French it was imperative to strike at the coalition's keystone, Great Britain. Everything depended upon Villeneuve.

On 5th August Villeneuve had despatched the frigate *Didon* to find the Rochefort squadron, temporarily commanded by *Contre-amiral* Allemand. She had not returned by the time that Villeneuve had to sail but, on the 14th, the latter sighted three ships. Two were British frigates and one of them, the *Phoenix*, was towing a disabled prize — the *Didon*. Making no attempt to retake her, Villeneuve then spoke a neutral, which informed him that the British were attached to a force that included 25 of the line. The dispirited admiral, with even the winds against him, decided to exercise a long-lapsed option and to make for Cadiz. Vice-Admiral Collingwood moved his small force aside to let the allies enter, whereupon the watch was resumed.

With 35 enemy ships now concentrated it was the Royal Navy's urgent task to keep them locked in Cadiz. Collingwood was joined by further detachments under Bickerton and Calder then, finally, by Cornwallis. By 30th August Villeneuve, still railing against the quality of his ships and crews, was precariously contained by a force of 26. Napoleon's rage at Villeneuve was absorbed by his opening a decisive military campaign against the Austrians.

The huge allied fleet soon emptied the Cadiz arsenal of its material and the surrounding district of its food. Its sick over-filled the hospitals. With his Emperor

Battle of Trafalgar: The end of the action (Nicholas Pocock)

By about 5.00 pm on 21 October 1805 the Battle of Trafalgar was effectively over. No British ships were lost but half were more or less immobilised. At left, the French *Achille* is blazing, soon to blow up. In the distance, Dumanoir makes his escape with the Allied van. Collingwood, faced with deteriorating weather, has to bring in seventeen prizes and over 7,000 prisoners. Of his own crews, 1,700 are casualties.

Far left: Trafalgar

The chaos of a major fleet action is here well conveyed, as was its point-blank nature. We see the *Victory* locked with the *Redoutable*. Note the studding sail boom irons on the *Victory*, the fittings that first fouled the Frenchman. And the French sharpshooters at her foretop, from where they did so much damage. The tangle of the *Victory's* rigging, fallen on the disengaged side. Note the peppered topsails of the ship on the left, presumably *Téméraire*, and her missing topgallant mast ...

apparently already discounting an invasion of Britain, Villeneuve received conflicting instructions to assist in Italian waters and to operate against trade, the latter hardly a task for a battle fleet.

On 28th September Collingwood handed over the Cadiz blockade to Vice-Admiral Lord Nelson, who had arrived with another pair of 74s. His policy was to keep his main strength well out to sea, linked visually by frigates to a small force cruising off the base approaches thereby, it was hoped, enticing Villeneuve to make a break. New arrivals brought Nelson's strength to 33 but, as groups of six were sent in rotation to Gibraltar for fresh water, available strength was 27.

Villeneuve knew that a replacement, *Vice-amiral* le Comte de Rosily-Méros, was on his way to Spain and that he would shortly have to return to explain his actions. As Napoleon had written to Decrés, the Minister of Marine, referring to the admiral's 'excessive pusillanimity', it is fair to assume that Villeneuve expected to be faced with imputations of cowardice.

As the wind shifted to a favourable easterly quarter on 19th October 1805, the allied fleet weighed, prior to a move into the Mediterranean. Warned by his frigates, Nelson moved to block the Gibraltar strait. In company were captains who had fought with him at the Nile and at St. Vincent, trusted friends who understood him implicitly. They knew well his plan of attack, which was to cut the enemy line at two points, at about 12 ships from the rear and about three ships ahead of the centre or where the flag was to be found. The centre and rear were then to be turned and destroyed as the van was blockaded by the British rear. On the main business having been achieved the enemy van would be engaged if circumstances permitted.

On the 20th the allied fleet was steering north and west in a south-westerly breeze, gaining the necessary offing to lay a course directly through the strait but also keeping Cadiz to leeward as a refuge for ships damaged in a battle that appeared inevitable. The main body of 21 comprised the van, under the Spanish Vice-Admiral Don Ignacio Maria de Alava, and a rear under the French *Contre-amiral* Dumanoir le Pelley, about Villeneuve's centre. The remaining 12 of the line, under Admiral Gravina, were located to windward, as a 'mobile reserve'. They were organised in two divisions of six, the junior division commanded by the French *Contre-amiral* Charles Magon de Médine.

During the night of 20/21st October Villeneuve ordered the fleet to wear together to form a line of battle. This reversed the order, and daylight found a ragged formation with Dumanoir leading Villeneuve and Alava, with Gravina formed up as rearguard. Villeneuve had thrown away an initial advantage conferred by superior numbers. Villeneuve's written instructions show that he anticipated Nelson's chosen form of attack, yet he persisted in meeting it with an over-long and unwieldly line of battle. This now headed southward on the starboard tack with Cape Trafalgar some ten miles distant on its port beam. It was a pleasant autumn morning, with very little wind, although a long swell from the west presaged a blow.

Characteristically, Nelson wasted no time in formal manoeuvre, signalling at 6.40 a.m. to form two columns and to clear for action. With the advantage of the west-north-westerly breeze, the British bore down at a stately two knots, the weather column of 12 ships led by Nelson in the *Victory* and the lee column of 15 headed by Collingwood's *Royal Sovereign*. At 8.30 a.m., Villeneuve again ordered his line to wear together. This took until 10.00 a.m., reversing its order and putting it on a roughly northerly heading. The British steered more to the north to cut off their access to Cadiz.

Nelson's final approach was risky as it exposed his lead ships to a raking fire, against which they could little reply. His intention to mitigate this by virtue of a slightly oblique

Santa Ana
The 112-gun *Santa Ana*, flagship of de Alava, lay in the centre of the Allied line at Trafalgar. Heavily engaged by Collingwood's *Royal Sovereign* and the *Belleisle*, she was eventually dismasted. She struck but was one of the prizes that the British fleet could not secure, and was retaken by Cosmao's frigates on 23 October.

Téméraire

Temeraire is seen here near the end of the battle. Captain Harvey was immediately astern of the *Victory* when she broke the French line. Damaged by the French *Redoutable* and *Neptune*, she succeeded in grappling the former. On her disengaged side she disabled the *Fougueux*, which also fell aboard her. Forty-seven of her crew were killed, but both enemy ships were taken.

Euryalus towing the Royal Sovereign

As dusk drew in, the victors of Trafalgar were threatened as much as the vanquished. A rising gale from the southwest was accompanied by an unpleasant sea, while only seven miles to leeward of the many dismasted ships lay the shoal waters off the cape itself. Here, Henry Blackwood's *Euryalus* frigate is struggling to tow Collingwood in his badly-damaged *Royal Sovereign* further offshore, later handing over to the larger *Neptune*.

run-in was confounded by the light conditions. On the other hand, the allied fleet's generally disordered formation decreased the possible concentration of their fire. The allied line stretched for some five miles. The approaching British columns were about a mile apart. Four of Nelson's five lead ships were three-deckers; Collingwood had only the one. Nelson's mark was Villeneuve's flagship, the 80-gun *Bucentaure*, twelfth in line and conspicuously led by the giant 130-gun *Santissima Trinidad*. Collingwood's aiming point was Alava's flagship, the *Santa Ana* 112, six ships to the right. The British ships were under full canvas, with studding-sails and royals, while their bands played rousingly.

Almost on the stroke of noon the *Fougueux* 74, immediately astern of Alava, opened fire on the approaching *Royal Sovereign*. Others joined in but their poor practice little hurt Collingwood, who deigned no response until, passing at last under the *Santa Ana*'s counter, he raked her with a crashing, double-shotted broadside that dismounted 14 of her guns and inflicted nearly 400 casualties. Freshly coppered, the *Royal Sovereign* had drawn well ahead of her next-in-line, *Belleisle* which, with barely steerage way, took a further quarter hour to arrive. Thus unsupported Collingwood fought the *Santa Ana* muzzle to muzzle on one broadside while, on the other, endeavoured, not altogether successfully, to keep four others, two French and two Spanish, from approaching to a raking position.

By 12.30 p.m. the leading eight of Collingwood's lee division were heavily engaged. Dense powder smoke hung in the still air, stabbed by the red-orange ripple of regular broadsides. Confusingly, many ex-prizes carried their original names, so that the British *Tonnant* was engaged with the French-manned *Algeçiras*, while the British *Colossus* fought it out with the French *Swiftsure*. Uncertain of the identity of Villeneuve's flagship, Nelson continued to steer at the towering *Santissima Trinidad*. For the half hour after midday the *Victory* attracted fire from all quarters. Without reply, both ship and company suffered badly. As custom demanded, her officers moved calmly about, commending the waiting guncrews while setting a disciplined example.

Not until nearly 1.00 p.m., sails and rigging shredded, decks already bloodied, did the British flagship finally get into action. Double-and even triple-shotted, her port broadside slammed through the stern galleries of the *Bucentaure*, causing carnage the length of the gundecks. There was no gap for the *Victory* to exploit: the French *Neptune* and *Redoutable* had closed virtually into contact with their admiral. Grazing the *Bucentaure*, yard to yard, the *Victory* rounded gently, laid alongside and grappled the *Redoutable*. The upper decks of both ships became untenable, *Redoutable*'s swept by the *Victory*'s 68-pounder carronades, firing langridge, *Victory*'s the target of French sharpshooters stationed in the tops. In full uniform, and coolly walking his quarterdeck with Captain Hardy, Nelson made an attractive and easy target. He was fatally wounded by a musket shot about a quarter hour from the commencement of the duel.

Supported briefly by the French *Neptune*, the *Redoutable* made to board the *Victory* but, with the intervention of the British *Téméraire*, was eventually obliged to strike with over 300 of her people dead. Although in a good position to assist their Commander-in-Chief, the *Neptune* and the *Indomptable* 80, together with two Spanish Third Rates, took it upon themselves to fall out and to assist the rear. None was eventually taken but their action opened a crucial gap, fully exploited by Nelson's powerful lead ships, which disabled the *Fougueux* as she attempted to close off the breach.

As the allied line ghosted northward the British lee column assumed an increasingly acute angle relative to its rear. Collingwood signalled for a line of bearing to starboard, having sufficient ships to engage opposite numbers as well as to double the tail and attack from leeward. Despite their centre and rear being heavily engaged, Dumanoir and the ten allied van ships remained beyond the action for two hours. At about 2.00 p.m. Villeneuve ordered them to come about and ease the pressure. A heavy swell and still fitful breeze caused them to take an hour to comply. Most of them survived, but their inaction enabled the British to destroy the allied centre.

Although many ships of the allied fleet — the *Bucentaure* herself, the *Santissima Trinidad*, the *Intrépide* and *Neptuno* —fought courageously, they struck their colours by mid-afternoon. By holding off the indecisively-led allied van, the British had created a local numerical superiority. Individual French and Spanish ships often had to face two or more opponents.

At the extreme tail of the line, Gravina, in the 112-gun *Principe de Asturias*, suffered badly in trying to prevent Collingwood doubling the rear. He himself had suffered what

The frigate Canonnière v. HMS Tremendous (Crepin)

The *Tremendous* 74 and *Hindostan* (sic) 50 were escorting a convoy of eleven Indiamen off the South African coast when, on 21 April 1806, they were cheekily accosted by the French 40-gun frigate *Canonnière*. Out-manoeuvring the 74, the frigate caused her considerable damage aloft before being chased off. Built as the French *Minerve* in 1794, then captured by the British and serving under the same name, she ran aground and was re-captured by the French, taking the name *Canonnière*. Sold out in 1809 and renamed *Confiance*, she was captured again in 1810 by the British.

In July 1805 Sir Robert Calder was cruising about 100 miles west of Cape Finisterre and had the good fortune to fall in with Villeneuve. In line ships the British were outnumbered 20 to 15 but Calder tried to cut off the enemy rear. The weather was very foggy and the fleets proved to be uncontrollable. Calder took two prizes but was considered by a subsequent court martial to have concentrated too much on preserving these and not sufficiently to bringing the enemy to decisive action. For this he earned a severe reprimand. The *Prince of Wales* 98 here wears Calder's flag as Vice-Admiral of the Blue, flanked by the *Repulse* (left) and *Defence* 74s.

proved to be a fatal wound and, at about 4.30 p.m., seeing that Villeneuve had been obliged to surrender, he decided to break off the action. Five French and five Spanish ships accompanied him in the direction of Cadiz and safety. The British were left undisputed masters of the field. They had taken 17 and sunk one, but hard fighting had left many with severe damage. The wind, so fickle during the action, rose steadily to a southerly gale and, nursing injured spars, British and prizes alike slowly pulled to the westward to gain sea room.

Taking advantage of British difficulties, Commodore Cosmao-Kerjulien on the 23rd led five of the Cadiz survivors back to sea to retake several prizes that were still clearly in sight under tow. As small compensation, Alava's great *Santa Ana* was recovered from her small prize crew, but at the cost of two others wrecked. Only four prizes were actually brought in by the British, the remainder foundering or cast adrift, abandoned to their complements or destroyed.

The allied defeat at Trafalgar was profound, but not yet fully done. Off Ferrol lay Captain Sir Richard Strachan with five of the line and four frigates. His brief was to apprehend Allemand's Rochefort squadron and, when his frigates sighted a group in southern Biscay at the end of the month, it was assumed at first that Allemand had been found. It was, however, Dumanoir, still endeavouring to reach safety with four of the line, two of which were much injured. In the stormy conditions, his only hope lay in flight. Strachan's force was much scattered by the weather but his frigates worried at the enemy until he formed a line of battle. This wasted so much time that, off Cape Ortegal, they were obliged to stand their ground to Strachan's main force. All were taken.

The final balance for Trafalgar, therefore, was a loss of 22 ships to the allies, with no British loss. Against 250 British dead and 1,200 wounded the allies, subject to contradictory reports, suffered between 5,000 and 7,000 all told. Many were drowned with the loss of the prizes subsequent to the action. Idolised and mourned by the nation, Nelson had died a hero's death. Not so Villeneuve. Repatriated in 1806, he was forbidden to return to Paris. Awaiting official instructions, he committed suicide, paying with his life for his single catastrophic failure. Dismissively, his Emperor pronounced his final verdict: "A gallant man but without talent".

Trafalgar confirmed British naval supremacy but did not end the war. With invasion no longer an option, the French concentrated on the ruination of the British economy.

As a strategy it was never likely to work, but resulted in a further decade of dour struggle in which two great nations edged toward bankruptcy rather than submit. Napoleon sought on the one hand to embargo British goods through cowing or cajoling European states, while on the other maintaining a direct assault on British shipping through the French talent for privateering.

The smashing of Austro-Russian military power at Austerlitz in December 1805 re-emphasised French supremacy on land. France and Britain were akin to the tiger and the snake, each dominant in its own element but ill-matched for a mutual trial of strength. By decree, Napoleon declared that Britain and her spheres of interest be blockaded. The so-called Continental System was designed to shut off her trade, with all the rigours of confiscation for any neutral flouting the rules. Britain, however, since the beginning of the Industrial Revolution was effectively the world's workshop, and French industry was yet too narrowly-based to compensate. In addition, French sea power was insufficient to sustain an effective blockade.

British resolve suffered a major setback in January 1806 with the early death of Pitt. In the divided 'Ministry of all the talents' that followed, Charles James Fox was the influential Foreign Secretary charged with seeking an accommodation with Napoleon. Fox had admired the Emperor for having steadied his nation following what he considered to have been a justifiable revolution. He was disillusioned, nevertheless, as Napoleon, far from dispirited by events at sea, became ever more demanding in his conditions for peace. Each military success made him more intractable and Fox himself died, frustrated, in September 1806.

Britain countered French decrees with Orders in Council that required, in turn, the search and clearance of all neutral shipping. The difference, of course, was that she was well able to enforce such conditions. After Trafalgar there was a shift of emphasis away from the main battle squadrons, which now lacked an opponent worthy of the name, toward smaller ships capable of harassing the enemy's business right up to his shoreline, and to cruisers necessary both to apprehend his privateers and to escort the convoys by which friendly trade was protected. An immediate result was a rapid increase in the number of commanders, lieutenants and masters populating the Navy list, for this was a young man's war and commands were readily available. The drudgery of convoy work would be leavened by the occasional prospect of a cruise, with its promise of prize money. Once condemned by an Admiralty Court, the proceeds of the sale of a prize and her cargo went to her captors and their Commander-in-Chief. Prize money was the mainspring of incentive, particularly after the Crown decided to waive its share in perpetuity.

While the trade war resulted in a great rise in the number of single-ship actions, the line squadrons were far from inactive. The Brest fleet, spared the disaster of Trafalgar, was re-organised into two raiding squadrons to carry the war to distant British trade and her overseas territories. The first, six of the line under *Contre-amiral* Jean-Batiste Willaumez, was to head for the Cape before returning via the West Indies and St. Helena. The other, of five ships under *Vice-amiral* Corentin-Urbain Leissègues, was to reinforce French military strength on San Domingo before annoying the British in the area of Jamaica. Should the Royal Navy prove here to be in too great a strength, Leissègues was to proceed to Newfoundland to disrupt the fisheries.

A storm on 13th December 1805 allowed both squadrons to emerge together as Cornwallis' blockaders were forced out to sea. Believing that only seven French line ships were out, the British Admiralty was slow to react, although the measure of its response suggested good intelligence. Vice-Admiral Sir John Borlase Warren was to proceed with seven of the line to Madeira for orders, probably to the West Indies. Six more line ships would, under Rear-Admiral Sir Richard Strachan, head for the Cape, via St. Helena. The alarm had been raised by the frigate escort of two convoys which had sighted the French shortly after they had separated on 15th December. One frigate encountered a squadron of six of the line commanded by Vice-Admiral Sir John Duckworth. On his own initiative (for which he was later heavily criticised) he had lifted the Cadiz blockade to investigate a reported sighting of the much sought-after Rochefort squadron. He actually found Willaumez but, although in adequate strength, he failed to keep contact on the grounds that his ships were scattered. Short of water, he then made the curious decision to move on to the West Indies to top up. At St. Kitts he was joined by a pair of 74s, then a sloop which brought news of French activity at San Domingo.

Arriving there on 6th February 1806, Duckworth discovered Leissègues' squadron, complete with supply ships. Slipping their cables, the five French ships hurried to sea, forming line as they went. Duckworth formed two columns, of four and three respectively. With a brisk following wind, events proceeded quickly, the numerically superior British cooperating efficiently. Within two hours, Leissègues' flagship, the 120-gun three-decker *Impérial* (late *Vengeur*) had been crippled by exchanges with up to four British and, together with a 74, was run aground. Both were later burned by boarding parties. The remaining three were taken although one foundered from the damage she had received. It had been a smart little action, but credit was due primarily to the initiative of individual captains; Duckworth himself used the *Superb* flagship very cautiously.

Willaumez, meanwhile, had reached the Cape. Finding it to be in British hands, he moved on to the West Indies. Having taken a handful of small prizes, he had the good fortune, on 6th July 1806, to arrive off St. Thomas, where the British were assembling a large convoy of some 180 sail. Its cover, a squadron

Hibernia
Completed in 1805, the *Hibernia* was
intended to be a sister ship to the *Ville de
Paris*, the first British-built 110-gun First
Rate. During construction she was
lengthened to accommodate 120 guns in
the standard disposition of 32-pounders on
the gun deck, 24-pounders on the main
deck and 18-pounders on the upper deck.
She enjoyed a 50-year active life, followed
by a near equal period on harbour service.

Sidney Smith

Ever a free spirit, William Sidney Smith defies categorisation. Born in 1764, he joined the Royal Navy at 13 but made such an impression at the battles of Cape St. Vincent and the Saintes that Rodney made him a post-captain. He was then just 18. Rather than face half-pay in 1789-91, Smith advised the Swedes in their war with Russia. Rewarded with a knighthood by the Swedish King, the 27-year old had the honour recognised by George III and, thereafter, was known to his many detractors as the 'Swedish Knight'.

With war again against the French in 1793, Smith volunteered to destroy their many ships laying in Toulon, when that base was about to be abandoned by the Royalists to the victorious Republicans. Although risking life and limb, however, Smith and his party could destroy only a quarter of the 60-odd ships present.

His boldness was legendary. In 1795 he sailed the frigate *Diamond*, under French colours, into the Brest approaches, actually speaking an unsuspecting anchored enemy 74. To better interdict coastal traffic he seized and garrisoned two small offshore islands. Personally leading the *Diamond*'s boats to cut out a French privateer, Smith was captured. He spent 1796-8 in a French jail but then, typically, escaped.

As a commodore in 1799, Smith commanded a squadron working against the French army in Egypt. Involved, through his brother, with the Turkish Porte, he used ships and shore parties, led by himself, to thwart the French siege of Acre.

Unorthodox inshore operations, whether in the Levant or in French and Dutch waters, were Smith's forte. In 1805 he gained flag rank, commanded a squadron under Collingwood in the Mediterranean, and was with Duckworth when he forced the Dardanelles in 1807. In that same year, as Napoleon moved against Portugal, Smith's powerful squadron, led by the *Hibernia* 120, blockaded the Tagus and transported the Portuguese royal family to Brazil. Smith's behaviour in Brazil was, however, so high-handed that he was recalled and, in 1810, was appointed Pellew's second-in-command in the Mediterranean.

Following the war with France, Smith, a full admiral, retired from the sea and settled in France. He died in 1840.

under Rear-Admiral the Hon. Sir Alexander Cochrane, was too weak to attack but its aggressive stance caused Willaumez to move on, missing a great opportunity. The French admiral seemed content to cruise but, where neither Warren nor Strachan had brought him to action, occasional sightings and reports of his presence caused the British some anxiety. In August 1806 Strachan arrived again in Barbados with seven of the line and was close enough for both squadrons to encounter the same great seasonal storm. One of the French 74s, the *Vétéran*, commanded by the Emperor's younger brother Jérôme, simply headed for France, while four more suffered considerable rigging damage. One of them, the *Impétueux* 74, was sighted limping northward by three of Strachan's ships. She was pursued into the Chesapeake where, in fine disregard for American neutrality, the British took and burned her. Four more of Willaumez' squadron sought refuge in American ports, only two ever returning.

The greatly-expanded Royal Navy list of the time included a number of officers who, in addition to achieving flag rank, could also be described as 'characters'. Sidney Smith and Thomas Cochrane spring immediately to mind but, lesser known, is Rear-Admiral Sir Home Riggs Popham. Highly unconventional, Popham had already incurred Their Lordships' displeasure with a little private enterprise during the earlier war, but had expiated his sin somewhat by developing the useful, vocabulary-based flag signalling system which, carrying his name, was adopted officially in 1803.

The month before Trafalgar, Popham, still a captain at 43, sailed for the Cape with a scratch squadron and 6,000 troops, more than adequate for the task of seizing Capetown from a Dutch garrison of only one-third that number. After Trafalgar Popham, who styled himself as 'Commodore', found himself with considerable forces but little threat. Before he sailed, he had tried to interest the First Lord, Melville, in an organised intervention in South America, where the various states were chafing under continued rule by Spain. Melville was not in favour but Popham now had both the means and the opportunity. His motive remains obscure, a mixture of adventurism and altruism, with a chance for personal gain.

Borrowing a regiment of men and some artillery Popham left for the Plate estuary. By the time that his declared intentions reached the Admiralty he was, of course, beyond the recall that immediately followed. Arriving in mid-June 1806, in the depths of the southern winter, Popham found that his deeper-draught ships could not easily navigate the poorly-charted, shoal-strewn and extremely shallow estuary. He used them to blockade Montevideo (on the north bank) and the main approaches while his smaller ships landed a naval brigade near the opposite settlement of Buenos Aires. This was taken and successfully ransomed for one million silver dollars, despatched immediately to Britain.

The army contingent was left ashore without any real policy or objective.

The Spanish rallied in the August and counter-attacked. Stormbound offshore, the Navy could not assist and the British had to surrender. Unable to approach Montevideo, Popham responded by seizing nearby Maldonado in October 1806. During the following month Popham's nemesis arrived in the person of Rear-Admiral Charles Stirling. Popham was sent home, court-martialled and severely reprimanded for leaving the Cape station without authority. It affected his career but little, for the City of London made him a presentation in recognition of his defence that he was engaged in seeking new markets and, before the war's end, he was elevated to flag rank.

The Plate campaign stumbled on into 1807. Montevideo was eventually taken but a bad failure against Buenos Aires resulted in abandonment and a general withdrawal. Had the British come promising early independence, they would have been hailed as liberators. As things were, the local population saw itself as about to exchange one set of colonial rulers for another when, in reality, what they desired was neither.

In the course of 1807, Britain began again to be concerned about Napoleon's access to a battle fleet. Through conquest, treaty and general intimidation, Spanish, Portuguese, Dutch and Russian, and soon, Swedish and Danish fleets could conceivably be available from states too weak militarily to resist French demands. As in 1801, Britain moved to pre-empt the possibility, again against Denmark first.

On 1st August 1807 Admiral James Gambier arrived off the narrows with a fleet of 17 of the line and a score smaller, later considerably reinforced. A demand to the Crown Prince for custody of his fleet was refused, so Gambier moved down to confront Copenhagen, where he was joined by troop transports. As discussion dragged on, the

Duckworth's action off San Domingo 1806 (Nicholas Pocock)

Late in 1805 two French squadrons, commanded respectively by Willaumez and Leissègues, were on the loose. On 1 February 1806 some of Leissègues' ships were sighted off San Domingo (now the Dominican Republic) where they had landed troops. A British squadron under Sir John Duckworth intercepted them on the 6th but the Admiral lacked resolve. Two French, including their flagship, the 130-gun *Impérial*, were driven ashore. Here, the French flagship duels with the *Northumberland* 74.

Far left: Hood's action off Rochefort 1806 (Francis Sartorius)

Five French frigates and two corvettes broke out of Rochefort on 25 September 1806, with troops and supplies for the West Indies. They were intercepted almost immediately by Commodore Sir Samuel Hood with a 98 and five 74s. This superior force took four of the enemy, although the *Monarch*, in engaging three of them at once, was badly cut up about the rigging.

Bucenataure

Completed in Toulon in 1804, the 80-gun *Bucentaure* became the flagship of Vice-Admiral Villeneuve. Her first real action was the indecisive brush with Calder in July 1805. At Trafalgar, however, she became the objective of several British ships and, considerably damaged, she finally struck to the *Conqueror*. The British prize crew were then overpowered by the *Bucentaure*'s men, only for the ship to be wrecked in the gale that followed the battle.

military was landed to set up siege batteries. The 1st September saw a final British ultimatum rejected, resulting in a week's bombardment of the capital. Following much damage and loss of life, the Danes capitulated. It had been a most distasteful task but Gambier took control of over 70 Danish warships, including 18 of the line.

Toward the end of 1806 France had begun to put diplomatic pressure, backed by implicit military threat, on the Turks to close the Black Sea exit to the Russians. The latter, allies of the British, had internationally-agreed treaty rights to navigation through both the Dardanelles and the Bosphorous. As the Porte vacillated, the British brought in a small squadron detached from Collingwood's Cadiz blockading force. Under Rear-Admiral Sir Thomas Louis, it based itself outside the Dardanelles, on the island of Tenedos. As relations worsened, its frigates brought out the ambassadors, theirs staffs and commercial communities.

Under pressure from the Admiralty, Collingwood sent reinforcement and a more senior commander, Vice-Admiral Sir John Duckworth. On the 10th February 1807 Duckworth arrived at Tenedos, bringing the total force to eight of the line and four smaller. His brief was to 'do a Copenhagen' by anchoring off Constantinople and securing custody of the Turkish fleet on pain of bombarding the city. Duckworth, despite having in support able subordinates such as Sidney Smith, Dacres and Blackwood, appeared to be seized by self-doubt, his communications with Collingwood being reminiscent of those of Villeneuve.

Aware that the Turks were adding to the fortifications of the straits, he was concerned that, if the squadron forced its way up to the capital, it would then be unable to extricate itself. Rapid action was called for, but there came only procrastination. Eventually leaving Tenedos on 11th February 1807, Duckworth lay inside the Dardanelles for a period awaiting a fair wind. Further progress then involved a desultory exchange of fire with forts until, at Nagara, the force encountered a Turkish squadron. First to open fire, it was forced ashore and burned, the adjacent fortifications being blown up by landing parties. Thus reasonably heartened, Duckworth arrived off the capital on 20th February. He and the ambassador then conducted a feeble exchange of discussion with the Turks, who merely played for time. Exasperated, Duckworth sailed past the city in line of battle, a warning completely ignored by the Turks, whose available naval force was greatly inferior. Thus, snubbed, the admiral took no further action, withdrawing down the straits pursued by a hail of shot from every fort. For this miserably-conducted affair the well-connected Duckworth was never called to explain himself.

The wearying watch on Brest was being conducted early in 1809 by Admiral Lord Gambier. Seasonal gales forced him offshore in the February allowing *Contre-amiral* Willaumez to slip out with a powerful group comprising the 120-gun *Océan*, two 80s, five 74s and four smaller. His orders were to chase off the British force blockading Lorient, release the French ships within and then, combined, repeat the process at Rochefort. Thus suitably reinforced by six more of the line and eight frigates, Willaumez was to sail without delay for Martinique and Guadeloupe, both badly in need of re-supply.

As Willaumez sailed coastwise a British 74 raced ahead to warn Captain John Beresford off Lorient. With only three ships he was obliged to stand off. Willaumez was here disappointed, however, for the wind and tide were not suited to allowing Commodore Troude's force to sail. Not daring to delay, Willaumez pressed on for Rochefort. He arrived during the night of 23/24th but, again, a patrolling British frigate had warned the blockaders, here three of the line under Rear-Admiral the Hon. Robert Stopford.

Watching the French squadron enter the Basque Roads, the anchorage to seaward of Rochefort, Stopford despatched the *Naiad* frigate to appraise Gambier of the situation.

Cochrane

Probably the greatest proven leader never to have commanded a British fleet in battle, Thomas Cochrane was born in 1775, son of the ninth Earl of Dundonald in Lanarkshire. He first went to sea with the Royal Navy at 18 but, as lieutenant, was censured by court-martial for disrespect. Given command of the 14-gun brig *Speedy* in 1800, Cochrane was in his element. Having taken several smaller French and Spanish craft, he went on to capture the 32-gun frigate *El Gamo*. Unorthodox in every way, Cochrane made many enemies and, as captain, still held command of the *Speedy*. When she was captured by a French squadron in 1802, he was again tried by court-martial for her loss.

Appointed in 1805 to the command of the *Pallas* 32 and, in the following year, to the *Impérieuse* 38, his exploits along the French Biscay coast were the stuff of adventure stories. Cochrane was made KB and was, by 1806, also a Member of Parliament. He engaged in bitter public controversy with his Commander-in-Chief, Lord Gambier and, when the latter was absolved by court-martial for his conduct in the Basque Roads, began a personal crusade against corruption in high places. The Admiralty brought him ashore.

Involved himself in a City fraud in 1814, he was quickly dismissed by both Service and Parliament. He therefore took employment abroad, fighting with distinction in the liberation struggles of Brazil, Chile, Peru, and Greece. He succeeded to the family title in 1831 and, in the following year, was reinstated into the Navy with the rank of rear-admiral. A full admiral by 1851, his final service was as Commander-in-Chief on the North American station. Although in his late 70s, he was keenly disappointed to have his offer of service in the Crimea refused. In old age, he busied himself with scientific invention. He died in 1860.

She immediately signalled the approach of three sails. These proved to be large French frigates. Commanded by Commodore Pierre Jurien, they alone of Troude's Lorient force had managed to sail and, according to orders, were making to join the concentration at Rochefort. Already dogged by two of Beresford's ships, Jurien now saw Stopford coming up in response to the *Naiad*'s call. He thus made for the nearest haven, the tiny port of Sables d'Olonne, where he anchored under the cover of shore batteries. They stood little chance, however, against the larger British ships; all drove ashore and were destroyed. Both Stopford and Beresford then resumed their watch on Rochefort. Here Willaumez had found Commodore Faure's group simply not ready to sail. It was imperative that he break out while the watching British were still in inferior force and a major squabble developed between the French commanders. They were relieved, the overall command being given to the capable *Vice-amiral* Allemand.

French opportunity finally evaporated on 7th March 1809, when Gambier arrived. Eleven line ships now blockaded 11 but the British were joined by two dozen assorted frigates, sloops, gun-brigs, bombs and cutters. Neither Gambier nor Allemand were aggressive commanders. The Admiralty urged Gambier to use fireships to smoke out the French but this served mainly to encourage him to take elaborate precautions against similar attack on himself.

Allemand, meanwhile, arranged his fleet at anchor so as to resist assault. All major ships sent down their upper masts and yards and were moored in a staggered, double line so placed as to give mutual support and to cover each gap. The approach was blocked by a stout boom, tended by armed launches. On 19th March Captain Lord Thomas Cochrane was summoned by the First Lord, now Lord Mulgrave. They were in full agreement about attacking the French with fireships and Cochrane was asked to lead the operation under Gambier's direction. Aware that his lack of seniority would cause friction, he accepted only with reluctance. Cochrane was also on poor terms with Gambier. A nephew of Admiral the Hon. Sir Alexander Cochrane, he was also a Member of Parliament and, in a politically-divided navy, he and Gambier were on opposite sides. He was, however, familiar with the

Cheerful

A widely used type in the Royal Navy and a cutter in the classic sense, the *Cheerful* spreads a gaff mainsail on a boom, main course and topsails, a fore staysail and two jibs. For good measure, she has also set studdingsails. Her substantial rig and armament of twelve 12-pounder carronades demanded a crew of fifty. Completed in 1806, she was sold out in 1816.

Basque Roads and was an inspirational leader. He joined Gambier's force on 3rd April, followed by William Congreve (of rocket fame) on the 6th, and a dozen fireships on the 10th. Although having adequate force Gambier, in his despatches to the Admiralty, betrayed, like Duckworth, a fundamental lack of confidence.

The attack went in on the night of 11/12th April 1809. The boom was breached by a pair of 'explosion vessels' whose crews, including Cochrane as a volunteer, bravely stayed aboard until the last minute, suffering burns and injuries while experiencing great difficulty in reaching their designated rescue craft. Immediately following the disintegration of the boom came a line of fireships. Although a fearsome sight, fireships are imprecise and the correct procedure for the French would have been to shift only if directly threatened. Three of their frigates, stationed as pickets inside the boom, were unable to halt the blazing ships by gunfire. Soon, they were under fire from their own ships which, one by one, were panicked into slipping their cables. With little means of manoeuvre, they ran foul of each other.

By first light the bulk of Allemand's force was aground with just two (*Cassard* and *Foudroyant*) at anchor, having kept their heads. None had yet been destroyed, yet all were defenceless to a rapid follow-up. From 6.00 a.m., Cochrane, close in aboard his frigate *Impérieuse*, urged Gambier to attack but his admiral only eventually closed for further bombardment. By midday, French ships were refloating and moving up-river to safety. Cochrane, beside himself, engaged an enemy 50 without orders but this precedent encouraged others in support so that, by 4.00 p.m., several of the enemy were taken. The opportunity was gone and the protesting Cochrane was eventually recalled by Gambier and packed off home with the despatches. Achieving nothing further of note, Gambier withdrew on the 29th.

Having put themselves in an entirely hopeless position, the French had been let off with the loss of four of the line and a frigate. Cochrane let it be known that, through Parliament, he would oppose any public recognition of Gambier. The latter then demanded a court-martial to clear his name. A compliant Admiralty convened a sympathetic court which granted Gambier an honourable acquittal. Cochrane was given no further sea appointment by the Admiralty for over 20 years. Napoleon, as usual, summarised the affair succinctly, labelling the French admiral an 'imbécile', the British as bad. Cochrane, like Sidney Smith, had fallen victim to his talent for self-promotion and a natural ability to make enemies in high places. Like Smith, however, he was highly valued elsewhere and, between 1817 and 1827, he successively held high rank in the fleets of Chile, Peru, Brazil and Greece as these nations fought for, and achieved, their independence.

The imposing edifice of Napoleon's continental Europe was, by now, showing signs of instability. Denmark and Portugal had been intimidated into his 'Continental System' but, once again, the Danish fleet had been taken from his control. A French army corps, entering Lisbon, found that here, too, the British had spirited away the fleet, this time with the Court and the Treasury. Spain, France's long-standing ally, had allowed rights of passage for this force and had, indeed, tolerated the presence of French garrisons on her soil. Now, however, Napoleon exploited a rift between King and infante to pass the throne to one of his younger brothers, Joseph Bonaparte. As his troops moved in to underpin the situation, the Spanish revolted, formally declaring war on France on 4th June 1808. The Spanish looked to Britain for support and France embarked on the long, debilitating Peninsula War.

A first French loss was the squadron of *Vice-amiral* François Etienne Rosily, whose *Neptune* 80 and four 74s had long been blockaded in Cadiz by a British force. The last survivors of Trafalgar, they were commissioned into the Spanish fleet.

During late 1808 Napoleon overran northern Spain at the head of some 300,000 troops. The overall plan was to secure the capital before fanning out to occupy the provinces and Portugal. It was disrupted by comparatively small British military forces, commanded by Lt. Generals Wellesley and Dalrymple. These had been landed by the Royal Navy during the previous August, and it was upon the Navy that the British Army depended for support during the long campaign to come.

Whether Napoleon still entertained a distant prospect of invading Britain is not clear but the Scheldt river now harboured the reality of the completed 'Escadre du Nord'; ten 74s under *Contre-amiral* Bourgues-Missiessy. A major marine arsenal had been created at Antwerp but lack of water required Missiessy to be based down-river at Flushing (Vlissingen). This had been arranged with the 'King of Holland', another of Napoleon's brothers, Louis. As a further ten ships of the line were building on the river, Britain resolved on military action, with troops advancing along either bank, supported directly by the Navy.

From May 1809 was assembled an enormous force. With little threat at sea, the Navy was able to concentrate 37 ships of the line (several partly disarmed for the carriage of horses), two 50s, 26 frigates, 60 minor warships and 120 tenders. The army of 39,000 and its impedimenta required 400 transports. The naval operation was to be conducted by Rear-Admiral Sir Richard Strachan and the military by Lt.General the Earl of

Caledonia

In Exmouth's opinion 'the finest ship of war in the British Navy' the 120-gun *Caledonia* was a superb sailer and extensively copied. As completed in 1808, she shipped the classic 32/24/18-pounder armament. She was soon upgunned to mount 24-pounder Congreves in place of the 18s, and was then spoiled by adding one foot to her beam in order to accept an all 32-pounder battery. Not finally paid off until 1856, she served in a variety of roles for a further twenty years.

Chatham (Pitt's brother). Involving months of preparation, the impending operation became one of the war's worst-kept secrets, allowing the French more than adequate time for preparation. The Scheldt estuary was good defenders' country. Its north bank comprised islands, the south extensive marshland. The apparently spacious lower reaches were cluttered with shoals. Ten miles below Antwerp the river contracted suddenly at Lilloo, where the French constructed a substantial boom and fortifications manned by naval gunners.

The British began operations on 28th July 1809 and took only three weeks to occupy the lower reaches, the south bank and the islands. This large area, however, had greatly attenuated Chatham's forces, while the unhealthy flooded flat-lands caused a rash of 'polder fever', with 14,000 men stricken. Missiessy's squadron had retreated up to Antwerp and it was learned that, suitably lightened, they could be taken up a further 15 miles. Chatham, described by the French as a 'temporiser' and by the British as being occupied 'exclusively by his health and his turtle soup', brooded on his faltering progress, reports of the strength of the Antwerp defences and of the 35,000-strong French garrison on his flank at Bergen-op-Zoom. Before the end of August he had convinced his subordinate commanders of the futility of proceeding further. Slowly, over several months, in good order and to the disbelief of the French, Chatham's forces withdrew.

The year of 1810 was comparatively uneventful at sea. True, the French had in commission nearly 60 ships of the line, but these were well dispersed and, with no discernible policy, enjoyed little sea time. British squadrons maintained their watch - Strachan on the Scheldt, Gambier on the Channel ports, Collingwood and, later, Cotton in the Mediterranean. Spare capacity was employed profitably, to seize again Martinique and Guadeloupe, Cayenne in French Guiana, the Ile de France (Mauritius), a major haunt of privateers, and much of the Dutch East Indies including, eventually, the huge island of Java.

A dearth of major fleet action made more brilliant that fought by Captain William Hoste. His three frigates and a 22-gun Sixth Rate comprised the sole Royal Navy strength in the Adriatic. Based on Ancona was a Franco-Venetian squadron of six frigates and four smaller, commanded by a noted cruiser captain, Bernard Dubourdieu. On 13th March 1811 the British, based on the island of Lissa, sighted the enemy approaching. He was carrying troops to take the island and, considerably outnumbering Hoste, formed a double line of battle and attacked.

Hoste hoisted the inspiring signal 'Remember Nelson' and maintained an exceedingly tight line which, supported by excellent gunnery, the enemy proved unable to break. In brisk conditions the British moved together like a drill line, even managing to force Dubourdieu's ship aground. Hoste's line was doubled and his ships considerably damaged, although his carronades caused considerable execution. With Dubourdieu out of the action it was his force that finally broke, although the British were too heavily damaged aloft to obey Hoste's signal for 'General Chase'. The enemy lost two ships and a third, which had struck, escaped as she could not be boarded, an action deemed at this time to be thoroughly dishonourable. Unusually for a small-ship engagement, all four British captains were awarded gold medals and, as was customary, their first lieutenants were each advanced to the rank of commander.

The French Navy continued to grow but was manned, if manned at all, by a high proportion of raw conscripts. Many trained seamen were drafted into the insatiable maw of Napoleon's armies. There was increasing unrest throughout

Saturn

Along with her sisters, *Elephant*, *Excellent* and *Goliath*, the *Saturn* was cut down from a two-decker 74 to a 58-gun frigate in 1813 as an interim response to the large American frigates. Although she appears at first sight to be still a two-decker, the upper is only a light spar deck, retaining longitudinal hull strength and strong enough to support 42-pounder carronades.

France at the expenditure of manpower - 600,000 into the Peninsula (where half died) then, in June 1812, a further 600,000 into Russia. Nations tired of French domination and the constrictions of the 'Continental System'. Britain was no longer able to bring naval power to bear so effectively but things began to go her way. As she wearily pursued the wholly unnecessary war with the United States (see following chapter) she could count on having ranged Denmark and Sweden, Spain and Portugal, Austria and Prussia, Russia and the new United Netherlands against the French. Despite the odd brilliant success, Napoleon was now tasting military defeat, even having to face Wellington on French soil. His great dream soured, he abdicated in April 1814. Appropriately, it was the British *Royal Sovereign* yacht that returned Louis XVIII to France, and a British frigate, the *Undaunted* 38, that carried the ex-Emperor to Elba.

Napoleon's sudden return in February 1815 caused the Royal Navy, already running down, to go again onto a war footing. It had little to do, however, before Waterloo in the June settled the issue finally. A month later, off Rochefort, Napoleon presented himself to Captain Maitland of the *Bellerophon* 74. His final voyage was from Plymouth to total exile at St. Helena in the *Northumberland* 74.

The British Foreign Secretary, Castlereagh, took the realistic view that a lasting peace would result only from imposing upon France conditions which France herself considered fair. The Treaty of Paris, signed in November 1815 was, therefore, less than onerous. She was confined to her old frontiers of 1790 but had restored the majority of her lost colonies, Britain retaining the small but key territories of Malta, Tobago, St. Lucia and the Indian Ocean islands. Britain shielded her from the harsher demands being made for reparations, but her fleet had to be reduced by one third. Holland and Belgium were linked, the Scheldt and Antwerp being opened at last to general trade. Britain retained the Cape and Guiana but restored Java to the Dutch.

The French Navy during the Napoleonic War had not performed near as well as in earlier hostilities. Its ships were designed as well as ever; the problem lay in the legacy of the revolution, with its lasting effect on the officer corps, the crews and the support structure. Close blockade worked well for British policy, greatly controlling the

Forcing the passage of the Sound 1807 (Robert Dodd)

In 1807 it appeared that Napoleon's pressure on Denmark might intimidate her into closing the Baltic to British trade, and even into handing over her fleet. Admiral James Gambier was despatched at the head of a powerful British fleet to put the Danish fleet beyond French reach. On 3 August Gambier exchanged gun salutes with the fortress of Elsinore as he headed for Copenhagen.

maritime war at tactical and strategic levels, and also, through confining the French to their ports and protected roadsteads, denying them the exercise of seamanship and gunnery that the Royal Navy could take for granted.

Major failings, however, came right from the top. Napoleon himself little understood the principles of sea power. His choice of Minister of Marine, Decrés, was also unfortunate for, as commodore of the French frigate squadron at the Nile, he had had to watch, helpless, as Nelson savaged his battle line. Traumatised by the experience, he advised his Emperor in a negative manner, with little evidence of boldness. The adoption of full-scale *guerre de course*, although damaging to British interest was, itself, an admission of defeat for, as a policy, it could never win the war. Further, the privateers always attracted the best seamen who, taken in large numbers by British cruisers, spent the remainder of the war languishing in prison hulks.

Napoleon aboard the Bellerophon (John James Chalon)

A month after Waterloo Napoleon, unable to escape to the United States, surrendered himself to Captain Frederick Maitland of the *Bellerophon* 74, anchored in the Basque Roads. Maitland sailed immediately for Torbay, thence Plymouth, from where the defeated emperor sailed in the *Northumberland* for St. Helena and exile. Hopes of a glimpse of the *Bellerophon*'s guest produced these regatta-like scenes.

CHAPTER 9: *The War of 1812*

The long years of turmoil in Europe enabled the United States to prosper. French mercantile activity was greatly reduced by the Royal Navy and new trading opportunities were created for neutral carriers. Of these, many were Americans who, able to move freely without recourse to the restrictions of convoy, began to challenge the pre-eminence of British operators in areas where near-monopoly had previously been taken for granted. By the beginning of the new century, France had effectively ceased to challenge British naval superiority and sought, by all possible means, to destroy the British economy, notably by closing Continental Europe as a market and by a direct onslaught on her merchant marine.

Various Napoleonic decrees were countered by Orders in Council, edicts which carried the authority of the King and his principal advisors. These defined the nature of 'contraband', those cargoes owned by enemy interests or which, once imported, would further his ability to continue warlike activities. They defined also the rights that, as a belligerent, Britain assumed to stop and search neutrals for such cargoes, and the means of their ultimate disposal. While neutrals could not be punished for exercising their trading rights in international law, Britain did not shrink from firm means of persuasion to discourage a neutral carrier from again trading with the King's enemies. Trading patterns were already hostage to restrictions imposed by either warring faction but were well worthwhile because of the huge hikes in freight rates resulting from the wars.

The greatly-expanded Royal Navy suffered a chronic manpower shortage. On the North American station this situation was exacerbated by men jumping ship to seek a new life, often using their skills in American-flagged ships. As a result, American merchantmen were frequently stopped by British warships for the impressment of British subjects. The practice enjoyed dubious legality and was resented deeply by Americans for its high-handedness. New states are notoriously prickly about their rights but, here, the Americans also felt helpless to oppose what they held to be an infringement of their rights. Resentment erupted into anger when, on occasion, a British deserter was removed only to be summarily hanged or, all too often, when a crewman removed was in fact a bona fide American citizen.

Following the secession of the colonies, British Orders in Council barred American ships from trade with the West Indies and British ports, while limiting the range of goods that could be American-sourced. The expanding American merchant marine thus sought markets further afield, largely in the Mediterranean. Like other maritime nations, it here suffered the attentions of Barbary Pirates. Operating out of ports from Morocco to Libya, these skilled corsairs virtually supported their states through preying on shipping in the narrow confines of the western Mediterranean. Regular traders either paid 'protection money' or found their ships and crews seized for ransom.

American operators demanded armed escort in vain, for, as noted above, the Continental Navy had been dissolved in 1785. There were no warships. George Washington's election in 1789 was, however, followed quickly by the adoption of a national constitution which, among much else, provided for the maintenance of a navy, to be funded from commonly-contributed taxation. Nothing happened immediately as a result of widespread hostility to the creation of permanent armed forces. A final stimulus, however, was an accommodation reached between European powers and the

Constitution

The most famous of the American heavy frigates, the 44-gun *Constitution* earned the nickname of 'Old Ironsides' when her massive construction defeated British 18-pounder shot. During her career she captured or sank the British frigates *Guerrière* and *Java*, and the sloops *Cyane* and *Levant*. Note the portlids on the upper, or spar, deck, concealing 32-pounder carronades.

Algerines, resulting in the latter concentrating their attentions on others, notably Americans. In March 1794 Congress thus passed the Navy Act, which marked the foundation of today's US Navy.

The core of the fleet was to be a half dozen frigates. Few in number by European standards they were, however, carefully considered. Three were to be nominally of 44 guns and three of 36. Technically frigates, being single-decked, they were, however, larger and more heavily armed than was customary. The 44s were reported to have been built with the size and scantlings of a 74 but with a metre or so less beam. They were single-decked by virtue of the forecastle and quarterdeck not being connected, and they carried a main battery of 24-pounders (compared with the 18s of conventional frigates). On a light 'spar deck' they mounted a score of 32-pounder carronades. The three smaller frigates were usually armed with 28 18-pounders and ten carronades. They were designed to out-fight anything they could not out-run.

A considerable American advantage lay in its navy being small and providing good conditions of service. Its crew were, therefore, almost all volunteers, with few of the 'landsmen' that composed a large proportion of the complements of British ships. Between 1798 and 1800 the new navy was blooded by the so-called 'quasi-war' fought to dissuade France from persecuting American trade. Captures had swelled the US Navy to 34 ships by the close of hostilities.

During 1801 the pacifically-minded Thomas Jefferson, who had assumed the presidency, began again to

Xebec

Much favoured by the Barbary pirates, the xebec differed from the polacre largely in her hull form, but shared the same concept of rig interchangeable between lateen (for close-hauled performance) and square rig for running free. In calms, she could be rowed. A large crew was required to handle the complex rigging, man the guns and board their victims.

dismantle the service. Increased demands from various of the Barbary rulers, however, gave the United States the choice of purchasing peace or pursuing the honourable path and fighting it out. Early expeditions were ineffective by dint of insufficient strength but, in 1803, Tripoli itself was successfully subdued by a force under Commodore Edward Preble. The navy thereafter did its best to maintain a presence in the Mediterranean.

Despite the acquisition of warships the Americans were still subject to British impressment. In this the Americans were not entirely blameless, for they did little to discourage the employment of British deserters, clearly a contentious issue. In June 1807 a small British squadron, detached from the Halifax command, was anchored just inside the Virginia capes. Its purpose was to watch two of Willaumez' squadrons which, storm-damaged, were laying farther up the Chesapeake. On the 22nd Commodore James Barron sailed in the frigate *Chesapeake*, en route to take command of the Mediterranean squadron. His ship was certainly not 'ready in all respects for sea', being cluttered and encumbered by a mass of unsorted and unstowed stores.

She was preceded to sea by the British frigate *Leopard* which, once beyond limits, sent over a boat to demand that Barron muster his crew to facilitate the identification and recovery of four known deserters. As the captain of a warship of a sovereign state, Barron rightly refused, whereupon the *Leopard* recovered her sea-boat and delivered three full broadsides. Defenceless, and having already incurred 21 casualties, the unfortunate Barron was obliged to strike his ensign.

This insult brought popular demands for war. Jefferson resisted these but pushed through an Embargo Act, prohibiting trade with either Britain or France. This move, understandably, hurt American trading interest the most and, in 1810, the Americans offered that, if either power ceased its activities against their shipping, 'non-intercourse' would be rigidly enforced against the other. Here, Napoleon saw his chance and, where normal trade was resumed with France, Britain was embargoed by the new president, James Madison. Under the authority of Orders in Council, however, British action proceeded as before.

Matters deteriorated considerably when, on 16th May 1811, the American frigate *President*, commanded by Commodore John Rodgers, encountered the British sloop *Little Belt*. Darkness was falling and the discharge of a gun (the Courts of Inquiry differ regarding the culprit) resulted in a 15-minute engagement. It was no contest, with the *President*'s 32 long 24-pounders and 24 42-pounder carronades matched with the *Little Belt*'s 18 32-pounder carronades and two long 9-pounders. Seriously damaged, neither able to manoeuvre nor return fire, the *Little Belt*'s captain, Commander Arthur Bingham, refused to strike, even to what was truly 'overwhelming force'. Rodgers ceased fire but had his offer of assistance declined. The British sloop patched her hurts and made Halifax successfully.

Rodgers was lionised as the avenger of the *Chesapeake*; the British Admiralty's opinion was encapsulated by Bingham's promotion to post-rank. Both encounters had demonstrated, however, that the two nations, populated largely by kinsmen, were spoiling for a fight. An additional factor was that states outside New England were powerfully in favour of annexing Canada. Congressional representatives from the south and the west of the Union formed a lobby known as the 'War Hawks', urging Madison to end the pacifist legacy of Jefferson and to take a strong line. Ironically, as the nation drifted towards war on a plank of 'Free Trade and Sailors' Rights', it was these states that consistently voted against increases to the US Navy. Where the Secretary of the Navy called for 20 additional frigates and a dozen 74s to meet what would clearly be a maritime war, just ten frigates were approved.

In February 1811 Madison demanded that Britain revoke the relevant Orders in Council. Not to be hurried, the British Government agreed to this in mid-June, to be effective from 23rd July. On the 18th June, in ignorance of this, Congress voted for war.

From the outset, the 'War of 1812' would be one of limited objectives. It was unpopular with many on either side. With the Atlantic separating the factions, settling the war by invasion was never an option; the Americans had not the means while the British, already fully occupied with Napoleon, had all-too-fresh memories of the difficulties inherent in large-scale military operations in the United States. As the US Navy could not contemplate defeating the Royal Navy, an assault on British trade was its inevitable policy. Only on the United States-Canada border did the British need to feel uncertain for, right up to the President himself, there existed the belief that simply to invade Canada was to take it. Its acquisition was, in many quarters, the major objective of the war.

'Steady Marines...'

All warships of any consequence carried a Marine detachment as an integral part of their complement. From 1802 the force was known as the Royal Marines, soon afterward adding artillery to their infantry skills. In normal routine they were responsible for ceremonial duties and the enforcement of discipline aboard. Their lack of seamanship skills made them the butt of much lower-deck humour.

The US Navy had in commission six large frigates, one small frigate, a corvette and eight smaller craft, a force that appeared insignificant to many against the might of the Royal Navy. The latter, almost continuously at war for decades, had achieved an unparalleled run of success which had bred a service-wide belief in its own invincibility. The Navy did not contemplate defeat; it rarely experienced it.

At the beginning of 1812 its strength included 102 commissioned ships of the line, half dozen Fourth Rates and 121 frigates.

At this time the Royal Navy was only just beginning to experiment with the 24-pounder frigate, a type for which it saw little use. Building were two big 44-gun types, the *Endymion* (based on the captured French *Pomone*) and the smaller *Cambrian*. Six 40s, also 24-pounder ships, of the Severn class were on order at Blackwall. Even though built of softwood, these would not be completed until 1814. For general cruising duties, the Navy simply needed smaller ships.

Despite the Royal Navy's disproportionately greater size, it could spare few resources for the quiet backwater of the North America stations. These, Halifax, Jamaica and the Leeward Islands commands, had been lumped together under the flag of Admiral Sir John Borlase Warren. In all, he commanded three of the line, 21 frigates and 37 smaller vessels. One third of this force, under Vice-Admiral Sir Herbert Sawyer, was deployed in the Halifax-Bermuda sector.

On the grounds that British naval strength could be rapidly reinforced in a crisis, the

American Secretary of the Navy first proposed that the US Navy should remain in port as a fleet-in-being. His senior commanders, Rodgers and Stephen Decatur, disagreed, stressing the need to get rapidly to sea to avoid the certainty of blockade. The two disagreed mutually on strategy, Rodgers espousing concentration of strength while Decatur favoured independent operations.

On 21st June 1812, three days into hostilities, Rodgers sailed with a squadron to intercept a reported British West Indies convoy. Two days later they sighted the British frigate *Belvidera* whose captain, Richard Byron, had heard of the likelihood of war. Wisely, he took refuge in flight, so closely pursued that he exchanged chase fire with Rodgers' own ship, the *President* 44. Through skilful manoeuvre and the jettisoning of all excess weight, including potable water, Byron escaped to bring the first news of war to Sawyer at Halifax.

Sawyer's response was to despatch a squadron comprising his only line ship, the *Africa* 64, and three (later four) frigates under the overall command of Captain Philip Bowes Vere Broke in the *Shannon* 38. On 16th July 1812 these encountered the American *Constitution* 44 off the coast of New Jersey. In an almost compete calm her captain, Isaac Hull, used every device to avoid capture. Over three days, occasionally within cannon shot, both sides used towing with ships' boats and kedging with anchors in order to make progress. Finally, a fair breeze developed and the longer *Constitution* made her escape.

Because of the nature of the War of 1812, it is convenient to consider in turn activities in three separate categories, i.e. at sea, along the Canadian border and along the United States' seaboard.

Troops embarking near Greenwich (William Anderson)

Ultimately, wars were won mainly through the occupation of enemy territory. This was a task for the military, the conveyance and convoying of which was an important part of the duties of all fleets of the time. Anderson's scene is full of interesting detail - the crude solidity of the transports, the loading of horses by sling and the rigging of the extra tackle, the laid-up ships 'in ordinary', and the distant vista of Greenwich itself.

En route to join Rodgers' two frigates (*President* and *Congress*) the 18-gun ship-rigged sloop *Wasp* encountered on 18th October the British brig-sloop *Frolic*. The latter correctly engaged the *Wasp* to allow her convoy to proceed to safety. Both ships were armed with 32-pounder carronades. Conditions were brisk with lively ship motions but the British vessel, although firing three broadsides to the enemy's two, aimed consistently high. Keeping her shooting deliberate and low, the *Wasp* caused carnage aboard the *Frolic* which, first crippled, then heavily raked, was boarded. With nobody left to resist them, the Americans lowered the ensign themselves. That a British 74 (The *Poitiers*) then arrived and captured both victor and vanquished did not alter the fact that another British ship, although fought to the last (62 of her 110 crew were casualties), had been simply outfought.

Admiral Warren engaged in acrimonious correspondence with the Admiralty. His concerns were at the swarms of American privateers and the fact that their frigates were of an individual fighting strength that meant that his own had to operate in company. He was, in turn, reminded that, despite commitments elsewhere, the Admiralty had given him 97 warships, including 11 of the line and 34 frigates. In their Lordships' opinion the Admiral should have met his particular points of concern by disposing blockading squadrons outside each American port, using small ships as escorts for an organised convoy system. The Admiralty was particularly unhappy that, because Warren had failed to blockade the American squadrons in their ports, a further seven of the line and seven frigates had had to be deployed in the enemy's areas of operation. Further unpleasant surprises were, however, forthcoming for the remainder of the year.

Rodgers and Decatur had sailed together for mutual protection on 8th October 1812, their squadrons separating three days out. Cruising to the Cape Verdes and back, Rodgers took only a handful of merchantmen. The 16-gun brig-sloop *Argus* became separated from Decatur in the *United States* and, pursued for three days by a British frigate, was obliged to return, having had to jettison much gear in order to lighten ship and escape. On 25th October, cruising alone south of the Azores, Decatur met the British 38-gun frigate *Macedonian*, one of a large and successful class, and completed at Woolwich only the year previously. She was known as an efficient ship and her captain, John Carden, was a taut disciplinarian.

Carden had the faster ship but, manoeuvre as he might, he could not close to the effective range of his 18-pounders without being battered by Decatur's 24s. A combination of heavier metal and disciplined fire from a larger and steadier platform proved, again, to be superior. Hardly touched herself, the *United States* reduced the *Macedonian* to a bloodied wreck. With 104 of his 301 crew casualties, over a hundred shot in his hull and his ship unmanoeuvrable, Carden struck his flag after about one hour of action.

It was a strange war. Decatur and Carden were already acquainted. Many of the American crew that boarded the *Macedonian* to claim her were recognised and greeted by the British as earlier shipmates. Quickly learning of the excellent conditions in the US Navy many promptly volunteered to serve in it, only to be refused by Decatur. Again, undoubted courage on the part of the British had been entirely negated by poor gunnery and uninspired manoeuvring, for the *United States* had suffered only a dozen casualties and a few hits to the hull. With no British blockade in place, Decatur was able to bring his prize safely to port. As the first to capture a regular British warship he was accorded full honours, the *Macedonian* going on to serve for a further 23 years in the US Navy.

Commodore William Bainbridge, meanwhile, had sailed in the *Constitution* on 26th October 1812. Accompanied by James Lawrence in the 18-gun ship-sloop *Hornet*, he was due to rendezvous in the Cape Verdes with the *Essex* 32. Smallest of the American frigates, she was commanded by David Porter. The rendezvous was not kept, and Bainbridge sailed for Brazil. At San Salvador (now Bahia) they found the *Bonne Citoyenne*, a British ship-sloop captured from the French in 1796. Conforming to contemporary manners, Lawrence challenged her to battle, with Bainbridge pledged not

US Gunboat

This attractive little craft was one of hundreds that resulted from President Jefferson's passionate belief that standing armed forces were a 'menace to liberty'. State militias and coastal gunboats were all that he held necessary to defend a nation 'separated by nature and a wide ocean from the exterminating havoc (of Europe)'. The War of 1812 proved him to be wrong.

to interfere. The British ship was, however, loading a large quantity of specie and refused the invitation. As the *Hornet* stayed to blockade the Briton, Bainbridge cruised the coast sighting, on 29th December, the British frigate *Java*. Also captured from the French, she was previously the noted sailer *Renommée*. Commanded by Captain Henry Lambert, she was carrying 28 18-pounders, 14 32-pounder carronades, and a pair of carronades and two long 9-pounders as forecastle guns.

Although an agile ship, the *Java* exhibited the chronic manning problems then plaguing the Royal Navy. Of her 397 crew, 50 had been drafted en bloc from a disaffected Portsmouth sloop, 60 were raw Irishmen who had never before been to sea, while many of the remainder were impressed landsmen or convicted prisoners. In addition to her establishment of 23 boys was a draft of lads from the Marine Society (a charity founded for the purpose). When, before sailing, Lambert had made representations regarding the quality of his complement, he had been informed that a voyage to the East Indies would knock them into shape. Having escorted down a couple of Indiamen, Lambert was calling for fresh water. His guncrews had not been regularly drilled, neither could his 18-pounders match 24s. Although the *Java* was well-handled, the *Constitution*'s greater range was decisive. A shot carried away the British ship's jib boom and headsail. As she was caught in stays, her adversary was able to cross her stern and pour in a destructive broadside.

Outgunned, Lambert attempted to board but the now un-handy *Java* only presented her vulnerable ends for two more raking broadsides. At close range, her foremast and main topmast were shot away while the crew, mustered for boarding, were badly cut up by langridge and musketry. Lambert was mortally wounded. After four hours, the *Java* was totally dismasted and Bainbridge placed his ship athwart her bows to indicate that further resistance was futile. Lambert's scratch crew had fought like heroes but, with 22 dead and 92 injured, including himself, his first lieutenant lowered the colours in submission.

It is probable that many British ships, on long and distant commissions, were unaware of this series of setbacks and had taken no remedial action. The traditional tactics of getting in close to pour rapid broadsides into an opponent's hull were obviously not practical when faced with ships with heavier scantlings and armament, manned by cool and disciplined crews.

Moved on from San Salvador by the arrival of a British 74, Lawrence was off the Demerara River on 24th February 1813 when he fell in with the British sloop *Peacock*. The latter's colleague, the sloop *Espiègle*, failed to support her, remaining at anchor as she was totally outgunned by the *Hornet*. Sunk outright in a quarter-hour, the *Peacock*'s survivors were taken by Lawrence to New York. Here, they presented him with written thanks for the excellent manner in which they had been treated. Although the fighting at sea was hard, it was marked by a general respect and a lack of ill-will between opponents.

This first phase of the war lasted until early in 1813. By the previous October, however, it had been apparent that repeal of the offending Orders in Council would not, in itself, be sufficient to end hostilities and British armed forces were instructed to institute general reprisals. In November, Admiral Warren was ordered to rigorously blockade the Delaware and Chesapeake. This blockade, once in place, was extended southward in stages to the far Florida border. Excepted was New England which, not in favour of the war, was still trading actively with Britain and Canada.

Finally accepting that the dispute was rather more than a sideshow, Britain also began to divert more powerful resources. Cruisers, particularly, were required to counter a veritable plague of American privateers which were reported to have seized up to 1,300 merchantmen. These corsairs were slowly reduced to the best and the boldest which, to an extent, embarrassed their regular navy by attracting the cream of the seamen, a problem earlier faced by the French.

Newcastle

As a direct answer to the American 24-pounder frigates, the *Newcastle* and her near-sister *Leander* were completed in 1814. Also spar-decked frigates, they shipped 30 x 24-pounders on the upper deck and a mix of 24-pounders and 32/42-pounder carronades on the spar deck. For rapid completion they were built of softwood, and only enjoyed short service lives.

The Admiralty also took measures to match the offensive power of the large American frigates. Draughts had been produced, possibly on reports of their building, some two years before the war. These were for 50-gunners, possible through linking forecastle and quarterdeck with a light spar deck. Two prototypes, *Leander* and *Newcastle*, were built, each with 32 24-pounders on the gun deck, and two to four 24-pounders and lighter 32/42-pounder carronades on the spar deck overhead. Probably ordered early in 1813, they were commissioned in the following year, followed by a new, 50-gun *Java*. Such ships were denoted 'large frigates' and, warship development being cyclic, brought about the re-invention of the 'small' frigate of 24 or 26 guns, though latterly of 32-pounders. As stop-gaps the Admiralty also cut down, or 'razeed', three old 74s. These, the *Goliath*, *Majestic* and *Saturn*, were ready in 1813 but their more portly proportions rated them closer to 50-gun Fourth Rates than to genuine frigates, and their lives were short.

Admiral Warren and his deputy, Rear-Admiral Sir George Cockburn had, meanwhile, tightened their grip on the eastern seaboard. Decatur had taken the *United States* and the *Macedonian* prize to New York, but there and in New London they were confined for the remainder of hostilities. The *Constellation* was similarly blockaded at Norfolk, Virginia. Rodgers, in the *President*, was luckier for, with his blockading force blanketed by fog, he broke out of Boston in May 1813 after a four-month delay, in company with John Smith in the *Congress*. The *Essex* had been taken to the Pacific by Porter but the *Chesapeake*, which had cruised the Cape Verdes, equatorial South America and the Caribbean, had enjoyed little luck in the face of a by now effective British convoy system. As continuous blockade of the huge length of the United States' coastline was never practical, however, the *Chesapeake* was able to slip back into Boston where, in May 1813, she became the command of a newly-promoted Captain James Lawrence.

Watching Boston was the British frigate *Shannon* whose commander, Philip Broke, already disappointed at the escape of the *President* and *Congress*, detached the supporting *Tenedos*, the better to entice the *Chesapeake* to sea. Broke was a gunnery zealot and, despite a recent influx of raw replacement officers and hands, ran an efficient ship with a comparatively benevolent regime. Ambitious, and keen to stem the series of British reverses, Broke sent Lawrence a personal challenge. Despite being under separate orders, the American was spoiling for a fight and, on 1st June 1813, he sailed, accompanied by so many local craft that it appeared to be a popular event.

One of the smaller American frigates, the *Chesapeake* had 28 18-pounders, exactly matching the *Shannon*. In 32-pounder carronades and chase guns too, neither ship had a distinct advantage. Lawrence's crew of 370 was 50 stronger than Broke's, which would have been an advantage in boarding.

In a good manoeuvring breeze Lawrence sought only to get to close quarters. Ignoring an offered chance to rake the *Shannon* he rounded

General Pike

Also built on Lake Ontario, but considerably larger than the *Oneida* (145 feet between perpendiculars compared with 85.5), the *General Pike* was a corvette armed with 28 x 24-pounders, two of them pivot-mounted. Launched in 1813 after only 63 days under construction, she served until about 1824. The appearance of her hull is conjectural as only the sail plan has survived.

up on her starboard quarter at less than 50 yards. Broke had loaded his broadside guns with, alternately, one ball and one double-headed shot, and two balls and one canister. At 5.50 p.m., as the *Chesapeake* obligingly bore in, the *Shannon*'s guns fired in succession, instantly echoed by a crashing American broadside. Survivors spoke of the murderous showers of wood splinters and the results of grenades and musketry loosed from the tops. Two-thirds of the 150 men on the *Chesapeake*'s weather deck were felled. Lawrence was severely wounded in the leg. Broke, his own ship hulled and leaking, sought to keep clear water between the ships until his gunners had established a discernible advantage. Damage to the rigging of each, however, saw them come together involuntarily. The British boatswain immediately ran a stout lashing about the riggings, only to lose his arm to an American cutlass.

Lawrence, in full uniform, was shot by a British marine. As he was carried below, dying, he gave the immortal order "Don't give up the ship!". Broke himself led the boarding party, forcing below the few left topside. Those on the main deck tried to reach the weather deck but were at a hopeless disadvantage. Several volleys directed down open hatchways decided the issue.

Just fifteen minutes from the first shot Broke, himself badly injured by a sword cut to the head, had won the day against what he described as a "desperate but disorderly resistance". In these few minutes, 43 British and 62 Americans had died, and 39 and 73 respectively were wounded. Britain greeted the result with relief and extravagant joy, Broke being created a baronet. In truth, the victory was logical in that, for the first time in these frigate duels, the British had opened on something like equal terms. During the following month, indeed, it appeared that the earlier trend might finally have been reversed.

Rattlesnake

Built as a 14-gun privateer, the *Rattlesnake* was acquired by the US Navy in 1813. As a regular warship she carried out a successful cruise in the North Sea in company with the *Scourge*, taking about 22 prizes. She was captured in June 1814 off Cape Sable by the British heavy frigate *Leander* which, in a blow, was able to out-run her.

The American sloop *Argus*, engaged on commerce raiding, was caught by the *Pelican* off St. David's Head. On this occasion, British success was due to a combination of heavier metal and superior ship-handling. Brig-rigged sloops fought a similar action off New England in September 1813. The American *Enterprise* and the British *Boxer* had a primary armament of 18-pounder carronades, supplemented by a pair of long chase guns. At close range, the carronades were mutually very destructive but it was the British ship that suffered the damage that left her unmanoeuvrable. Raked repeatedly, she had to strike. Both commanding officers were killed and, fittingly, were interred side-by-side at Portland, Maine.

Under Admiral Warren and his successor, Vice-Admiral Sir Alexander Cochrane, the blockade of the American coast had now been made effective, but being regulated so as to avoid too great a hardship on commerce as hopes still lingered for a settlement. The issue of impressment, however, defied all solution. From April 1813 the Royal Navy was in sufficient strength to commence using the many deep-water bays and estuaries to mount increasingly destructive raids which the American militias were powerless to prevent.

As mentioned above, Captain David Porter of the frigate *Essex*, having failed to rendezvous with Bainbridge, headed for the Pacific. In the Atlantic, prizes were few and provisions hard to come by, and a sortie against the British whaling industry proved attractive. Arriving in March 1813, he found a complex situation. South American territories were in revolt against Spanish rule. Britain was sympathetic to their cause, which emboldened local privateers to operate against the also-numerous American whaling fleet. In the Galapagos, Porter captured a group of well-found British whalers. Arming one as an auxiliary he despatched the whole as a convoy to Valparaiso under her escort. She returned with a rumour that the British Admiralty had already despatched ships to apprehend the *Essex*. As the frigate required refit, Porter made for the Marquesas where, between September and December 1813, he used for the purpose resources from captured ships.

Returning to the South American coast, the *Essex* entered Valparaiso early in February 1814. Five days later the British *Phoebe* 36 arrived, accompanied by the ship-sloop *Cherub*, of 18 guns. A second sloop, the *Racoon* 18, had been detached on search. Under Captain James Hillyar, the British were on a mission similar to Porters' own. Already acquainted, but both in neutral waters, Hillyar and Porter exchanged formalities, followed by customary social contact between the officers. Both ships ran up large white flags bearing political slogans, but there was no disguising that the *Essex* was now hostage to superior force. Following rest and recuperation, Hillyar's force set up an offshore blockade. Porter knew that he had a problem inasmuch as, against his will, he had been given a main battery of 40 32-pounder carronades but only six long 12-pounders. His adversary had a conventional, outfit of 30 18-pounders and 16 32-pounder carronades. The *Cherub*'s all-carronade armament comprised 18 32-pounders and six 18-pounders. Porter had repeatedly sought single-ship combat with Hillyar, banking on offsetting his lack of range with superior speed and manoeuvre. The British captain, however, was not given to romantic notions of duelling. His orders were to apprehend the *Essex*, which could either capitulate or face whatever force could be mustered against her.

On 28th March matters were decided by a squall, which parted the *Essex's* anchor cable. Obliged to seek sea room, she lost her main topmast to a further heavy gust. Crippled, she was moved by Porter into neutral water for repair. Ignoring diplomatic niceties, Hillyar moved in and, manoeuvring beyond carronade range, used his long guns to reduce the *Essex* to a wreck. Damage to his rigging prevented Porter from running his ship ashore and, when his spare anchor cable was shot away, he allowed those who would to swim ashore, then struck his colours. His hopeless defence had cost the lives of 58 of his 255 crew, a further 30 going missing on attempting to escape. His auxiliary cruiser was disarmed and used for the survivor's repatriation.

Because of the British blockade, prizes taken by the remaining American privateers had to be destroyed at sea. Of the frigates, the *Congress*, which had returned in December 1813, made no further contribution. When Commodore Rodgers relinquished command of the *President* in May 1814, she was taken over by Decatur, who brought with him the crew of the blockaded *United States*. She was under orders to sail, accompanied by the sloops *Hornet* and *Peacock*, against British trade in the West Indies. Stationed just inside Sandy Hook, however, was a British squadron comprising the 56-gun razee *Majestic*, the 24-pounder frigate *Endymion* and the 18-pounder *Pomone* and *Tenedos*.

Although the peace treaty ending the war had been signed at Ghent on Christmas Eve 1814, news had not reached the United States by 14th January 1815, when a north-westerly gale forced the British offshore. Decatur took immediate advantage in sailing but his intentions were well anticipated by Captain John Hayes, the British senior officer. A tail-chase developed, the *President* hampered somewhat by leakage, caused by bumping heavily in Decatur's anxiety to cross the estuary bar. She was overhauled by the *Endymion*, which skilfully yawed from quarter to quarter, loosing a broadside on each pass but being answered only by chase guns. Decatur was obliged to alter course to allow his broadsides to bear. This slowed his escape, but he succeeded in damaging the British ship's rigging sufficiently to again head for the open sea. Toward midnight, however, the *Pomone* caught up and, with the *Tenedos* not far behind, Decatur acknowledged the hopelessness of his position by striking his flag after only a nominal couple of broadsides.

This was not the only action to be fought after the official cessation of hostilities for, on 20th February 1815, the *Constitution*, which had succeeded in breaking out of Boston, encountered two British sloops near Madeira. These, the *Cyane* 22 and the *Levant* 20, were unwisely pitted by their commanders against the formidable victor of the *Guerrière* and *Java*, probably to deflect attention from a couple of convoys that were in the area. The sloops were nimble, but their armament was of carronades, with a pair of small chase guns. Neither this nor their light construction suited them for the action. In the lumpy conditions, the larger ship also proved to be the better sailer and the British craft were quickly reduced to manoeuvring to cover each other as far as possible, neither being able to escape. Inevitably, a 24-pounder broadside eventually went home and the *Cyane* was obliged to strike. Her consort, having effected some emergency repairs to her rigging, returned to the action only to find herself unsupported. Out-manoeuvred she, too, was beaten into submission.

The *Constitution* took her prizes into Porto Praya for refurbishment and, on 11th March, was there surprised by the arrival of the new 50-gun frigates *Leander* and *Newcastle*, supported by the *Acasta* 40. The Americans slipped with commendable rapidity and it is apparent from their and the *Acasta's* logs that their opponents' class and strength were correctly assessed. The captains of the two big British frigates, which were built expressly to counter the Americans, apparently mistook the captured ship-rigged sloops as frigates, however and, in pursuing them, lost the *Constitution*. Despite the *Levant* being recovered, this farcical outcome was never satisfactorily explained.

Java

One of three American 44-gun frigates ordered in 1813, the Baltimore-built *Java* (like the *Guerrière*) carried a prize name. The third, *Columbia*, was burned on the stocks when British forces took Washington. Both of those completed carried 33 x long 24-pounders on the main- deck and 20 x 42-pounder carronades on forecastle and quarterdeck. The *Java* was scrapped in 1842

Constitution v. Guerrière

Meeting on 19 August 1812, the larger *Constitution* was handled deftly, yawing sufficiently to escape a series of raking manoeuvres by the *Guerrière*. Ranging parallel, the American's 24 pounder broadside splintered the lighter British ship, whose mizzen mast went by the board. The ships fouled briefly and, in wrenching apart, the *Guerrière* lost her weakened fore- and main masts, obliging her to strike. Her loss was a great blow to British morale.

In the far reaches of the oceans, hostilities dragged on. On 23rd March 1815 the American sloop *Hornet* arrived at remote Tristan da Cunha only to counter there the British sloop *Penguin*. Their similar carronade armaments dictated a destructive, close-range duel but the *Penguin*'s commander was mortally wounded and his first lieutenant decided to board. A misjudgement in ranging alongside carried away the *Penguin*'s bowsprit, which in turn brought down her foremast. In striking her flag, the *Penguin*'s commander brought to a close the final action at sea. It was the last of a series which had given the Royal Navy much to reflect upon.

War on the Great Lakes

As Britain and the United States moved closer to hostilities, James Monroe, the then American Secretary of State, declared that: "In case of war, it might be necessary to invade Canada, not as an object of the war, but as a means to bring it to a satisfactory conclusion". The Americans bore no particular animosity toward the Canadians but the latter, as British subjects, automatically became enemies once war was declared. In terms of military strength, the Americans were superior to the point where Jefferson could make, with confidence, his unfortunate remark that: "The acquisition of Canada ... will be a mere matter of marching". The application of this superiority proved, however, to be no simple matter, despite the sizeable lobby advocating the territory's annexation.

The boundary between the then United States and Canada was defined for the most part by a median line along the eastern Great Lakes. The two easternmost, Lakes Erie and Ontario, are linked by the St. Lawrence river to the open sea, and formed the primary barrier to invasion by either side. Because of the lack of

Prometheus

Described as a hermaphrodite schooner, the *Prometheus* was built in 1814 to private account as the privateer *Escape*. Purchased new by the US Navy, her designed 14-gun armament was reduced to one long 32-pounder, four long 9-pounders and four 18-pounder carronades. She was sold out in 1819.

alternative communications, control of the lakes was of crucial importance. British presence there was dependent upon access via the rapid-strewn St. Lawrence while, once again, the Americans looked to the natural line of the Hudson valley, the long finger of Lake Champlain and the Richelieu to enable them to reach the St. Lawrence and to cut the British supply line below Montreal.

The American militia was of variable quality, as was some of its leadership, and they suffered two early reverses, at Detroit and the Niagara, as they attempted to advance into Canada by the land bridges between the lakes. On each of the eastern lakes the British operated half a dozen armed brigs and schooners. Like similar American craft, they were manned and commanded by non-regular personnel, described as 'lakes' sailors', but a stiffening of regulars soon began to arrive. In September 1812 Captain Isaac Chauncey, US Navy, arrived from New York with a first draft of seamen and, with a flotilla of mainly commandeered craft, subjected the British to a series of raids. Captain Sir James Lucas Yeo was consequently appointed to the British lakes' command, arriving on Lake Ontario in the spring of 1813 with 500 men. Throughout the winter, which had brought sea-borne operations to a halt, there had been frantic construction activity in both camps.

On Lake Erie, the British Commander Robert Barclay enjoyed initial superiority with the existing 17-gun *Queen Charlotte*. His opposite number, Master Commandant Oliver Hazard Perry, arriving early in 1813, set to with furious energy to redress this situation. By the end of July he had overseen the completion of two brig-sloops, *Niagara* and *Lawrence*, each armed with 18 32-pounder carronades and a brace of long 12s. Rather more leisurely, Barclay was building the brig *Detroit*, for which he was assembling an ad hoc armament purloined from various forts. He was thrown on the defensive pending her completion, scheduled for the September.

On 10th September 1813 the two squadrons met to decide control of the lake. Perry had the heavier metal but needed to get in close. With the advantage of the weather gauge he succeeded, having endured the damage inflicted by the *Detroit*'s long cannon. For some reason his second-in-command, Lieutenant Jesse D. Elliott, failed to engage the *Queen Charlotte*, leaving her free to come to the *Detroit*'s assistance. The *Lawrence* was reduced to a wreck, Perry having to transfer by boat to Elliott's ship, *Niagara*. He then charged the two British ships, panicking them into fouling inextricably. Able then to rake them at will, he quickly effected their surrender. After his victory Perry was able to signal his superiors: "We have met the enemy and they are ours".

Elliott's conduct had been such as to lead to a full-scale enquiry and, shortly afterward, Perry left the lakes' service for a sea-going appointment. British reverses in frigate duels had been of little importance other than in terms of morale but Perry's victory on Lake Erie had a strategic effect on the war. Although on a small scale, it deprived the British of the free waterborne movement necessary to support larger military operations such as those against Detroit and the Michigan territory. British positions facing Detroit at the lake's western end were effectively isolated. Although the British were not able to again contest mastery of the lake for the duration of hostilities, they did not allow the Americans to relax. Cutting-out expeditions, using small armed craft, subsequently took at least five American auxiliary warships. Throughout 1813, however, Chauncey and Yeo brushed, in general, ineffectively and with excessive caution.

With events in Europe moving at last toward a conclusion Britain was able to transfer to North America many of the seasoned regulars of the Peninsula army. The general plan was to conduct two offensives, one heading northward from the Gulf coast, the other southward from Montreal, via Lake Champlain and the Hudson valley. The latter movement would be subject to the same topographical restrictions as was that of the earlier war and the assembly of an 11,000-strong army on the St. Lawrence during the summer of 1814 did not pass unnoticed by the Americans. To oppose this force was one of only about 3,000, half of whom were sick. This disparity was, however, offset by the extremely narrow front upon which the British could advance.

By the end of August the Americans had dug in around Plattsburg, about half way down the lake. Here they were supported by a naval squadron under Master Commandant Thomas Macdonough, whose command comprised the 27-gun corvette *Saratoga* (whose broadside included eight long 24-pounders), the brig-sloop *Eagle* 20, the 17-gun schooner *Ticonderoga*, a small seven-gun craft and ten armed rowing galleys.

In Canadian waters at the extreme northern end of the lake the British 16-gun brig *Linnet* was supported only by a pair of schooners, *Chub* and *Finch*, with 11 guns apiece. With otherwise only a dozen galleys the force was badly outclassed until completion of the 37-gun frigate *Confiance*, which was being built at a furious pace. Yeo could not challenge the American position without her support and attempts to disrupt their preparations were easily repulsed by shore batteries. The *Confiance* was delayed by the interception of a couple of consignments of her spars. These were being supplied by the good citizens of Vermont, who were also conducting a thriving cross-border trade in provision of beef on the hoof for the British Army.

This latter force, under the Governor-General of Canada, General Sir George Prevost, crossed the border on 31st August. Covered on its flank by Captain Pring's naval flotilla, it met only sporadic opposition and occupied Plattsburg on 7th September. American regulars and militia had retreated over the Saranac River, which marked the town's southern boundary and, having destroyed the bridge, were dug in on low bluffs beyond. Plattsburg stands on a bay, sheltered by Cumberland Head, which curves around to the east, some two miles distant. Macdonough's squadron was moored in the bay in a close line, head to tail, the ends of the line abutting on shoal water. His larger ships were secured to several anchors, permitting them to be slewed to redirect their broadsides.

With the *Confiance* in company, Pring could have defeated Macdonough in open water but he was not powerful enough to cut him out from under the shore batteries. Had Prevost advanced quickly, crossed the Saranac and seized the bluffs, his own artillery could have driven the American squadron from the bay without the need of a battle. The British commanders were, however, at loggerheads. Yeo had differences with Pring, his deputy, and had just had him replaced by Captain George Downie. The latter was immediately instructed by Prevost, and in the most intemperate terms, that he would cover the army's flank as it advanced to secure the bluffs, implying that Downie would first have to neutralise Macdonough.

Prevost was chafing due to the lateness of the season. The *Confiance*, launched on 25th August, first fired her guns in test on 7th September. Prevost had been well appraised that, lacking naval superiority, he could not advance down the lake, yet he used his rank to intimidate Downie into premature action on unfavourable terms. Early on 11th September Downie stood down the lake with a north-north-easterly breeze, rounded Cumberland Head and, though seeing no discernible movement by Prevost's forces, went ahead with the attack. In the lee of the land the breeze was fickle and the loftier *Confiance*, initially in line abreast with her colleagues, forged ahead. She attracted raking fire from the whole American line and, the wind deserting her, she anchored. At about 500 yards she opened fire on the *Eagle* with a double-shotted broadside that killed or injured nearly a quarter of the American's crew. Downie himself, however, was killed soon afterward. The *Linnet* arrived to the assistance of the *Confiance* but the *Chub*, her rig much cut about during her slow approach, lost control, drifted onto the American line and was taken.

While the galleys, manned by soldiers, kept the *Ticonderoga* occupied, the battle devolved much on the *Confiance* and *Linnet* trading broadsides with the *Saratoga* and *Eagle*. Steadily, all four were reduced to wrecks and, critically, it was Macdonough's foresight in mooring arrangements that decided the day. As the *Confiance* settled visibly, the *Saratoga* warped herself around to present her uninjured broadside. The British ship attempted to follow suit but, with her ground tackle much damaged, succeeded only in presenting her vulnerable bows. Heavily raked, she had to strike her colours, followed quickly by the *Linnet* and the grounded *Finch*.

The battle on Lake Champlain was as fiercely contested as any at sea but the British defeat caused Prevost's immediate withdrawal. The obligatory naval court-martial only exposed all the more the problems created by Prevost. Ordered home for an inquiry, he died before the event. The military situation along the natural barrier of the lakes thus became stalemated long enough for the eventual peace agreement to confirm the line as the national boundary.

THE SAILOR'S JOURNAL ..Sung by Mr Incledon, at Covent Garden Theatre, &c

The Sailor's Journal…

A professional seaman's lot, now as then, is a working lifetime of farewells and reunions. Commissions could, until recently, mean three or more years parted, with children growing up unfamiliar with their father. Chances of a safe return were diminished as much by disease and malnutrition as by enemy action. All hoped for a good prize that the Admiralty would decide to purchase.

Seaboard operations

Early in 1814 the British Admiralty changed its policy of combining the North American, Jamaica and Leeward Island stations under one flag officer. Responsibility for the American Atlantic and Gulf coasts accordingly passed from Admiral Sir John Borlase Warren to Vice-Admiral Sir Alexander Cochrane. The lakes remained a separate command under Captain Sir James Yeo.

Cochrane assumed his duties with a grim enthusiasm. "I have it much at heart", he wrote to the Secretary for War and Colonies, "to give them (i.e. the Americans) a complete drubbing before peace is made". With the United States' seaboards now both effectively blockaded and wide open to combined operations, Cochrane's intention was to bring home to ordinary citizens the realities of their government's having declared war.

Warren had shown some residual sympathies toward the ex-colonies but Cochrane was not so minded. Ordered to divert American resources from Prevost's planned line of advance, Cochrane gave his captains instructions "to destroy and lay waste such towns and districts upon the coast as may be found assailable". The precedent for such an order was the burning of Canadian lakes' settlements, notably Newark, by American militia. It was fortunate for local citizens that the British military commander did not concur and only naval personnel were involved in such subsequent activities.

There operated in Chesapeake Bay a flotilla of armed rowing galleys commanded by Captain Joshua Barney of the US Navy. While they constituted a threat to any of the British blockading force unwise enough to become embayed, they were

Oneida
Despite her lofty appearance the Oneida brig was built on Lake Ontario. Constructed for a reported '$20,505 and 110 gallons of spirits' she shipped a single 32-pounder on a pivot

mounting forward, and either 18- or 24-pounder carronades, or long 9-pounders, in the waist. Considered to be a fast craft she served throughout the War of 1812 but, subsequent to 1815, her fate is uncertain.

about to become the catalyst to a larger British enterprise. Cochrane assembled inside the Capes a varied force of warships, together with 3,500 troops and further marines. Simultaneously with feints, he moved into the Patuxent River, up which Barney was based. On 19th August, troops were put ashore 25 miles up-river, along which they advanced, flanked by armed naval tenders.

Under Major-General Robert Ross, the force marched quickly, opposed only by uncoordinated militia groups. Trapped, Barney's crews burned their galleys and joined local infantry units. At this point Ross's force turned westward toward its true objective, Washington, which lay only 20 miles distant. Brushing aside a militia stand at Bladensburg the force entered the capital, spending the 24th firing public buildings, newspaper offices and some private property. The Navy Yard and vessels within were burned by the Americans themselves. British frigates had ascended the Potomac River and, finding the defences abandoned, seized merchantmen laying at Alexandria.

This punitive expedition had a greatly sobering effect on remaining American enthusiasm for the war, even though a parallel raid on Baltimore, situated further up the Chesapeake, was abandoned. The idealised concept of a citizen army, rising ready-armed against an invader, had been found wanting in the face of a seasoned foe with the means to land seemingly anywhere at will.

As part of the territory of Maine protruded between the Canadian provinces of New Brunswick and Quebec, it was occupied to enforce boundary changes. This action yielded the bonus of the destruction of the American 28-gun corvette *Adams* which, damaged, was laying in the Penobscot River below Bangor.

Following operations against Washington and New England, British military forces were re-deployed on the Gulf coast. Major-General Ross having been killed in action, command devolved on Major-General Sir Edward Pakenham, who delayed some months to give military training to disaffected local Indian tribes. His primary objective was New Orleans, an important port in its own right but with the added attraction of being stocked with three seasons' worth of cotton and sugar crops from Mississippi and neighbouring Louisiana, stranded by virtue of the British off-shore blockade.

Vice-Admiral Cochrane's force arrived off the Mississippi delta with the military on 8th December 1814. A considerable force of ships' boats was then armed and adapted to penetrate the saltwater Lake Borgne, which flanks New Orleans to the east. Here, following a stubborn resistance, they neutralised a similar improvised American naval force on 14th December. The clearance of the gunboats permitted the disembarkation, on the 23rd, of an advance force directly from one of the bayoux, or creeks. This location was still some 15 miles distant from the American positions and over extremely difficult, boggy country. On Christmas Day, Pakenham landed with the main body, bringing the British strength to about 5,000.

The approaches took a week over the few dry tracks, all of which were subject to ambush and skirmishing. Any attempt to light a fire in this wet country produced a smoke column that was immediately targeted by enemy artillery. Casualties mounted as morale dropped. General Jackson's defence line could not be directly outflanked, its right abutting the Mississippi River and its left impenetrable wetland. The line was fronted by a substantial bank and ditch. On the opposite riverbank was an American gun battery, sited to be able to enfilade any frontal attack on the line.

Pakenham considered the neutralisation of the battery to be an essential preliminary to his assault, planned for 8th January 1815. The task was given to a force of 400 marines and 200 seamen, whose timetable was badly delayed by a sudden drop in river level. They carried the position, however, successfully spiking the guns before using their boats to advance further to a point well beyond Jackson's positions on the opposite bank, a potential advantage apparently not appreciated by Pakenham.

The latter was killed in the frontal attack on Jackson's line, as was another major-general, Gibbs. A further, Keane, was severely injured. At point-blank range, the ditch proved a major obstacle and, less their leaders, the attackers faltered and fell back. The operation to date had cost over 2,400 casualties and it was decided to abandon it, a last action being to secure Fort Bowyer, which commanded Mobile Bay. At this point, news of the preliminary peace put an end to the campaign.

Weary of war, Britain sought honourable peace conditions. The Duke of Wellington, offered the army command, had declined on the interesting grounds that the Americans, perceiving his appointment, would assume the British military state to be worse than it really was. What was required, he advised, was "not a general, nor general officers, nor troops ... (but) naval superiority on the lakes. If we cannot, I shall do you but little good in America, and I shall go there only to prove the truth of Prevost's defence, and to sign a peace which might as well be signed now". British inability to establish control of the lakes and the twin victories of Perry and Macdonough had effectively cost them the war. The Duke also commented that, with the then-current state of the war, the British would be ill-advised to press for territorial concessions as a condition for peace.

By the terms of the Treaty of Ghent, signed on 24th December 1814 and ratified on 17th February 1815, both sides were content to return to the so-called status quo ante bellum. Both had undergone chastening experiences. Harried by commerce destroyers and privateers, British trade had again suffered despite the best efforts of the Royal Navy. That service itself had encountered superior ships, superior ship-handling and superior gunnery. Having lost the myth of its own invincibility, it set-to to correct its deficiencies.

For its part the US Navy had proved unable to prevent the British maintaining an ever-tighter blockade that caused considerable hardship and damage to the national economy. Where, militarily, the Americans had proved generally deficient, their navy had shown itself, man for man, ship to ship, a worthy equal of the old masters. It had gained genuine new heroes and a new confidence in its abilities (although it still had to wait until 1845 for the creation of the essential US Navy Academy). Borders established, the two nations settled down to co-exist in grudging harmony.

USS Essex 32 guns 1799

1.	Captain's cabin	18.	Pump
2.	Captain's day room	19.	Mast foundation
3.	Wardroom	20.	Ballast
4.	Officers' cabins	21.	Ammunition rack
5.	Tiller	22.	Water
6.	Mizzen mast	23.	Sail locker
7.	Capstan		
8.	Quarter deck		
9.	Tiller room		
10.	Main deck		
11.	Berth deck		
12.	Gangway		
13.	Net supports		
14.	Store		
15.	Magazine		
16.	Rope		
17.	Shot locker		

24. Cable locker
25. Flour store
26. Stanchion
27. Forecastle
28. Galley
29. Small arms store
30. Prow
31. Mizzen topsail
32. Mizzen topgallant
33. Mizzen upper topgallant

34. Main mast
35. Main sail
36. Main topsail
37. Main topgallant
38. Main upper topgallant
39. Fore mast
40. Fore sail
41. Fore topsail
42. Fore upper topgallant
43. Jib
44. Outer jib
45. Bowsprit
46. Rudder

The *Essex* was destroyed by the British who ignored Chilean neutrality to sink her in neutral waters. *Essex* was armed entirely with carronades, giving her incredible firepower at close range, but the British kept beyond their reach, using long 18 pounders to batter her into submission.

CHAPTER 10: *The Post-war Royal Navy*

Once the French ceased to contend mastery at sea, and the prospect of invasion of the British Isles had receded to improbability, the reduction of the Royal Navy commenced, despite a continuing state of war. The impetus was a combination of factors, but notably the need to reduce the punitive level of taxation that the long wars had forced on the country, and a requirement to release men (many impressed against their will) to service the national economy.

Again, there was no room for sentiment and the rundown was swift, as demonstrated by comparative figures for 1808 and 1815.

Rates		1st	2nd	3rd	4th	5th	6th	Sloops
1808	In Commission	4	7	102	10	116	29	179
	In Ordinary	2	4	7	-	23	3	12
1815	In Commission	-	2	45	7	95	37	174
	In Ordinary	8	5	49	2	29	5	11

It will be noticed that, with the reduction in battle squadrons, all but two of the three-deckers were laid-up. Of the ubiquitous 74s, over half went into reserve, many relegated to harbour service from which only another emergency would rescue them. It was becoming a peacetime service of small-ship commands, with the total of frigates and below declining only marginally. Personnel strength, sailors and marines, dropped initially from 130,000 to 90,000 before a strategic review slashed it dramatically to 35,000.

Significant numbers of foreign-built ships appeared in the Navy's order of battle, a source both of economy to the exchequer and of design refinements. Most were refurbished prizes, some of which went on to take prizes of their own. An example of this was the *Rivoli* 74 which, captured by the *Victorious* 74, later took the *Melpomène* 40.

Following so many years of emergency, the Royal Navy had been employing many over-age and outdated ships, some in need of considerable attention. To assist in servicing the hugely increased National Debt, the government had, by 1818, reduced the naval estimates by two-thirds. It was a time for the naval administration to carefully review the Service's commitments and its future form. There would inevitably be a wide-ranging cull.

A major requirement was the protection of a huge increase in trade. Although many acquired territories were returned by the conditions of peace treaties, many strategic locations were retained. New colonies at the Cape, in Ceylon, Trinidad and Mauritius (late Ile de France) not only excluded the influence of earlier colonial powers but provided the springboards for further territorial expansion through private initiative, which proved to be a more powerful impetus than even official policy.

In addition to safeguarding territorial interests, and the trade routes that served them, it was apparent that the maintenance of law and order to newly-imposed standards would require frequent intervention by British armed forces, for which warships would be indispensable. Such activities pointed up the need for considerable numbers of smaller cruising ships but, in addition, a battle fleet was still required in home waters to act as the nation's major deterrent.

British foreign policy was in the skilled hands of Lord Castlereagh who quietly ensured that France, in addition to losing key colonial holdings, also lost control of those foreign

Montebello

One of a class of three Sané-designed 120-gunners, the *Montebello* was launched in 1812. As built, the last two exceeded 5,000 tons by contemporary measurement. Unlike British First Rates of the period, the *Montebello* carries guns over the waist on the deck connecting forecastle and quarterdeck. In 1852 she was fitted with steam propulsion and, as such, fought at Sevastopol. In the Crimea she is recorded as having lost 140 of her complement to cholera within the space of three days.

Careening

Experiments with copper-sheathing began about 1760, both to defeat wood-borers and marine fouling. Lightly-fouled ships could be scrubbed-off by careening, which alarming-looking operation is here seen. Stout timbers have been passed through the gunports to provide grounding for extra bracing for the lower masts, used to haul down the ship. Teak-built in Calcutta for the East India Company, the *Hastings* was purchased for the Royal Navy in 1819. As a 74 she was, in 1840, a unit of the Mediterranean fleet being prepared for the French war scare. In 1855 she was converted to a steam blockship.

arsenals, notably Antwerp, Genoa, Naples and Venice, that Napoleon had used to alleviate the effects of British blockade. Treaties saw them pass to the control of powers with little interest in their development or who would turn to Britain in a dispute.

France, although surrendering some of her best ships, had not been stripped of her fleet by the peace. Some 50 sail of the line remained but, once again, the system that supported them had dissolved into chaos. The restoration of the monarchy had encouraged the return of large numbers of officers, aristocrats and royalist sympathisers who, during the years of revolutionary turmoil, had been obliged to flee their country. Advanced in years and with no recent command experience, they promoted something of a naval schism. Who, after all, had been truly loyal to France — those who had sacrificed home and career, forced abroad in order to remain true to the King, or those who had stayed on to fight and die for the Republic? At a time when the officer corps was being reduced by a third, the King was morally obliged to reward many who were elderly and incompetent with reinstatement and command. As in Britain, hundreds of good men were retired on half pay, many finding their way into the merchant service.

With the loss of many of her colonies, France saw a decline also in her merchant fleet. This, together with a lack of grand imperial design, made many question the need for a regular navy at all. Ministers of Marine came and went, unable to cope on inadequate budgets, while the home dockyards lost the efficient system of administration that had been put in place during the Empire. French naval policy was now based on an acceptance that superiority to the Royal Navy was unattainable. Its latent strategy would, therefore, be the time-honoured *guerre de course*, for which frigate squadrons would be the main instrument. A home-based battle fleet would maintain the threat of invasion while being available alternatively to deal with events elsewhere.

British plans for a post-war navy had to take into account not only the French but also other continental powers, envious of Britain's new pre-eminence in Europe. In Russia's influence in the Balkans, the Black Sea and the eastern Mediterranean lay potential conflict with British interests. The United States were developing their battle fleet in parallel with an aggressive expansion in trade. British policy, therefore, adopted the so-called 'two-power standard', maintaining a fleet capable of defeating those of a combination of the two most powerful foreign powers acting in concert.

The First Lord, Melville, was instrumental in the appointment of Rear-Admiral Sir Thomas Byam Martin as Controller. Together, they formulated the response to political demands that the Service's future size should be based on the estimates voted prior to the late wars. Their starting point was the maximum manpower that could be mobilised in an emergency. Spread over both support and manning, this would permit 100 sail of the line and 160 frigates, totals which more than met the required two-power standard. Surveys, much neglected during the years of war, nonetheless showed that many ships, particularly frigates built in mercantile yards, were fit only for scrap or dismantling. Through increased standardisation on new buildings, they eased the problems of supply of major timbers.

Dockyard-built ships were superior in using seasoned timber and in allowing a new construction settlement time while on the ways. To increase the proportion of such construction the government agreed to fund extra building slips and to roof over those dedicated to major units. To maintain the required establishment of warships, a certain proportion had to be built and refitted each year. Spread between the three large and four small royal yards, this workload required a skilled workforce of definable size. The extent of the Service and its infrastructure was thus accurately specified; the problem was that the government cut funds to the point where realisation of the programme would take a decade.

The tendency of wooden ships to 'work' in a seaway was long considered a necessary evil. Strains imposed by sailing, interaction with the waves and the considerable distributed weight of the armament acted on the ship over long months of blockade or cruising, loosening joints and bolted connections throughout. The result was a weakened and leaky hull, damp and unhealthy for the crew and prone to rot at a thousand inaccessible points. Dockyard repair could be on a huge scale, often involving the dismantling of the whole structure. Quicker solutions could sometimes be found in fitting extra knees and stanchions (now almost invariably of iron) or additional riders.

Despite the preceding half century of scientific interest and enlightenment, British ship design still favoured the empirical. Trial and error, copying and developing hull forms with proven qualities was the preferred approach. In France, by contrast, there was a scientific interest in reconciling the conflicting requirements of strength and stability, speed and affordability. The French objective was to distil knowledge gained into a set of universally applicable mathematical principles.

A first attempt to remedy the unscientific British approach was the private-initiative Society for the Improvement of Naval Architecture. Founded in 1791, its lifespan was less than a decade but brought together some of the most influential minds of the time. One, Charles Middleton (later Lord Barham), succeeded as First Lord, soon discovering that the majority of his senior administrators were poorly educated. The selection and the conditions of employment for shipwright apprentices were thus reformed to identify 'superior' individuals for education at a specialist school to be attached to the Naval Academy at Portsmouth. This institution opened in 1811 as the School of Naval Architecture which, though itself superseded 20 years later, produced alumni who were eventually hugely influential in a variety of maritime areas.

Where the humblest of medieval cottage builders understood the need to incorporate diagonal members in order to confer rigidity to a timber frame, it remains something of a mystery why shipbuilders were reluctant to follow suit. As things were, transverse framing supported longitudinally-laid wales and planking, with the whole offering very little resistance to racking loads except by edge-to-edge friction between the planks. Instances of the use of diagonal members were known to the British by their captures from the French, Russian and Spanish fleets. The ships concerned were constructed between 1766 and 1794.

It fell to Sir Robert Seppings to gather these concepts into a coherent building strategy. Surveyor of the Navy from 1813 to 1832, Seppings appreciated (where many did not) that it was not the quantity of material in a hull that decided its stiffness so much as the

Morris

Encouraged during time of war, the privateering spirit carried over into peace as a thriving smuggling tradition. The American Revenue Service therefore built a succession of classes of fast cutter (not necessarily cutter-rigged), some of which served with the regular navy. The *Morris*, built post-war in the New York Navy Yard, was thus pierced for fourteen guns but, in normal service, carried only six 6-pounders.

disposition. Gabriel Snodgrass had earlier stiffened weakened Indiamen by the addition of transverse diagonal bracing and by doubling the planking. Seppings moved the process forward from what were essentially remedial measures to the incorporation of diagonal frames in the lower hull, diagonal deck planking where possible, and the use of continuous shelves to better link beams to frames. Remaining spaces between bottom frames were solid-filled with timber coated with a mixture of linseed and coal tar.

Having proved his ideas on three elderly 74s during 1810-11, Seppings was allowed to incorporate them into the 120-gun *Howe*, building during 1812. In frigates, Seppings successfully added iron diagonals. He showed by measurement that the breakage, or hull movement, of ships built to his methods had been virtually eliminated. Efforts to reduce the concept to a simple mathematical solution were unsuccessful, although subsequent trial and error did demonstrate that some members were redundant and could be eliminated. Being a single girder rather than a collection of loosely connected elements, Seppings' hulls were stiffer and could be made longer. Their extra strength also permitted the shipping of the heavier armaments then being favoured.

As part of the re-modelling of the fleet, some older First and Second Rates were slated to be cut down to two-deckers. As built, the main bow structure extended upward only to the middle deck (i.e. the centre of the three gun decks), the upper deck terminating at its forward end in a light transverse bulkhead which had long been shown to be vulnerable to the effects of raking fire. In removing the upper deck, Seppings saw no need to lower the bow structure in turn, creating, virtually by chance, the first two-deckers with high bows. This was quickly adapted to the so-called 'round-bow', much stronger and better able to resist the pounding of sea and enemy fire alike. Suitably designed, it also permitted the inclusion of further gun ports to improve chase fire.

Seppings then addressed the stern, where the discontinuity of structure to provide a counter capable of supporting the huge expanse of galleries and glass had long been a weakness. His 'round stern' provided a sound, coherent structure but met with wide disapproval on aesthetic grounds and reduce habitability. Variously 'round' or 'elliptical', the new sterns undeniably improved resistance to damage and, again, increased axial fire.

Sailing performance was a great design variable and, in these days before experimental modelling had been introduced, improvements were the responsibility of the Squadron of Evolution (or 'Experimental Squadron'). Although British naval tradition was aggressively to seek combat, forcing action on a reluctant opponent was not always possible. Foreign-built ships often had superior sailing qualities which enabled them to decline or terminate an action. On occasion, particularly in single-ship duels, superior manoeuvre decided the outcome. Experimental sailing was intended simply to determine, by empirical means, why certain ships sailed better than others. Even today, with powered ships, this is no simple matter. For a sailing ship it was virtually impossible, for there were too many variables: the changing asymmetry of the hull under varying angles of heel; the area, disposition or trim of the rig; the experience of the sailing master. With two otherwise identical powered ships sheer horsepower will decide the faster but, in the case of sailing ships, the skill of an individual crew was all-important. Not surprisingly, therefore, many, including Seppings himself, set little store by the squadron's activities, even though it evaluated several of his own designs in comparative tests.

Seppings' creation of stronger and larger hulls was timely for, as mentioned, there was a general movement towards heavier armament. The 32-pounder was recognised by the British as approaching the ideal when destructive power was set against weight and crew size, and both the French and American navies were working to mount this weapon, or its equivalent, on all gun decks. More reliable materials and improved manufacturing techniques had made possible the carronade. These qualities were now employed to reduce the weight of metal in larger guns, in effect to merge the characteristics of cannon and carronade.

A contemporary French treatise on gunnery shows their equivalent to a standard 32-pounder cannon to have a barrel weight of 200 times that of its solid round shot. The equivalent 32-pounder carronade, in contrast, had a weight factor of only 69, or one third. Between these two weapons with their respective long and short ranges, were now inserted two further 32-pounder variants of intermediate length and barrel thickness. These had weight factors of 116 and 142, equal to 18-and 24-pounder cannon respectively. Mounting such variants on the middle and upper decks retained the same weight distribution as before while giving the ship a homogeneous 32-pounder armament.

The hitting power of the big American frigates had made a considerable impression on British thinking. Traditional, bruising, close-range combat should, it was proposed, be abandoned in favour of fighting with the maximum weight of metal delivered at the maximum range. It would be 1826 before the British adopted an all-32-pounder armament, experimenting first with 24-pounders bored out and shortened to create two new variants, namely the 32-pounder 50 hundredweight (cwt) and the 32-pounder 41cwt. Reduced barrel thickness demanded lighter firing charges. Greater elevation was thus required to attain a given range. This, and the guns' reduced weight, resulted in a more severe recoil with consequent damage to the ship's fabric, not least to Seppings' newly-introduced, diagonally-laid decks. There was also no question of firing the new guns double-shotted although, with the general tendency away from short-range engagement, this was of reduced consequence.

Calls began to be heard for the creation of a permanent gunnery establishment. It was apparent that it was already possible to engage and defeat an opponent at 2,000 or even 3,000 yards, and the trend toward even greater ranges required that gunnery be taught as a science. This was anathema to a core of more senior officers who had been nurtured on a regime of continuous success through point-blank engagements and who stoically refused to believe that this state of affairs could ever change. While it would be 1830 before the old razee *Excellent* became the Navy's floating gunnery school, change was imposed on the Service by outside forces.

Since the end of the 18th century bomb ketches had been lobbing explosive-

Delaware
One of an intended class of six 74s, the *Delaware* was laid down in 1817 by Norfolk Navy Yard. Only three were ever completed as planned, the *New York* remaining so long on the ways that she was destroyed when the Norfolk yard was burned during the civil war. This same fire claimed the *Delaware*.

filled spherical projectiles over the walls of fortifications. Carronades also fired hollow spherical shot and it is surprising how the two concepts were not earlier combined. Always ready to experiment, the French had long supplied their fleet with spherical explosive shells that were interchangeable with solid shot. As these were activated by a protruding length of fuse, lit by the gun's discharge, it was possible for them to detonate almost instantaneously on firing. Such an accident has, indeed, often been cited as the cause of the catastrophic explosion that destroyed Brueys' flagship at the Nile.

Renewed interest in the shell-firing gun is credited to the French General Henri Paixhans and the development of more reliable fusing. Cannon were re-bored to accept a larger-diameter shot, leaving a chamber for the firing charge at the inboard end. Between the charge and the shell was located the usual wad, together with a specially configured 'sabot'. This both aligned the shell and separated it from the firing charge.

To the French the shell gun, or *canon-obusier*, promised superiority over the British fleet by making its wooden warships vulnerable to fire and explosion. During ensuing decades they would also advance armour protection, steam power, the torpedo, torpedo boat and submarine as further means of rendering the Royal Navy obsolete. Each failed, because the French could never match the British technical and manufacturing base, which could simply out-build them. Embarking on a protracted period of freedom from major war, the Royal Navy introduced the shell gun at a leisurely pace, the period of its development falling after the reign of King George III.

As part of the review of the required numbers and types of warship, the nominal firepower quoted for each rate was, from 1816-17, increased to include the carronades that had always been carried. A Third Rate 74 might thus now be referred to as an 'eighty' or an 'eighty-two'. The kernel of a British battle squadron had long been the 100-gun First Rate three-decker, prodigious in action but ponderous to the extent that admirals keen to force battle had been known to shift their flags to 74s.

George IV aboard the Lightning (Huggins)

This exquisite painting shows King George IV making a historic royal 'first' by sailing from Holyhead to Dublin in the steam packet *Lightning* in August 1821. The vessel was renamed in his honour, *Royal Sovereign* later being contracted to *Sovereign*. When the Post Office packet service was taken over by the Admiralty in 1837, she was renamed yet again, becoming the *Monkey*.

Experience at Trafalgar, however, had convinced the French of their value and their subsequent building programme stimulated a British response. The growth in the size of First Rates really began with the British-built *Ville de Paris*, a 110-gunner completed in 1795. Commenced as a sister, the *Hibernia* was lengthened during construction, entering service in 1804 as a nominal 120-gunner. The first ship actually designed to this establishment was the *Caledonia* which, on completion in 1808, turned out to be a superlative sailer. Her lines were the basis for successive classes of First Rate clear through to Victoria's reign. As these great new ships commissioned, older units, worn out or unable to be up-gunned, were broken up, relegated to harbour service or razeed to Third Rates.

In 1793 the active fleet list included just five First Rates, all of 100 guns, together with 15 Second Rates of 98 guns and one of 90. By 1820, the final year of the King's reign, this had changed to 16 First Rates- five of 120 guns, two of 112, two of 108, one of 106 and six of 104. Seven more (four of them 120s) were on order or under construction. Three-decked Second Rates had disappeared, the class being usurped by two-decker 80s or 84s, nine of which were active with 12 building.

The ubiquitous British 74 could not simply be up-gunned if the gun deck sills were to remain a reasonable height above the waterline. A model, however, already existed in the 80-gun *Canopus*, built in Toulon in 1797 as the *Franklin*, and taken at the Nile. Fast and a steady gun platform, she was over three metres longer than her British equivalents and sufficiently dimensioned all round to accommodate the heavier armament required by the Board of Admiralty. She was copied as the *Formidable*, a new-style 84-gun Second Rate which was then developed further over many classes. Sané's design, combined with Seppings' strength, produced a hull that could ship 32 32-pounders on the gun deck, the same number of 24-pounders on the main deck and four more on the quarterdeck. She could take on a pair of earlier 74s with their 18-pounder main deck batteries. Heavier again were the small razeed three-deckers, which had the size and scantlings to carry a uniform armament of 32-pounders on both the gun and main decks.

The French built a number of 32-pounder frigates but the Royal Navy mounted such heavy weapons only on cut-down 74s. There were in addition a few 52-gun heavy

H M S Active — with Capt Burtons wheel Portsmouth harbour

frigates with 24-pounders and a far greater number of 18-pounder 44s, classified as Fourth and Fifth Rates respectively.

For the professional seaman, who had as yet no provision for continuous service, the end of the war was a calamity. Of 140,000 personnel serving in 1813 only 19,000 remained just four years later. Thousands of officers were thrown on to half pay, the lists being so long that only exceptional ability or influence would find a post aboard one of the decreasing number of active ships. Officers of commander rank and below could be retired but post-captains remained on an interminable list (nearly 900 names) that, theoretically, led by seniority to flag rank. Unfortunately, the list of flag officers was equally congested by many of exceedingly advanced years, a situation that was to greatly reduce the efficiency of the Service when, in mid-century, it was faced with hostilities against Russia.

For the greater part, the 19th century was a period where naval action was confined to peacekeeping and punitive expeditions. Despite occasional chastisement by the major powers, the inhabitants of the Barbary Coast still found piracy, extortion and slavery to be a useful means of supplementing their income. Following their war with Britain the Americans expanded their fleet and, in May 1815, Commodore Stephen Decatur led a

HMS Active with paddles (John Schetky)

Paddles in 1817 were well proven, but the machinery to drive them dictated a ship's layout. Ryder Burton, supported later by Sir Charles Napier, devised an auxiliary arrangement, whereby wheels could be rigged for manoeuvring and worked by the abundant manpower of a sailing warship. Surprisingly, perhaps, they worked, this sketch by the Court's marine artist, Schetky, showing the *Active* frigate in 1819.

Pennsylvania

Laid down in 1822, the 120-gun *Pennsylvania* was intended to make it impossible for an enemy of America to impose a close blockade on the US coast. Not completed until 1837, her sheer size greatly taxed the resources of the Philadelphia Navy Yard that built her. Manning her was also expensive, and she continued to be a target for cost-cutters until she was finally burned at Norfolk in 1861.

force of nine warships on a show of strength. This was followed up by Commodore William Bainbridge with a further squadron, including the new 74-gun *Independence*. Guarantees and indemnities were received from Algiers, Tunis and Tripoli.

The Algerines, however, read restraint as weakness, and continued their depredations. The British, therefore, assembled a force under Sir Edward Pellew, who had assumed the post of Commander-in-Chief, Mediterranean on Collingwood's untimely death in 1810. Pellew, noted for his action with the *Droits de l'Homme* back in 1796 was, in 1816, 60 years of age. From his flagship, the *Queen Charlotte* 100, he commanded a 98, three 74s, one heavy and four smaller frigates, five sloops, four bombs and an 'explosion vessel'. On arrival at Gibraltar on 14th August 1816, the force was joined by five Dutch frigates and a sloop.

Pellew arrived off Algiers on the 27th and, after a brief ultimatum, stood into the harbour. Somewhat crowded, his heavier ships moored in bombardment positions and, from 3.00 p.m. until 10.00 p.m., battered the fortifications at close range with over 45,000 round shot. In parallel, the bombs fired much of the city with their explosive ordnance, while the explosion vessel was expended alongside a battery. Both British and Dutch squadrons inflicted and suffered considerable damage and casualties. Predictably, the Algerines agreed terms but, as no military force was ever landed, their activities were never completely suppressed. Pellew, however, was created Viscount Exmouth.

From 1807, slave-trading was progressively abandoned by the major European powers, but there still existed a hugely-profitable illicit trade, the suppression of which was to occupy leading fleets for decades to come.

Having played such a pivotal role in the successful outcome of years of war, the sailing warship was about to enter its final phase. Already, tall smoking stacks and a new breed of seamen with oily hands and strange terminologies had signalled the arrival of what would become the new order. Steam, in the context of marine propulsion, had been exercising the minds of innovators since the 1780s. Symington's craft, *Charlotte Dundas*, successfully towed canal barges in 1802 to claim her title of the world's first commercial steamship. It fell to the American engineer Robert Fulton, however, to first apply steam power to warship propulsion. Having failed to impress either the French or the British governments in the concept of submersibles, Fulton built the commercially-practical *Clermont* in 1807. With the United States at war, he went on to build a large, paddle-propelled catamaran warship, named *Demologos*. Heavily armed and protected, she was intended to drive off close-blockading British squadrons. Completed too late, she was never proved in action but would probably have been too cumbersome. Fulton's death in 1815 brought such ventures to a premature end.

The British Admiralty adopted steam power slowly and logically, first applying it to dockyard machinery and to non-propelled dredgers. Having for so long suffered from squadrons being unable to sail owing to contrary winds, the Admiralty saw an immediate application for steamships in towage, which craft could also double as despatch boats.

The Admiralty also supervised the construction of prototype steam packets for the Post Office. As the first two, *Lightning* and *Meteor*, were building during 1820, the old King died. It fell to his successor, George IV, to make the first royal passage by steamship, crossing by packet to Ireland in August 1821.

INDEX

The Aesthetic Movement

The Aesthetic Movement

PRELUDE TO ART NOUVEAU

Elizabeth Aslin

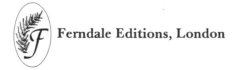 Ferndale Editions, London

This edition published 1981 by Ferndale Editions
Brent House, 24-28 Friern Park, London N12 9DA,
under licence from the proprietor.

Copyright © Elizabeth Aslin 1969

ISBN 0-905746 29 5

Printed and bound in Hong Kong by South China Printing Co.

Contents

List of plates

9

List of plates

Front of jacket: Detail of a piano cover embroidered in gold thread and *appliqué* on silk damask, designed by C. R. Ashbee, about 1889. *London, Victoria and Albert Museum.*

Back of jacket: Tile, designed by Kate Greenaway, made of earthernware, transfer printed in colours and made by T. & R. Boote, Birmingham, 1883. *London, Victoria and Albert Museum.*

Front endpaper: Wallpaper registered 7 June 1870, made by Gillow & Company, 176 Oxford Street, London. *London, Patent Office.*

Back endpaper: 'Gold, black and brown' wallpaper made by Jeffrey & Co., Islington, 1878. *London, Patent Office.*

List of figures in the text

Chapter 1

INTRODUCTION

In recent years, despite the popularity of certain aspects of Victorian art, the belief has grown that the Victorian period as a whole was a Philistine age in which the low standards in all the visual arts was relieved only by the work of William Morris and that *fin de siècle* Art Nouveau, with its own brand of poetic gloom, heralded the dawn of the enlightenment of the twentieth century. Admittedly a high proportion of what was produced in England during the nineteenth century in the fields of the decorative arts and of architecture was unattractive, but this oversimplification is open to question on at least two grounds. It presupposes that the work of the twentieth century is of necessity superior to that of our immediate forebears and it completely ignores the genuine modern style of the Victorians, the Art or Aesthetic Movement of the eighteen-seventies and 'eighties when it could be said that 'there has assuredly never been since the world began an age in which people thought, talked, wrote and spent such inordinate sums of money and hours of time in cultivating and indulging their tastes'.[1]

The movement, beginning with the work of a few architects and designers in the 'sixties, gathered force until, in the 'eighties, it embraced every art form from the greetings card to domestic architecture. It introduced Japanese art to children's story books and red brick Queen Anne architecture to the streets of London; it led to changes in fashionable dress, to the first garden suburb and to the vogue for painted dark green or Venetian red front doors and railings which lasted for half a century in England. People described themselves as 'going in' for 'High Art', for Art Decoration, Art Embroidery or Art Furniture, this last expression becoming so general that by the mid 'seventies the *London Trades Directory* lists 'Art Furniture Manufacturers' quite separately from ordinary cabinet-makers and furnishers. The tone of the whole movement is recorded in a conversation which William Morris had with a lady who said, 'You know I wouldn't mind a lad being a cabinet-maker if he only made Art Furniture'.[2]

In terms of architecture and the applied arts the movement was confined to the English-speaking countries, that is to the British Isles and the United States, though it would seem that the fashion for aesthetic clothing spread briefly to France, in the early eighteen-eighties. By this time 'aesthetic', a word virtually unknown in the early part of the century, had become the adjective for almost anything that was currently fashionable.

The term was invented or adapted from the Greek by the German philosopher Baumgarten whose work *Aesthetica* was published in 1750. The word, defined as meaning the science of the beautiful or the philosophy of taste, was brought to England at the beginning of the nineteenth century together with its opposite, 'philistine', which in this context meant one deficient in liberal culture whose interests were bounded by material and commonplace things as opposed to the high-minded spiritual and artistic values of the aesthetes. By the middle of the century the two terms were in general if somewhat ill-defined use. The naturalist, Charles Darwin, for instance, described birds as aesthetic, meaning that in his view their taste for beauty was similar to that of man, while another writer thought that the term aesthetic covered 'the adoption of a sentimental archaism as the ideal of beauty'. By 1880, however, the Aesthetic Movement in the arts was a well-established fact and the name itself part of everyday speech.

One of the origins of the movement, and that to which its name can be attributed, was to be found in a long-standing literary and philosophical dispute as to whether an object was actually beautiful in itself or whether it merely appeared so to those whose sensibilities and training enabled them to appreciate it. Assuming the latter to be the case it was obviously necessary to establish principles or standards by which the beauty of any work of art or domestic utensil could be assessed and 'hence', wrote a contemporary author, 'the essence of the movement is the union of persons of cultivated tastes to define and decide upon what is to be admired'.[3] This meant that in the centre of the movement there was a closely-knit group of self-appointed *cognoscenti* with carefully cultivated sensibilities and that some sort of publicity was needed by them to pass on to their followers the standards to which they should aspire. Aesthetes laid down standards of colour, of ornament and of form for all aspects of art and domestic decoration which, reduced to the basic essentials, were simple, sensible and a considerable improvement on the elaborations of the design of the High Victorian period. The public, however, naturally tended to associate aesthetic ideas with the more extreme elements in the movement and this led to a great deal of simple fun and even ridicule in the press which obscured the overall serious and significant effects which influenced many aspects of everyday life. These benefits were explained in an article in the short-lived periodical *The Burlington*, sub-titled 'A High Class Monthly Periodical', which was the mouthpiece of the movement in 1881 and 1882. Having dealt with the recent improvements in the costume of an imaginary Mrs Jones, the author proceeds to Mr Philistine Jones who

'dubs all aesthetes idiots, while he also adopts their ideas. A dozen years ago his dazzling carpets and wallpapers were enough to give a templar a fit of delirium tremens – his furniture was a roughly hewn mass of ponderous mahogany, his walls were hung with abominations encircled in tawdry gilt frames – which he called pictures, he delighted in waxen fruit under glass covers; his crockery, his glass, in fine everything he possessed and especially admired was a violation of good taste. But somehow he has changed all this – the human eye may now repose upon the neutral tints of his carpets and walls. He has a dado, and blue and white china may be espied in nooks and corners – he has eschewed gilt – he has ceased to care for stucco – he lives in a Queen Anne house and actually has begun to think about the shape of his jugs.

'This improvement is rapidly spreading through all classes of society – good taste is no longer an expensive luxury to indulge in – the commonest articles of domestic use are now fashioned in accordance with its laws and the poorest may have in their homes at the cost of a few pence cups and saucers and jugs and teapots, more artistic in form and design than were to be found twenty years ago in any homes but those of the cultured rich.

'And to whom are we indebted for these advantages? Why, to the Aesthetes, the fools and idiots of Philistine phraseology.'

Even allowing for the exaggerations of an enthusiast such sweeping changes, which were also recorded by other writers, must obviously have been based on something more than the fancies of a few artistic cranks and exhibitionists whose languid manner, based on the drooping figures of Burne-Jones, disguised a sincere attempt to bring some beauty into an increasingly ugly world. Despite the reforming spirit which inspired both designers and writers on the decorative arts, this beauty took diverse forms and the unifying element of the movement was one of mood and atmosphere rather than any immediately obvious common visual quality. Each designer strove for a practical interpretation of the new ideas which at the same time was personally satisfying.

The actual artistic origins of the movement were far more complex than something compounded of these abstract theories and a feeling for Burne-Jones, and they date back to the beginning of Queen Victoria's reign, if not even earlier. In the eighteen-thirties and 'forties it was fairly generally agreed by thinking men that English design in all branches of the industrial arts was at a very low ebb. Ornament was lavish and overwrought and the exciting possibilities of new materials, new industrial processes, new dye-stuffs for fabric printing and, above all, an expanding market merely led manufacturers to the indiscriminate production of ever increasing quantities of singularly ill-designed and elaborate objects. Design motifs were picked at random from the many published 'cribs' the most distinguished of which, Owen Jones' *Grammar of Ornament*, contained examples of every known historical style. Eclecticism was rampant and the simple elegances of the eighteenth century were scorned. It was not only those professionally involved, such as artists and designers, but other public-spirited men who became alarmed at design standards and addressed themselves to matters of taste and in particular to the form and type of decoration and ornament. In early Victorian terms this problem was one of how to apply 'art' to industrial products.

Henry Cole (1808–82) was an early and influential reformer who later became the moving influence behind the Great Exhibition of 1851 and the first head of the South Kensington Museum. Cole's remedy was the employment of painters and sculptors to design objects of everyday use. He also recommended the use of naturalistic 'appropriate' ornament. This meant that instead of the indiscriminate use of design motifs culled from a variety of historical sources, designers were to confine themselves to renderings of natural forms which symbolized the use of the object in question. Thus ears of corn were suitable for bread boards, bunches of grapes for wine jugs and hops for beer tankards, irrespective of the material used. Appropriate ornament became a popular form of early-Victorian decoration but obviously it had little effect on the basic shape of the objects, as opposed to the ornament applied to them.

The average manufacturer's panacea for these design ills was to make strenuous efforts to emulate the French both in design and quality of manufacture. This was not a piece of disinterested idealism but a practical attempt to increase exports and reduce imports; as French goods were popular so it seemed sensible to imitate them. It was no doubt with this aim in mind that the first exhibits purchased for what is now the Victoria and Albert Museum were objects selected from the Paris Exhibition of French Industrial Arts held in 1844. These included examples of Sèvres porcelain, as well as elaborate pieces of metalwork, and they were intended as models for British manufacturers and artisans; they seem to have achieved the required effect all too thoroughly. Reporting to the Select Committee on the School of Design in 1849, Henry Cole said that 'the best of our metal ornamental designs are plagiarisms from the French; as respects the Potteries, the best of the pottery are imitations of old Dresden and Sèvres designs' and the list continues through all the other categories of industrial design. Another witness on the same occasion stated that all the English wallpapers were direct copies from the French production. Fresh impetus was given to this trend by an influx of foreign artisans and tradesmen around 1848, particularly into the cabinet-making trade, and by 1851 almost all the English exhibits in the industrial design sections of the famous Great Exhibition of that year were based on French models, both in form and colour. Furniture was carved and gilt, metal mounts abounded, and rich, strident colours were used for carpets, textiles and wallpapers.

This imitation of French design continued through the 'fifties although efforts were made through various Select Committees, Government Reports and, above all, Exhibitions held up and down the country to improve public taste and native design standards. A small victory was won for England by a very large exhibit at the Paris International Exhibition of 1855. On this occasion, despite the reported 'incontestable pre-eminence of France in many sections'⁴ an English cabinet-making firm won an award for a giant buffet or sideboard. Even this was in the style of Louis XVI and designed by a Frenchman though made by English craftsmen, no less than forty of whom laboured to produce this small English triumph. The real turning point came with the International Exhibition held in London in 1862. Less well-known than the earlier Great Exhibition, it was of infinitely greater significance in the development of nineteenth-century taste and design. In all the contemporary writing on that exhibition there was a remarkable self-congratulatory tone admitting by implication the previously unsatisfactory state of affairs. 'It is a pleasure to report a most unmistakable advance in almost every direction since the exhibition of

1 Corner cupboard; ebonized wood with incised decoration designed by Alfred Waterhouse and painted in colours on a gilt ground by Mrs Alfred Waterhouse, 1878. *London, Victoria and Albert Museum.*

2   Buffet in ebonized wood with silver-plated fittings and inset panels of embossed Japanese leather paper, designed by E. W. Godwin, 1867. *London, Victoria and Albert Museum.*

3   Sideboard in various woods with metal mounts designed by Alfred Waterhouse, about 1872. *The Rt Hon. the Earl of Selborne.*

4   Chair, with turned and ebonized decoration, designed by Alfred Waterhouse, 1872. *The Rt Hon. the Earl of Selborne.*

5   Armchair in ebonized wood with rush seat combining Japanese and English traditional design, about 1870. *The Rev. Michael McLean.*

6   Side chair in golden oak, 'Eastlake' style, about 1880. *New York ; Courtesy of the Brooklyn Museum ; Gift of Mrs Otto Gretz*

2

3

4

5

6

7 Buffet of ebony, with marquetry of various woods and carved boxwood panels, designed by B. J. Talbert and made by Gillow's, 1873. *Vienna, Österreichisches Museum für Angewandte Kunst.*

8 Detail of plate 7 above.

9 Original design for 'Sunflower' wallpaper by B. J. Talbert. The wallpaper was made by Jeffrey & Co., 1878. *London, Victoria and Albert Museum.*

10 'Apple Blossom', hand-printed wallpaper designed by Lewis F. Day, 1878, and made by Jeffrey & Co., for W. B. Simpson & Sons. *London, Victoria and Albert Museum.*

11 'Trellis dado', hand-printed wallpaper designed by Lewis F. Day for W. B. Simpson & Sons, about 1877. *London, Victoria and Albert Museum.*

7

8

15

On previous page

12   Wallpaper designed by B. J. Talbert and exhibited by Jeffrey & Co., Paris 1878. *London, Victoria and Albert Museum.*

13   Wallpaper, frieze, filling and dado designed by B. J. Talbert and made by Jeffrey & Co., 1877. *London, Victoria and Albert Museum.*

14   'The Sleeping Beauty', machine-printed nursery wallpaper designed by Walter Crane and made by Jeffrey & Co., 1875. *London, Victoria and Albert Museum.*

15   Original design for part of 'Swan, Rush and Iris' dado, by Walter Crane. The paper was printed by Jeffrey & Co., 1877. *London, Victoria and Albert Museum.*

16

16 Original design for a wallpaper
by E. W. Godwin. The paper
was printed by Jeffrey & Co., 1872.
London, Victoria and Albert Museum.

17 Decorative panel in carved
boxwood from a piano designed by
H. W. Batley and made by James
Shoolbred & Co., 1878. *London,
Victoria and Albert Museum.*

18

19

18 Chair in ebonized wood with split-cane back and seat designed by E. W. Godwin and made by William Watt about 1877. *In the author's possession.*

19 'Jacobean' armchair made by Collier and Plucknett, Warwick, from a design by E. W. Godwin of about 1877. *London, Victoria and Albert Museum.*

20 Sussex chair of ebonized beech with a rush seat made by Morris & Co., from about 1865. *London, Victoria and Albert Museum.*

20

21

22

23

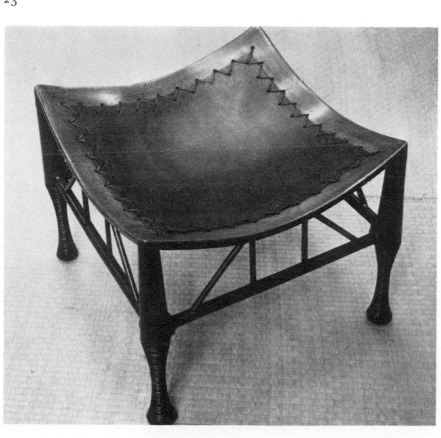

21   Table in ebonized oak,
designed by E. W. Godwin and
made by William Watt, 1876. This
table was originally owned by
Ellen Terry. *Bristol, City Art
Gallery.*

22   Chair probably designed and
made for Liberty & Co., 1884.
*Walthamstow, William Morris
Gallery.*

23   'The Thebes stool', in
mahogany with a leather seat
designed and made for Liberty &
Co., 1884. *London, Victoria and
Albert Museum.*

24   25

24   Chair and coffee table
designed by E. W. Godwin, 1875
and 1867 and made by William
Watt. *London, Victoria and Albert
Museum.*

25   Chairs with ebonized frames
and mahogany panels inlaid with
light wood. Part of a set of bedroom
furniture made by Herter Brothers
for William T. Carter of
Philadelphia, 1876. *Philadelphia,
Museum of Art.*

1851'[5] wrote one commentator, and others spoke of the disappearance of meaningless ornament and the development of a new lightness and grace in English work. In both learned professional journals and the popular press all were agreed that English designers and artisans had at last established themselves as the equals of their foreign rival in almost all trades.

In addition to this newly acquired self-confidence in English design and manufacture in the industrial arts, there appeared in the 1862 Exhibition other new elements which were to have a profound influence on later nineteenth-century taste. The first was that William Morris (1834–96) and the colleagues with whom he was associated in the newly-formed firm of Morris, Marshall, Faulkner and Company, exhibited publicly for the first time. Their painted furniture and rich embroideries had previously only been seen by close friends in the privacy of their homes. Now they were available to a wider audience and as Morris's associates included such men as Burne-Jones, Rossetti and Ford Madox Brown who painted on furniture at this date, Pre-Raphaelite painting reached a wider, new public. The second new influence was that of Japanese art which was to have a widespread effect on the domestic arts in the latter part of the Victorian period and was one of the most important contributory factors in the Aesthetic Movement. It was the first time that the Japanese had shown at one of the great European exhibitions and, although their display appears to have been quite small and rather cluttered by modern standards, the simplicity of the individual exhibits had a profound and inspiring effect on a small group of architects and painters whose own work eventually led to a mania for almost anything Japanese.

Thus the foundations on which the new 'Art' movement was built were first, a certain national self-confidence in design which made it unnecessary to play safe and emulate the French; secondly, there was the Pre-Raphaelite revolution against the false in painting accompanied by a similar revolt in the decorative arts against the false in decoration, a reformation which stressed the novel idea that an object could derive elegance from its very usefulness and need not be overburdened with superfluous ornament. Thirdly, the enthusiasm for Japanese art was also due in part to its comparative simplicity. Finally the influence of Ruskin and that of William Morris were all important, though at the outset Morris's influence was by example rather than precept. He had been designing for many years before he wrote or spoke, publicly campaigning against the debased standards of mass production which he traced to the disappearance of honest and satisfying craftsmanship.

It is also, in some degree, to William Morris that the missionary aspect of the aesthetic movement can be traced. In one of his earliest published works, a lecture on 'The Decorative Arts' given in 1878 to the Trades Guild of Learning, Morris said 'I do not want art for a few' and likened the artist working for his own delight to the rich man eating in the presence of 'starving soldiers in a beleaguered fort'. The marked difference between this and other art movements was that it was essentially educational and 'improving' in intention. The designers and painters wished not only to work in a new way but to convince the general public of the rightness of their views. Hence one of the most influential figures of the whole movement was Oscar Wilde, who lectured and spread the views of his more creative associates. And even Whistler, who had no interest in the social aspects of art, felt it his duty as an artist to uphold good taste and impose it on others.

As part of the same process, books on the decorative arts appeared in quantities in the 1870s and '80s. Obviously they were nothing like the lush, coloured publications of the twentieth century but none the less these books were very fully illustrated and their authors were concerned to inform their readers of the standards at which they should aim in furnishing and decoration. The authors were not in complete agreement in their exact interpretation of 'art' but there was a consensus of opinion on the need for an alteration in design of all kinds.

The earliest and one of the most influential of these guides for the amateur was C. L. Eastlake's *Hints on Household Taste*, originally published as a series of articles in the *Cornhill Magazine* and first issued as a fully illustrated book in 1867. In the introduction Eastlake wrote 'half the effect of every room which is planned must ultimately depend on the manner in which it is fitted up and, if our national taste is ever to assume a definite character, let us hope that the inside of our dwellings will reflect it no less than the walls by which they are enclosed'. Other books and articles followed in profusion, some dealing with interior decoration in general, others with individual rooms such as a series which included *The Bedroom and the Boudoir* by Lady Baker (1878), *The Dining Room* by Mrs Loftie of the same year. But authors did not confine themselves to interior decoration. Mrs Haweis, a popular author, wrote on *The Art of Beauty* and concerned herself with every aspect of decoration, dress and jewellery and even considered the colour of hair which was aesthetically acceptable. Mrs Haweis had in her writing the same objective as Eastlake and others of her contemporaries though she did not think of herself as an aesthete and did not think highly of Queen Anne architecture. Similarly another influential writer and lecturer, Lucy Crane, the sister of the better-known Walter, while putting forward many aesthetic ideas, spoke scornfully of 'art embroidery, art decoration and the like tautological expressions' and suggested that they had been invented by shopkeepers to please that part of the public which was attracted by fashion and novelty.

In addition to books on every aspect of decorative art, new periodicals abounded and the old-established ones such as the *Art Journal* were re-designed in a new format with a new type of illustration often printed in soft browns and sepias, colours second only in popularity to the aesthetic green –

'No tint which common blue and yellow mingled make
 But green y wrought of sepia without stint
 With indigo and lake.'[6]

Two of the earliest periodicals in this field were *The Architect* and *The British Architect* first published in 1869 and 1874 respectively. Both voiced advanced opinions and were illustrated by reproductions of pen drawings instead of the tight engravings of earlier architectural publications. The only two

Victorian periodicals devoted to furniture started at the end of the 'seventies, as did *The Magazine of Art, The Journal of Decorative Art, Decoration* and *The Artist*, subtitled 'Journal of Home Culture'.

The emphasis on home culture and on amateur work of all kinds sprang naturally from the aesthetic concept of art embracing every aspect of life and several of the periodicals were as much concerned with the amateur artist and craftsman as with professional work. Another aspect of the movement was the proliferation of art groups and societies and of amateur craft workers. One of these bodies was the Home Arts and Industries Association, dedicated to 'spread knowledge of Art Handwork among the people', whose members carved woodwork and made repoussé copper vessels. The lady amateur made her appearance in the eighteen-seventies, painting panels on furniture and decorating plates and vases in addition to her traditional pursuit of embroidery. One firm of artistic tradesmen, Messrs Howell and James, organized an annual exhibition of painting on pottery at which amateurs and professionals showed their skill and prizes were awarded by a selection committee of Academicians. At the Paris International Exhibition of 1878 Howell and James actually included amateur work in their exhibit.

At this distance the eighteen-seventies and 'eighties seem to have an atmosphere quite unlike any other part of the Victorian period. Coupled with the artistic activity was a certain sense of excitement at new scientific developments that encroached on home life. Electric light, the telephone and new methods of transport produced as much copy for the cartoonist as did the Art Movement itself. *Punch* encouraged its readers to laugh at scientific jokes, which have proved eventually not fantasy but fairly accurate prophecy, and similarly though the Aesthetic Movement had its ludicrous aspects it did contain the seeds of ideas which later gained general acceptance.

Over forty years ago, when early Victorian bric-à-brac was already fashionable in some circles, Roger Fry forecast that later generations would become sentimental about the 'eighties, a period which he regarded with horror, having been brought up in an artistic home surrounded by 'black polished wood with spidery lines of conventional flowers incised in the wood and then gilt'.[7] At least one piece of furniture in this manner survives which was decorated by Roger Fry's aunt (plate 1). Writing in 1919 Fry said 'we at this moment have no inkling of the lies they (our successors) will invent about the 'eighties to amuse themselves. We only know that when the time comes the legend will have taken shape and, from that moment on, the objects of the time will have the property of emanation.' With this warning in mind and the wealth of available evidence it should be possible to establish the reality beyond the legend of the 'eighties, beyond the vision of artistic interiors in which elegant drooping figures on spindly Morris chairs gazed at their blue and white china or sketched sunflowers.

Chapter 2

RED BRICK AND SUNFLOWERS

The architectural innovation of the 'seventies and 'eighties was the introduction of an entirely new style called, somewhat inaccurately by both admirers and critics, 'Queen Anne'. It was essentially a domestic and secular style and, like other aspects of the Aesthetic Movement, was confined to England and America. While the rest of Europe continued to produce variations on the flamboyant and relatively cumbersome forms associated with the 'High Victorian' period, the English-speaking countries embarked on a revival of domestic building with some concern for comfort and convenience as well as for picturesque effect. It is to the aesthetes and their associates that we owe the red brick houses of Chelsea and Kensington, the great blocks of mansion flats embellished with terracotta sunflowers and many more modest urban dwellings each with its own garden.

Until the eighteen-seventies, though a version of Italianate classic was the accepted style for banks, club houses and the more pretentious type of town house, architecture was predominantly Gothic in one form or another. Even the reformers such as Pugin, Morris, Street or Butterfield, remained convinced Gothicists throughout their careers, believing that English architecture had gone astray at the end of the sixteenth century or even earlier when pure Gothic was abandoned and foreign influences contributed to the eclectic elaborations of Elizabethan and Jacobean building. It was felt that the national traditions of architecture had been still further damaged by the introduction of Palladian classicism and that only by turning the clock back to the days of pure medieval Gothic and by ignoring the intervening regrettable foreign-inspired developments could a truly English style be evolved. A desire for a genuine style expressing the aspirations of the nineteenth century inspired much architecture that in retrospect appears mere plagiarism. However, while the revived Gothic or 'pointed' architecture was considered appropriate for places of worship and could be applied with success to such large buildings as guildhalls, town halls and law courts, it led to curious and inconvenient results as a domestic style.

As early as 1857 in his *Remarks on Secular and Domestic Architecture* Gilbert Scott (1811–78), though advocating building based on a serious understanding of Gothic architecture, expressed the hope that 'the practice of building abbeys for gentlemen's residences is gone' and 'that the use of castles having long since gone by, people will henceforth be content to live

26 'Honeysuckle', designed by William Morris, 1876, and printed on Indian tusser silk by Thomas Wardle, Leek. *London, Victoria and Albert Museum.*

27 Part of a bedspread in indigo-dyed linen embroidered in coloured silks, designed by William Morris, 1877. *London, Victoria and Albert Museum.*

28 Detail of a curtain with *appliqué* and embroidery in crewel wools. Designed by H.R.H. Princess Louise and worked at the Royal School of Art Needlework, 1877. *Manchester, Town Hall.*

29 'Tulip' chintz, designed by William Morris, 1875. *London, Victoria and Albert Museum.*

32

in houses'. The practice, however, continued for some years longer and one of the first architects to rebel against it was J. J. Stevenson (1831–1908) who was able to take the revolutionary step of abandoning Gothic when he built a house for himself in London in 1871. Not only was the house of red brick but it was built in present-day Bayswater Road in an area of stucco houses in the classical taste. Stevenson called it the 'Red House' like another landmark in the history of domestic architecture, the William Morris house designed by Philip Webb ten years earlier. Stevenson's house was actually of brownish brick with brighter red details and mouldings and with sash windows; it was designed with some thought for comfort and convenience as well as style. Whatever the architect's intentions, he launched a fashion which by 1880 had reached such proportions that it was said that 'cheap builders are possessed by the idea that red brick, a blue pot and a fat sunflower in the window are all that is needed to be fashionably aesthetic and Queen Anne.' This comment and an account of an interview with Stevenson appeared in the periodical *The Queen* in 1880 and was later published with other descriptions of artistic houses in book form as *Beautiful Houses*. It is amusing to note that while the author, Mrs Haweis, a popular arbiter of taste, poured scorn on the Queen Anne fashion, her own little book was printed in a simulated eighteenth-century format and in pseudo-Queen Anne type face which incidentally makes it extremely difficult to read. Mrs Haweis described how 'Mr Stevenson began by following enthusiastically the Gothic Renaissance movement but transferred his affections when practical experience convinced him that Gothic architecture and decoration have many demerits when applied to modern houses, especially town houses. The waste of space, the frequent inevitable darkness which complicate the difficulties of Gothic domestic architecture when it has to be combined with nineteenth-century ideas of comfort and luxury are avoided by the adoption of the classic, of course in its more picturesque forms.' This note on the inevitability of the picturesque exactly sets the mood of the late 'seventies and 'eighties when 'picturesque' was a favourite term of commendation and a necessary attribute of any successful design.

While Stevenson's house was the first considered architectural work in the new idiom, the first of the red brick houses in London had actually been built in 1861 by the novelist Thackeray for his own occupation. A modest and relatively undistinguished house it was soon to be overshadowed, as it still is, by its larger neighbour, Number 1, Kensington Palace Green, designed in a semi-Gothic manner by Philip Webb (1831–1915). Thackeray's novel *Henry Esmond*, subtitled 'A Colonel in the Service of Her Majesty Queen Anne' had appeared a few years earlier, rapidly becoming a best seller. Thackeray clearly regarded the period as his own and it was natural that he should provide himself with a pseudo-Queen Anne setting in a house that may well have provided the name for the new style. That this literary origin of the name was accepted even by architects is proved by an article in *The British Architect* in 1875 in which William Burges wrote: 'It has been said and with great truth that the real restorer of medieval art was Sir Walter Scott – in the same way Thackeray, by means of his writing, has made Queen Anne's style popular.' Burges, whose own work was based on

30 'Tanjor Lotus', tusser silk damask, made by T. Wardle, Leek, for Liberty & Co., about 1875. *London, Victoria and Albert Museum.*

31 Panel of tiles painted in 'Persian' colours by William de Morgan about 1885. *London; Courtesy of the Trustees, Old Battersea House.*

32 Tiles, transfer printed and painted in colours, made by T. & F. G. Booth, Church Bank Pottery, Tunstall, Staffordshire, dated 1883. *In the author's possession.*

33 Earthenware tiles painted in colours, with the mark of W. B. Simpson on the reverse, 1878. *West Berlin, Kunstgewerbemuseum.*

French thirteenth-century architecture, went on to give an uncharitable but not wholly inaccurate recipe for the new style. 'To take an ordinary red brick house and to put as many gables and dormers and bow windows as possible – in fact to cut up the outlines; the great object being to get the picturesque by any and every means. The windows should be long and narrow and filled with lead glazing or with small frames divided by straight bars painted white – the ornamental parts consist of a few scrolls in the brickwork and coarse woodwork occasionally verging on the Jacobean.' The observations on narrow windows and gables came rather strangely from one who was literally still building castles as residences.

The main characteristics of the Queen Anne style can be clearly identified whether on large or small buildings. The most prominent feature, of course, was the use of red brick of all kinds. As one lyrical enthusiast put it: 'He must be strangely insensible to the charms of the picturesque who has not felt his mind refreshed and his daily load lightened by their glow of unwonted colour.' A dark red brick was usually used for the main structure, finely-jointed, smooth brickwork of a lighter, brighter red for porches, gables, mouldings and other projections and moulded terracotta for more elaborate ornament. This frequently incorporated the date of erection of the house and almost always used the sunflower as the main decorative motif. The sunflower appeared either as a repeating pattern, as in Cheniston Lodge (plate 43), or growing in an urn-like plant pot (plates 35, 37, 38). One of the earliest panels of this kind is on the gable of Norman Shaw's Lowther Lodge, built in 1874, now the Royal Geographical Society in Kensington Gore (plates 39, 40). A rare variation in decoration was the use of Japanese motifs exactly similar to those found on contemporary embroidery or silver (plates 36, 41, 42). Chimneys were very tall and ornamented with projecting vertical ribs of brickwork emphasizing the height of the building. Gables were curved and shaped or stepped in the Dutch manner producing a variation of the style which came to be known as 'Pont Street Dutch' from the area of Chelsea in which it was most prevalent. One of the most impressive houses of this 'Dutch' kind was built in Harrington Gardens, South Kensington, in 1884 for W. S. Gilbert (1836–1911), who like so many other Philistines, was much involved in the movement he lampooned.

Apart from the gables themselves, smaller gable-shaped panels were incorporated in the Queen Anne buildings and the broken pediment was a popular form, much like that used in contemporary furniture design. The other important innovation which radically changed the appearance of houses, both inside and out, was the introduction of large sash windows instead of the small windows previously dictated by the mullions of the Gothic style. These larger windows were relatively tall, adding to the vertical emphasis of the whole design, and the glass was divided into small panes by wooden glazing bars painted white. Another characteristic feature of the windows was that the upper part was further subdivided and filled with plain coloured glass or sometimes painted in grisaille. The style usually involved a quantity of external woodwork in the form of balconies, balustrades and supporting brackets and this, like the window bars, was painted white.

The same component parts were used in varied ways by a number of architects who between them produced an essentially domestic architectural form in which the façade, though consciously picturesque, reflected the interior arrangement of the building. A decorative feature which was particularly popular for smaller houses in rural settings was tile-hanging on gables and window bays. This innovation can be attributed to W. Eden Nesfield (1835–88) whose first essay in the new manner was a modest little lodge in Kew Gardens. Built in 1866, it was described at the time as an archaeological exercise in early eighteenth-century brickwork and, like most of Nesfield's work, was an entirely personal solution to the particular problem on hand. He was one of the very few architects whose work was influenced by Japanese design and the decoration of some of his buildings incorporates a frieze of stylized sunflowers or discs which Nesfield himself called his 'pies'! While Nesfield was responsible for one or two large buildings, such as Cloverley Hall in Shropshire, his main contribution was in the realm of modest buildings in the small towns and villages of southern England where his combination of original forms and traditional picturesque detail blended with the existing brick houses of the eighteenth century.

By the early eighteen-seventies the existence of the Queen Anne school of architecture was thoroughly established, whether its origins were literary or architectural. An editorial article in *The Architect* for 24 May 1873 explained that 'the name has been in vague use for three or four years past' but that with the sending of Queen Anne designs to the Royal Academy by Norman Shaw (1831–1912) and G. F. Bodley (1827–1902), both previously known for their Gothic work, the movement could be assumed to have become respectable and established. The writer then listed the 'principal leaders of the new school' including Norman Shaw, Bodley, Nesfield, Philip Webb, J. J. Stevenson, William Butterfield and others all of whom were said to have repudiated the thirteenth century for everything but ecclesiastical work. To the list was added another, unexpected name which linked Queen Anne and the Aesthetes. The unknown author referred to Dante Gabriel

Fig. 1 Drawing of a blacksmith's forge and cottage designed by W. Eden Nesfield at Cheavely Hall, Cheshire, 1881.

Rossetti as 'one more moving spirit artistic rather than architectural'. Rossetti's name was also mentioned in the following year, 1874, in a lecture given to the Royal Institute of British Architects by Stevenson himself, when he explained the new movement to his fellow architects. He asserted that the Queen Anne school was no mere fashion but a genuine style, 'the outcome of our common want picturesquely expressed'.

As it happened one of the common wants of the time was a great number of new schools and a major factor in the spread of the new style was a most unusually enlightened piece of official patronage. As a result of the Elementary Education Act of 1870 the School Board for London was established and Stevenson's partner, E. R. Robson (1836–1917), was appointed architect to the Board. There were no precedents for an elementary school architecture and after considering the problem from all angles Robson began by the selection of brick as the best and cheapest material for use in London. He decided also that, even had it been convenient, Gothic with its ecclesiastical associations would be inappropriate for school architecture at a period when education had begun to be recognized as a secular and non-sectarian responsibility. Starting from the simple brick style of the late seventeenth and early eighteenth century, many modest examples of which were still extant in most of the older London boroughs, Robson evolved the type of Board School with which Londoners are still familiar today. These schools were consciously intended to form the nucleus of a good modern style expressive of the second half of the nineteenth century. They were tall buildings with large windows, Queen Anne detail and the same vertical emphasis found in artistic red brick houses, and each varied according to the requirements of the site. Like the houses each school had its panel of decorative terracotta and was surmounted by white painted ornamental woodwork or ironwork. Two hundred and sixty such schools were built in London between 1870 and 1881.

Clearly this was too much work for one architect but Robson did retain responsibility for the overall design policy as well as designing himself many of the buildings, such as that in Wornington Road in North Kensington (plate 65). In an article characteristically called 'Art as Applied to Town Schools' Robson explained his missionary approach to school building and related it to the Aesthetic Movement as a whole. 'It must always be among the high purposes for which Art exists to make any home brighter and more interesting, nobler if you will. We have seen how abject are the homes of countless thousands. If we can make the homes of these poor persons brighter, more interesting, nobler, by so treating the necessary Board Schools planted in their midst as to make each building undertake a sort of leavening influence, we have set on foot a permanent and ever active good – this is no mere theory – it is already proved by the manner in which builders of ordinary houses are imitating the Board Schools in every direction.' It seems unlikely that the homes of the poor were actually made brighter by these 'picturesque temples called Board Schools' but they did dominate the London townscape, as they still do in some areas, and the speculative builders produced terraces of red brick houses in the same idiom. Even the more drab tenement buildings were sometimes decorated, as an afterthought, by a single sunflower as a modest conciliatory gesture to Art and Queen Anne (plate 34).

Bedford Park today looks, to the casual passer-by, much like any other residential area of West London but on closer inspection it is apparent that all the houses are similar in character and in date and some, those with extra large windows, suggest that they may well have been intended as homes for artists. In fact this was the first garden suburb, the Utopian home for aesthetes, which set the pattern for the main English contribution to late nineteenth-century architecture, the detached house in its own garden. While others concerned themselves with improving the living conditions of artisans, Mr Jonathan T. Carr (1845–1915), a property speculator with artistic inclinations, decided to build a village which would provide ideal living conditions for the professional classes. He purchased a hundred acres of well-established garden and orchard land, close to the Thames and served by a railway from the City but considered far enough out to avoid the fogs of London. Between 1876 and 1881 he built there 'a little red town made up of the quaintest Queen Anne houses' employing as his architects E. W. Godwin and Norman Shaw.

Picturesque houses had previously been the prerogative of the rich since any deviation from the conventional, even in interior decoration, had been too expensive for the average householder. Carr decided that if sufficient numbers wanted interesting houses and artistic decoration it should be possible for his architects to produce varied results from materials sufficiently alike to be bought in large quantities. Thus the picturesque could be made accessible, if not actually cheap. So on roads curved or straight, according to taste, and all lined with blossoming trees were built three hundred and fifty red brick houses, all slightly different and all engaged in 'pleasing competition as to which could be the prettiest' (plate 55).
To quote a contemporary verse:

'Thus was a village builded
For all who are aesthete
Whose precious soul it fill did
With utter joy complete.'

This is part of the 'Ballad of Bedford Park' published in *St James's Gazette* in 1881 and one of the many both flippant and serious poetic efforts inspired by the project.

In the manner of later garden cities, Carr provided other amenities for the artistic tenants of his picturesque houses. There was a village store, an inn or tavern, a club house and a church which was one of the few attempts at the use of the new style for a place of worship. Everything was consistently Queen Anne and quaintly old-fashioned with interior decoration in keeping with the red brick architecture. It seems likely that Carr was responsible not only for the first garden suburb but indirectly for many an 'olde worlde' teashop and inn influenced by his personal vision of Old England.

The first eighteen houses were actually completed in 1876 from designs by E. W. Godwin (1837–86) whose published work had suggested to Carr that he was one of the only architects practising at the time who was capable of combining artistic detail, practical design and economy. One of the first families to occupy a Bedford Park artistic home was that of the poet W. B. Yeats who, in later life, described the initial wonder of living in a house 'like those we had seen in pictures and even [meeting] people dressed like people in story books'. It is recorded elsewhere that the inhabitants of Bedford Park, whether artists or members of the professional classes, were inclined to affect aesthetic dress and on occasion actually wore eighteenth-century costume. Another observer, the artist Edwin Austin Abbey, said that Bedford Park 'made him feel like walking through a watercolour sketch'.

There were a number of criticisms of Godwin's designs on practical rather than aesthetic grounds and after a somewhat acrimonious exchange of views in the professional press architect and client parted. In 1877 Norman Shaw was engaged as the main architect for the project. He or his associates designed the remainder of the houses as well as the public buildings. The overall effect of the Tabard Inn and its adjoining buildings still suggests the seventeenth century not least because Shaw ignored the new development of plate glass windows and equipped his store with large bays divided into small panes of glass. The inn sign outside was painted by an artist resident in one of the nearby houses and internally the inn was decorated with tiles designed by William de Morgan and Walter Crane in glowing colours said to be 'all of Early English and most pronounced Aesthetic type'. This comment throws interesting light on the misleading character of contemporary description. The surviving tiles at the Tabard Inn are essentially of their times, the design of the de Morgan ones being built on the typical structural form of a William Morris wallpaper design and totally unrelated to 'Early English' design of the Queen Anne period or any other date. The birds and flowers echo the gardens of the surrounding houses as do de Morgan's sunflower tiles of a similar date (plate 31). Socially the most important building of the community was the Club which differed from others of its date in catering for both ladies and gentlemen. It had a domestic atmosphere with flowers in all the rooms, china and glass ornaments about the place and 'the prettiest of all possible ladies' drawing rooms'. Apart from the more usual amenities of billiards, cards and games rooms, the Club had a library in which the newest books were available and accommodation for the concerts, dramatic performances and fancy dress parties which were an essential part of the community's life. From the beginning a high proportion of the residents were practising artists and the Art School, the interior of which seems to have had a slightly discordant Moorish flavour, was one of the centres of the life of Bedford Park. The students, reported to be 'of decidedly aesthetic type both as to mode of dress and fashion of arranging their hair', worked at all the usual art school subjects as well as the more specialized ones of art needlework, art pottery and art tile painting.

In architectural spheres, the aesthetic approach did not preclude the consideration of practical details. It was in a Bedford Park house that one of the first air-conditioning systems in England was installed and the whole project was advertised as having not only artistic but sanitary advantages over any other housing development. This example seems to have been followed elsewhere, as for instance in Eastbourne where in 1881 a combined 'Aesthetic Fine Art and Sanitary Exhibition' was held, with public lectures on both subjects. The whole Bedford Park scheme embodied the aesthetic concept of art embracing all aspects of life. The resident artists shared the social life of the businessmen who travelled daily from the City; all lived in honest brick houses, uncamouflaged by a covering of conventional stucco, in which paint was not used to imitate marble or grained woodwork; and almost everyone chose to live with Japanese prints and William Morris wallpapers. The purchasers and lessees of the houses were able to choose their own decorations but there seems to have been such unanimity of view on the virtues of green or terracotta paintwork and Morris papers that at one time it was suggested that a branch of Morris and Company could with profit be set up at Bedford Park. After a remarkably successful start the project proved either impractical or unprofitable as a business venture and the original company was dissolved, but much of its character has survived as a unique and practical demonstration of the aims of the Aesthetic Movement.

Around 1880, American enthusiasm grew to such an extent that, inspired by the example of Bedford Park, it was proposed to build not a mere village but an 'aesthetic city'. The project, however, did not materialize. One writer in the English press suggested that 'we are convinced that the harmless enthusiasts who at present imagine themselves enamoured of existence in a town inhabited by none but aesthetes will, before they have paid their second quarter's rates, be ready to rush from the place as if it were stricken by the plague.'

Examples of Queen Anne architecture can still be found all over London where it was particularly favoured by prosperous artists. There are 'quaint red mansions' in such areas as Melbury Road, Kensington, where Lord Leighton's house was at the centre of a colony of artists. E. W. Godwin built numbers of red brick houses and studios in Tite Street, Chelsea (plate 63), in addition to Whistler's famous 'White House' (plate 64). This was recently demolished but the others, with their large studio windows and restrained terracotta ornament, survive (plate 62). Godwin became a specialist in studio architecture and in 1878 built one in the grounds of Kensington Palace for Princess Louise, Queen Victoria's sculptress daughter. The largest concentration of artists' houses was in the Hampstead area and of these a fairly considerable number were designed by Norman Shaw, for instance 39 Frognal built for Kate Greenaway in 1885. Outside London red brick Queen Anne is, aptly enough, principally associated with art schools and other educational buildings.

Queen Anne or the picturesque classic did not prove the answer to the problem of an English national style but for a decade or so it did produce some pleasant and fresh domestic architecture based loosely on the vernacular of the eighteenth century. In the latter part of the century red brick architecture was adopted for larger domestic buildings, such as blocks of mansion flats, and the style degenerated into heaviness and pomposity overburdened with elaborate terracotta ornament.

Chapter 3

THE AESTHETIC INTERIOR

The adjective 'Victorian' as applied to English furniture and decoration still conjures up for most people a vision of over-elaborate, over-furnished interiors filled with carved mahogany sideboards, plush curtains, turkey carpets and papiermâché. As far as can be judged from the surviving evidence and from first-hand descriptions, this is a fair picture of furnishing by the prosperous in the first part of Queen Victoria's reign and of the style which continued until the end of the century in many middle-class homes. For different reasons both the furnishing trade and the buying public were conservative in their tastes and understandably preoccupied with increasing domestic comfort. In considering style there is a tendency to forget the social changes embraced by the Victorian period which made it possible for manufacturers in the latter part of the nineteenth century to compete in selling ornamental domestic paraphernalia of all kinds to the humbler householders whose early Victorian forebears had only rudimentary furniture and had eaten from wooden trenchers or pewter plates. Stylistically the term 'Victorian' covers everything from the simple classic forms of the late Regency to the curves and fantasies of the Quaint or Art Nouveau.

In the late eighteen-sixties and early 'seventies a new style of interior decoration arrived with the Aesthetic Movement and was given the name 'art' to indicate that its exponents were opposed to the crude commercial colours and vulgar display of High Victorian decoration. The name was also proof of the division which had arisen in the middle of the century between art and manufacture. In the eighteenth century a well-made chair or table was accepted as an artistic object within the obvious limitations of its kind. With the coming of the new mass-producing manufacturing industries came the new idea that art had to be added after the mere maker had done his job. This conception applied to all forms of household equipment but particularly to furniture. Whereas, before the industrial revolution, there had been furniture of varying quality made by either urban or rural craftsmen, in the latter part of the nineteenth century there were three quite separate categories. These were commercially made furniture, art furniture, and pieces made by rural craftsmen; both the latter categories were assumed to be necessarily superior to the former.

The term 'art' furniture seems traceable, like so many other names of the period, to C. L. Eastlake's *Hints on Household Taste* first published in England

34   Victoria Dwellings,
Clerkenwell Road, London.
Detail of brickwork, 1882.

35   Sunflowers in terracotta,
Fitzjohn's Avenue, London,
about 1878.

36   Detail of the decoration of
Barclay's Bank, Saffron Walden,
designed by W. Eden Nesfield,
1874.

35

34   36

Overleaf

37   Central façade of Carlisle
Mansions, Cheyne Walk, London,
1886.

38   Another detail from the
central façade of Carlisle
Mansions, Cheyne Walk, London,
1886.

39

39   North-facing façade of
Lowther Lodge, designed by
Norman Shaw, 1874; now the
Royal Geographical Society,
Kensington Gore, London.

40   Part of north-facing façade of
Lowther Lodge, showing in detail
the sunflower motif in the gable.

Overleaf

41   Panel in the façade of
Carlisle Mansions, Cheyne Walk,
1886.

42   Another panel in the façade of
Carlisle Mansions, Cheyne Walk,
1886.

in 1867. Its influence can be appreciated from the fact that there were four English editions and six published in the United States. The title 'art' furniture was not in general use until the mid 'seventies but the first 'Art Furniture Company' was established in 1867. Obviously a little before its time, it was reported to be failing a year later because, although its products were well designed, they were too expensive and not appreciated. Even before the publication of his book Eastlake associated art with craft and regarded both as the opposite of fashion and commerce which he held to be the joint villains of the contemporary scene. He complained of the quality of the design of industrially produced furniture and suggested that simplicity could only be achieved by individually designed pieces specially made by rural craftsmen. 'We have at the present time no more artistic workman in his way than the country cartwright. His system of construction is always sound and such little decoration as he is enabled to introduce seems appropriate because it is in accordance with the traditional development and necessary forms.'[1] This passage contains in brief all Eastlake's novel recommendations for good design. Furniture and other domestic equipment should be simple and soundly constructed, the decoration should be minimal and the whole design should be based on function or purpose. 'Every article of manufacture should indicate by its general design the purpose to which it will be applied.'[2] The theme of simplicity runs through all Eastlake's written work. It is a little difficult to reconcile the illustrations in *Hints on Household Taste* with the text but this is a problem with so much nineteenth-century design in all media. New principles were applied by designers to existing forms as they were known and the interiors or individual pieces of furniture chosen to illustrate these principles were interpreted by contemporary artists or draughtsmen in the manner fashionable at the time. The resulting drawings look Victorian to a modern eye while the text is often remarkably in accord with twentieth-century ideas of design.

In America the influence of Eastlake's book was such that a form of restrained Gothic furniture, still known as 'Eastlake style', was made there (plate 6). In fact C. L. Eastlake (1836–1906), though an architect by training, was not a practising designer. He was involved in a variety of activities and ultimately became Keeper of the National Gallery in London. His book contains some designs attributed to him but the text reveals that they were individually created pieces for his personal use and presumably made by his country cartwright. The contemporary American author, Mrs Harriett Prescott Spofford, writing in 1878, recorded that the popularity of the book produced a demand for Eastlake style furniture.[3] As such furniture did not exist the New York upholsterers, book in hand, were compelled to devise some. Mrs Spofford continued, 'The Eastlake style is from solid wood unvarnished and usually without veneer, made in the simplest manner that conforms to the purpose of the article, with plain uprights and transverses slightly chamfered at the corners.' Popular as this furniture may have become in some circles it was not universally admired in the United States. A writer in *The Cincinatti Trade List* of 1874 condemned the leading New York houses for their folly in adopting English Gothic styles after designs by Eastlake and hoped that the regrettable fashion would not extend to their

43   Cheniston Lodge, Marlowes Road, Kensington, 1885. Typical 'Queen Anne' town house with sunflower decoration in the brickwork.

city. While some people saw Eastlake in the forefront of an advanced move-ment the Cincinatti writer took the opposite view. 'Of all the clumsy, ugly inventions, or rather copies, the sort advocated by Eastlake deserves most to be condemned. There may be some use of medievalising household articles in England where this movement is but parallel to the reassertion of conservatism as proclaimed by the recent parliamentary elections – but whereas in our country comfort and beauty are the only guides, the manifest incongruity and unsuitableness of the fashion give it but small chance of being extensively adopted.'

While these views may have seemed convincing from the other side of the Atlantic, in England, the home of the Aesthetic Movement, it would have been impossible to find in contemporary life the political equivalent of the many styles covered by the general term 'art' decoration. Furniture alone ranged in name, if not in form, over almost every English and European historic style. Art furniture illustrated in such periodicals as *The Cabinet Maker* and *The Furniture Gazette* appeared with the labels 'Tudor', 'Jacob-ean', 'Anglo-Japanese', 'Italian Renaissance' or 'Queen Anne' and one of the fashionable cabinet-making firms of the day was described as a pioneer of the 'Backward-Ho' movement. 'Queen Anne' was the most popular label but this covered almost anything, as one writer defined it, that possessed 'remarkable simplicity and quietness of old work together with great picturesqueness and quaintness.'[4] However diverse their approach almost all designers were actually aiming at 'an avowed Victorian or New English style which need not be ashamed to acknowledge itself as such'[5] and all furniture of the period has a common recognizable flavour.

The fashionable woods were black or ebonized baywood, basswood or black walnut. These replaced the long popular, highly polished mahogany and dark Danzig oak. Bright, almost orange, mahogany and satinwood had a certain vogue around 1880 and oak seems to have been acceptable if light in colour and often even unpolished. Other light woods used for chairs, such as the many variations on the rush-bottom chair made popular by William Morris (plate 20), were stained green, dark blue or black. The fashion for ebonized furniture, which lasted about fifteen years, was introduced when Collinson and Lock showed their first ebonized cabinet in 1871 at the International Exhibition held in London (plate 54). Designed and produced with painted decoration of semi-classical languid ladies, it was regarded as an artistic novelty which started a fashion; ten years later, in 1881, ebonized cabinets 'were legion and so like each other that none can claim any special merit over the others.'[6] The original design was remade and exhibited in Europe and America and one version, with decoration designed by Burne-Jones, was bought by Prince Johannes Liechtenstein. The legs, supports, balusters and other uprights of art furniture were slender and turned, characteristics that create an air of comparative instability, and this led to much of the simple fun made of the aesthetic home (plate 67). Carving was confined to formal, repeating designs in thin incised lines, often gilt, to give emphasis in the black wood (plate 1). The accepted method of decoration of more elaborate pieces was painting which completely replaced the rich carving of the High Victorian period (plate 52). 'One good painted panel

A door in the Drawing-room

a bit of the finger plate

Fig. 2 Drawing of a painted door in the drawing-room of the home of an architect.

is worth ten thousand times more than all the meretricious carving with which so much of our modern furniture is filled'.[7] From the painting of panels on furniture the idea spread to the painting of actual interiors; vases of flowers and other artistic subjects were often painted on door panels (plate 49). Another popular form of decoration was the carving of little balustrades, echoing the turned decoration of legs and other structural members, round the tops of cabinet furniture and round the edges of shelves (plate 1). While most art furniture design was rectilinear, one curved feature survived and is characteristic of the period: this was the over-hanging support of the upper parts of cabinets and sideboards (plates 3, 53), a shape which also appeared in overmantels and sometimes as the frieze around a complete room.

The keynote of aesthetic interior decoration was the use of subdued or even dull colours, particularly a range of dull greens, and the comparatively lightweight furniture was usually set against wallpaper in these tones by one of the accepted designers, such as William Morris, Bruce J. Talbert or Lewis F. Day. The use of secondary or tertiary colours was the aesthetic reaction to the bright, harsh colours favoured in the middle of the century. Technical advances had made possible a new range of colours which were considered by artistic critics, with some justice, to be 'hideous through their extreme purity'[8] and most writers on interior decoration particularly warned their readers against the use of white for either walls or ceilings. On the other hand some enthusiasts went rather too far in the other direction and many light and fresh wallpaper designs, notably those of Lewis F. Day and Bruce J. Talbert (plates 9, 10, 11), were sold most successfully in dreary versions printed in shades of dull green and khaki. William Morris advised against the use of pure colour but also said 'on the other hand do not fall into the trap of a dingy bilious yellow-green, a colour for which I have a special hatred because I have been supposed to have somewhat brought it into vogue. I assure you I am not really responsible for it.' One aspect of the aesthetic interior for which Morris was almost certainly responsible was the use of painted woodwork and this often in a dark green. The first important interior decoration projects undertaken by Morris and Company in about 1866 were the Armoury at St James's Palace and the Green Dining-Room at the Victoria and Albert Museum. Both these rooms had dark painted woodwork and a dull green predominated in the decorative schemes. While the rooms in St James's Palace were obviously comparatively unknown, the Green Dining-Room was in daily use by architects, designers and art students of all kinds, and one architect at the heart of the aesthetic move-ment, E. W. Godwin, is known to have derived his ideas for painted wood-work from that room. The colour of the woodwork was an important feature of the average room as it was customary at this date to divide walls hori-zontally in at least three parts often separated by bands of wood moulding. Whereas today most interior walls would be covered by a single paper or colour the aesthetic practice, which became generally accepted in late Victorian times, was to divide a wall into a dado some three feet high sur-mounted by a wooden moulding which protected the wall from chairs and other furniture, a filling for the main upper wall, and a frieze (see plates 12,

13). Between the filling and the frieze there was either a picture rail or, more often, a narrow shelf on which porcelain or other bric-à-brac could be shown (plate 51). This led to a series of patterned wallpapers being used in association with each other (plates 12, 13) and occasionally to the use of the same paper, such as Morris's well-known 'Pomegranate', in three different colourways in the same room (plate 58). Another result of this wall division was the production, for use on staircases, of curiously angled papers, designed to fit the treads of the stairs and the sloping dado.

The word dado had long been in use as an architectural term but it seems to have entered the domestic vocabulary in the mid eighteen-seventies and for some reason it became one of the key words of the aesthetic fashion, its mere mention providing a source of merriment for the Philistines. Another innovation for wall covering at this date was the use of Indian matting and Japanese leather paper, both first imported into England in the mid eighteen-seventies. The fine matting was used for covering the lower wall or dado and was also recommended for floors. Its soft golden colour provided a pleasantly warm background for lightweight furniture. The imitation leather paper, slightly embossed and gilt, was hung on the main wall or on the frieze and it provided a rich background for blue and white china or Japanese lacquer trays. This type of paper was also pasted on furniture, being a cheaper and more durable alternative to painted panels (plate 2).

Broadly speaking it can be said that the aesthetic interior contained less furniture and far fewer ornaments than had been customary in the middle of the century. Heavily carved furniture, large mirrors in gilt frames, white ceilings and bright colours were regarded as vulgar, while shades of soft green, blue and white porcelain, Japanese fans and peacock feathers, and William Morris wallpaper were the marks of an enlightened home. However there was considerable variation within these broad outlines and it is of some interest to read some contemporary descriptions of actual rooms or methods of decoration recommended by arbiters of taste who wrote handy guide books for amateurs or articles in professional papers.

An article in *The Furniture Gazette* of 1875 typically entitled 'The Moral Influence of Decoration' gives a detailed description of a recently-decorated pretty house. In the dining-room 'the walls are a dark drab with a high dado of mauve and drab in alternate bands and a frieze of sober hued stamped leather . . . the furniture shows sufficient variety to avoid monotony while harmony is yet preserved throughout . . . over the fireplace is a mantelpiece of oak and walnut with ebonised mouldings . . . a curtain that divides the dining room from the small ante chamber or reception room beyond. This curtain which is the work of the lady of the house is a quite perfect work of art. In colour it is a dark, bluish green, and it is crossed by broad bands of pale yellow and black velvet beneath which are embroidered at intervals circular devices of peacock's feathers. These, with the rare blue china, Salviatti vases, the choice brass work and bronzes and other *objets d'art* sprinkled about serve as points of positive colour to brighten the room.' Mrs Haweis, in her little handbook *The Art of Beauty*, provided a general rather than a specific recipe for room decoration also based on a mixture of colour. 'Doors should be tall and should match in effect, if not in colour, the walls and ceiling – that is a room with a deep blue ceiling and walls of Vandyck brown and similar dark colours may have doors black or deep sage green; a room whose walls and ceiling are chiefly coloured with tertiary citrine (a mixture of orange and green, a yellowish colour) may have doors of a very dull green or brownish purple; a room papered with scarlet deeply indented to break the monotony of that tint may have black or sage green doors and wainscott.' It is easy to see from this last fashionable description with its air of authority how *Punch* came to define the aesthetic interior as one on which dust was allowed to accumulate so that colours should be suitably subdued.

In contrast to these popular ideas of art decoration the real aesthetic interiors devised by the architect E. W. Godwin and J. McNeil Whistler (1834–1903) must have been of astonishing elegance and simplicity. Whistler's work as an interior decorator, apart from the famous Peacock Room (plate 59), was principally in devising settings for his own pictures when they were exhibited. On one occasion the gallery was decorated in shades of brown, on another in white and yellow with the chairs painted yellow and even the door attendant dressed in a white and yellow livery. One of his subtlest colour schemes was for an exhibition 'Notes, Harmonies, Nocturnes' held in 1884, when he decorated the gallery with delicate rose-coloured walls, a white dado, white chairs and pale azaleas in rose flushed jars. Such decoration could be regarded as pure showmanship, but Godwin on the other hand was responsible for the decoration of numbers of domestic interiors and descriptions of some of these survive though the houses have gone.

When clients permitted it, Godwin designed not only the house and the furniture but chose the wallpapers, often of his own design, supervised the mixing of the paint and finally selected pictures and ornaments. In 1874 he decorated a conventional London terrace house for his own occupation. The entrance hall and all the ground floor rooms were uncarpeted and the bare floorboards were oiled and waxed. The dado was of Indian matting and the upper part of the wall covered with a paper in a conventional pattern in umber and vellum colour. The ceiling was also pale, creamy vellum colour and all the paintwork a light red. In a series of articles published in *The Architect* in 1876 Godwin gave detailed descriptions of every room, even to his exact recipe for the mixing of the paint. In the drawing-room he used 'a rather dark-toned yellow of which yellow ochre is the base, but combined with white, sprinkled with gamboge, Prussian blue and vermilion' and so on through each room. The overall effect was so unusual that it was recorded by various contemporaries, such as the actor Forbes-Robertson who remembered that 'the floor was covered with straw-coloured matting and there was a dado of the same material. Above the dado were white walls and the hangings were of cretonne with a fine Japanese pattern in delicate grey-blue. The chairs were of wicker with cushions like the hangings.'[9] According to the designer there were also a few Japanese fans against the skirting and on the ceiling, some Japanese vases and a few light-weight pieces of furniture. 'No description, however, except perhaps that which may be conveyed in the form of music, can give an idea of the tenderness and, if I may say so, the ultra refinement of the delicate tones of colour which form the background to the few but unquestionable gems in this exquisitely sensitive room.'[10]

These few words contain the essence of the aesthetic approach to design or 'Art Work' as Godwin called it, with the implied interrelationship of the arts and everyday life. None but an aesthete would have contemplated the description of his London drawing-room in terms of music. But while they provided the material for artistic settings, all the designers of the day were not aesthetes.

One of the most prolific and influential designers was Bruce J. Talbert (1838–81) who seems to have been an essentially practical man though a sensitive draughtsman with positive views on design. A professional industrial designer, trained as an architect in his native Scotland, Talbert's first move south was to Manchester where he began to design for the cabinet-making firm of Doveston Bird and Hull in 1862. He quickly established a reputation as one of the leading furniture designers in the simplified Gothic manner which was then fashionable. In 1867 he had published a book of designs, *Gothic Forms Applied to Furniture*, which contained details of individual pieces and suggestions for complete rooms as well as a preface in which Talbert explained his approach to design which was similar to that of Eastlake. The same authoritarian note was struck in Talbert's writing on design as in that of most of his contemporaries. Readers were not offered suggestions but firmly told what was right and proper for each room of their house. As far as is known, Talbert was only designing furniture and metalwork at this date but he advised on all aspects of decoration and even took into consideration current fashion, suggesting that adequate contrast to horizontals and verticals would be supplied by 'the ever-changing curves' of those for whom rooms were designed.

Based on a sound practical knowledge of materials and structural principles, his furniture was relatively simple for its date and incorporated geometric designs in inlay, a little low-relief carving and sometimes small enamels (plates 7, 8). This was Talbert's alternative to the more popular painted panels which he regarded as impractical unless the paintings were inset in such a way as to avoid constant rubbing in use. Small enamel panels of birds and animals introduced a pleasant colour note into his designs. Talbert worked for a number of leading cabinet-makers but his book and a later publication, *Examples of Ancient and Modern Furniture*, were so widely studied that by the mid-'seventies a casual observer would have imagined that he had a hand in far more than he could possibly have actually designed. A fellow designer and chronicler of style development, J. Moyr Smith (working 1870–89), writing soon after Talbert's death, attributed the beginning of public interest in 'art furniture' to a single plate in *Gothic Forms*. This was a design for a drawing-room which, with its curved frieze, sunflower decorations and comparative spaciousness, may well have been ahead of its time, but it is difficult to see in it the seeds of revolution.

Talbert's wallpaper and textile designs, however, are as attractive to modern eyes as they must have been when they were first produced. As he worked anonymously for a number of firms it is not possible to be certain of the extent of Talbert's work but enough has been identified to realize the freshness and originality of his flat pattern design (plates 70, 71). His characteristic style, much imitated after his early death, involved the use of sharply-delineated flowers, fruit and leaves, all without shading, arranged formally on a ground ornament often derived from a Japanese source. His surviving drawings show that, though the final effect was somewhat stylized, his work was based on a detailed observation of natural forms. Talbert's most popular papers were the 'Sunflower' series exhibited at the Paris Universal Exhibition of 1878. In addition to the conventional printed papers these included designs for embossed leather and flocks in the usual dull green colour (plate 9). These designs were awarded a Gold Medal and were much illustrated and imitated. During the late 'seventies and early 'eighties Talbert-type sunflowers appeared on woven and printed fabrics of all kinds and were particularly popular in stamped velvet or plush. Talbert's own designs for printed textiles actually predate the better known ones of William Morris.

Morris did not design for textiles until the early 1870s and the actual fabrics were first marketed about 1875 after a period of experiment with dyes in which he joined forces with a dyer and printer from Leek in Staffordshire, Thomas Wardle. Together they revived the lost art of indigo dyeing and attempted, with the use of vegetable dyes, to achieve the 'repose of tint' found in native printed Indian fabrics as opposed to the vivid colours current in Europe. These fabrics printed with native dyes had recently been rediscovered and proved, once more in practical form, the aesthetic contention of the superiority of craft processes over commercial products. The desired result was achieved by printing Morris's designs in soft subdued colours on the newly discovered tusser silk, hand-woven in India (plate 26). A collection of these fabrics, together with others commissioned by Liberty and Co., was also shown at Paris in 1878. Morris's prime influence on the aesthetic home, however, was through the medium of his wallpapers which, unlike the fabrics, were amongst the earliest productions of Morris and Company. Almost all designed by Morris himself and printed by the principal art wallpaper firm, Jeffrey and Company, these papers were an immediate success. The 'Daisy', dating from 1862, was the first Morris wallpaper and, with its formal, almost stiff, treatment of the simplest of flowers in flat colours, it was the complete antithesis of the lush two-dimensional papers in the French style then popular with the trade. The other contribution of the Morris firm was their lightweight rush seated chair, which was based on a traditional Sussex country type. It could be bought for only a few shillings and thus was well within the reach of the most modest aspiring aesthete.

Lewis F. Day (1845–1910) was an artist and a prolific writer on design subjects and, like Talbert, some of his most attractive designs were for wallpapers (plates 10, 11). Day entered the art world by way of a firm of glass painters where he was employed as a clerk. He moved to another firm where he graduated to actual glass design, a subject in which he retained a critical interest all his life. In 1870 he started his own business and produced designs for wallpapers, pottery, glass, textiles, furniture and virtually everything for the artistic home. In the latter part of the century he exerted considerable influence in various official capacities; he was art director of a textile firm, a Master of the Art Workers' Guild and an examiner for the Royal Society of Arts, but in the aesthetic period it was by his own work that he influenced public taste. His flat, pattern designs for wallpapers and textiles were usually based on a strictly geometric diaper form but the end product has a remarkable freedom and flow of line in which it is possible to see the seeds of Art Nouveau, a development which Day lived to see and deplore. It is no doubt the sinuous and flowing line which has made subsequent reprints of his textiles so popular. In all his flat patterns Day was particularly successful in disguising the repeats so that a geometrically-based design could appear to be an apparently random arrangement of daisies or apple blossom. Much of his work was based on the ubiquitous sunflower and his most original contribution to the aesthetic home was a series of designs for mantelpiece clocks in which the sunflower was used as the dial. These were all designed for the firm of Howell and James, whose work is described in Chapter VII. These attractive little clocks, many of which can still be found today, contain in miniature all the elements of the larger pieces of art furniture. The cases are usually of ebonized wood with simple turned or incised ornament and surmounted by galleries and turned terminal knobs. The clock faces are of ceramic tiles painted in blue and white in a variety of charming designs with the sunflower as the central feature (plates 44, 45). Lewis Day's furniture design was confined to relatively large exhibition pieces, aesthetic only in their use of painted panels.

Art furniture of considerable charm was produced by numbers of lesser figures few of whose names are known. One of the best of these was H. W. Batley (working 1873–93) who produced a handsome volume of etchings recording his own work[11] (plate 53). The plates were drawn and etched by the designer and some of them illustrated actual schemes of decoration while others were works of imagination, such as the room of 1872 in which Batley described his aim of adapting Egyptian ornament to modern use. The book typifies the aesthetic search for some practical basis for a new Victorian style. The plates were printed in artistic sepia, the text was in a Gothic typeface and there are traces of Egyptian, Jacobean and Japanese influence in the designs themselves, as well as a very personal treatment of plant form almost suggesting the first stirrings of Art Nouveau. On the evidence of surviving pieces of furniture, Batley hardly did himself justice in his etchings. A piano in the Victoria and Albert Museum, originally shown at the Paris Exhibition of 1878, is a modest and attractive piece of furniture in bright mahogany with low relief carving based on Japanese motifs (plate 17). Its comparative simplicity and restraint make it easy to see why English art furniture made such an impact on the Continent where heavy, dark carved pieces were still the order of the day.

Art furniture and decoration were also designed by some architects whose eminence in their own profession has tended to overshadow their domestic work. Norman Shaw in his Queen Anne period was associated with the London joinery firm of W. H. Lascelles for whom he designed a range of lightweight furniture stained blue or deep red and decorated with panels

44   Clock in ebonized wood with incised decoration and painted porcelain face, probably designed by Lewis F. Day, 1880. *London, Victoria and Albert Museum.*

45   Clock in ebonized wood with painted tile face and brass panels, designed by Lewis F. Day and made by Howell & James about 1878. *Private collection.*

46   Firescreen made in mahogany, inset with tiles, made by W. B. Simpson & Sons, about 1880. *Walthamstow, William Morris Gallery.*

50 Hanging cupboard and painted wall panels from The Grove, Harborne, Birmingham, designed by J. H. Chamberlain, 1877; from a contemporary photograph.

51 Billiards room, designed by Thomas Jeckyll, 1870; from a contemporary photograph.

52 Cabinet in ebonized wood with painted panels and turned and fret decoration; probably made by Collinson & Lock about 1875. *David Verey Esq.*

Within the drawing:
A lacquer panel by Mr Eaton

A Cabinet by R. Norman Shaw R·A
green stain
+ panels in gold lacquer

Fig. 3   Drawing of a cabinet designed by R. Norman Shaw and shown at the Furniture Exhibition, 1882.

53   Design for a drawing-room mantelpiece in satinwood, inlaid and carved, the backing panelled in silk. Exhibited at the Paris Exhibition, 1878. Plate 6 from *A Series of Studies for Domestic Furniture and Decoration* designed and etched by H. W. Batley, 1883.

painted in colours and gilt. These pieces were exhibited from 1875 until the mid eighteen-eighties in a gallery run jointly with the Royal School of Needlework in that centre of all art work, South Kensington. Contemporary opinion seems to have been divided on the quality of this furniture but there appeared to be no doubt about the virtues of the design, each article appearing what it really was, 'neither the usefulness nor the ornamentation clashing with each other'. In 1877, despite his growing architectural practice, Shaw became a partner in the firm of Aldam Heaton whose work included embroidery, stained glass, carpets, wallpaper, embossed leather-work and furniture all designed in Shaw's office. J. Aldam Heaton had previously been responsible for some of the painted decoration of Shaw's furniture. The trend of furniture designing towards the end of the century is indicated by the fact that the later pieces produced by this partnership were often faithful reproductions of actual Chippendale and Hepplewhite.

None of Shaw's art furniture is known to have survived but pieces by another eminent architect, Alfred Waterhouse (1830–1905), exist today. Waterhouse, by no means an aesthete but certainly a leader of fashion, was responsible for some interesting interior decoration conforming to aesthetic standards and for some original furniture design. One of his most complete schemes of decoration was that for Blackmoor House in Hampshire built for the Earl of Selborne and completed in 1872. Externally the house is slightly Gothic and a little forbidding but a wrought iron sunflower surmounting one of the gables gives a clue to the interior. The rooms were all oak panelled to dado height and covered with Japanese leather paper or stencilled decoration above. Art tiles with figure subjects were used in each of the individually-designed fireplaces but it was in the furniture that the architect showed his skill and originality. The larger pieces (plate 3), like the house itself, have slight Gothic echoes but the smaller pieces, notably the chairs, were completely original in design and carried out in practice Eastlake's theories. In light oak or ebonized wood, upholstered in natural leather, these chairs owed nothing to any traditional forms and yet they exploited the best of traditional craftsmanship (plate 4).

By the mid 'eighties the Aesthetic Movement was spent but it left a permanent mark on interior decoration. Even the most conservative critics of the Movement admitted that the long-term effects on design were beneficial in correcting the excesses of the High Victorian period. The statement that 'it would be difficult now for anyone buying furniture and domestic utensils of any sort to avoid becoming possessed of a considerable number of objects which were really good in form and colour' appeared in *The Spectator* in 1881,[12] and was echoed by other writers. The more extreme products of the Art Movement died a natural death, speeded by impracticability, but the best survived and passed into general use. Two new furniture styles had been added to the designer's repertory: so-called Queen Anne settled into a neo-Georgian vein, generally accepted for drawing-rooms well into the twentieth century, and the simple rustic style, typified by Morris chairs, unexpectedly provided the basis for the Quaint or English Art Nouveau. Some of the earliest essays in this style were drawing-room chairs, made north of London in High Wycombe, based directly on old craft traditions. But probably the most important legacy of the Art Movement was the concept of fitness for purpose which led eventually to the functional design of the twentieth century.

Chapter 4

THE JAPANESE TASTE

The impact of Japan on the decorative arts in England in the second half of the nineteenth century has never been fully explained though the influence itself passed through three clear phases each of which conveniently falls into a decade. In the eighteen-sixties it was a matter for individual collectors and enthusiasts, both in England and in France, and in this period Whistler produced his earliest Japanese-inspired paintings, Rossetti designed a Japanese bookbinding and a few amateurs began to collect lacquer, porcelain, glass and prints. In the 'seventies, the fashion was in full swing amongst informed people and Japanism and the Aesthetic Movement were virtually synonymous, while the Philistines scoffed. Interior decoration and furniture design were based on what were believed to be Japanese principles, rather than on the superficial forms and ornament which were the hallmark of the 'eighties when what had been a movement became a mania. Every mantelpiece in every enlightened household bore at least one Japanese fan, parasols were used as summer firescreens, popular magazines and ball programmes were printed in asymmetrical semi-Japanese style and asymmetry of form and ornament spread to pottery, porcelain, silver and furniture. To the great British public – as one writer explained in the trade periodical *The Cabinet Maker and Art Furnisher* – 'Japanese art has taught the advantages of asymmetrical arrangements so that one need not always have pairs'. By the 'nineties the fashion for anglicized Japanism had gone and Japanese art, together with other characteristics of the Aesthetic Movement, had become one of the contributory elements in Art Nouveau.

It has long been assumed that Japanese objects were first seen in London and Paris in about 1860, mainly on the basis of varied apocryphal stories of pots wrapped in superb Japanese prints which were treasured by their finders. These discoveries were followed by the exhibition of the arts of Japan at the International Exhibition in London in 1862 when the first British Minister in Japan, Sir Rutherford Alcock, showed his personal collection of lacquer, bronze and porcelain. This exhibit certainly made a considerable impact on the informed visitor as an art of relative simplicity and restraint in the midst of High Victorian elaborations but it was really not the beginning of the story. Even during the centuries when Japan was cut off from the rest of the world, there had been a trickle of trade through the Dutch and Chinese who had limited trading rights at Nagasaki. As a result of this, when the Department of Practical Art, the forerunner of the present Victoria and Albert Museum, was established in London in 1852, two thirds of its tiny collection in Class V, 'Furniture and Upholstery etc.', were either japanned or papiermâché and nearly all were directly ascribed to Japan or China. These pieces were small and not of the highest quality and presumably the only people influenced by them in 1852 were the makers of fashionable papiermâché who traditionally imitated Chinese lacquerwork of earlier centuries. Two years later in 1854 a complete exhibition of Japanese applied art was held in London in the gallery of the Old Water Colour Society in Pall Mall East, from which the Science and Art Department made fairly extensive purchases on the recommendation of those eminent critics, Messrs Richard Redgrave and Henry Cole. Though this seems to have been the first large display of Japanese wares in London it would appear to have made little mark and in contemporary press comment there was no suggestion that the exhibition was an event of any significance. Clearly the mood of the times was not receptive to this new art form.

The exhibition may well have been one of the results of the first expedition to Japan made in July 1853 by the American Commodore Perry. From then until 1858, when both the British and the Americans achieved a limited commercial treaty with Japan, there was intermittent contact with the country and indeed representatives of the British navy and some civilians were continuously resident in Yedo for six months in 1857, becoming fairly well acquainted with life and art. A charming little book *Japanese Fragments* was written in 1860 by Captain Sherard Osborn, one of the English officers on this expedition. It is fuller than the title suggests, providing a general history of Japanese relations with Europe and an account of everyday life and arts and is illustrated by facsimile reproductions of Japanese colour woodcuts of landscape subjects. The book did not appear until 1861 since Captain Osborn had difficulty in finding a printer of sufficient skill for this work. He finally settled for Bradbury and Evans, the printers of the illustrated periodical *Once a Week*.

This period of negotiation in Japan no doubt explains the Hokusai prints seen by Whistler in Paris in 1856 and a series of roller-printed cottons with designs lifted direct from Japanese prints which were produced and marketed by Daniel Lee of Manchester in 1858, fully four years before the normally accepted date for the introduction of Japanese goods into England. Obviously some Japanese goods were known in Europe in the sixteenth and seventeenth centuries but the figures on these chintzes were taken directly from wood block prints of a type not produced until the middle of the eighteenth century when Japan was firmly closed to foreigners. In other respects these are typical Victorian furnishing prints but the usual floral wreaths happen to contain Japanese figures rather than some picturesque rustic or rural scene.

One of the curious things about the whole Japanese mania is that it seems to have been sparked off, not by long-haired aesthetes who were the products of the movement rather than initiators, but by a staunch devotee of medievalism. This was the architect William Burges, amongst whose private papers are preserved some of the first Japanese prints to be collected in England and all dating from the 1850s. These include some of the usual single figure prints and several sheets of rather crudely executed popular prints of children's games, badges and figures of Europeans, as well as book wrappers, one of which is a repeating pattern of what came to be Whistler's butterfly. The combination in Burges of an enthusiasm for thirteenth-century France and nineteenth-century Japan, so superficially curious, is easily explained. It was not primarily the form of Gothic architecture which appealed to Burges but a romanticized view of the conditions which produced it, and so it was with Japanese art. 'To any student of our reviving arts of the thirteenth century', wrote Burges of the 1862 International Exhibition, 'an hour or even a day or two spent in the Japanese Department will by no means be lost time, for these hitherto unknown barbarians appear not only to know all that the middle ages knew but in some respects are beyond them and us as well'. Here, Burges felt, was perfect medieval art. He was particularly impressed by the success of the audacious asymmetrical ornament, or the Japanese 'horror of regularity' as he called it, and by the beauty of their patterned papers.

After the South Kensington Exhibition of 1862, some of the exhibits were disposed of by Messrs Farmer and Rogers in the Oriental Department of their Great Cloak & Shawl Emporium, of which young Mr Lasenby Liberty, subsequently the founder of Liberty's, became manager in the following year. Another large consignment of Japanese goods was sold by public auction having arrived too late to be exhibited.

Arthur Lasenby Liberty (1843–1917) was Oriental Manager for Farmer and Rogers for twelve years and on 17 May 1875 he opened his own small shop at 218a Regent Street. The timing of the venture seems to have been exactly right for, with an increasing demand for Oriental art amongst a small and informed public, the venture was so successful that within twelve months he was able to extend, first to the adjoining premises and later into another shop at 120 Regent Street. His own knowledge and taste was based on experience of the best and highest quality goods as they came into the country during the first years of contact with Japan and before increasing public demand led to the inevitable vulgarization, and the whole project was based on Liberty's personal enthusiasm for the goods he sold and a genuine desire to improve public taste.

The customers in the first years of trading included William Morris, Carlyle, Ruskin, the Rossettis, Burne-Jones, Whistler, the architects Norman Shaw and E. W. Godwin and numbers of other figures associated with the arts. The initial enthusiasm for the venture can be assessed from some of the contemporary press accounts. Godwin writing in *The Architect* of 23 December 1876, only eighteen months after the opening, describes the excitement when it was rumoured that a new importation of Japanese fans was expected and 'that certain cases of them would be opened in a certain little shop near the top of Regent Street'. The waiting crowd agog for the opening included, apart from 'a bevy of ladies', three distinguished painters with their wives, a distinguished traveller, a well-known baronet and 'two architects of well-known names'. On this occasion unfortunately the waiting crowd was disappointed as the cases were delayed until the evening but this left the author free to explore the shop, from ground floor to attics, which were 'literally crammed with objects of oriental manufacture'. These included carpets, matting, embroideries, small pieces of bamboo and lacquered furniture, porcelain, bronzes, dress fabrics and curios of all kinds and even 'Tokio Tooth Powder', to the beneficial properties of which the maidens of Japan owed the pearly whiteness of their teeth. Already in Liberty's first catalogue of 'Eastern Art Manufactures' there are objects described as Anglo-Japanese and clearly specifically made for the European market and Godwin confessed with misgiving that a certain coarseness was creeping into some Japanese work. 'The fans of ten years ago are for the most part lovely in delicate colour and exquisite in drawing, but the great majority of the fans of today that have come under my observation, are impregnated with the crudeness of the European's sense of colour, and are immeasurably beneath the older examples in both qualities mentioned.' Clearly the mania of the 'eighties for cheap and tawdry bric-à-brac was already on its way. On the whole, however, Liberty continued to maintain the high standards he had set himself not only in Japanese goods but also in those from other parts of the Orient. Silks and dress fabrics were imported from Persia, China and India, as well as from Japan, and such care was taken over design that the Indian silks were produced especially for Liberty only after consultation with the authorities at the newly-established Indian Museum. Only a year after the shop opened Liberty were selling Indian silks, woven to their own specifications and printed in England with vegetable dyes 'in artistic, aesthetic and useful colours', in the same way as some of William Morris's designs.

Other Japanese warehouses were set up in various parts of London, notably a distinguished and short-lived venture in Farringdon Street in the City started in 1879 by Dr Christopher Dresser who had the unique distinction amongst English designers of the day of having visited Japan. Other smaller oriental departments were opened in some of the new large stores, such as William Whiteley's, Swan and Edgar and Debenham's but these, like Liberty's fabrics, were more concerned with fashionable costume than with Japanese *objets d'art*. It is to Liberty's that the main credit must go for maintaining the flow of high-quality Japanese blue and white porcelain, bronzes and lacquer objects, collected by the followers of the Aesthetic Movement in the 'seventies, as well as the cheap fans and toys which filled every mantelpiece in the 'eighties.

It seems likely that the original collectors of Japanese objects, having no shop to turn to, acquired them from the post-exhibition sale in 1862. This may well have been the source of William Burges's prints and leather paper, Dante Gabriel Rossetti's porcelain and screens, and where the architect E. W. Godwin bought the colour prints with which, in the same year, he decorated his Bristol home, reputedly the first house in England to be decorated according to Japanese-inspired principles. It is curious that Godwin's name and work are so little known and he is remembered mainly as the father of Gordon and Edith Craig. In fact he was an original architect, a prolific architectural journalist, an authority on various aspects of Gothic building, a designer of theatrical productions, furniture, wallpaper, textiles and almost every aspect of interior decoration and, in a large measure, was responsible for the Victorian enthusiasm for things Japanese. In addition he was something of a personal publicist and he was generally regarded by his contemporaries as one of the leaders of the Aesthetic Movement, together with his friends Whistler and the young Oscar Wilde.

In his early days as a conventional church architect Godwin had designed some stained glass and embroidery but his first large furniture commission was for the Guildhall at Northampton. The building was designed in 1861 but by the time the furniture was ordered he had come under the influence of Japanese art. Consequently the Gothic building was equipped with original, simple furniture owing almost nothing to contemporary furniture design. Godwin's next major work was Dromore Castle in County Limerick where one of the aesthete's trademarks, the peacock, taken directly from a Japanese crest, made its first appearance in Godwin's work. All the furniture, of simple rectilinear structure, was made in 1867 to the designer's specifications in oiled wainscot oak, the material a concession to the Gothic building, or ebonized mahogany, his favourite furniture wood. From the early 'sixties onwards, or from the time of his first contact with William Burges, Godwin devoted as much time to the study of Japanese art and its principles as he had in the previous ten years to the medieval. It was not his exclusive study, however, as his notebooks are filled with drawings from a variety of historic sources and from nature itself. This eclectic approach, which produced Japanese ornament in an Irish castle, is explained by Godwin's advice to students that they should study all that they could and take what good they could from every country and age but work in no particular style. If asked what style their work was – a reasonable Victorian enquiry – they should say: 'It is my own.' This is certainly true of all Godwin's furniture designs and such pieces as have survived. His most characteristic pieces were usually described as Anglo-Japanese but in their elegant simplicity they have little or nothing in common with the rickety imitation bamboo of the 'trade' productions of the latter part of the century.

From 1867, when he made his first furniture designs, until his death twenty years later Godwin designed considerable quantities of furniture, much of it, such as the well known elegant coffee table or the ebonized sideboard (plates 24, 2), originally for his own use and subsequently put into production. The sideboard, like the contemporary pieces for Dromore Castle, is a perfect example of Godwin's declared aim of basing his designs on the grouping of solid and void without additional ornament. The only ornaments he allowed himself were panels of Japanese leather paper, as in this case, or the occasional use of panels of actual Japanese carving, both commodities available at the time from Liberty's.

Possibly the most influential of Godwin's furniture was the group designed for the Paris Exhibition of 1878. This seems to have been the occasion on which real and pseudo-Japanese design came into its own. Not only were there actual Japanese exhibits, but such an august building as the official English Pavilion erected for the use of the Prince of Wales contained a morning room of 'exceptionally modern character' with Anglo-Japanese furniture, stained glass windows (plate 120) and an embroidered frieze of

Japanese motifs made by the Ladies' Work Society. Godwin's furniture was decorated on this occasion by James McNeil Whistler. The two men had first met in about 1863 when both had already been infected with an enthusiasm for Japanese prints and they were in close touch for the rest of Godwin's life. The most famous piece of work with which their names were jointly associated was Whistler's own house in Tite Street, Chelsea, designed by Godwin in 1877 (plate 64). On the occasion of the Paris Exhibition the next year Godwin did not use his favourite ebonized mahogany and instead of the usual black the whole exhibit was in shades of yellow described by the designers as a harmony in yellow and gold. A combination of the work of an architect and a painter in this form was most unusual though it was a logical extension of their mutual study of Japanese interior design. Early Morris and Company furniture existed, which was merely a vehicle for a series of pictures, but here for the first time were purely decorative abstract paintings which were intended to complement the furniture design. The group included elegant lightweight chairs, occasional tables, a sofa, a case for music and 'The Butterfly Cabinet'. It has been suggested that it was ultimately intended for Whistler's own use but unfortunately none of the pieces seems to have survived. However, there are various contemporary descriptions of the group, some wholly admiring and some like that by the writer in the *Society of Arts Reports* who admired Godwin's Japanese-type furniture but had distinct reservations about the glaring yellows ranging from citron and sage to orange and gold.

This variation on a single colour, using only plain painted surfaces, was one of Godwin's particular enthusiasms and his usual method of work for individual clients. In 1884, when the general practice was to mix a variety of positive designs and sombre colours in one room, he designed a subtle room for Oscar Wilde in shades of white. It is easy to see why painting was an expensive form of decoration, as compared with the more usual wallpaper, when Godwin's instructions for the decorators were: 'The whole of the wood-work to be painted in enamel white and grey to a height of five feet six inches. The rest of the walls to be finished in lime white with a slight addition of black to give a greyish tone.' All these subtle gradations of pale, clear colour were inspired by Japanese colour prints.

In another room designed for himself in 1872 when he was living with the actress Ellen Terry, Godwin based the entire décor on the pineapple. For example the woodwork was 'painted the pale green sometimes seen at the stem of a pineapple leaf when the other end has faded' which seems an instruction of extraordinary subtlety to give to the average housepainter. Another of his rooms was decorated in shades of blue and 'almost entirely furnished with Japanese things', a statement supported by his own house-hold inventory in the 'seventies and by Ellen Terry's memoirs in which she records the exceptional upbringing of the children, whose nursery walls were lined with Japanese prints, who wore tiny kimonos which made them look as Japanese as all that surrounded them and who, as a suitable treat, were taken to see an itinerant band of Japanese conjurors.

While his furniture was, as Godwin wrote himself, 'more or less founded on Japanese principles' (plate 56) his flat pattern designs, whether for wall-

54 Cabinet in ebonized wood with painted panels designed by T. E. Collcutt and made by Collinson & Lock, 1871. *London, Victoria and Albert Museum.*

55 'Tower House and Queen Anne's Grove' from a set of lithographs of Bedford Park published in 1882. *London, Victoria and Albert Museum.*

56 Watercolour sketch for a 'Japanese' cabinet, by E. W. Godwin, 1876. *London, Victoria and Albert Museum.*

57 Sketch design for a Town Hall in the 'Queen Anne' style, by E. W. Godwin, about 1876. *London, Victoria and Albert Museum.*

55

56

57

papers, tiles or textiles, were usually lifted directly or elaborated from Japanese sources. A page in one of his sketchbooks covered with detailed drawings of Japanese badges provided the motifs for several of his wallpaper and tile designs as well as obvious inspiration for textiles, such as the silks woven by Messrs Warners to Godwin's designs in about 1874 with names such as 'Nagasaki' (plate 75). This latter silk is a fairly complex design with angular linear ornament on the leaves and the ground 'full of detail but quiet', a subordination which Godwin found and admired in Japanese pattern design. The wallpapers were more diverse in character, ranging from those like the stylized 'Peacock' (plate 73) to the almost random asymmetrical designs such as the 'Bamboo' filling (plate 16), for use with the 'Peacock', and the 'Sparrow and Bamboo', all produced in the same year, 1872. This last paper, which Godwin intended to be printed in pale blue and pale green on a white ground, was usually sold in shades of the gloomy paper-stainer's green which was the hall mark of cultured taste in the 'seventies and was described by Godwin as an artistic mistake, ruining as it did the effect of his light, fresh designs as well as those of other Japanese enthusiasts like B. J. Talbert. The full range of Japanese wallpapers designed by Godwin has not yet been identified but the number can be appreciated from the fact that in 1872, when he was arranging the interior decoration of one of his larger houses, the builder's specifications enumerated at least a dozen rooms including the hall and stairs to be papered 'in different patterns at different prices all papers to be had of Messrs Jeffrey and to be Mr Godwin's patterns'.

Another 'Japanese' designer of the 'seventies was Thomas Jeckyll (1827–81) who, like Godwin, began his professional life as a Gothic architect and who had a considerable quantity of church building and restoration to his credit before he first came into contact with Japanese art and decoration. In Jeckyll's case this happened, not in London, but at another International Exhibition, that held in Paris in 1867. Architecture was singularly untouched by Japanism throughout the whole Aesthetic Movement. There was a certain asymmetry of fenestration, the deliberate use of undecorated surfaces and some rather superficially applied ornament but it was on interior decoration and furniture that the mark was made and thus after his conversion from the Gothic it was to domestic work that Jeckyll's energies were directed. His first important commission in 1870 was for a new wing of a house at 1 Holland Park for that enlightened patron and collector, Alexander Ionides. The house already included decoration by Morris and Company and Walter Crane quite apart from the owner's collections of painting and objects of virtue. Jeckyll designed a sitting-room, a billiards room, a bedroom and a servants' hall, all in the Anglo-Japanese manner, and was responsible for most of the furniture. This was much more closely related to actual oriental furniture than the designs of some of his contemporaries, both in detail and form, though obviously adapted to European use. The most distinctive feature of the sitting-room was an elaborate but elegant overmantel into the framework of which were set pieces of carved coral-coloured lacquer as a background for a collection of porcelain. The blue and white pieces were housed with style and elegance if

58 The dining-room at 18 Stafford Terrace, Kensington. The wallpaper 'Fruit and Pomegranate' by William Morris was new in 1874, the year in which the house was decorated. The sideboard was painted by Linley Sambourne. *The Countess of Rosse.*

59 The Peacock Room. Designed by Thomas Jeckyll and painted by J. M. Whistler for F. R. Leyland, 1877. *Washington, Freer Gallery.*

60 'Blossoms' by Albert Moore, 1881. Oil on canvas. *London, Courtesy of the Trustees of the Tate Gallery.*

61 'The Pelican'; pastel by Edward Burne-Jones, 1881. *Walthamstow, William Morris Gallery.*

somewhat impractically, on shelves running from floor to ceiling set against yellow walls, in the servants' hall. Judging from surviving illustrations and descriptions, however, the most successful and consistently Japanese room in the Ionides house was the billiards room (plate 51). The ceiling and walls were covered by a system of oak framing, related in proportion to the mullions and transoms of the windows. Within this framework, the cornice, dado and ceiling were made of lacquered Japanese trays and the openings in the walls were set with colour prints and paintings on silk, all of bird and flower subjects.

It was presumably as a result of this successful scheme of decoration that Jeckyll was commissioned by F. R. Leyland in 1876 to decorate his diningroom and to make it a suitable setting both for his collection of porcelain and for Whistler's 'Princesse de la Paye du Porcelain'. Overpainted with blue and gold peacocks by Whistler, it is often forgotten that Jeckyll was the designer of this remarkably original room (plate 59). In form it is a skilful blending of elements from a variety of sources. The fan-vaulted ceiling was almost a direct reproduction of the Tudor ceiling of the Watching Chamber in Hampton Court Palace with light fittings replacing the original pendant finials; the walls were lined with Spanish leather as a backing to the delicate shelving, with a strong vertical emphasis in their arrangement to counteract the restricting effect of their practical horizontal line. The only truly Japanese motif was that of the sunflower firedogs of wrought iron (plate 114). It was in the design of ironwork that Thomas Jeckyll excelled and it was the material in which he produced his most delicate and highly-wrought Japanese designs.

Soon after his conversion to the Japanese vogue, Jeckyll was employed by Barnard, Bishop and Barnard of Norwich to design for them a great cast-iron pavilion to be shown at the Philadelphia Centennial Exhibition of 1876. Transported back across the Atlantic it appeared two years later at the Paris Exhibition where it was admired both as a technical *tour de force* proving the skill of the manufacturer and as a perfect example of the application of Japanese design to contemporary use. An extraordinary structure, the pavilion was intended by the manufacturers for use upon a lawn or in ornamental grounds and it ultimately came to rest in a public park in Norwich, the town of its manufacture (plate 66). This two-tiered structure was supported on a series of cast-iron columns, with brackets and roof panels also of cast-iron, enriched with elaborate designs in low relief of birds and foliage, all of Japanese inspiration. The railing of the upper floor was of wrought iron of a fairly severe Japanese fret design but the most successful part of the whole structure was the surrounding railing, each unit of which was the aesthetic symbol, the sunflower, described at the time as 'one of the boldest and at the same time the most successful examples of modern wrought-iron work'. The treatment of both the foliage and the flower itself showed an intimate knowledge of the natural form of the plant and of the resources of the craftsman, as did the individual designs for the supporting brackets. The original drawings have a remarkable sensitivity of feeling and are some of the most attractive products of the Japanese vogue (plates 115, 116). The pavilion itself was merely an exhibition piece but the individual components were adapted by Jeckyll for use in stoves and firegrates and were in production for many years, finding their way into many an aesthetic interior, as did the sunflower in its adapted form as a firedog. The most popular of Jeckyll's cast-iron designs was that for a stove front consisting of a series of decorated circles, each containing a formalized flower and set on a ground of Japanese key diaper pattern, and he also designed cast-iron seats ornamented with Japanese cloud forms for use on railway stations in East Anglia.

Probably the most attractive form of Japanese design and one that was well within the reach of the general public was that for pottery and porcelain. Spectacular exhibition and display pieces were made by a number of manufacturers, notably the Worcester Royal Porcelain Company, but around 1880 almost every maker of table wares registered a 'Japanese' design with the Patent Office. The keynote of all these designs was an asymmetrical arrangement of fans, birds, sunflowers and almost anything remotely oriental, within the framework of the circular plate.

Another feature of this type of design was the practice of running a band of design obliquely across a circular plate or the cutting up of the whole pattern area by such bands meeting at acute angles. Occasionally the printed decoration included a European figure or landscape subject but always set in a fan or box shape placed off centre in the design indicating the oriental sympathies of the designer. One of the earliest complete services was called 'Sparrow and Bamboo' and was first made by Wedgwood in 1879. Except that the body was of Wedgwood's usual cream earthenware, the service was quite unlike their normal production (plate 83). Jugs and other vessels were straight-sided and angular and the decoration was a combination of relief moulding and transfer printing. The bamboo of the title was used as the motif for the handles of the various jugs and cups and the surface decoration was of fans moulded in relief and with a printed fan superimposed in relief only. In between the fans were sparrows and a type of kingfisher perched on boughs of plum blossom. While many designs of this kind on pottery were merely self-consciously asymmetrical and different from the conventional production, some of the more restrained examples are most attractive with painted or moulded decoration of a very high quality. Possibly the most successful were relief-decorated stoneware jugs made by such firms as W. Brownfield and Pinder, Bourne who, keeping up with fashion in this form of popular art, substituted for their usual narrative or commemorative subjects, storks or plum blossom applied seemingly at random (plates 85, 86). Some makers occasionally made objects in direct imitation of oriental forms, such as the attractive little angular teapot made by the Worcester Royal Porcelain Works in 1877 (plate 78).

The Japanese mania reached the silver trade in the mid-'seventies though in a comparatively restrained form. No attempt was made to imitate actual Japanese metal forms in original design, though one firm, Hukin and Heath of Sheffield, supplemented the real pieces of metalwork available to collectors by producing reproductions of actual Japanese and Persian metalwork by the electrotype process. As far as domestic silver was concerned the fashion took the form of the production of straight-sided or very simply curved vessels decorated with engraved designs of natural plant and bird forms derived from Japanese sources (plate 90). The only elaborations of form were in handles which, like the pottery jugs, were often based on growing bamboo. A later development of the eighteen-eighties in both domestic silver and jewellery was the use of applied gilt fans or birds on the main engraved silver ground in imitation of Japanese damascened metalwork (plate 89). Some of the pieces of relatively cheap jewellery of this kind were among the most attractive products of the fashion, possibly because of their comparatively small scale.

It seems curious that in a period of outward show and opulent display, an art which was opposed in every way to these ideas should have been popular, but the reasons for the existence of the Japanese taste seem to have been as diverse as its varied manifestations. It was the elements of understatement and restraint that appealed to Godwin, Whistler and the Aesthetic Movement, and this was explained in high-flown terms by Oscar Wilde in one of his lectures. 'Only a few have learned the secret of those high hours when thought is not. The secret of the influence of Japanese art here in the West is that it has kept true to its primary and poetical conditions and has not laid upon it the burden of its own intellectual doubts, the spiritual tragedy of its sorrows.'

On the other hand, Burges and his medieval followers admired Japanese ornament for the conditions which they believed produced it and without any real understanding of purpose or aim they opened up a rich new source of design motifs for trade. With the architect's enthusiasm for light colours and elegance on the one hand and for Japanese-derived ornament on the other, plus the great flood of Japanese goods reaching Europe after the Japanese revolution of 1868, the mania knew no limits. The Japanese made their contribution to the Queen Anne interior just as surely as they did to asymmetrical magazine layouts. There were provincial exhibitions of Japanese art, Japanese balls, a Japanese village set up briefly in Knightsbridge, Japanese furniture, Japanese books and, of course, Gilbert and Sullivan's opera *The Mikado*.

By 1878 a writer in the *Society of Arts Journal* explained that 'there has been such a rage for Japanese design of late that we are tolerably well acquainted with it. From the highest to the lowest, from the Worcester Royal Porcelain Works to Parisian children's fans we have had imitations of Japanese style.' Directly or indirectly Japan was the strongest external design influence in England from the mid-'sixties until the end of the century.

Chapter 5

OSCAR WILDE AND AMERICA

The most notorious figure of the eighteen-eighties was Oscar Wilde (1854–1900) who became in his early twenties the butt of most of the fun poked at aesthetes and was lampooned as one of the central figures in Gilbert and Sullivan's *Patience*. This notoriety was remarkable in that Wilde was not the originator of any of the ideas then current; though he did claim some responsibility for initiating an artistic movement he designed nothing, painted no pictures and his creative work at the time was confined to some rather weak poetry and an early play apparently never actually staged as it was unacceptable to the Lord Chamberlain, not for aesthetic excesses but because of its democratic or left-wing sentiments. Wilde's poetry was somewhat overpraised by a small group of the more intense aesthetes probably as much for its presentation as for its literary merit. The paper, the printing and above all the binding were most considered and as one reviewer of 'Poems' of 1881 wrote 'the cover is consummate, the paper is distinctly precious, the binding beautiful and the type is utterly too'.[1]

Wilde was a most effective apostle of aestheticism, writing and lecturing on all aspects of the decorative arts and on dress reform with such zeal that, while the more serious aspects of the Art Movement are forgotten, the mention of the eighteen-eighties conjures up an image of Wilde, lily in hand, attired in a velvet knickerbocker suit. This picture is unfair to his contribution to the movement though it does seem possible that he was responsible in some degree for the choice of the aesthetic symbols of the sunflower, the lily and the peacock feather symbolizing respectively constancy, purity and beauty. The origins of the adoption of these signs or badges of right-thinking are very obscure. As early as 1882 Walter Hamilton wrote 'why the sunflower, lily and peacock's feather have become identified with the movement is not easy to explain . . . in this minor matter I believe the example of Mr Oscar Wilde has had a considerable influence'. Again this is a question of publicity rather than an original idea. In one of his published lectures Wilde said, 'You have heard, I think, a few of you, of the two flowers connected with the aesthetic movement in England and said (I assure you erroneously) to be the food of some aesthetic young men. Well let me tell you the reason we love the lily and the sunflower . . . It is because these two lovely flowers are in England the two most perfect models of design, the most naturally adapted for decorative art – the gaudy leonine beauty of the one and the precious liveliness of the other giving to the artist the most entire and perfect joy.'² In fact the use of both the sunflower, 'that bright emblem of constancy', and the peacock feather originate from the study of Japanese ornament and were popular motifs throughout the 'seventies and 'eighties, the sunflower in particular occurring in every conceivable material from cast-iron and brickwork to embroidery 'as if it were the sum total of all beauty'.³ The lily motif with its fairly obvious symbolism is said to have originated with Rossetti's Blessed Damozel who leant out from the bar of Heaven with three lilies in her hand, but it was also used *ad nauseam* as a subject for design in all media and forms one of the links between aestheticism and Art Nouveau; and of course Rossetti kept peacocks in his London garden.

Another possible origin of the enthusiasm for the lily can also be traced to Oscar Wilde. In 1879 as a young man recently down from Oxford he conceived a great admiration for the society beauty, Lily Langtry. She recorded in her memoirs that Wilde was in the practice of bringing her flowers and on several occasions he visited Covent Garden Market, purchased a single, giant Amaryllis and proceeded down Piccadilly to present the flower to the object of his affections. Lily Langtry reported that this was at the time construed as a pose and the theory is given credence by the famous lines by W. S. Gilbert, written only two years later, about the young man who walked down Piccadilly with a poppy or a lily in his medieval hand.

Oscar Wilde was born in Dublin in 1854 and after a fairly conventional education he went up to Oxford in 1874. There, unlike his fellow undergraduates, he became infected by the current artistic enthusiasms for Pre-Raphaelite painting, for engravings and blue and white porcelain. Before he had been long at Oxford his rooms in Magdalen were popularly considered to be one of the show places of the college and of the university. The three rooms were panelled, he had the ceilings and dados decorated with painted ornament and the walls were hung with old engravings. His considerable collection of blue and white porcelain was housed on shelves and it was at one of his many entertainments in these rooms that Wilde is said to have made the well known remark, 'Oh, would that I could live up to my blue china'. He seems to have worked briefly under Walter Pater, whose influential *Studies in the History of the Renaissance* was published in 1873, and attended Ruskin's lectures on Florentine art. It was these lectures and Ruskin's personal influence that launched Wilde into a veritable crusade for art. Incidentally Wilde, like Ruskin many years earlier, won the Newdigate Prize for English verse, in his case with a weighty work called *Ravenna* celebrating both the splendours of Italian art and the new political unity of Italy.

Wilde himself gave several accounts of how a group of undergraduates attended one of Ruskin's lectures in which the Master expounded on his regrets that the best physique and strength of the young men of England were wasted on the cricket field or the river instead of being directed into noble work that would do good for other people. The audience was so moved that as a result, under Ruskin's direction, they spent some part of the

Fig. 4 Portrait of Oscar Wilde from an original photograph by Elliott & Fry, about 1881. *London, Victoria and Albert Museum.*

following winter building a road between the villages of Upper and Lower Hinksey, divided in those days by a swamp. After two months of hard work Ruskin departed for Venice and the road ended abruptly in the middle of the swamp. Oscar Wilde, however, felt that all the energy previously devoted to the road should be harnessed, as he said, 'to create an artistic movement that might change . . . the face of England. There was none of us idle; poets most of us, so ambitious were we: painters some of us, or workers in metal or modellers, determined that we would try and create for ourselves beautiful work, for those who love us, poems and pictures, and for those who love us not, epigrams and paradoxes and scorn.'[4] With the exception of the sting in the tail for enemies of art, these aims were clearly inspired by the works of Ruskin and William Morris. It was at about this time during 1877 that Morris delivered his first lecture on 'The Decorative Arts' and a number of his ideas appear in Wilde's lectures masquerading as original thought, notably the famous injunction to 'have nothing in your houses which you do not know to be useful or believe to be beautiful'.[5] Despite Wilde's claims there is no evidence that any of his energetic Oxford companions made any more effective contribution to art than they had done to road making but Wilde himself embarked enthusiastically on a career as an art critic and poet.

Coming down from Oxford in 1878 with a brilliant reputation, Wilde's tall, elegant figure and flowing hair made him the personification of a type of the Pre-Raphaelite movement. He was 'the rage' socially and his youth seemed to excuse his pose as an artistic reformer. Wilde in his turn came into contact with some of the figures whom he had admired from afar. He met Burne-Jones through Comyns Carr, the director of the Grosvenor Gallery, and the two became good friends, and for some years he was the constant companion of Whistler who had long been his hero, personifying as he did all the undergraduate theories of living beautifully amongst blue and white porcelain. Their mutual image was so confused in the public mind that Bunthorne, the Fleshly Poet in *Patience*, though intended as a caricature of Wilde, was made up with the black curls, moustache and eye glass of Whistler. During their association Wilde wrote poetic versions of the Thames Nocturne paintings and absorbed many of Whistler's ideas. When he married in 1884 he bought a house in Tite Street, Chelsea, close to Whistler and had it altered, decorated and furnished by their mutual friend, E. W. Godwin. Few of Whistler's friendships lasted long and Wilde and he finally parted company over some suggestion of plagiarism in Wilde's much publicized lectures.

But in the meantime Wilde had made his greatest contribution to the Art Movement – a lecture tour of the United States of America. Interest in the aesthetic school had spread to the United States largely through the influence of such books as Eastlake's *Hints on Household Taste* and cheap reprints of the aesthetic poets. The movement was obviously fairly widely known as *Patience* opened to an appreciative audience in New York only five months after its London première. One contemporary account of the trip suggested that Wilde himself felt that it was necessary to explain real aestheticism to the Americans, as opposed to the stage interpretation, and

99

'possibly instruct and elevate our rich, clever but not particularly cultured transatlantic cousins'.[6] This attitude was also suggested by the press account of Wilde's departure from England on Christmas Eve 1881 when he declared himself to be carrying culture to a continent armed only with his genius. This rather supercilious view was obviously modified by contact with the transatlantic cousins who were most enthusiastic in their reception of the young lecturer and who proved, en masse, to be better educated than their English counterparts.

An alternative suggestion for the origin of the lecture tour was that it was arranged by D'Oyly Carte to advertise the opera. It seems unlikely that Wilde, even if he was prepared to laugh at himself, would have agreed to be used as an advertising agent for a work which professed to ridicule all that he most admired in both art and poetry. In addition he would appear to have financed the trip himself as he said on arrival in New York that his subsequent movements would depend on the financial success of the first lecture. In fact the lecture tour lasted for eighteen months while *Patience* ran to packed houses in New York and another company took the show on the road. Whatever the original intentions the whole affair was a considerable personal triumph for Oscar Wilde both as prophet of the revived domestic arts and as showman. Thousands flocked to his lectures, crowds gathered at wayside railway stations for a view of this strange European phenomenon and hundreds of copies of his photograph were sold to admirers, and last but not least he inspired popular songs and music. Some of these songs originated in England, such as *Quite Too Utterly Utter*, *A New Aesthetic Roundelay* and were later also published in the States but most of them were written there for his new admirers. These included *The Oscar Wilde Gallop*, *Oscar Polka Mazurka* and *Oscar Dear* published by F. W. Helmick of Cincinatti in 1882. The words of this latter song are typical of many of the outpourings in verse form inspired by Wilde's appearance and charm.

> 'I'll sing to you of a nice young man
>   Of virtues rich and rare,
> Of stature tall and ankles thin
>   And long and curly hair.
> Aesthetic to a great degree
>   In actions sweet and mild
> Sublimely lank and nonchalant,
>   But just a little wild!

The pictorial covers of this sheet music invariably showed languid young men with lilies, in supposedly artistic settings, or Oscar Wilde himself in his famous knickerbocker suit. There must rarely if ever have been a serious artistic endeavour which so captured the imagination of the great mass of the public at all levels, from the undergraduates of Harvard to the purchasers of popular songs. Wilde's importance in the history of the Aesthetic Movement is in fact a direct result of this popularity which ensured that all his doings were recorded; complete lectures were published in the popular

E·W·Godwin·f·s·a· Architect ·   x R·W·Edis·f·s·a·Arch⁻ · x   E·W·Godwin·f·s·a· Architect ·

62

62   Artists' Houses in Chelsea; a view of Tite Street drawn by Thomas Raffles Davison from *The British Architect*, May, 1880.

Overleaf

63   Front elevation of the House and Studio in Tite Street, designed by E. W. Godwin for Mr F. Miles, 1879, as published in *The British Architect*, July 1880.

64   The White House, Tite Street, Chelsea, designed by E. W. Godwin for J. McNeil Whistler, 1878. Revised front elevation, as published in *The British Architect*.

E·W·Godwin·Arch!·

C·P·Edwards·del·

SCALE of 0   5   10   15   20   25 FEET

House & Studio for J·A·M^cN·Whistler Esq·Chelsea

Section through Ground Floor.

Street

E·W·Godwin·Arch^t

ÆSTHETIC LOVE IN A COTTAGE.

Miss Bilderbogie. "YES, DEAREST JOCONDA! I AM GOING TO MARRY YOUNG PETER PILCOX! WE SHALL BE VERY, *VERY* POOR! INDEED HOW WE ARE GOING TO *LIVE*, I CANNOT TELL!"

Mrs. Cimabue Brown. "OH, MY BEAUTIFUL MARIANA, HOW *NOBLE* OF YOU BOTH! NEVER MIND *HOW*, BUT *WHERE* ARE YOU GOING TO LIVE?"

Miss Bilderbogie. "OH, IN DEAR OLD KENSINGTON, I SUPPOSE—EVERYTHING IS SO CHEAP THERE, YOU KNOW!—PEACOCK FEATHERS ONLY A *PENNY A-PIECE!*"

67   'Aesthetic Love in a Cottage',
cartoon by George du Maurier
published in *Punch*, Volume 80,
1881.

68   'Sweet Little Buttercup' or
Art Embroidery, cartoon by
Linley Sambourne published in
Punch, Volume 76, 1879.

"SWEET LITTLE BUTTERCUP;"

Or, Art-Embroidery, 1879.

Text within the illustration:
LIBERTY & Cᵒ LONDON
INDIA, CHINA, JAPAN, MERCHANTS

69   Ornament from Liberty's
Eastern Art Catalogue, Dec. 1880.

press while the words of his less flamboyant contemporaries have been lost.

The first lecture on 'The English Renaissance of Art' was given in New York on 9 January 1882, soon after his arrival. The arrival itself was recorded very fully in the New York press and in a splendid burlesque interview in *Punch*. In this the poet was described as 'dressed in a long, snuff-coloured single breasted coat which reached his heels, and was relieved with a seal-skin collar and cuffs rather the worse for wear while a small daisy drooped despondently in his buttonhole'. He was said to be leaning against a chimney piece which had been painted pea green with panels of peacock blue pottery let in at uneven intervals and 'we may state, that the chimney piece as well as the seal-skin collar is the property of Oscar and will appear in his lectures on the Growth of Artistic Taste in England'.[7]

The *New York Tribune*, however, was kind about the lecturer's appearance and enthusiastic enough about the content to print a very long précis on the morning after the lecture and its lead was followed subsequently by other papers. There are numerous versions of these lectures, all of which differ to some extent. This is understandable as in the eighteen-months' tour Wilde lectured in New York, Boston, Omaha, Philadelphia and many other smaller towns before moving to Canada where he spoke in Montreal, Ottawa, Kingston, Quebec and to 1,100 persons in Toronto's Grand Opera House. He seems to have given three basic lectures at all these places: on the 'English Renaissance', 'House Decoration' and 'Art and the Handicrafts-man' but they were given from notes and each lecture obviously varied according to the circumstances and the type and size of audience. When the lectures were first published in book form, some years after Wilde's death, the editor found four copies of the first lecture all varying in some degree from each other and from the published press accounts.

However the main burden of the message of the lectures is clear and it can be assumed that it represented the approach of the aesthetes of the 1880s. Wilde was a little muddled in his exposition but the essence of his views was contained in the first lecture – 'Love art for its own sake and then all things that you need will be added to you'. The same lecture concluded with the observation that 'the secret of life is art'. This broad conclusion led logically to every aspect of life being related to art. 'Stately and simple architecture for your cities, bright and simple dress for your men and women; those are the conditions of a real artistic movement. For the artist is not concerned primarily with any theory of life but with life itself.' In Wilde's view a noble work of art could only be produced in a healthy, clean atmosphere and not in the polluted air of grimy industrial cities. From this followed a need for improved social conditions producing healthy young men and women, for 'sickly or idle or melancholy people do not do much in art' or in any other field of creative work. These healthy people in their turn must be individualists and in the last extreme Wilde equated re-publicanism and socialism with good art, proving his point by derisory reference to the products of France under Louis XIV. He poured scorn on the French decorative arts which had for so long been admired in England. 'The gaudy, gilt furniture writhing under a sense of its own horror and ugliness, with a nymph smirking at every angle and a dragon mouthing on every claw' he attributed directly to the follies of the nobility and monarchy of France. This was obviously a good approach in his attempt to spread culture in republican America and many of his other views were tailored for an American audience.

Wilde was clearly enormously impressed by the natural beauty and size of this new continent. He travelled extensively in the course of his tour and recommended to his audiences the magnificent materials that were available on their own doorsteps. Whereas in England native materials were relatively simple and more exotic things had to be sought abroad, his American audiences had to hand 'marble richer than Pentelicus and more varied than Paros' with which it was wrong merely to build great square houses. The material should be worked by noble workmen into marvellous forms. Similarly the various precious stones could give impetus to much-needed new designs and jewellery and, above all, Wilde suggested that it should be easy for American craftsmen to produce magnificent goldsmiths' work. A little optimistically he declared 'the gold is ready for you in unexhausted treasure, stored up in the mountain hollow or strewn on the river sand, and was not given to you for barren speculation. There should be some better record of it left in your history than the merchant's panic and the ruined home.' Similarly he advocated the use of native flowers and animals as design motifs rather than the repetition of those chosen by Greeks, Goths or even the contemporary Japanese.

These ideas were reiterated in various forms in his American lectures, notably one first given in May 1882 with the cumbersome title 'The Practical Application of the Principles of the Aesthetic Theory to Exterior and Interior House Decoration with Observations upon Dress and Personal Ornaments'. He further encouraged his American audiences by pointing out that the commercial spirit upon which their great cities were based was no barrier to art, as might be supposed, drawing a parallel with the similar spirit which was responsible for the development of the great cities of Renaissance Italy. On the other hand he did not hesitate to chide when he felt the occasion warranted it, for instance telling the citizens of Omaha that their houses were ill-designed and shabbily decorated in poor taste. One of the only recorded instances of difficulty with an audience was in Boston when some sixty Harvard students attended a lecture dressed in imitation of Wilde and 'having lilies in their buttonholes and sunflowers in their hands'. Wilde is recorded as having achieved a real triumph by ignoring the intended affront and offering the students a gift of sculpture for their gymnasium.

While he was clear and precise in his advice to his audiences Wilde's exposition of the origins of the new English Art Movement was somewhat confused. He saw it as an outcome of the combined forces of the French Revolution, the poetry of Keats, some Ruskin, and the Pre-Raphaelite movement, coupled with the more practical work of William Morris, the sum total being 'the union of Hellenism – with the intensified individualism, the passionate colour of the romantic spirit'. Despite his overwhelming enthusiasm he seems never to have fully understood his subject, so that on one occasion he could recommend Queen Anne architecture as being the most suitable for England while saying on another that the secret of all good architecture and furniture was the combination of the Greek line with Oriental phantasy. Side by side with this comparative nonsense comes the advanced idea, and a heretical one for a follower of Morris, that 'all machinery may be beautiful when it is undecorated even. Do not seek to decorate it. We cannot but think all good machinery is graceful, also, the line of strength and the line of beauty being one.'

This sort of original observation gives the lie to some of the accusations of plagiarism by Whistler and others. It is to Wilde that the idea of 'Art for Art's Sake' can be traced, a conception which was completely revolutionary in the 1880s when the content of painting had for so long been more important than the painting itself. In one of his lectures he said 'nor in its primary aspect has painting any more spiritual message for us than a blue tile from the wall of Damascus or a Hitzen vase. It is a beautifully-coloured surface, nothing more, and affects us by no suggestion stolen from philosophy, no pathos pilfered from literature, no feeling filched from a poet, but by its own incommunicable artistic essence.'

After the American trip Wilde continued his lectures in London, dressed rather more conventionally in a good dark suit and well-polished boots but still with the symbolic lily in his lapel. He practised what he had been preaching with great enthusiasm in the decoration of his own home in which the dining-chairs were described by the owner as sonnets in ivory and the table as a masterpiece in pearl; but with his appointment as editor of *The Woman's World* he gradually withdrew from active participation in the movement for which he had worked with such feeling.

Chapter 6

SATIRE AND COMMENT

The rise of the Aesthetic Movement and its impact on everyday life was best recorded in that chronicle of English social history, the periodical *Punch*. In its early days *Punch* virtually disregarded the arts except in so far as some of its elaborate and verbose jokes were set, for instance, at a Royal Academy private view but they might equally have been at a race-meeting or a dinner party. Artistic trappings appeared in the domestic interiors of some cartoons in the mid eighteen-seventies but it was not until 1877, when the movement was well established, that Art made its appearance as a subject of mirth. The preface of the complete volume of that year includes 'China-Mania' and 'Oxford Aesthetics' in the list of assorted movements afflicting England in the fortieth year of Queen Victoria's reign and, in the same volume, there are a number of cartoons by George du Maurier (1834–96) on aesthetic topics, one of which is a fully-developed comment on the idea of art for art's sake. An artistic young man is explaining to what is described as a 'matter-of-fact party' that, despite a repulsive subject, poor drawing and beastly colour, the painting which they are both studying is beautiful.[1] The joke clearly presupposes that *Punch* readers were familiar with this sort of situation and it must have been equally well-known in the United States as most of du Maurier's drawings were pirated or appropriated soon after their appearance in England by American illustrated papers, notably the *New York Daily Graphic*.

In 1877 du Maurier's young man was dressed in conventional town clothing and only the text explained his artistic leanings. It was not until 1879 that du Maurier introduced his famous artistic family, the Cimabue Browns and their aesthetic young friends, Postlethwaite and Maudle. The Browns, mother, father and children, aspired to live an artistic life in which they were guided by their admiration for the poet, Postlethwaite, and the painter, Maudle, who in their turn admired each other and their respective arts. In appearance the artistic pair were based roughly on Wilde and Whistler with a touch of Swinburne. They drooped and were lionized in drawing-rooms filled with spindly black furniture, Japanese fans and screens covered in bulrushes and sunflowers. In due course du Maurier became so absorbed in his creations that their own supposed work began to appear in *Punch*. One such piece was a design, 'A Love Agony', said to be the work of the fictitious Maudle and accompanied by some curious verses by Postlethwaite who was reported to have posed for the picture.[2] Maudle's comments on current affairs appeared in articles in *Punch* in 1880 and 1881 and many readers must have believed that he actually existed. One of du Maurier's most attractive drawings (fig. 5) shows four little girls dressed in Kate Greenaway-style costume with peacock-feathers in their hats proudly carrying sunflowers on their afternoon walk. These are the young Cimabue Browns and more conventionally dressed children attribute their dress and bearing to aesthetic exclusiveness. Many of the jokes about adults were based on the self-assumed superiority of the aesthete busily setting standards by which other less enlightened mortals were to live. On their second appearance in *Punch* the smug little Cimabue Brown children shocked their conventional grandfather by expressing a preference for the National Gallery and Bach's 'glorious Passionsmusik' rather than a proffered trip to the Zoo and a pantomime.[3] du Maurier excused the Philistine grandfather by explaining that he had only recently returned from Ceylon and must presumably have been unaware of the rise of the cult for existing beautifully even amongst young children. Most contemporary evidence suggests that the Aesthetic Movement had reached its peak by the early 1880s and this theory is also supported by du Maurier's drawings (plate 67). Always the most careful observer of the social scene, direct reference to aesthetes had disappeared from his cartoons by 1882 and Postlethwaite and Company withdrew from *Punch* late in 1881 in a short poem entitled *The Downfall of the Dado*.[4] It is in the form of a drawing-room operetta and the stage instructions at the end of each verse describe the breaking of blue and white china, the rending of aesthetic flowers and the final ascent of the company including Maudle, Postlethwaite and Mrs Cimabue Brown from 'The Dismal Depths of Dadocracy to the Coral Caves of Common Sense'. The aesthetes faded quietly from the pages of *Punch*

Fig. 5 'The Height of Aesthetic Exclusiveness', an original drawing by George du Maurier for a cartoon published in *Punch*, Volume 77, 1879. *The caption reads* MAMMA: 'Who are those extraordinary-looking children?' EFFIE: 'The Cimabue Browns, Mamma – they're *Aesthetic*, you know!' MAMMA: 'So I should imagine. Do you know them to speak to?' EFFIE: 'Oh *Dear* no, Mamma – they're most *exclusive* – why, they put out their tongues at us if we only *look* at them!' *London, Victoria and Albert Museum*

Fig. 6 Caricature of Oscar Wilde
by Linley Sambourne from *Punch*,
Volume 80, 1881. *The caption reads*
'O.W.'
'O, I feel just as happy as a bright
sunflower!'
Aesthete of Aesthetes!
What's in a name?
The poet is WILDE,
But his poetry's tame.
London, Victoria and Albert Museum

though the arts, and in particular the amateur artist, remained as subjects for cartoons and jokes.

The other *Punch* artist most concerned with witticisms at the expense of aesthetes was Edward Linley Sambourne (1844–1910). Unlike du Maurier, who relied for his work on the careful observation of society and coupled his drawings with verbose jokes, Linley Sambourne (1844–1910) worked almost entirely from imagination producing what were described as quaint and fanciful drawings with captions so brief that the editors of *Punch* sometimes provided explanations for their less quick-witted readers. Thus a portrait of O. W. (fig. 6) as a sunflower was accompanied by an editorial note explaining that this particular 'Fancy Portrait' was of Oscar Wilde. Linley Sambourne's first sunflower appeared without comment in the Almanac for 1877 and his subsequent political cartoons and fanciful drawings often had an aesthetic note. One of the most successful and self-explanatory drawings poked fun at 'Art Embroidery' (plate 68). This shows a charming young lady dressed rather suggestively in a William Morris type fabric surrounded by the paraphernalia of contemporary embroidery. *Punch* derived a lot of simple fun from the possibilities of combining aesthetic enthusiasms with fashion, such as the lady who carried her feeling for blue and white porcelain to the lengths of wearing applied plates on her gown and a delicate little teapot on her head (fig. 7). Linley Sambourne's own position in relation to the Art Movement was somewhat ambiguous. The evidence suggests that in 1877 it became editorial policy to attack aesthetes in *Punch* much as it had previously dealt ruthlessly with other movements and individuals. Sambourne, who worked for the paper, obviously conformed with its views but his own house which was decorated and furnished in 1874 remains today as one of the most perfect examples of an artistic interior (plates 49, 58). There are Morris wallpapers, art embroideries, art furniture, Japanese ornaments from Liberty's and decorations designed by Linley Sambourne himself. The main feature of the drawing-room is a handsome stained-glass window in which birds flit amongst giant sunflowers and potted palms.

Quite apart from providing visual copy for his one-time friend, du Maurier, Whistler was an early butt for *Punch* in its literary campaign against the aesthetes. The 1877 volume contained a poem on Whistler's newly completed Peacock Room (plate 59) as well as a series of rather puerile suggestions for future paintings such as 'a depravity in scarlet, an impertinence in any colour or an optical illusion in invisible green'. The Peacock Room theme recurred over the years, culminating in a poem published in 1881, the first verse of which ran:

'Her blue-green dress on the grey-blue floor
    Lay in folds all tumbled and hilly,
Like the waves that break on the smooth sea shore
    Or the crumpled leaves of a floating lily.'

From this example it can be deduced that the literary standard maintained by *Punch* was by no means equal to that of its drawings. Verse was one of its

CHINAMANIA MADE USEFUL AT LAST!

Fig. 7 'Chinamania made useful at last!' from *Punch*, Volume 78, 1880. *London, Victoria and Albert Museum*

most popular weapons for satire but it was of a poor quality, except on the rare occasions when it was actual parody. One of the more successful pieces in this vein was a parody of the poem by Edward Waller *Go Lovely Rose*:

The Aesthete and the Rose

Go flaunting Rose!
Tell her that wastes her love on thee,
    That she nought knows,
Of the new Cult Intensity,
If sweet and fair to her you be.

    Tell her that's young,
Or who in health and bloom takes pride,
    That bards have sung
Of a new youth – at whose sad side
    Sickness and pallor aye abide.

    Small is the worth
Of Beauty in crude charms attired,
    She must shun mirth,
Have suffered fruitlessly and desired,
And wear no flush by hope inspired.

    Then die, that she
May learn that death is passing fair,
    May read in thee
How little of Art's praise they share
    Who are not sallow sick and spare.[5]

The pale, sad and melancholy manner adopted by would-be aesthetes gave infinite scope to the satirists. To indicate right-thinking it seemed necessary to droop limply in imitation of the pale characters in Pre-Raphaelite paintings. *The Decorative Sisters*, an amusing little book on this subject, was published in New York in 1882 (plate 107). The format was similar to that of children's books of the time but in this case it was directed at aesthetically-minded adults and told the sad story of two previously ordinary young ladies who became 'intense' and spent their days sketching sunflowers and looking at lilies instead of pursuing a healthy, rural life.

Some of the artistic jokes in *Punch* which may well have been amusing at the time have misfired in the long run. In the same volume in which cartoons ridiculed the possibility of flying from London to Paris or bottling and storing music for later enjoyment, *Punch* published an Art Utilitarian Examination Paper. The questions ranged from designs for posters and suggestions for the best way of advertising a new soup to the conversion of a stucco villa into a Queen Anne Mansion. Today no one would think it strange that a student should be required to design a poster or promote the sale of soup and the basic joke, that the applied arts might ever be a subject of higher education, has proved to be very wide of the mark.

F. C. Burnand (1836–1917) became the editor of *Punch* at the height of its campaign of ridicule aimed at art in general and aesthetes in particular. Realizing that the subject was still popular with the public he wrote a play or, to be more precise, converted an existing French one, in which the aesthetic characters were represented not only as fools but as knaves. The joke would seem to have failed to some extent because the sets and costumes, at which the audience were expected to laugh, were so attractive that several critics regarded the play *The Colonel* as an excellent advertisement for aestheticism. After seeing the play E. W. Godwin wrote that the set 'presented to us as wrong, we find is furnished with artistic and simple things; a charming cabinet in walnut designed by Mr Padgett for the green room, some simple inexpensive Sussex chairs like those sold by Messrs W. Morris and Co., a black coffee table after the well known example originally designed in 1867 by the writer of these notes; a quite simple writing table, matting on the floor, a green and yellow paper on the walls, a sunflower frieze, a Japanese treatment of the ceiling and a red sun such as we see in Japanese books, and a hand screen, make up a scene which if found wanting in certain details and forced in sunflowers, is certainly an intriguing room with individuality about it, quiet in tone and what is most important, harmonious and pleasing.' He also reported seeing the leading lady outside the theatre where she passed unnoticed though 'her private costume was modelled line for line on that she had just worn as an aesthete in the comedy, and which the audience had been invited to ridicule'.[6]

This view of *The Colonel* (see plate 97) was taken by other and presumably more detached commentators such as the dramatic critic of *The London Illustrated News* whose enthusiasm was such that he visited the play twice in the first month of its production, February 1881, and wrote about it at length on both occasions. He thought the plot trivial but found the performance excellent and the settings and costumes the best that had been seen on the London stage for many years. This anonymous critic, not unnaturally, took exception to the suggestion implicit in the play that an admiration for the work of the artists of the Italian Renaissance automatically led to the picking of pockets or the telling of lies. He was, however, delighted by the subtle education of the Philistines who came all unsuspecting to enjoy a gay evening in the theatre little thinking that they were absorbing the philosophy at which they were laughing. The critic felt that the whole thing was quite harmless because in his view culture was rapidly winning the day 'over stupid and vulgar Philistinism'. The play had a long and successful run in London and in the autumn of 1881 gained the distinction of a Royal Command performance before Queen Victoria at Abergeldie Castle in Scotland. The new ideas were so generally accepted by this time that it was reported that furniture for the aesthetic scene was purchased expressly in Edinburgh to save the cost of transport from London and additional pieces were borrowed from the Prince and Princess of Wales.

Dramatic entertainments were not the exclusive prerogative of the aesthetic opposition. In 1875 Comyns Carr, friend of many artists and director of the Grosvenor Gallery in London, the shop window of aesthetic painters, helped in the production of *A Cabinet of Secrets* at St George's Hall

70 'Marigolds and Blossom', chintz designed by B. J. Talbert and roller printed in colours by Stead, McAlpin & Co., 1873. *London, Public Record Office.*

71 'Sunflowers and Vetch',
chintz designed by B. J. Talbert
and roller printed in colours by
James Back, Glasgow, 1875.
London, Public Record Office.

72 'Flower Pot' panel,
embroidered in coloured silks on
white flannel and designed by
William Morris about 1880.
London, Victoria and Albert Museum.

in Portland Place. This was a small hall or theatre which specialized in 'select' and intimate entertainments, in character somewhere between domestic charades and musical plays. *A Cabinet of Secrets* was a skit on china collecting, a pastime of the *élite*, which by the mid-seventies had assumed the proportions of a fashionable craze. The theme song of the piece concluded with the line 'we revel in the form and glaze of every cup and saucer' and the plot was based on the idea that a world-wide passion for porcelain might break down international barriers and ultimately cure the ills of the world. It would appear that 'select' artistic audiences were quite prepared to laugh at their own enthusiasms.

The culmination of all the aesthetic fun was the production of Gilbert and Sullivan's new comic opera *Patience or Bunthorne's Bride* at the Opera Comique in London on St George's Day, 1881. Subtitled 'An Aesthetic Opera', it was an immediate success, acknowledged by all but the *Punch* critic who ignored its very existence, presumably because he regarded the opera as unfair competition for *The Colonel*. Richard D'Oyly Carte, the impresario, had already had some years of success with Gilbert and Sullivan's comic operas but *Patience* was to be a milestone in his career. With its 'Fleshly and Idyllic Poets', chorus of lovesick maidens in aesthetic draperies playing mandolins and, of all improbable things, 'cellos, it exactly fitted the mood of the times. The text was witty enough to amuse the converted and cruel enough for the Philistines. As in *The Colonel* before it, while the aesthetes were held up to ridicule, the costumes were elegantly and genuinely artistic. These were designed by the author himself, W. S. Gilbert (1836–1911), and made from fashionable Liberty textiles which were actually advertised on theatre programmes printed in the fashionable asymmetrical Japanese way. After a successful run at the Opera Comique in London, D'Oyly Carte elected to open his new Savoy Theatre, itself an artistic landmark, with the same opera but, as he announced, with 'new scenery, costumes and increased chorus'.

Opened on 14 October 1881, the Savoy Theatre had the distinction of being the first public building 'lit permanently and in all departments' with electric light. A gas supply was available in case of emergencies though it does not seem to have been necessary to use it. The theatre was artistically decorated in keeping with the times with rich embossed wallpaper in tones of Venetian red and the seating upholstered in peacock blue plush in the stalls and stamped velvet for the rest of the house. The only other colour used was a pale, soft yellow and the usual painted drop scene was replaced by a gold satin curtain.

The real innovation was the almost simultaneous opening in London and New York of the same comic opera. Earlier Gilbert and Sullivan pieces such as *H.M.S. Pinafore* had been ruthlessly pirated in the United States and D'Oyly Carte decided to overcome this complimentary but financially unrewarding practice by launching an official version before sub-standard productions could get under way. To this end the Carte Bureau was established in New York conveniently near to the Standard Theatre and a publicity campaign was launched. So successful was the new venture that during the latter part of 1881 and the whole of 1882 D'Oyly Carte had two

73 'Peacock', wallpaper designed by E. W. Godwin and hand-printed by Jeffrey & Co., 1873. *London, Public Record Office.*

74 Wallpaper, anonymously designed, printed by Corbiere, Son & Brindle, 1877. *London, Public Record Office.*

75 'Nagasaki', silk damask made by Warner & Sons about 1874, and probably designed by E. W. Godwin. *London, Victoria and Albert Museum.*

76 Upholstery fabric in worsted wool and silk by an unknown designer, about 1880. *London, Victoria and Albert Museum.*

77 Detail of a piano cover embroidered in gold thread and *appliqué* on silk damask, designed by C. R. Ashbee, about 1889. *London, Victoria and Albert Museum.*

Fig. 8 Monogram of Richard D'Oyly Carte combined with the sunflower, Union Jack and Stars and Stripes from the programme published by the Standard Theatre, New York, on the occasion of the 100th performance of *Patience*. *London, Victoria and Albert Museum*

Patience companies touring England in addition to the London production and in America there was a company at the Standard Theatre, New York, as well as a touring company. So close was the liaison between the two productions that on 29 December 1881 a souvenir programme was published celebrating jointly the 250th London show and the 100th in New York. But, despite all the precautions, two pirate companies were also presenting *Patience* in Chicago. Clearly aesthetes were prevalent enough in the United States to be found amusing.

Always at his best as a satirist, W. S. Gilbert produced some of his most sparkling writing in *Patience* and dealt with almost every aspect of the art craze. It is made quite plain throughout the whole piece that to be fashionably aesthetic it was necessary to droop despairingly, and to be visibly soulfully intense. The contrast between aesthetes and the others was made the more pointed in that their rivals for the affection of the rapturous maidens of the chorus were army officers whose attentions were rebuffed initially because their uniforms were of gay, bright primary colours. It was suggested to the Dragoons that they would be altogether more attractive dressed in 'a cobwebby grey velvet, with a tender bloom like a cold gravy, which, made Florentine fourteenth century, trimmed with Venetian leather and Spanish altar lace, and surmounted with something Japanese – would at least be Early English.' This recipe could have been taken from almost any contemporary book on decoration but for the typically Gilbertian deflationary note introduced by the cold gravy.

At one point Bunthorne, the Fleshly Poet, admits to the audience in a recitative and song that he has no real love for languid lilies or things Japanese and that his whole attitude is a pose 'born of a morbid love of admiration'. He then gives a most useful list of requirements for those wishing to appear cultured, including what could almost be described as the fashionable architect's motto –

'Be eloquent in praise of the very dull old days which have long since passed away,
And convince 'em if you can, that the reign of good Queen Anne was Culture's palmiest day.'

The transformation of the Dragoons into acceptably fashionable young men gave Gilbert the opportunity to pour scorn on the taste for the medieval, for blue and white china, lilies and all the other trimmings of the movement and he concluded with a sparkling lyric pinpointing the whole fashionable craze:

'A Japanese young man,
A blue and white young man,
Francesca di Rimini, miminy, piminy,
Je-ne-sais-quoi young man!

A pallid and thin young man,
A haggard and lank young man
A greenery-yallery, Grosvenor Gallery,
Foot-in-the-grave young man!'

126

Scornful though they may have been, others cashed in on the whole affair. The eminently respectable Worcester Royal Porcelain Company took the opportunity to issue a remarkable teapot composed of the head and torso of a male and a female back to back dressed in costumes derived from the stage presentation of *Patience* (plate 101) and inscribed underneath 'Fearful consequences through the laws of Natural Selection and Evolution of living up to one's teapot'. It was an expensive and complicated but apparently successful joke. The pot is actually beautifully and ingeniously modelled, the elegantly drooping arms of the figures providing the spout through which the tea was poured. Both parties wear 'yallery' green garments with puce hats and both have fashionable red hair.

Patience ran in London for 578 performances and though it provided excellent entertainment it did considerable disservice to the serious aspects of the Art Movement, as did all the other public jibes at the outward appearances of the fashionable few. *The British Architect*, one of the periodicals which led the way in serious design reform in many fields, chose the occasion of the 500th performance to philosophize on the little that had been achieved thus far. 'If there is nothing else to illustrate the fact, the sickening repetition of the sunflower in all sorts of decorative work (as though it were the sum total of all beauty) would be enough to show how little the general public have yet derived from the increased study of art.'[7]

Chapter 7

'ART' INDUSTRY

Initially one of the motivating forces of the Aesthetic Movement was the antipathy of the art world to the products of industry and the machine but, ironically enough, by the early 1870s 'art' was becoming a profitable adjunct of many an established business. Trade was imitating what had been begun by artist-craftsmen and by 1880 the movement had snowballed to such an extent that any successful retailer or maker of household goods included the word 'art' somewhere in the description of his business. In the early stages in the late 1860s there seem to have been certain hazards in the art business. Trade periodicals record a number of short-lived firms, such as the first of the Art Furniture Companies with which E. W. Godwin was associated and which began and ended in 1867, and Christopher Dresser's 'Art Furniture Alliance'. This was a showroom in New Bond Street for the sale of metalwork, furniture and other objects mostly designed by Dresser himself and 'attendants robed in many aesthetic costumes of the period, in demure art colours, added a certain air to the place, which set it absolutely apart from a shop'.[1] It must have been so unlike any other shop that it was not a successful commercial venture. However by the late '70s, art was no longer a risk. Trade directories list dozens of Art Furniture Manufacturers and Art Metal Workers and other trades, many of which were old-established firms who thought it politic to add 'art' to their other activities. W. B. Simpson, the tile- and glass-makers, became art tile painters in 1873. In 1876 Gillow and Company listed themselves both as cabinet-makers and as Art Furniture Manufacturers and many other firms followed suit. In 1880, Walter Crane, whose business abilities seem always to have equalled his skill as a designer, became Art Superintendent of the London Decorating Company, a firm with a capital of £100,000, specializing in encaustic tiles. The prospectus of the new company showed Art, Science and Health as the three graces. Walter Crane and many others were able successfully to combine commerce and arts and crafts.

In some cases tradesmen merely produced parodies of fashionable designs or conventional goods in supposed art colours. In 1880 one firm produced a series of 'Early English' leather goods 'of a new tint of green called Elizabethan'. An entry in the same year in *The Artist* recorded that Messrs William Collins, makers of wood and fancy boxes, were making a 'Queen Anne' writing desk fitted with 'the new sea-green Queen Anne notepaper and sundries'. It is difficult to visualize the subtle difference between these two new and original royal greens. Other firms made and sold goods genuinely inspired by the real spirit of the new movement. Pottery, textiles, wallpapers, silver and furniture of quality, which have had a lasting effect on design, were made between 1870 and 1885.

The first and most important of these enterprises was William Morris's own firm. It was established in April 1861 with the name Morris, Marshall, Faulkner and Company as a direct result of Morris's personal furnishing difficulties. Finding nothing that pleased him on the market, he and his friends set to and designed their own furniture, embroideries and wallpaper. The firm had its first modest success at the 1862 International Exhibition in London at which goods were sold to the value of £131. The business moved to its own premises at 26 Queen Square in 1865, was renamed Morris and Company in 1875, in April 1877 opened showrooms in Oxford Street, London, and in 1881 showrooms were opened in New York,[2] slightly predating the arrival of Oscar Wilde and *Patience*. Morris and Company were both retailers and manufacturers, or at least supervisors of the manufacture of the goods they sold. Cabinet furniture was made in their own small workshops and the well-known chairs were made to the firm's specifications probably at High Wycombe. All the wallpapers were printed by the leading art wallpaper firm, Jeffrey and Company, who also worked for a number of other retailers and designers. Both woven and printed textiles were ultimately made in the Morris workshops at Merton Abbey, which were taken over in 1881, but in the earlier years of the firm the designs were woven or printed on commission by outside firms. Silks were woven at Macclesfield and wool tapestries and lenos made by Alexander Morton at Darvel in Scotland. Before Morris embarked on the weaving of hand-knotted pile carpets himself, his earliest carpet designs were for machine-produced floor coverings made by the Heckmondwike Manufacturing Company in Yorkshire and the Wilton Royal Carpet Works. The earliest chintzes were printed on commission in about 1868–70 and after his experiments with vegetable dyes some printing on silk was done at Leek by Thomas Wardle. But the bulk of Morris's textile dyeing and printing was carried out after the establishment of the firm's own workshops at Merton Abbey. The only part of the company's activities almost exclusively executed on their own premises from the inception was embroidery, though some of the more elaborate designs were worked by skilled needle-women amongst Morris's clients. In addition to actual embroideries the firm supplied patterns traced on cloth or silk and either sold their own specially-dyed silks and wools or advised on the colours to be used.

The retailer whose name has remained most closely associated with the Aesthetic Movement is, of course, Liberty. In addition to the oriental goods that Liberty's originally imported and sold, the business was expanded to include the sale of pottery, textiles and metalwork, designed and made exclusively for their various shops both in England and abroad, and their influence on the art world continued into the Art Nouveau period. The Italian name of the later movement, 'Stile Liberty', derived from the popular identification on the Continent of Liberty's with the flowing curves of Art Nouveau.

Fig. 9 Drawings of some
'Burmantofts Pottery' made for
Messrs Howell & James, from the
British Architect, October 7, 1881.

Possibly the largest business in London concerned with art manufactures
was that of Howell and James of Lower Regent Street. By the mid 'seventies
their galleries were the gathering place of artists of all kinds and their
annual show of 'Painting on Pottery and Porcelain', instituted in 1875,
seems to have rivalled the Royal Academy as a social and artistic event of
the London Season. Established as early as 1820, Howell and James sold
both antique and modern silver and jewellery as well as most of the requirements of the fashionable furnishing trades. By the early 1860s they had their
own pottery mark and by the 1870s they described themselves as 'Silk
Mercers and Proprietors of an Art Pottery Gallery' and, in another trade
list, as Art Metal Workers. While Howell and James had their own metal
workshops most of their other Art products were made on their behalf by
other manufacturers. Their stand at the Paris Exhibition of 1878 included
lace and various wooden articles in addition to the pottery for which they
were well known by this time. The pottery was in every case made by some
reputable firm, such as Minton or Doulton, but marked with the Howell
and James mark, and they also patronized individual art potteries, such as
that of Charles H. Brannum of Barnstaple. While the firm was internation-
ally 'known for their efforts to popularize works of high art and good taste'
their secondary purpose was a social one 'to supply graceful, appropriate
and at the same time profitable employment for ladies'.

The employment of female labour in their pottery painting establishment
seems to have grown from the annual exhibitions at which both amateurs
and professionals showed and competed for prizes. The standing of the
whole enterprise can be gauged from the fact that the first prize for amateurs
in 1878 was presented by the Crown Princess of Germany and was won by
the Countess of Warwick for a dish painted with a charming head set
against apple blossom. The second prize-winner on this occasion was a
professional painter whose plate was exhibited at Paris and subsequently
acquired by the Kunstgewerbemuseum in Berlin (plate 82). The exhibitions were judged by members of the Royal Academy and it appears that
some attempt was made to divide the prizes equally between amateur and
professional painters. The most popular vehicles for decoration were large
dishes or plaques, some as much as a yard in diameter, and the subject
matter was as diverse as in any contemporary exhibition of painting with
landscape subjects, often including children, heading the list of popularity.
One of the leading professional artists in this field was a Mrs Sparkes, wife
of the head of the Lambeth School of Art, a school much concerned with
the development of Art Pottery. Her work was usually exhibited *hors concours*
and it was said to be as freely painted as if it would have been on canvas.
In addition to decorated and painted wares, Howell and James also sold
blanks and colours for both over- and under-glaze painting for amateurs. It
seems possible that some of these blanks had designs traced on them ready
for colouring but Howell and James usually confined themselves to suggesting suitable subjects, such as the copying of Walter Crane's picture-books
for the decoration of a nursery.

Another professional artist and designer associated with the firm was
Lewis F. Day (1845–1910). He produced a series of formal designs for

plates and vases which he painted himself. In addition he designed a range of 'Early English' and 'Queen Anne' clocks in ebonized wood – one of Howell and James's most distinctive 'art' lines. The faces, in blue and white earthenware, were designed by Day (plate 45) and by R. Phené Spiers and Walter Crane. These were intended to accompany the ubiquitous ebonized and painted cabinets of the artistic home.

W. B. Simpson and Sons were established in London as housepainters and decorators in 1833. In the nature of their work they were involved with tiles and other decorative materials and eventually they became agents for the sale of these goods. By 1873 the business seems to have expanded considerably and W. B. Simpson and Sons described themselves, amongst other things, as 'art tile painters' and 'art glass painters'. With a large showroom in St Martin's Lane, they not only painted tiles but commissioned distinguished designers to work for them. Tile blanks were made by Minton Hollins and by Maw and Company of Jackfield in Shropshire and were painted, glazed and fired on Simpson's premises at 456 West Strand. The decorated tiles were marked with W. B. Simpson's own mark. Unfortunately much of the design was anonymous, like the attractive tiles in the Kunstgewerbemuseum in Berlin (plate 33) which were included in Simpson's display at the Paris Exhibition of 1878. This particular set of tiles is very freshly painted and illustrates craftsmen in an idealized medieval setting busy at their various pursuits. Narrative tiles of this type were particularly popular in the 1880s in fireplace surrounds, some being designed for the purpose and others using subjects from children's books illustrated by such artists as Kate Greenaway (plate 105) and Walter Crane (see also plate 46). In addition to tile painting W. B. Simpson were responsible for the actual tile and mosaic work in a number of important buildings, in particular the tiled refreshment room and grill room at the Victoria and Albert Museum decorated in 1874. This latter room included a series of large figure subjects designed by E. J. Poynter (1836–1919), as well as a series of more routine tiles on which the inevitable sunflower was painted in blue and white. Messrs Jeffrey and Company of Islington printed a set of wallpapers exclusively for W. B. Simpson, notably those designed by Lewis F. Day of which one of the most attractive was the 'Apple Blossom' (plate 10). The wallpapers, like the tiles, were marked with the Simpson monogram. A commentator on the Paris Exhibition of 1878 described the W. B. Simpson exhibits as being 'of much grace, originality and beauty as well as being examples of pure and good Art'.

While some manufacturers and retailers were temporarily involved with the needs of their aesthetic customers, the Art Movement made an enduring impression on English pottery. During the last thirty years of the nineteenth century there was a clear division between ordinary commercial production on the one hand and 'art' pottery, the forerunner of modern studio pottery on the other. In most industries the term 'art' implied a new approach to decoration or design but in some branches of the pottery industry it implied a radical change in methods of production based on the principles of the Arts and Crafts Movement, with its dual respect for the nature of materials and the dignity of the individual craftsman. The established firms, such as

Minton's, Copeland's and the Worcester Royal Porcelain Company, produced highly-finished, sophisticated wares often of considerable elaboration based on increasing technical efficiency. In addition, though the English designers had come to the fore in the 1860s, this was the one industry which continued to rely heavily on foreigners particularly for prestige exhibition work. Current fashions were reflected in some painted decoration but had virtually no effect on shapes, with the exception of some of the Japanese-inspired porcelain made at Worcester, and the occasional oddity such as the Worcester 'Patience' teapot (plates 101,103).

The first actual art pottery was saltglaze stoneware made by Doulton of Lambeth and exhibited at the International Exhibition held in London in 1871. Doulton had been making ornamental flasks, and a variety of basic domestic equipment in brown stoneware, from the early part of the century. The brown material with its rough surface had become increasingly unpopular with the mid-Victorian public who preferred the comparative sophistication of porcelain or white earthenware so that by the middle of the century production was confined to oven-ware and large containers of various kinds. An important new development occurred in the 1860s after John Sparkes, headmaster of a flourishing School of Art at Lambeth, became a friend of Henry Doulton, the head of the firm. Sparkes was later appointed as the Principal of the National Art Training School at South Kensington and his wife was one of the best known of the professional art pottery painters. As a result of this personal association, Doulton embarked on the novel experiment of allowing selected students from the School of Art to work on stoneware, under the direction of John Sparkes.

The pottery was thrown and turned by skilled craftsmen and from their production vessels were selected for decoration by the students, each of whom signed his or her finished work. This practice continued at Doulton for some years and one of the results is that their pots are of particular interest to collectors. Each designer's work can be recognized and identified by the individual marks, usually composed of initials. A group of decorated saltglaze stoneware was first shown to the public at the International Exhibition of 1871 and George Wallis, the Keeper of the Art Collections at South Kensington, wrote of them with considerable enthusiasm. 'The forms are admirable, and the decorations, whether incised or in relief, are always thoroughly well considered, and especially adapted to the material, the mode of production and the use of the object. There are no affected imitations of antique types. The spirit of true design is caught with admirable perception and insight; and it is not too much to say that in Messrs Doulton's case of stoneware in the Pottery Gallery there is not an article that can be deemed in any sense common-place. When colour is introduced it is done sparingly, and with a view to enhance the form of the object and the natural beauty of the material, rather than to conceal the one or the other.' This is high praise for any new venture but the Doulton's saltglaze stoneware of the period incorporated all the aesthetic virtues. Another writer on the same occasion even went so far as to say that 'in many cases they merit the high favour of those who collect pure works of Art'. The production of saltglaze stoneware was peculiarly suited to the combined

78

79

78 Teapot; porcelain, transfer printed in blue and made by the Worcester Royal Porcelain Works, 1877. *In the author's possession.*

79 'Bamboo and Fan', earthenware plate, transfer printed and painted in enamel colours. The design was registered Dec. 1875 and made by Minton's, with the factory date mark of April 1880. *In the author's possession.*

87 Jug in saltglaze stoneware,
designed by Frank A. Butler, 1882,
and made by Doulton's in
Lambeth. *London, Doulton & Co.
Ltd.*

88 Jug in saltglaze stoneware,
designed by George Tinworth
about 1870, and made by Doulton's
in Lambeth. *London, Doulton & Co.
Ltd.*

89

90

89   Wine jug in silver with
engraved and applied ornament;
Birmingham hallmark for 1880 and
maker's mark of Frederick
Elkington. *London, Victoria and
Albert Museum.*

90   Jug in silver with engraved
decoration; London hallmark for
1881–2 and maker's mark of
John Aldwinkle and James Slater.
London, Victoria and Albert Museum.

91 Jug in saltglaze stoneware
with incised and coloured
decoration by Emily J. Edwards,
and made by Doulton's, 1871.
London, Victoria and Albert Museum.

92 Plates in earthenware, transfer
printed and painted. The design
was registered in March 1870.
Printed mark on the reverse is
'W. S. Coleman. Inv. & del.' and
'Minton' impressed. *Mrs Barbara
Morris.*

efforts of technically unskilled students and skilled artisans, as the firing was completed in a single operation and all the decoration was carried out while the pot was in the clay state. This gave considerable freedom of expression to the individual artist. Most of the pottery was moulded in relief, some artists chose to use applied slip decoration, others stamped or impressed ornament and others used freely-drawn incised line emphasized with colour (plate 87). For technical reasons colour was limited to shades of blue and brown but these had a satisfactory quality in their relationship with the clay and were in keeping with the aesthetic demand for soft, earth colours, in marked contrast to the sharp colours of commercial porcelain decoration. One of the earliest and best known of Doulton artists was Hannah B. Barlow who specialized in incised or sgraffito animal subjects, drawn freely on straight-sided vessels. By modern standards Hannah Barlow's representational work bears little relationship to the pottery but it was much admired for its freedom of expression. Some of the most attractive pottery produced by the Lambeth studio were the small pieces by another female artist, Emily J. Edwards (plate 91). She specialized in leaf motifs, directly related to the form of the pottery and set off by boldly-drawn formal background ornament, a type of design found in the best of contemporary wallpaper and textile design and almost certainly derived from the study of Japanese ornament. A key pattern which could almost be described as the trade mark of art pottery, and which was used by a number of Doulton artists, was composed of applied beads or dots of white slip emphasizing the main lines of a design (plate 88). Following the success of the saltglaze stoneware, Doulton enlarged the scope of their Art Studio and introduced Lambeth Faience. This was earthenware painted in colours with a brush at the biscuit stage and the success of this new type of art pottery was said to have inspired Howell and James to organize their exhibitions of painting on pottery. Doulton Art Pottery of both kinds was shown with great success at all the international exhibitions of the 1870s, notably the Philadelphia Centennial, at which they were awarded a number of medals for their work, and at Paris in 1878, when it was written that 'the exquisitely chaste and delicate tints and the wealth of artistic feeling, which pervade these new productions . . . have won for them a fame which will assuredly endure so long as beauty is valued or art is cherished.'[3]

In 1871 at approximately the same time as Doulton's new venture, Minton and Company opened their Art Pottery Studios in South Kensington. Ground was leased from Her Majesty's Commissioners for the Exhibition of 1851 and Minton's built a studio and a kiln 'so arranged as to consume its own smoke'[4] with the intention of persuading eminent artists, 'especially ladies', to paint on porcelain and majolica. It is curious that all the art pottery enterprises seem to lay emphasis on the employment of female artists and painters. The nucleus of the workers at the Minton Art Studio was a group of male professional artists from their factory at Stoke-on-Trent where the biscuit pottery was made and from where it was then transferred to London for decoration and final firing. In addition to its technical equipment the Studio was provided with every amenity to attract and encourage decorative artists in their work. The inspiration of both

Fig. 10 Drawings of 'Burmantofts Pottery' available at Messrs Howell & James's in Regent Street, from *The British Architect*, October 7, 1881.

nature and art were to hand: the Studio adjoined the gardens of the Royal Horticultural Society and was near to both the South Kensington Museum collections and to the School of Art. The Studio manager, William Stephen Coleman (1829–1904), was an artist who began his professional life as a naturalist but had already moved to pottery painting and had had at least one exhibition of his work in this medium before the opening of the Minton Studios. His work had been acclaimed as 'High Art' and a worthy example for others to emulate. While Coleman's boldly painted figure subjects were much admired, they contributed relatively little to the development of art pottery, as can be judged from the fact that his designs were used quite arbitrarily on plates (plate 92), greeting cards or any other art product (plate 106). The wares produced here were normally impressed with the mark 'Minton's Art-Pottery Studio, Kensington Gore', to distinguish them from the normal production at Stoke. Unfortunately it has not proved possible to discover the identity of many of the Minton Studio artists, such as the painter of obvious skill, identified only by the initials E.J.S., who painted a handsome portrait of a fashionable young lady, and enriched it with applied slip, on a large dish or charger (plate 104). The Studio soon became one of the show places of London but unfortunately the venture was only short lived. Coleman left in 1873 and the premises were destroyed by fire in 1875. Though the Studio was not rebuilt, as there was a fairly close association between Doulton and Minton, some of the artists continued their painting on Doulton's Faience.

Wilcock and Company of Leeds were makers of drain-pipes and fire-bricks but in the late 1870s, no doubt inspired by Doulton's example and that of other firms who had 'striven to bring Art to bear on their commoner produce', they embarked on a new art ware, Burmantofts Faience.

The body was of fine clay, found locally, and all the wares relied for their decoration on elaborate modelling and rich, brilliantly coloured glazes. They were stocked by Howell and James and despite their elaborate form were much admired in aesthetic circles. The artist and commentator, T. Raffles Davison, wrote in *The British Architect* in 1881 that 'those aesthetes who can get pitched up high with exquisite sensitive emotion of colour, will do well to take a bit of "Burmantofts Ware" home with them and sit and look at it. It would last them a long time.' Each of the pieces was unique but all were unsigned and bear only the factory mark.

Numbers of small art potteries were established in the 1880s in various parts of England, notably in Devonshire and in the Midlands where there was a long-standing tradition of pottery-making. One of the most interesting of these, both for its origins and its connections with the Aesthetic Movement, was that of C. H. Brannam of Barnstaple in North Devon. In the seventeenth and eighteenth centuries Barnstaple had been an important pottery centre from which traditional domestic earthenware with slip and sgraffito decoration had been exported direct to America. By the mid nineteenth century Brannam's pottery was still making bread ovens and other large domestic wares on the site of its seventeenth-century forerunner. C. H. Brannam himself attended Barnstaple School of Art and later combined the new art teaching with the surviving craft tradition making art pottery. All the pieces were executed in rich red earthenware coated with creamy slip and with some sgraffito decoration. In the late 1870s, under the influence of a visiting artist who admired the 'quaint' shapes, Brannam's work grew bolder and more original in form and the glazes became richer with the introduction of dark greens and browns. For many years C. H. Brannam designed, threw and decorated all the pieces himself and each piece was signed and dated. These decorative vases and jugs, each a unique piece with slight irregularities of form and decoration but informed by 'art' principles, were the embodiment of the ideas of the Arts and Crafts Movement and the complete antithesis of contemporary commercial production. Howell and James sold some of the first pieces but in 1882 Liberty became the sole London agents for Barum Ware, as it was called, and the association continued for some years forming a link with the Art Nouveau period. Later Brannam Pottery was marked as being made for Liberty and the traditional method of slip decoration seems to have been peculiarly well suited to the sinuous line demanded by Art Nouveau decoration.

Cast-iron seems, at first sight, to be a most unlikely material for an 'art' industry but the work of Barnard, Bishop and Barnard of the Norfolk Iron Works proved the contrary. Cast-iron was a popular material during the whole of the Victorian era, lavishly and skilfully used, but many of the industrial products were so conspicuously ill-designed that it was an obvious field for design reformers. Barnard, Bishop and Barnard produced both cast- and wrought-iron as well as wire goods of various kinds. Their work was of the highest technical quality and, unlike many other English exhibitors, at the 1851 Exhibition, their work was highly commended and they were later described as having initiated a renaissance of English metalwork. By the 1870s their work seems to have been universally praised in the most fulsome terms. The *Iron Age* of New York, writing of their exhibit at the Philadelphia Centennial, spoke of wonderful casting and brilliant design and, on the occasion of the Paris Exhibition two years later, another writer

Fig. 11 Cast-iron grate, designed by Thomas Jeckyll about 1876 and made by Barnard, Bishop & Barnard, Norwich. Reproduced from J. Moyr Smith, *Ornamental Interiors.*

143

said that 'by the exercise of a delicate fancy they may be said to have raised again the working of wrought-iron to its legitimate position amongst the Fine Arts.' This seems to have been a combination of the skill of the firm and the foresight of Alfred Barnard in employing Thomas Jeckyll as his designer. Thomas Jeckyll, a 'Japanese' designer, seems to have worked almost exclusively for Barnards during the last ten years of his life. Their mutual *pièce de résistance* was the Japanese exhibition pavilion (plate 66) but it was the ornamental and decorative stoves and grates which were the significant contribution to the Art Movement. They were well designed with pleasant and most effective ornament and they were launched on a long and successful career by the Prince of Wales. A stove, set with blue and gold art-painted tiles with a mantelpiece of American walnut, was the Prince's first personal purchase from the Paris Exhibition of 1878. The Prince of Wales also bought a pair of gates for Sandringham Park in Norfolk and another pair were bought for the then recently established Decorative Art Museum in Vienna. It is possible that Jeckyll's designs form another direct link with the later Art Nouveau as the sunflower railings for his Japanese pavilion bear a striking resemblance to one of the earliest designs for metal by the Spaniard, Antonio Gaudi (1852–1926). The Jeckyll design, dating from 1876, consists of repeated sunflowers with softly drooping leaves contained by firm vertical and horizontal lines (plate 116). They were the subject of one of the earliest experimental photographs published in the periodical *The British Architect*. The Gaudi railings for the Casa Vicens, designed in 1878, consist of repeated open palm leaves, extraordinarily similar in form to Jeckyll's sunflower petals.

In the late 1860s a small number of firms were producing well-designed goods for a small, informed public but as the Art Movement degenerated into a veritable mania for sunflowers, strange colours and terracotta ornaments, so almost any manufacturer with a feeling for publicity climbed on the artistic bandwaggon. On the credit side, it became much more general to employ designers for industrial products but by the mid eighteen-eighties only a few firms were maintaining the standards and the ideals which had originally inspired the Art Movement.

Chapter 8

THE FASHIONABLE AESTHETE

Aesthetic costume is a somewhat tantalizing subject of study. Unquestionably such clothing existed and was worn by many cultured women and their children and by some eccentric men in the late 1870s and early '80s but virtually no illustrations of it survive except in the form of caricature. One fashion journal was reported to have adopted what was called 'a startling innovation' in early 1881 in the form of large, full-length figure cartoons entitled 'Fashions for Art Folk' intended for ladies who chose to wear tasteful costumes of medieval suggestiveness, but this venture was clearly unusual. Fashionable, Paris-inspired dress of the same period was probably as elaborate in construction and as heavy to wear as at any time in the Victorian era. Bodices were tight-fitting, moulded to heavily-boned corsets, and skirts of the most complex construction consisted of layer upon layer of varied fabric and were further complicated by the addition of elaborate trimmings. Such garments called for individual professional dressmaking and considerable quantities of material so that there were obviously sound commercial reasons for the fashionable women's magazines, which had close ties with the retail trades, to confine their illustrations to these French fashions. The colour fashion plates published with each number all showed ladies and children in rather stiff attitudes in unbelievably elaborate garments. But the texts of these periodicals did occasionally give some hint of another, more individual approach to dress. In the summer of 1880, one Cicely, a reader of *The Queen*, was advised that she 'might embroider her bluish green art dress with peacock's feathers, the pattern carried from the shoulder down both sides of the front of the dress over the side darts as in the newest style of tennis aprons'. This lady and many others must have accepted this advice, for a writer in another periodical two years later reported that 'we have seen ladies wearing serge dresses embroidered with crewel wools but the effect was not happy'. Also in 1882 the aesthetic fashion was reported to have reversed the usual processes and passed across the Channel to Paris from London, as well as to New York, where 'women have begun to indulge in that chromatic misery, the green and yellow melancholy which is supposed to distinguish the Aesthetic habit of attire.'[1] It was an entirely new idea for London to influence Paris fashions, however briefly.

Despite the quips and criticism a very real change had come over the style of English fashionable dressing during the mid 1870s. Just as a variety

Fig. 12 'An Impartial Statement
in Black and White' by George du
Maurier from *Punch*, Volume 80,
1881. *Left*, Aesthetic Lady and
Woman of Fashion. *Right*, Woman
of Fashion and Aesthetic Lady.

of forms of architecture and interior decoration were socially acceptable, so two versions of fashionable dress existed side by side; one group of ladies favoured simple gowns, with flowing folds, while others wore the elaborate, stiffened, overweight fashions dictated by Paris and the modistes (fig. 12). These changes were produced by a number of factors working simultaneously, some artistic but possibly even more related to changing social conditions. Physical comfort had always been the last consideration involved in the design of fashionable female attire. Convenience, comfort and practicability were continuously sacrificed for the extremes dictated by each season's fashion whether it was currently to be under or over dressed. In the 1870s, however, a comfortable form of utilitarian dress became a necessity for some respectable young ladies who for the first time were beginning to work outside the home. Women were making great educational strides and were becoming nurses, teachers and social workers and even contemplating the professions of medicine and architecture, if a little tentatively. Stiff-boned garments might appear elegant for social functions and their wearers might be prepared to put up with some discomfort for the sake of fashion but such garments were totally impractical for an active life outside the drawing-room. Another factor was increasing female participation in active sport, although only in a very mild form by modern standards. Thus by 1881 *The Queen*, in an editorial comment, came to the somewhat obvious conclusion that 'during recent years most girls have become convinced that tight stays and sleeves and tied-back skirts are incompatible with success in rowing or tennis'. A freer, looser form of sports costume was needed.

These pressing practical problems led to the establishment of The Rational Dress Association with the aim of reforming the taste of both the purchasing public and the designers and makers of clothing of all kinds. Their prospectus laid out the requirements of perfect dress and gave the names of the few firms willing to make dresses 'as far as possible in accordance with these requirements'. It is interesting to notice from the prospectus that one Parisian establishment had been recruited to the Rational Dress Movement. The requirements for perfect dress as enumerated were:

1. Freedom of movement.
2. Absence of pressure on any part of the body.
3. Not more weight than is necessary for warmth and both weight and warmth equally distributed.
4. Grace and beauty combined with comfort and convenience.
5. Not departing too conspicuously from the ordinary dress of the time.

This last cautionary provision marked the difference between artistic dress and the purely rational. Aesthetes were very much concerned with rational dress, just as they were concerned with the improved form of their dining-chairs, but their ultimate aim was beauty whereas the Rational Dress enthusiasts were primarily concerned with health, an understandable pre-occupation given the extremities to which the modiste had carried her clients in the mid 'seventies. This aim was reflected in the displays at the Association's exhibition held in 1883. According to the catalogue the exhibition included a few garments which were intended for formal occasions but quite the largest number were for sport of various kinds, such as swimming and bicycling, and there were even a number of discreet variations on the divided skirt. While this type of dress was commended for various practical virtues, as it was carefully disguised to give minimal offence, it did little to alter the appearance of the wearer. A change of shape of both dress and figure remained to be devised by the aesthetes.

The beauty with which they were primarily concerned was personified, in the first instance, by the flowing robes of the ladies in pre-Raphaelite painting. Mrs Haweis in her work on *The Art of Beauty* published in 1878 was even more specific and suggested that there should be a revival of the forms and colours of the years 1327–77. On the other hand, William Morris wrote, 'The period most worthy of reproduction is the ninth to the fourteenth century costume, perhaps those of 1250 being the most simple and elegant.'[2] Morris naturally took an interest in dress reform, one of 'the lesser arts of life', the increased beauty of which would make daily life more pleasurable. The recommended time span in itself gave a fairly free range of choice to the artistically inclined dressmaker but when the source of information on the period was confined to the few paintings available for study in public collections, and monochrome reproductions of others, the scope for invention was almost unlimited. The aim was to dress gracefully and to be in harmony with the domestic surroundings so that inevitably artistic fashions were governed by the current taste in art. Mrs Haweis wrote enthusiastically of the pre-Raphaelites: 'those dear and much abused painters whom it is still in some circles the fashion to decry who are the plain girl's best friends. They have taken all the neglected ones by the hand. All the ugly flowers, all the ugly buildings, all the ugly faces, they have shown us have a certain beauty of their own. Morris, Burne-Jones and others have made certain types of face and figure once literally hated actually the fashion. Red hair – once to say a woman had red hair was social assassination – is the rage. A

Fig. 13 'The Tidy Costume', from *Punch*, Volume 78, 1880.

pallid face with a protruding upper lip is highly esteemed – only dress after the pre-Raphaelite style and you will be astonished to find that so far from being an "ugly duck" you are a fully fledged swan.' The practical effect of the study of the pre-Raphaelites was to produce high-waisted flowing dresses with sleeves slightly puffed at the shoulders and always of soft fabrics in 'indescribable tints', tints dictated by current furnishing fashions and by the study of fourteenth-century painting.

The illustrated books of Kate Greenaway and Randolph Caldecott also provided models to be followed both by ladies and children of both sexes. The essential quality was that the wearer should appear as limp as possible and a contemporary account of an artistic 'at home' gave a graphic picture of the effects of this fashion. 'Two sad-eyed damsels with golden locks wore lank garments of white muslin, crumpled in a million creases; lilies in their hair and a long Annunciation lily carried in the hand. Another was dressed in a raiment of gold tissue with no vestige of waist or band; the two puffs on the shoulders gave the impression of being dilated by an immense sigh; the garment hung loosely about her long neck; tiger lilies were in her hair and crimson gloves reached midway up her arms.' In fact though some ladies looked a little strange, the mode was not inconsistent with grace and elegance, as is proved by Whistler's portrait of Mrs Leyland (plate 119), the wife of the patron of the Peacock Room. She was painted in soft pinks and greys and is shown in a gently-flowing, high-waisted muslin gown and standing on rush matting, the personification of the best of the Art Movement.

No doubt Mrs Leyland could afford the best advice and fabrics but one contemporary writer who actually favoured dress reform suggested that many artistic dresses deserved scorn and ridicule because the well-intentioned wearers lacked taste and their good ideas were clumsily executed. This criticism applied particularly to the use of embroidery on dress. 'Art' embroidery, 'a name recently introduced as a general term for all descriptions of needlework that spring from an application of knowledge of design and colouring, with skill in fitting and executing',[3] was usually worked in crewel wools in 'crewel' or 'Kensington' stitch, a form of irregular stem-stitch. While it could be attractive for furnishings, this type of work was far too coarse for clothing and the fact that truly artistic ladies were urged to make their own designs added a further hazard to the overall effect (fig. 13). Embroidery on a more modest scale seems to have been popular on the new tennis costumes and other art dresses were finished with broad bands of embroidery in silk on net, and by 1886 even shoemakers had adopted art embroidery. Ladies' boots with embroidered fronts were reported to be the rage, though not worked by the ladies themselves. Trade had stepped in at this stage and the work was commercially produced in Switzerland and Italy. Another innovation using embroidery was smocking on ladies' and children's dress. It was introduced as part of the 'Old English' revival, running parallel with similar tastes in architecture and decoration, but it was also favoured on health grounds particularly for children. A loose garment smocked at neck and wrist allowed more natural movement than more conventional clothing.

93

WITH EVERY GOOD WISH FOR THE NEW YEAR.

93 New Year Card, one of a set of prize-winning designs illustrating the seasons, by H. W. Batley for Hildesheimer & Faulkner, about 1880. *London, Victoria and Albert Museum.*

94 Christmas card by an unknown designer produced for Marcus Ward & Co. about 1880. *London, Victoria and Albert Museum.*

94

May you have a happy Christmas and many of them.

104   Dish of earthenware painted
in colours by an unknown artist at
Minton's Art Pottery Studio,
Kensington Gore, about 1871–2.
Marked Minton's and signed
E. J. S. on the reverse.
G. W. Hawkins (*Collection*).

Fig. 14 'Valeria', a Liberty Art tea gown from a catalogue of about 1885. *London, Victoria and Albert Museum*

A painter whose work both reflected and influenced fashion was Albert Moore (1841–93), whose elegant ladies were usually shown in flowing white garments of some muslin-like fabric. In Moore's case the inspiration was not medieval painting but Greek sculpture, a source recommended by both artistic and rational fashion experts. Albert Moore's models were far more shapely and robust than those favoured by the pre-Raphaelites but their attitudes were suitably languid and their garments fell in graceful, soft folds (plate 60). Mrs Haweis suggested in *The Art of Beauty* that her readers would do well to spend some time studying both the larger pieces of Greek sculpture and the small Tanagra figures in the British Museum. The classical-style garments evolved from these studies in the early 1880s were cut loose and flowing but were worn over tight-fitting 'Princess' style dresses usually with very un-Greek puffed shoulder sleeves as favoured by the medievalists.

Since one of the main precepts of artistic dress was that it should blend with the new furnishings, and that the artistically dressed lady should be in harmony with her surroundings, furnishing colours and indeed furnishing fabrics were recommended for garments of all kinds. Artistic ladies of sensitivity shunned the garish, bright colours of the Paris fashion houses and adopted dull greens, peacock blue and dull, rich reds, or mellow amber-yellows. Mrs Haweis advised dull grass-green, with a slight yellow in it, as a picturesque colour for a woollen day dress, or sage green accompanied by deep lake, primrose or dull greenish-blue, and Liberty and Co. offered to their customers, 'Persian Pink, Venetian Red, Terracotta, Ochre-Yellow, Sapphire and Peacock Blue, Sage, Olive, Willow Green, Soft Brown and Drab'. Yet another 'authority' suggested the equally gloomy olive-green worn with turquoise for evening wear or for day dress almost any patterned fabric intended for furniture coverings or curtains. It was this fashion, no doubt, that prompted the printing on soft Indian silk of some of William Morris's designs for chintz. Gloomy as the recipe for aesthetic dress sounds, it was responsible for the introduction of some very lovely fabrics because the relative simplicity of line and shape demanded good pure fabrics which would drape well. Modish dress had become so extravagant of material that few could afford to be dressed, for instance, in pure silk which, in any case, lacked the body needed to support the artificial outlines demanded by fashion. The aesthetes used soft, pure silks, printed or plain, shantung or tusser silk for evening wear, and for day dress plain materials, such as Brown Holland, cream cotton with a linen stripe imported from Algeria, or printed cottons from India. By 1881 these fabrics could be obtained readily from 'any art warehouse', according to a writer in *The Queen* in that year.

First and foremost of these art warehouses was that of Liberty and Company which soon made a speciality of 'the particular class of oriental silks (properly termed Liberty silks) which are distinctly adapted for light clinging robes and draperies'. The dress fabric catalogue issued by the firm from which this quotation is taken, advertised a great range of Indian, Japanese and Chinese silks all commended to potential buyers for various artistic qualities. They were described as diaphanous, exquisite, suitable in every case for drapery and above all as aesthetic and artistic with the further commendation that such fabrics had been used in the stage costumes for

Patience, The Colonel and *The Cup* in which Ellen Terry had appeared. Liberty's were the first commercial firm to use the term 'Art Fabrics' as early as 1876 though others followed suit in the 1880s. 'The Aesthetic Gallery' was opened in Bond Street by a former Liberty partner, F. B. Goodyer, who specialized in English silks, cashmeres and velveteens and a Regent Street firm, A. Stephens and Company, set up as importers of Indian silks 'to promote the use of these fabrics for tasteful and artistic costume purposes'.

These soft materials were a great improvement on the dressed, stiffened silks and hard, glazed cottons which had been in general use in the earlier part of Queen Victoria's reign. Heavy fabrics had been so popular that silks had actually been chemically weighted to give a completely artificial appearance of richness comparable with the weighty and bulbous mid-Victorian furnishings. By demonstrating the success of his Oriental fabrics, Liberty was able to induce English manufacturers to produce lighter, softer materials, such as woven and printed silks, silk *crêpes* and gauzes, though the imports remained popular with the convinced aesthetes largely because of the circumstances of their manufacture. Wild silk, prepared and woven entirely by hand processes, with 'the consequent accidental irregularity in threads and weaving', conformed with the principles of the Arts and Crafts Movement based on the ideas of William Morris. Liberty fabrics were equally popular with the Rational Dress reformers and were included in their Exhibition in 1883 as playing 'an essentially prominent part in connection with Rational and Healthy Dress'. Their healthiness was guaranteed by their purity and comparative simplicity of production.

Following the success of the 'Art Fabrics' Liberty's opened a dress department in which artistic clothing was available ready made for ladies and children, for the most part designed by architects and painters (fig. 14). Some of the costumes were intended for fancy-dress and may well have been worn by the residents of Bedford Park for their Queen Anne soirées, but many were also intended for everyday wear. In 1884 a branch of Liberty's was opened in Paris also selling ready-made aesthetic clothes and the famous silks. It was these silks, the product of the English Aesthetic Movement, which so inspired the great Art Nouveau designer, Henri van de Velde. He first saw them in 1891 and described them as bringing '*une sorte de printemps*' new to the continental scene. By 1895 a writer in *The British Warehouseman* was able to claim with some satisfaction that Liberty costumes had become the centre of a Parisian social craze.

Despite well-meaning efforts, men's dress was singularly unaffected by all attempts at reform. It started with fewer disadvantages than the strangely malformed female attire and could hardly claim to be so unhealthy and detrimental to the health of the wearers. Even Oscar Wilde, known for eccentric costume, appeared by day in conventional clothing and merely donned knee-breeches and silk stockings for his public engagements, and the Rational Dress Association exhibited nothing more outlandish than gentlemen's bicycle dress. During his American lecture tour at Salt Lake City Oscar Wilde claimed, a little optimistically, that all England would soon dress as he did since 'the Prince of Wales and some of his friends have already pronounced in favour of the velvet coat, ruffles, knee-breeches and silk hose' but this may well have been merely colourful embroidery of his topic as there seems to be no other evidence to support this claim of royal patronage of dress reform. It seems probable that Wilde tactfully adjusted his dress ideas to his audience as on another American occasion he advised all men to dress like George Washington 'whose attire was noble and good' and after his visit to Colorado decided that the miners' large hats, loose corduroys and soft leather boots were ideal for male costume.

As with interior decoration, the strange extremes of fashion disappeared, as they always will, but the ultimate influence of the Aesthetic Movement on the textile trade and on fashion was beneficial. Colours were softer and more becoming and shapes were in some measure actually related to the female form.

Chapter 9

KATE GREENAWAY AND COMPANY

The eighteen-sixties and 'seventies saw a blossoming of art in the unexpected fields of children's illustrated books and of greetings cards and other printed ephemera. The two sorts of work were closely related as popular book illustrators also designed cards and both art forms were the direct outcome of the developing skills of the colour printer. English children had long been fortunate in the wealth and variety of their nursery literature but until the middle of the nineteenth century illustrations were usually small and tended to be subordinated to the text. The richly-coloured, well-designed picture book, accompanied by short verses or simple stories, was a product of the Aesthetic period and was produced in such quantity that by the early 1880s the contemporary child was said to be exceptionally well favoured in the matter of art. 'He may be said to be something of an art critic ere he leaves his cradle and an adept in style ere he sees fit to abandon long garments for short – his aesthetic opportunities are innumerable and the matter produced for the gratification of his pampered appetite is perhaps the daintiest ever seen.'[1] Children's reading matter had long been censored by parents and mentors on the ground of its moral content but the aesthetic parent was also concerned with the visual quality. Ellen Terry recorded in her memoirs the early training of her own two children, Edith and Gordon Craig, born in 1869 and 1871. 'They were allowed no rubbishy books but from the first Japanese prints lined the nursery walls and Walter Crane was their classic . . . this severe training proved so effective that when a doll dressed in a violent pink silk was given to Edy she said it was vulgar.'[2] Edith was some four or five years old at the time.

In some measure, this outburst of tasteful culture in the nursery may well have been due to a conscious attempt to instil right ideas about art but the credit is largely due to the enthusiasm and skill of one man. This was Edmund Evans (1826–1906), the engraver and colour printer, who was not only responsible for initiating and maintaining high standards of colour printing but was the first employer of such influential figures as Walter Crane and Kate Greenaway and he persuaded other established artists to work on coloured picture books.

After his apprenticeship as a wood engraver, Evans set up in business on his own account in 1851, engraving from the designs of a variety of artists and printing in black and white and colour from wood blocks. Apart from fine illustration, one of Evans's staple products was brightly-coloured book covers printed on yellow paper for the new railway bookstall market. It was as a designer of covers for sensational 'cheap railway novels' that Walter Crane (1845–1915) was first employed by Edmund Evans. The two men first met in 1863 when Crane was only eighteen and Evans recorded that he immediately recognized the young man's capabilities as a draughtsman and designer. In 1865, in association with the publisher Routledge, Evans embarked on a series of toy books. These were of a new, almost square format, with full-page illustrations in rich colours and the bold, vigorous design found in the best of contemporary popular or fairground art. It would appear that the subjects of these first books were suggested by Edmund Evans and a number of artists worked on them, including Walter Crane, but the actual illustrations were unsigned. The early toy book illustrations usually had solid, dark grounds with figures and animals in relief against them in vivid, plain colours, principally because the publishers were anxious to cater for the mid-Victorian taste for coarse colours and flamboyant design. After the proved success of the first toy books Walter Crane embarked on a series of children's books, some with his own text and some illustrating traditional fairy stories. He produced fifty complete books between 1865 and 1886 and continued with at least two a year almost until the end of the century. The designs were drawn direct on to the wood block by the artist who then added colour to the black proofs for the guidance of the block cutter and printer in the production of the finished illustrations. By 1869 or '70 Crane had evolved his personal and distinctive manner of illustration and was not only signing his work but his books were issued by the publishers in a separate category under the heading 'Walter Crane Toy Books'.

In his memoirs, Crane described the evolution of his style in which 'gradually more colours were used as the designs became more elaborate under various influences amongst which Japanese colour prints must be counted an important factor.'[3] First shown such prints in about 1868 by a naval officer who merely regarded them as curiosities, Crane immediately realized their relationship to his own woodcut illustrations and saw the further potentialities of the medium. A series of Crane's sixpenny and shilling picture books poured from the press of Edmund Evans during the early 'seventies, each bearing the stamp of the Aesthetic Movement in one way or another. The three bears, for example, grew sunflowers in their well-ordered garden and most of the characters in his stories used ebonized furniture and tasteful blue tiles in their homes. The covers of the shilling books carried a large version of the Japanese crane, adopted by Walter Crane as his signature just as Whistler had adopted the oriental butterfly. These covers, intended for the entertainment of children, were the epitome of the Art Movement, with their combination of assorted Japanese, Greek, Queen Anne and wilting aesthetic motifs, asymmetrically arranged. All the illustrations bore the mark of the influence of Japanese colour prints in their composition and colour while some, such as the colour plates for *Aladdin* in the shilling series, showed a sophisticated knowledge of oriental design with a rich profusion of Japanese motifs (plate 98).

Obviously Crane was familiar with the work of the pre-Raphaelites but at about the time that he embarked on his shilling books he first met Edward Burne-Jones. The impact of this meeting can be seen in many of the illustrations, particularly in those for *Princess Belle Etoile*, a fanciful tale in which Burne-Jones's figures were set in classical settings and ladies in aesthetic attitudes languished in Queen Anne interiors. A romanticized pre-Raphaelitism pervades the whole book but one illustration in particular derives directly from Burne-Jones's painting of 'St George and the Dragon', dating from some ten years earlier, with its graceful, willowy figure clad in armour encountering a dragon under Italianate trees (plate 108). A contemporary writer aptly commented on Mr Crane's decorative inventions as a combination of the medieval Hellas of Mr Burne-Jones and the medieval England of the architect of Bedford Park. Through the medium of his illustrations for children, Crane was one of the best publicists for the Aesthetic Movement to the principles of which he fully subscribed in the early days of his career. He was said to have refused to advise on the costumes and décor for *Patience* as he was reluctant to be involved in guying his own beliefs. Crane was well aware of his influence, even outside the nursery, as he recorded that it was his practice to put into the illustrations any sort of detail that interested him and to make use of any opportunity to demonstrate his ideas on furniture and decoration.[4] In fact this policy led directly to a number of commissions for interior decoration and in 1875 to his earliest wallpaper designs produced for Jeffrey and Company. This first design was for a nursery paper incorporating such nursery rhyme figures as Bo Peep and the Queen of Hearts and was followed by others, 'Little Queen Anne' and 'The Sleeping Beauty' (plate 14).

In addition to his book illustrations, Walter Crane designed greetings cards for the firm of art publishers, Marcus Ward, of which his brother Thomas, also a competent illustrator, was the art director. This was a Belfast-based firm, initially concerned with playing cards, which entered the greetings card business in about 1870 and eventually controlled much of the market, becoming a significant influence on the production of other art publishers. Christmas and other greetings cards had only come into general use in the middle of the nineteenth century and most of them were imported from the German states or France. Charming though they may appear today their florid style made them an obvious target for aesthetic reform. At the time of the Franco-Prussian war in 1870 when Paris was temporarily closed to trade, Marcus Ward and Company seized their opportunity and inaugurated a profitable venture into the greetings card market with such immediate success that by Christmas of the same year it could be said that 'their merest trifles are sound Art-teachers and they circulate nothing that endangers a true and pure taste for that which is excellent in art.'[5] This applied to the text of Marcus Ward's greetings as well as the designs. For example, one typical New Year card expressed the wish that the fairest forms of Art and Nature should surround the recipient in the coming year.

With Thomas Crane as their art editor Marcus Ward and Company employed numbers of artists subscribing to aesthetic ideas. Some were anonymous (plate 94) but others were already known for their work in other fields of aesthetic endeavour, such as H. Stacy Marks (plate 102) and J. Moyr Smith (plate 113) known for the painted panels on ebonized furniture or tile designs. Their Christmas card subjects were scenes of Old English revelry in which yule logs were carried or rich meals were prepared by worthy citizens clad in medieval dress. Basically they showed respectable Victorian families transposed into an Old English setting. Thomas Crane himself designed floral cards with ornamental borders incorporating aesthetic motifs as well as similar designs for some of the children's books which Marcus Ward began to publish in 1873. Two of these books, the joint work of Thomas Crane, his cousin Ellen Houghton and another artist, J. G. Sowerby, are some of the most charming publications of the period. Entitled *At Home* and *Abroad* they were published by Marcus Ward and Company in 1881 and 1882 respectively on the crest of the Art Movement. They record the home life in London and the travels in France of a family of children who lived in a Queen Anne house and dressed in shades of green, peacock blue and sepia that would have done credit to Mrs Haweis and other arbiters of taste. Each page of verse is surrounded by charming and appropriate borders designed, as were the endpapers, by Thomas Crane. The actual illustrations and figures are by Ellen Houghton and John Sowerby (see also plate 111).

As the popularity of artistic greetings cards grew other publishers entered the field, employing a variety of artists and even promoting competitions to find suitable designs for an ever-increasing range of occasional greetings. Emphasis was upon quality of design and printing rather than on illustration of the season or event celebrated so that, for instance, there were virtually no art cards with any religious significance. Asymmetry and aesthetic colour became the hallmarks of tasteful greeting for every occasion. Wilting aesthetes with sunflowers and teapots were sent at Christmas time (plate 109) and one publisher specialized in semi-nude nymphs in vaguely classical seaside settings, based on watercolours by W. S. Coleman (plate 106). H. W. Batley, a dedicated aesthete, better known amongst his contemporaries as an interior decorator and furniture designer, won a greetings card competition with a most original and charming group of cards illustrating the seasons (plate 93). Amateurs designed cards, just as they painted on pottery or designed embroidery, and their works were occasionally selected for actual publication. The standard of work seems to have been reasonably high and a critic commenting in the *Magazine of Art* on an exhibition of Christmas cards held in a London gallery in 1881, wrote of the proof given by the exhibits of the recent general spread of better taste in the daily life of the English. However he regretted that some of the designs were 'flaccid illustrations from Tennyson' and that still more were pale imitations of the work of Kate Greenaway. While less influential in the long term than, for example, the work of Walter Crane, Kate Greenaway's personal style was imitated more or less successfully by many of her contemporaries.

Kate Greenaway (1846–1901) began her career as an artist in about 1871 with Christmas card designs for Marcus Ward in which little girls in high-waisted frocks and sunbonnets skipped gaily surrounded by delicate garlands of flowers (plate 95). At about the same time she was employed on some bold and more conventional woodcut designs for *Aunt Louisa's Toy Books* published by Frederick Warne, but these were published anonymously and were quite unlike her later work. Kate Greenaway's father was an engraver and an acquaintance of Edmund Evans to whom he showed a group of his daughter's drawings and simple nonsense verses. Evans was so struck by their quality that he persuaded Routledge to publish the collection with the title *Under the Window* and on his own initiative printed a first edition of 20,000 copies. He was convinced that the charm, quaintness and originality of the drawings would make the book a popular success. His confidence proved well-founded for the first edition issued in 1878 sold out almost immediately and Kate Greenaway's reputation was established not only in England but also in America (plate 100). Following this success, she illustrated numbers of books in her own quaint style, often supplying her own brief text and sometimes co-operating with other authors. Her prettily-dressed little boys and girls played innocent games, gathered flowers or took afternoon tea in idyllic rural settings strongly reminiscent of the villages of Sussex and Kent whose red brick cottages had already inspired aesthetic architects. The children were dressed in an entirely original style which owed something to late eighteenth- and nineteenth-century children's fashions but was essentially 'Kate Greenaway', a style so admired that budding aesthetes were soon dressed to match the books, a unique achievement for a book illustrator. It was recorded that the clever Miss Greenaway actually made costumes to her own designs for her child models. Her illustrations were always in subdued tones with an extensive use of soft yellows and greens and Evans excelled himself in the skill with which he reproduced the delicate designs (plate 96). Charming as the illustrations were they were nonetheless pervaded by an extraordinary melancholy typical of the Aesthetic Movement. The children all have a subdued and somewhat depressed air even when accompanying gay verses but the designs were so in keeping with the mood of the times that they provoked a rush of imitators.

Typical of the best of these were the greetings cards of Mrs Koberwein Terrell but it is of some interest that no less than nineteen lithographically-printed colours were needed for the reproduction of her pictures to achieve a standard of printing comparable to Edmund Evans's wood engravings (plate 110). Evans himself refused to print one book offered to him by a Kate Greenaway imitator. This was *Afternoon Tea*, drawn and written by J. G. Sowerby and eventually printed by some half-dozen different printers and published by Frederick Warne in 1880 (plate 99). It is a pleasant book but the illustrations are neither as well drawn nor as well printed as in the real Kate Greenaway books, and it is easy to see how her personal reputation eventually suffered through the association of her name with the work of her imitators.

As a member of the family glass manufacturing firm of Sowerby of Gateshead, J. G. Sowerby (working 1876–1914) was a successful glass designer in his own right. The firm was an old-established one and it can be assumed that it was due to the influence of John Sowerby that their art glass was introduced in the mid 1870s. They were far in advance of other glass

105

105   Tile, designed by Kate
Greenaway, made of earthenware,
transfer printed in colours and
made by T. & R. Boote,
Birmingham, 1883. *London,
Victoria and Albert Museum.*

They would gaze upon a lily, s
utterably utter,"
With eyes distended wide as
blossom they'd devour;
'Twas easy to believe they had
quished bread and butter,
And really lived on nothing mo
stantial than a flower.

106 Original design for a
greetings card for Messrs de la Rue
by William Coleman, about 1880.
London, Victoria and Albert Museum.

107 Page from *The Decorative
Sisters*, a 'Modern Ballad' by
Josephine Pollard, illustrated by
Walter Satterlee and published in
New York, 1882. *London, Victoria
and Albert Museum.*

108

108   Illustration from *Princess
Belle Etoile*, one of Walter Crane's
Shilling Toy Books, published by
George Routledge, 1874. *London,
Victoria and Albert Museum.*

SPRING · SVMMER · THE · RAINBOW · CELADON & AMELIA · AVTVMN · WINTER · COMES · JOVIAL · ON · ON · SOVNDING · SKATES ·

113

113 'The Four Seasons'; tiles
designed by J. Moyr Smith and
made by Minton's, about 1880.
Washington, Smithsonian Institute.

manufacturers of the day in design and their catalogues were full of original ideas for opaque pressed glass, or what Sowerby's called 'vitro porcelain', incorporating aesthetic and Japanese motifs (plates 80, 81). Significantly a number of their smaller pieces were decorated with friezes of Kate Greenaway-type children and were first made in 1878, the year of publication of *Under the Window*.

The third of the distinguished illustrators who worked with Edmund Evans was Randolph Caldecott (1846–86). His background was entirely different from that of Walter Crane and Kate Greenaway. Born in Manchester, he moved to London in 1872 and immediately came under the influence of the Aesthetic Movement. Following a visit to the International Exhibition in Vienna in 1873 he began to paint Japanese-inspired compositions and ventured into the field of interior decoration while at the same time learning modelling from the French sculptor, Jules Dalou, then resident in Chelsea. While pursuing these varied interests his main source of revenue would seem to have been book illustration. It was his pen drawings, engraved on wood as illustrations to *Old Christmas* and *Bracebridge Hall* by Washington Irving, that so impressed Edmund Evans that he asked Caldecott to do some shilling toy books. The first two, *The House that Jack built* and *John Gilpin*, were issued by Routledge in 1878, a vintage year for children's books. These were followed by fourteen others before Caldecott's early death in 1886. All printed by Edmund Evans in ever-increasing editions, they were beautiful productions, skilfully printed in delicate watercolour-like tints. Caldecott was not only a skilful draughtsman but a most entertaining story-teller, even within the framework of each illustration, and his work is quite untouched by the melancholy of his contemporaries though bearing many of the trade marks of the Art Movement. One of his most attractive books was *A Frog he would a-Wooing go* (plate 112) in which the animal participants, though living in one of the late eighteenth-century houses which passed for Queen Anne and sitting on Morris Sussex chairs, are given scale by the occasional interpolation of human observers. Miss Mouse must be presumed to have subscribed to aesthetic views as her simple classic fireplace was ornamented with peacock feathers.

Caldecott's illustrations form an interesting link between the English Art Movement and the continental arts of the latter part of the century. It was Caldecott's practice to spend holidays in the Breton village of Pont Aven where it seems possible that he met Gauguin. There is a striking similarity between Caldecott's little terracotta figures of Breton peasants, made after his work with Dalou, and Gauguin's early pottery, both dating from the mid 'eighties. In addition the Scottish painter, A. S. Hartrick, also a frequenter of the Breton artists' colony, recorded that Gauguin possessed some of Caldecott's coloured books. On one occasion Gauguin 'produced one in which some geese were depicted in the artist's characteristic way. These he praised, extravagantly', and commented on the true spirit of the drawing.[6] It may well have been due to Gauguin's enthusiasm that Crane's and Caldecott's illustrated children's books were included, together with his own ceramics, in one of the first Continental Arts and Crafts exhibitions held in Belgium in 1891.

Regrettably the standard of design and production set by Edmund Evans in his work was not maintained by other printers and publishers but it is a measure of the quality of the artistic picture books of the 'seventies and 'eighties that many of them have remained continuously in print for almost a century.

Chapter 10

QUEEN ANNE TO ART NOUVEAU

'Tonight there passes away the most memorable quarter of a century in the annals of Art which this country has known since the brilliant periods of the Middle Ages.'[1] Thus wrote the editor of *The British Architect* on New Year's Eve 1875, voicing the new-found self-confidence and excitement about the future of English art that was felt by so many architects, designers and artists. The statement was obviously an extravagant evaluation of all but a few of the actual products of the period but, nonetheless, those twenty-five years did contain the germ of much that was to be of importance later in the century, both in England and on the Continent. It was the period that saw the rise of the pre-Raphaelites, the introduction of William Morris's first designs, of a new style of architecture, of Japanese influence, and with all this the Aesthetic Movement. These last two, coupled with the spread of the ideas of Ruskin and Morris and the consequent turning to nature as a source of inspiration, led directly to what is now known as Art Nouveau. It is significant that in England the style was first known as New Art as it was seen as a progression from the earlier Art Movement.

The relationship between the Art Nouveau and its English forerunner is intricate and complex and, while the two movements had many similarities, their differences are equally marked. The Aesthetic Movement was a self-conscious revival or renaissance of the decorative arts and, as it was in part inspired by a certain social consciousness, it was essentially missionary. Artists and designers worked simultaneously to improve the taste of their public, intending by this method to improve the actual conditions of life. As the sun gives colour to flowers so art gives colour to life, as one contemporary artist expressed it. The aestheticism of the 1870s and the Arts and Crafts Movement of the 1880s inspired designers with ideals and produced a way of working and an attitude to life rather than a style. There were similarities of form and some common decorative motifs, trade marks as it were, such as the lily and the sunflower, but the relationship between an ebonized sideboard, a Doulton Art pot and a Morris wallpaper is not immediately apparent on purely stylistic grounds.

On the other hand international Art Nouveau, which came to full and brief flower in the later 1890s, is immediately recognizable, identified by the sinuous organic line and sensuous curves of both form and ornament. As will be seen later, it was generally accepted that this evolved from the 'sentimental passion for a vegetable fashion' mocked by Gilbert and Sullivan and found in the English design of the 'seventies and even earlier. Like Aestheticism before it, Art Nouveau was a movement of pure individualism but this time there were no missionaries. The concept of Art for Art's sake was wholly accepted and artists and designers worked with an almost complete disregard for their public. In addition, the decorative arts adopted the conscious search for decadence which had been present in European literature, particularly in France and Belgium, during much of the second half of the nineteenth century. There were 'many young men eager for the distinction of decay'. The concept of decadence was in part related to the symbolism of the dying century. *Evergreen*, one of the many short-lived periodicals of the 1890s, gave this explanation saying that artists were seeking 'only to link the autumn of our age with an approaching spring and pass through decadence towards Renaissance' and that decadence was a mere 'autumn sickness and one of rapid growth and adolescence'. The intention was to create something new and fresh for the new century and the English Art Movement with its very different aims, and the writings of William Morris and some of his contemporaries, set the mood of all the work if not necessarily establishing its form. 'No more museum-inspired work; no more scruples about styles; no more dry as dust stock patterns . . . but instead designs by living men for living men. We must clothe modern ideas in modern dress, adorn our design with living fancy and rise to the height of our knowledge and capacity.' These are the words not of some wild revolutionary of the 'nineties but of a follower of William Morris, the architect and designer J. D. Sedding. As a good pupil of Ruskin and Morris, Sedding recommended an alternative source of inspiration. 'Drop this wearisome translation of old styles and translate nature instead.' It is this translation of nature in one form or another that provides the visual link between the Aesthetic Movement and Art Nouveau. There is obviously a danger in assuming that a similarity of shape or design necessarily implies a common source or influence but, though the relationship between an early Morris wallpaper and the wild floral swirls of the eighteen-nineties may not be immediately apparent, the one is a direct descendant of the other.

'The Daisy' wallpaper which was designed by Morris for the 1862 Exhibition was the trend-setter of its day. An obvious repeating pattern with the simplest of flowers directly observed as its motif, it was in marked contrast to the exuberant papers popular with the trade at the time. The principle of the strong main motif derived from nature, with a more rigid subsidiary one, giving an underlying flatness and stability, was one that was used later by Morris himself in more complex designs and by most English designers of the latter part of the century. It can be seen in the simple floral papers of Lewis F. Day (plate 10), the work of Walter Crane and many others. Even the Japanese-inspired work of E. W. Godwin contains the same elements used with increasing freedom. 'The Peacock' paper designed in 1873 consists of two motifs, the peacock and the textured background, both taken directly from Japanese badge or heraldic designs merely enlarged and simplified (plate 73). However the floral design intended for use with 'The Peacock' though Japanese in inspiration, is not based on any specific model.

It has the stability of a fairly rigid ground but the natural forms flow freely. This free-flowing quality which has been called Proto-Art Nouveau was characteristic of much of the English design of the 'seventies. An embroidery designed by Morris at the height of the aesthetic fashion (plate 27), with its sunflowers peeping from behind undulating leaf forms, is typical of the best of Morris's flat pattern design and clearly contains all the seeds of Art Nouveau. The same tendencies can be seen in an anonymously-designed wallpaper (plate 74). This and the embroidery both date from 1877, fully twenty years before the new movement acquired its continental name.

The strange fact is that having in effect created Art Nouveau in the 1870s England abandoned and even shunned the style once it had become a fashion. Lewis F. Day's simple sunflowers and sprays of apple blossom (plate 10) evolved into naturally-swaying forms such as those of the printed velveteen of about 1890 (plate 121). It is significant that this is one of the many examples of Day's work chosen for illustration in 1892 in one of the first German publications dealing with what were then called the modern naturalistic styles.[2] The first volume of this periodic survey contains dozens of designs by Morris, Lewis F. Day and Walter Crane, most of them originally published at least ten years earlier. Walter Crane's peacocks, swans and lilies led quite naturally to what he himself called 'that strange decorative disease known as L'Art Nouveau'. While Crane's much illustrated and exhibited work was an acknowledged source of inspiration for the continental movement he was one of the most violent critics of its 'wild and whirligig squirms', apparently quite unable to see the logical extension of his own work and that of his English contemporaries. Apart from the surviving visual evidence there seems to have been fairly general contemporary agreement that Art Nouveau had well-established roots in England. Alfredo Melani, the Italian critic, writing in 1902 on the occasion of the opening of the first International Exhibition of Modern Decorative Art, felt that there would inevitably be thousands of English visitors, as the exhibition was the greatest expression of 'the modern aesthetic movement the first ideas of which really originated in England'.

Art Nouveau was originally the name of a shop in Paris established in 1896 by Samuel Bing for the display and sale of work by all those with a 'distinct personal perception whose designs were not re-incarnations of the past'. A French visitor to Bing's shop in Paris said that she was able to see the influence of Morris and Burne-Jones in all the work there and an English critic in *The Art Journal* of 1897 felt so certain of his English superiority that he asserted that 'to the Parisian the decoration applied to the rooms might appear new but for those who know the English style now in vogue curiosity is certainly less.' This anonymous writer went so far as to accuse van de Velde of copying Mr Walter Crane but of rendering his ideas without charm.

There was in fact some foundation for this accusation as, of all the artists whose names were associated with Art Nouveau, it was van de Velde (1863–1957) who paid the most whole-hearted tribute to his English masters, specifically to the ideas of Ruskin and Morris and the designs of Walter Crane. Though he had come into contact with English design a year or two earlier, van de Velde first wrote of his new enthusiasm in the French periodical *L'Art Moderne* in 1893. Significantly he used the English language for the title, calling his article 'Artistic Wallpapers'. English art wallpapers had been shown in Paris at the International Exhibition of 1889 and were subsequently imported into Belgium together with Liberty textiles and other examples of artistic English household goods. In addition Walter Crane's illustrated children's books were amongst the English contributions to the 1891 salon of *Les Vingt*, the *avant-garde* group of Belgian sculptors and painters. This was the first occasion on which decorative arts were shown in what had previously been a fine art exhibition and it was at about this time that van de Velde himself abandoned his career as a painter and began to design furniture, textiles, metalwork and eventually architecture. First he set himself the task of becoming thoroughly familiar with what he described as the recent revival of handicrafts in England and to this end it seems likely that he visited the third annual exhibition of the Arts and Crafts Exhibition Society held in London in 1893, as he quoted extensively in the wallpaper article, from Crane's catalogue foreword. The Society, whose original name had been 'The Combined Arts', embodied all van de Velde's ideas for reform in the decorative arts and its president was Walter Crane. After acknowledging the debt of the Arts and Crafts Movement both in England and abroad to William Morris, van de Velde went on to list almost all the contemporary English pattern designers including Lewis Day, Sedding and C. F. A. Voysey but his final conclusion was that Walter Crane triumphed over all the others by virtue of the rhythmic vegetation in his designs and '*les lignes de très spéciale souplesse*'. These of course were the very qualities which marked the most extreme expression of continental Art Nouveau and it is obvious from van de Velde's detailed analysis of each of Crane's designs that these contributed significantly to his own decorative work in its formative stage in the early 1890s.

Curiously Crane was not alone in his aversion to Art Nouveau. Almost all the English designers whose work provided the basis for later developments in Belgium, France and, in particular, in Austria and Germany, turned from Art Nouveau around the end of the century almost with revulsion, adopting a national puritan view in the face of what they regarded as an unwholesome foreign disease.

There seems to have been only one artist whose career coincided at each stage with the apparently logical developments from the Art Movement of the 1880s, through Arts and Crafts to Art Nouveau and the twentieth century. This was the American Louis Comfort Tiffany (1848–1933). Trained as a painter, he continued painting throughout his life unlike others, such as van de Velde who made a complete break with fine art under the influence of the Arts and Crafts Movement. In the late '60s and early '70s Tiffany worked in Paris and visited North Africa and Palestine, experiences which affected his later decorative work. One of the main factors in Tiffany's diversion from fine to applied art was his association with Edward C. Moore, chief silver designer to the family firm of Tiffany and Company, and friend of Samuel Bing. Before opening his famous Art Nouveau shop Bing was a collector of oriental art, as was Moore, whose particular enthusiasm was near-Eastern glass. Under his guidance Tiffany embarked on his own collection of Japanese objects. An additional influence was that of Donald G. Mitchell, a relative of Tiffany who was actively engaged in the Art Movement and in this capacity was chairman of the judges of Decorative Arts at the Philadelphia Centennial Exhibition. There was a considerable quantity of English art work shown at Philadelphia and in his report of the exhibition Mitchell singled out for commendation to his countrymen the work of Walter Crane. Crane, Morris and Burne-Jones were also the inspiration behind the first of Tiffany's practical ventures into the decorative arts. He designed, advised and helped the New York Society of Decorative Art, a body principally concerned with art embroidery founded by Mrs Candace Wheeler in 1878 in imitation of the Royal School of Art Needlework in South Kensington.

Tiffany's next step in 1879 was to start his own firm, Associated Artists, to undertake complete interior design projects. At this stage the work of the firm was remarkably similar to that of English interior designers such as W. H. Batley, Lewis F. Day and Thomas Jeckyll, and Tiffany is known to have seen the Godwin and Whistler exhibit at the Paris Exhibition of 1878. The firm's first really original work was the decoration of the Veterans' Room of the Seventh Regiment Armory in New York completed in 1880, a rich, dark room in which Tiffany improbably but successfully combined motifs from Celtic, Moorish and medieval art into a completely unified

Fig. 15 Part of the decoration of the Lyceum Theatre, New York, designed by Louis C. Tiffany, 1884, from a contemporary drawing illustrated in *The Magazine of Art*.

scheme of decoration. The ceiling was of dark wood covered with a stencilled decoration in silver, a favourite motif at this date which was repeated in the interior of the Lyceum Theatre, New York, decorated by Tiffany in 1884. An English critic, writing in the *Magazine of Art* in the same year, was able to find Turkish, Arabian and even what he described as Louis Quinze details in the scheme but could also see the unifying effect of the personal quality of Tiffany's design in an ensemble rich with silver and gold stencilling and 'glittering with streams of silver paint'. The critic of the *New York Morning Journal*, obviously surprised by the originality of the design, commented that 'it belongs to no school unless the ultra aesthetic school of Wilde'.

Tiffany had used stained glass and had experimented with glass tiles in his earliest interiors but in the latter part of 1885 he established another firm, the Tiffany Glass Company, initially concerned exclusively with the production of stained-glass windows. It was this venture that provided the link between Tiffany's work and the European Art Nouveau Movement. When he visited Paris for the International Exhibition of 1889, Tiffany approached Bing with his ideas for stained glass and the two formed a lasting association which derived from their mutual admiration for William Morris and the Arts and Crafts Movement and which was to become a major influence on Art Nouveau. Early in the 1890s Tiffany began his experiments with blown glass, and the first pieces of iridescent Favrile glass were sold by Bing in his Art Nouveau establishment in Paris. Curiously the intention behind these experiments with blown glass was a desire to provide household objects of everyday use which would enrich by their beauty the lives of average American citizens. However from this worthy missionary aim evolved some of the most precious, elegant, exquisite and totally impractical products of Art Nouveau, sought by European collectors and museums and far beyond the pocket of the average householder. Thus objects personifying Art Nouveau were produced for the same reasons that had inspired the earlier aesthetes and under craft conditions based on the English Arts and Crafts Movement.

Tiffany's career demonstrates the extent to which Art Nouveau, of which he was one of the most distinguished exponents, was rooted in the innovations of the 1860s. Despite their obvious differences of both form and intention, the two linked movements proved to be equally important and related parts of the transition between the eclectic historicism of the early nineteenth century and the disciplined and purposeful style of the Modern Movement of the twentieth century.

114 Sunflower in wrought iron, designed by Thomas Jeckyll and made by Barnard, Bishop & Barnard, Norwich, 1876. *London, Victoria and Albert Museum.*

Overleaf

115 Pencil drawing of a bracket panel for the Japanese Pavilion by Thomas Jeckyll, 1876. *London, Victoria and Albert Museum.*

116 Pencil drawing of a bracket panel for the Japanese Pavilion by Thomas Jeckyll, 1876. *London, Victoria and Albert Museum.*

AESTAS

119 'Symphony in Flesh Colour and Pink'; portrait of Mrs F. R. Leyland by J. M. Whistler, 1872–3. Oil on canvas. *New York, Frick Collection.*

120 Drawing of a panel of stained glass from the Prince of Wales's Pavilion at the Paris Exhibition of 1878, made by J. Powell & Sons, Whitefriars.

Notes

CHAPTER I Introduction
1 *Furniture Gazette*, vol. v, 1876, p. 76. 2 William Morris, *Collected Works*, vol. 23, p. 154. 'Art, Wealth and Riches'. 3 Walter Hamilton, *The Aesthetic Movement in England*, 1882, p. vii. 4 M. Digby Wyatt, *Reports on the Exhibitions*, H.M.S.O., 1856. 5 *The Art Manufactures of Birmingham & the Midland Counties*, Birmingham, 1862. 6 *Punch*, 1879. 7 Roger Fry, *Vision and Design*, London, 1920, p. 27. 'The Ottoman and the Whatnot'.

CHAPTER III The Aesthetic Interior
1 C. L. Eastlake, *Hints on Household Taste*, London, 1872, p. 60. 2 *Ibid.*, p. 92. 3 Harriett Prescott Spofford, *Art Decoration Applied to Furniture*, New York, 1878. 4 Anon., *Artistic Homes*, London, about 1880, p. 75. 5 *The Artist*, vol. 1, 1880, p. 345. 6 *The Builder*, vol. XLI, 1881, p. 196. 7 J. Moyr Smith, *Ornamental Interiors*, 1887, p. 82. 8 Mrs H. R. Haweis, *The Art of Beauty*, London, 1878, p. 232. 9 J. Forbes-Robertson, *A Player under Three Reigns*, London, 1925, p. 66. 10 *The Architect*, Aug., 1876, p. 73. 11 H. W. Batley, *A Series of Studies for Domestic Furniture and Decoration*, London, 1883. 12 Harry Quilter, 'Fashion and Art or Spots on the Sunflower', 1881, reprinted in *Opinion on Men, Women and Things*, London, 1909.

CHAPTER V Oscar Wilde and America
1 'Swinburne and Water', *Punch*, vol. 81, 1881, p. 26. 2 Oscar Wilde, *The English Renaissance of Art*, Essays and Lectures, 6th edition, 1928, p. 154. 3 *British Architect*, vol. XVIII, 1882, p. 534. 4 Oscar Wilde, *Art and the Handicraftsman*, Essays & Lectures, 6th edition, 1928, p. 195. 5 William Morris, *The Beauty of Life*, Works, vol. XXII, p. 77. 6 Walter Hamilton, *The Aesthetic Movement in England*, 2nd edition, 1882, p. 100. 7 *Punch*, vol. 82, 1882, p. 14.

CHAPTER VI Satire and Comment
1 *Punch*, vol. 72, 1877, 'Modern Aesthetics', p. 51. 2 *Punch*, vol. 78, 1880, 'A Love Agony', p. 254. 3 *Punch*, vol. 77, 1880, p. 303. 4 *Punch*, vol. 81, 1881, p. 241. 5 *Punch*, vol. 81, 1881, p. 154. 6 *British Architect*, vol. XV, 1881, p. 379. 7 *British Architect*, vol. XVIII, 1882, p. 534.

CHAPTER VII 'Art' Industry
1 *Studio*, vol. XV, 1899, pp. 104–14. 2 *The Artist*, vol. II, 1881, p. 88. 3 *The Paris Exhibition of 1878;* An illustrated Weekly Review, Christmas, 1878, p. 634. 4 *Art Journal*, vol. IX, 1870, p. 381.

CHAPTER VIII The Fashionable Aesthete
1 *The Magazine of Art*, vol. v, 1882, p. xii. 2 William Morris, 'The Lesser Arts of Life', lecture delivered in support of the Society for the Protection of Ancient Buildings. 3 Caulfeild and Saward, *Dictionary of Needlework*, 1882.

CHAPTER IX Kate Greenaway and Company
1 'Art in the Nursery', *The Magazine of Art*, vol. VI, 1883, p. 127. 2 Ellen Terry, *Memoirs*, London, 1933, p. 66. 3 Walter Crane, *An Artist's Reminiscences*, London, 1907, p. 74. 4 *Ibid.*, p. 156. 5 *Art Journal*, vol. IX, 1870, p. 381. 6 A. S. Hartrick, *A Painter's Pilgrimage*, Cambridge, 1939.

CHAPTER X Queen Anne to Art Nouveau
1 *British Architect*, vol. LV, 1875, p. 361. 2 Ed. Julius Hoffman Jnr., *Für das Kunstgewerbe*, Stuttgart Bilderschatz, 1892.

121 Printed velveteen designed by Lewis F. Day, 1890. *London, Victoria and Albert Museum.*

Selected Bibliography

Anon., *Artistic Homes*. London, 1880.

Alford, Lady Marion, *Needlework as Art*. London, 1886.

Batley, H. W., *A Series of Studies for Domestic Furniture and Decoration*. London, 1883.

Baker, Lady, *The Bedroom and the Boudoir*. London, 1878.

Carr, Mrs J. Comyns, *Reminiscences*. London, about 1920.

Conway, Moncure Daniel, *Travels in South Kensington*. London, 1882.

Cook, Clarence, *The House Beautiful*. New York, 1878.

Crane, Lucy, *Art and the Formation of Taste*. London, 1882.

Crane, Walter, *An Artist's Reminiscences*. London, 1907.

Crane, Walter, *William Morris to Whistler*. London, 1911.

Day, Lewis F., *Everyday Art. Short Essays on the Arts Not-Fine*. London, 1882.

Eastlake, C. L., *Hints on Household Taste*. London, 1867.

Edis, R. W., *Decoration and Furniture of Town Houses*. London, 1881.

Garrett, R. & A., *House Decoration*. London, 1876.

Hamilton, Walter, *The Aesthetic Movement in England*. London, 1882.

Haweis, Mrs H. R., *The Art of Beauty*. London, 1878.

Haweis, Mrs H. R., *Beautiful Houses*. London, 1882.

Lockwood and Glaister, *Art Embroidery*. London, 1878.

Loftie, Mrs, *The Dining Room*. London, 1878.

Orrinsmith, Mrs, *The Drawing Room*. London, 1878.

Robson, E. R., *School Architecture*. London, 1874.

Sedding, J. D., *Art and Handicraft*. London, 1893.

Smith, J. Moyr, *Ornamental Interiors*. London, 1887.

Spofford, Harriett Prescott, *Art Decoration Applied to Furniture*. New York, 1878.

Stevenson, J. J., *House Architecture*. London, 1880.

Wilde, Oscar, *Art and Decoration*. London, 1920.

Wilde, Oscar, *Decorative Art in America*. New York, 1906.

PERIODICALS

Architect. London, 1849–   .

Artist and Journal of Home Culture. London, 1880–94.

Builder. London, 1842–   .

British Architect. Manchester, 1874–   .

Decoration. London, 1880–8.

Furniture Gazette. London, 1873–93.

Journal of Decorative Art. Manchester, 1881–   .

Magazine of Art. London, 1878–   .

Pottery Gazette and Glass Trades Review. London, 1879–   .

Punch. London, 1841–   .

Sylvia's Home Journal. London, 1878–91.

Index